GREAT
AUSTRALIAN
FOOTBALL
STORIES

Compiled by
GARRIE HUTCHINSON

VIKING O'NEIL

Viking O'Neil
Penguin Books Australia Ltd
487 Maroondah Highway, P.O. Box 257
Ringwood, Victoria 3134, Australia
Penguin Books Ltd
Harmondsworth, Middlesex, England
Viking Penguin Inc.
40 West 23rd Street, New York, N.Y., U.S.A.
Penguin Books Canada Limited
2801 John Street, Markham, Ontario, Canada L3R 1B4
Penguin Books (N.Z.) Ltd
182–190 Wairau Road, Auckland 10, New Zealand

First published by Currey O'Neil Ross Pty Ltd 1983
This paperback edition published by Penguin Books Australia Ltd 1989

10 9 8 7 6 5 4 3 2

Produced by Viking O'Neil
56 Claremont Street, South Yarra, Victoria 3141, Australia
A division of Penguin Books Australia Ltd

Printed and bound by The Book Printer, Victoria

National Library of Australia
Cataloguing-in-Publication data

Hutchinson, Garrie, 1949–
  Great Australian football stories.

  ISBN 0 670 90157 1.

  1. Australian football—Anecdotes. I. Title.
  II. Title: The great Australian book of football
  stories.

796.33'6

Contents

1. Introduction   1
2. The Beginning   2
3. The 1870s: 'The game is getting hot'   18
4. Respectable Opinions   24
5. The 1880s: 'One of our most brilliant football campaigns'   32
6. The split: the 1890s   58
7. 1900s: 'Oh, a bonzer, a bonzer, a boshter, a bontoshter'   93
8. 1910s: 'The call of stoush'   111
9. The Twenties: 'invincible dash and determination'   131
10. The Thirties: 'Victoria's Winter Industry'   146
11. The Forties: 'the smell of eucalyptus oil again'   191
12. The Fifties: a decade of heroes   210
13. The Sixties: 'you can buy anything in club colours'   237
14. Today 'A game of Russian roulette. The winner-take-all ethic rules supreme'   275

1
Introduction

Australian football is not renowned for its literature, but the amount of interesting, amusing, revealing and illuminating writing on and about it ought to be better appreciated. Some of it is in this book.

It has almost entirely been written in newspapers and magazines for an audience that, right from the beginning, was hungry for information. Such books as have been written were meant to survive a single season and then be forgotten. Reflective writing, sitting back and taking the longer view, has not been a characteristic form. Our football literature is immediate, meant to be consumed in a day and then consigned to the fish and chips. In the tradition of ephemera, it retains a terrific freshness.

The amount is daunting, when you consider that virtually every game from 1858 has been reported in some manner, in anything from three to thirteen places, by a talented, fascinated and enthusiastic line of writers.

The millions of words—from Free Kick and Peter Pindar, a hundred and twenty years ago, through Donald McDonald (Observer), R. W. E. Wilmot (Old Boy), Tom Kelynack (Kickero), John Healy (Markwell), Fred Ludlow (Forward) and John Worrall, to the present day—tells us as much about Australia, as about Australian football. Unhappily even a book of this size has to leave a lot out—but I hope that the material here gives some feeling, some taste of Australian football over its long history.

Another book could be put together with what's been left out, or lies undiscovered in the mountains of material in the library. But here's an impression—through games, heroes, stories, poetry, doggerel and barrackers—of our unique game.

2
The beginning

"AN OUNCE OF PRACTICE IS WORTH A POUND OF THEORY"

The origins of the Australian game are lost in the unrecorded activities of ordinary people who happened to have a football (probably a roundish one) in Victoria in the early 1850s. There have been acrimonious disputes about who should be given the credit for its invention from the first recorded game. We'll never know.

In Australia as well as England dozens of different games were played under all kinds of rules, or the absence of them, before 1858. Blokes kicked footies around the parks of Melbourne (and the goldfields), then as they do now, making up rules as they went along.

But for the sake of starting somewhere—because their activities were recorded in the papers—we have to give the honour of inventing the game to Thomas Wentworth Wills. He wrote the legendary letter, he organised the 'first' practice games, and had a quill in the first rules. And besides that he was a remarkable fellow, one deserving greater fame.

Captain of Rugby School in cricket and 'football', a great cricketer for Victoria, coach of many Aboriginal cricketers, five times football Champion of the Colony, he later became morose like Marcus Clarke and stabbed himself with a pair of scissors.

Wills' cousin Henry Harrison was later dubbed 'father of the game'. Four times Champion of the Colony, he was more celebrated, partly because he lived longer, and also because he was more industrious at meetings.

Certainly without him the game would not have prospered as it has.

TOM WILLS' LETTER

Bell's Life, July 10, 1858

Sir: Now that cricket has been put aside for some months to come and cricketers have assumed somewhat of the chrysalis nature (for a time only 'tis true), but at length will again burst forth in all their varied hues, rather than allow this state of torpor to creep over them, and stifle their now supple limbs, why can they not, I say, form a football club, and form a committee of three or more to draw up a code of laws. If a club of this sort were got up, it would be of vast benefit to any cricket ground to be trampled upon, and would make the turf firm and durable; besides which it would keep those who are inclined to become stout from having their joints encased in useless superabundant flesh. If it is not possible to form a football club, why should not these young men who have adopted this newborn country for their native land, why, I say, do they not form themselves into a rifle club, so as at any rate they may be some day called upon to aid their adopted land against a tyrant's band, that may some day 'pop' on us when we least expect a foe at our very doors. Surely our young cricketers are not afraid of the crack of the rifle, when they face so courageously the leathern sphere, and it would disgrace no-one to learn in time how to defend his country and his hearth. A firm hand, a steady heart and a quick eye, are all that are requisite, and, with practice, all these may be attained. Trusting that someone will take up the matter, and form either of the above clubs, or at any rate, some athletic games, I remain, yours truly,

T. W. Wills

A PRACTICE GAME

Bell's Life, July 31, 1858.

Football—We understand that a number of gentlemen interested in keeping the muscles in full vigour during the winter months, and also anxious for an occasional afternoon's outdoor exercise, have determined upon getting up a football club. Mr. Bryant of the Parade Hotel, on the principle that "an ounce of practice is worth a pound of theory", will have a ball on the Melbourne cricket ground, or adjoining portion of Richmond Park, to-day, at one o'clock. After the game, a committee will be formed to draw up a short code of rules. We wish every success to this movement in the right direction.

THE 'FIRST' GAME

Morning Herald, August 7, 1858.

A grand football match will be played this day, between the Scotch College and the Church of England Grammar School, near the Melbourne Cricket Club ground. Luncheon at the pavilion. Forty a side. The game to commence at twelve o'clock.

Morning Herald, August 9, 1858.

Richmond Park was unusually lively on Saturday. Under the auspices of a fine day and their respective magistrates, the juvenile presbytery and episcopacy came out uncommonly strong. Both masters and boys appeared to reach the acme of enjoyment, and most jubilant were the cheers that rang among the gum-trees and the she-oaks of the park when the Scotch College obtained a goal. This event occupied nearly three hours in its accomplishment. The compliment was shortly reciprocated by the opposition, who made a grand effort to do the deed. Evening's anxious shades cut short an amusement which, to judge by the evenly balanced scale of results, and the apparently inexhaustible physique of the combatants, must otherwise have been interminable.

Argus, August 9, 1858.

Football—A match of this excellent game was played in the Richmond Paddock on Saturday, between the scholars of the Church of England Grammar School and those of the Scotch College. The ground was visited during the afternoon by a considerable number of persons interested in the sport. Dr. Macadam acted in the capacity of umpire on the one side, and Mr. Wills on the other. The contest, which lasted until late in the day, was undecided, a game having been declared in favor of each party.

AN IMPROMPTU MATCH

Argus, August 16, 1858.

Football—The match at football between the Church of England and Scotch Schools, which was to have been completed in the Richmond Park on Saturday afternoon, remains undecided, as the members of the Church of England School did not appear upon the ground. An impromptu game was, however, organised among several members of the Melbourne Cricket Club and others who happened to be present, and was maintained with immense spirit for several hours. Football seems to be coming into fashion in Melbourne, and as it is a most manly and amusing game we hope that it may continue to grow in favor until it becomes as popular as cricket. To lookers-on a well-contested football match is as interesting a sight as can be conceived, the chances, changes, and ludicrous *contretemps* are so frequent, and the whole affair so animated and inspiriting. Let those who fancy there is little in the game, read the account of one of the Rugby matches which is detailed in that most readable work, "Tom Brown's School-days", and they will speedily alter their opinion.

NO WHITE FEATHER: A LETTER

Argus, August 17, 1858.

To the editor of the Argus. Sir,—A paragraph appeared in your columns, from which it might be inferred that the Church of England Grammar School Football Club broke an engagement with the Club of the Scotch College, with regard to finishing the match of the 7th inst. You thus inadvertently throw on us the imputation of showing the "white-feather". We beg to state that no such engagement existed, the match having been postponed *sine die*, and that we hope next Saturday to show that we are not wanting in pluck.

By inserting this you will oblige.
Your obedient servant,
The Secretary of the Church
of England Grammar School
Football Club.
Grammar school, August 16, 1858.

MANY CLUBS EXPECTED

Argus, August 30, 1858.

Football—The neighborhood of the cricket-ground in Richmond Park was rendered lively on Saturday afternoon by a match at football which was played by about 50 gentlemen—members of the Melbourne Cricket Club and others. The match between the Church of England and the Scotch schools has not yet been played out, but it is expected that next Saturday will witness its terminating game. At the close of the approaching cricket season it is anticipated that many football clubs of an extensive character will be organised in and around the metropolis.

MELBOURNE GRAMMAR v SCOTCH COLLEGE FINALLY ENDS

Argus, September 4, 1858.

The concluding game between the Scotch College and the Church of England Grammar School will be played this afternoon in Richmond Park. If no goal is kicked, the match will probably be abandoned for the season, as the weather will soon be too warm for football. There is a talk of establishing football clubs next season, so that a number of matches may be anticipated. It is a fine, manly game, which, regulated by good rules, deserves to be a popular winter recreation.

MELBOURNE v SOUTH YARRA

Argus, September 27, 1858.

Football match between Melbourne and South Yarra—A very animated match at football came off on Saturday afternoon, in Richmond Paddock, between 26 players of Melbourne and the like number of South Yarra. Among the antagonists on either side were several well-known public characters whose presence tended not a little to enhance the vivacity of the game, while it certainly increased the curiosity and amusement of the spectators. The game was most keenly contested for nearly three hours, and terminated about half-past 5 o'clock by the Melbourne men kicking through the goal of their opponents in capital style.

AN INSTITUTION IN THE METROPOLIS
Argus, April 18, 1859.

Football—On the 1st of May the cricket season closes. Even now rapidly shortening evening, cold winds, and frequent showers, warn the patrons of the bat that their reign is for the nonce nearly at an end. Not that they intend their physical energies to lie dormant until warm weather sets in again, for football clubs in almost all the suburbs are either being formed or re-organised. Whether that manly and healthy book, "Tom Brown's School Days", or the natural anti-American tendencies of Victoria, adult and adolescent, or a little of both, have produced such a love for robust exercise, it matters not to inquire. Football, like cricket, has become an institution in and about the metropolis, and it would not be surprising if the epidemic spread wider. There are many well-grassed valleys and plains in the immediate neighborhood of the various diggings, where the miners, cramped in their limbs with working in constrained positions, and whose lungs would be none the worse for a little extra oxygen, might enjoy themselves on Saturday afternoons in straining for goals of easier attainment than that which is the aim of their ordinary occupations. Mechanics, too, and artisans, would find their health much improved by a good game of football once a week. The advantages of supplementing summer by winter exercises for such as are chained to the desk, or are otherwise sedentarily employed, are too manifest to require comment. The buzz in the various metropolitan and suburban hives, which promises to end in swarming to the open spaces about the city during the winter months, shows that the necessity for exercise above alluded to is fully appreciated. Amongst the best football clubs who will shortly break ground may be mentioned the Melbourne and South Yarra. The latter, we understand, have already had some little practice together. Nor are the public schools lagging in the matter,—so that before the month is out we may, on all favorable occasions, expect to see every available portion of Richmond Paddock, and other "lungs of the city", dotted by animated groups in full pursuit of the leathern sphere.

THE GEELONG FOOTBALL CLUB
RULES, 1859

1. Distance between goals and the goal posts to be decided by captains.

2. Teams of 25 in grand matches, but up to 30 against odds.

3. Matches to be played in 2 halves of 50 minutes. At end of first 50 teams may leave ground for 20 minutes for refreshments but must be ready to resume on time otherwise rival captain can call game off or (if his side has scored) claim it was a win.

4. Game played with 200 yard wide space, same to be measured equally on each side of a line drawn thru the centre of the two goals, and two posts to be called the "kick off" posts shall be erected at a distance of 20 yards on each side of the goal posts at both ends and in a straight line between them.

5. When kicked behind goal, ball may be brought 20 yards in front of any portion of the space between the kick off and kicked as nearly as possibly in line with opposite goal.

6. Ball must be bounced every 10 or 20 yards if carried.

7. Tripping, holding, hacking prohibited. Pushing with hands or body allowed when player is in rapid motion or in possession of ball, except in case of a mark.

8. Mark is when player catches the ball before it hits the ground and has been clearly kicked by another player.

9. Handball only allowed if ball held clearly in one hand and punched or hit out with other. If caught, no mark. Throwing prohibited.

10. Before game captains toss for ends.

11. In case of infringements, captain may claim free from where breach occurred. Except where umpires appointed, opposing captains to adjudicate.

12. In all grand matches two umpires—one from each side—will take up position as near as possible between the goal posts and centre. When breach is made appeal to go to nearest umpire.

ST KILDA OBJECTS

Bell's Life, June 25, 1859.

Match between two sides of the Melbourne Club—The Melbourne Club held their usual weekly game in the Richmond

Paddock, on Saturday. Sides were selected by Mr. Hammersley and Mr. Bruce, and after some three hours' kicking three goals were obtained—two by Mr. Hammersley's side and one by that of Mr. Bruce. A match is talked about between the St. Kilda and Melbourne Clubs, but the first-named club objects to rule No. 7 of the Melbourne Club, which provides for "tripping" but not "hacking", whether over the ball or not.

The Coast Football Club will meet at Elsternwick this day (Saturday), at 2 p.m.

MELBOURNE v RICHMOND

Bell's Life, July 7, 1860.

On Saturday the Melbourne and Richmond clubs again met, the ground of the latter being the tryst. At the time appointed, several of those selected to play were missing, and the game had to proceed with those who were present—some fifteen on either side. The ball having been put in motion by Mr. Wills the game began in right earnest, neither party gaining much advantage, but at length Mr. Wray, who had made his debut for the present season, kicked the ball into the goal, and the Melbournites hailed this feat with an ecstasy which, alas, was only too soon to be dispelled, for the ball on passing, touched Mr. Bruce, who was keeping goal, before it went through the posts. A slight "talk" having been satisfactorily got over, business was again the order of the day, and a fierce onslaught was made by the Richmondites. Mr. Wills, their indefatigable and untiring captain, then tried a *coup de main*, and placing his men right down to the goal, by this means succeeded in getting the ball safely landed between the posts. The hitherto "unconquered whites" were not to be beaten yet, and the battle was resumed with greater vigour than ever; the "tussles" became more frequent, the "spills" less inviting, and the "scrimmages" thicker and thicker; the whites and the reds were everywhere in collision. The spectators, of which there were a large number, did not escape scatheless; many of them preferred standing in the middle of the field, and when a rush took place they were knocked over by the eager players, and were to be seen sprawling about in all directions. At length Mr. J. B. Thompson, who had only just joined the Melbourne ranks, contrived to obtain a goal for his side, thus rendering the game a tie. As some daylight still remained, Mr. Wills made an attempt to get through the conquering heat, but a very short time sufficed to show the impossibility of playing by twilight, for Mr. Thompson again took the ball in hand (we do not mean that he transgressed the rules), and safely escorted the encased bladder through the goal posts, without fear of opposition on the part of the Richmond keepers, who not having the fear of duty before their eyes, allowed the ball to pass them untouched and uncared for, thus leaving the Melbourne side to glory in their victory. The ground was very slippery, and scarcely large enough, thus causing the ball to go too often out of bounds.

GENTLEMEN MEET TO FORM A FOOTBALL CLUB

Bell's Life, May 21, 1859.

Football—The first game of the season was played on Saturday last, between two sides chosen by Messrs. Bryant and Smith. It was more of a scratch than a strict match, owing to there being no fixed rules of play; some of the parties engaged following out the practice of catching and holding the ball, while others strenuously objected to it, contending that the ball should never be lifted from the ground otherwise than by the foot. The difference of opinion did not, however, prevent the enjoyment of the sport, for the greatest good humour prevailed. A preliminary meeting of gentlemen interested in the game was subsequently held at the Parade Hotel, with the object of forming a Football Club. A list of fifty-one members was submitted, and from amongst them the following were selected as a committee to draw up rules, etc.:—Messrs. Wills, Hammersley, Bruce, Smith, and Wray. Mr. Sewell was appointed treasurer, and Mr. J. B. Thompson secretary of the club. A deputation was also appointed to wait on the Ground Committee of the Melbourne Cricket Club to obtain permission to play on their reserve, at such times as may be hereafter arranged.

The members of the Melbourne Football Club are requested by the secretary to assemble in Richmond Paddock at one o'clock this afternoon.

KICK DOWN, OR DIE! THE BRYANTS' BOLD REPLY

Bell's Life, June 4, 1859.

Scratch match between two sides of the Melbourne Club.

It was expected that a match would have been played between the Melbourne and the South Yarra Clubs on last Saturday, on the ground of the former club, but from some unexplained cause the meeting did not take place, much to the disappointment of the public, who hoped to add to the enjoyment of a stroll on a fine afternoon, the witnessing a match at this popular game. Every preparation had been made by Bryant; new boundary and goal posts and flags had been made, and the ground properly marked out. As there was no likelihood of the great match coming off, Messrs. Bryant and Hammersley proceeded to choose sides from the members of the Melbourne Club, and sixteen players on each side were entered, Bryant's men being distinguished by a red riband, while their opponents, the Hammersleys, adopted the "true blue", as they termed it. After a long struggle, in which the "blues" were twice nearly haling the ball, the "reds" were ultimately victorious in the first innings. After some little time devoted to refreshment, the rival force were marshalled for the second innings. All being in readiness—

> The ball went up—by Bryant strong 'twas sent—
> A wild haloo the blue-domed Heavens rents.
> Then rushed the boys the contest to pursue.
> The honor to sustain of red or blue.

After divers kicks, races and tumbles, the ball was caught by a "blue" within a few feet of his goal. "Mark" was instantly called, but before he could place the ball on the ground and kick it past the goal he was opposed by a massive and impenetrable human wall of "reds". He, however, made the attempt, and, as may be supposed, the ball failed to reach its intended destination but was sent, amid loud cheers, in the direction of the opposite goal.

> Like arrows from the Cretan archer's bow
> The raging 'blues' to battle onward go,
> They fly—they reach the mingled scene of fray.
> Each anxious to become the hero of the day.

11

The ball being kicked into the middle of the field, raised the hopes of the "reds", whose *corps de reserve* coming up at the time, a peneral *melec* ensued, and as

> Ere the storm, the rumbling thunder far
> Calls clouded heaven to black and lurid war,
> So 'Keep it up' is heard, the true blues cry;
> 'Kick down, or die!' the Bryants' bold reply.

The ball was soon afterwards made to curve in as many eccentric evolutions as a knight on a chess-board, till Hammersley, on this occasion most, undeniably "the right man in the right place",

> Swift as an eagle on the wing
> Holds fast the ball, then with a sudden spring
> He leaps high in air and kicks the volume round.
> The ball emits a hollow moaning sound,
> Obedient to this hero's skilful care,
> The football rushes whistling through the air.
> Then—as a bomb, by blazing powder thrown
> High in mid-air, when rapid it has flown,
> Describes a curving parabola there—
> So turns the ball its bending course and fair.
> It falls, and far beyond the 'true-blues' base,
> With many a bound it stops its headlong race.

Each side having obtained a goal, the members were anxious to play the conquering game. In this Hammersley's side were as nearly as possible winning on three occassions, but, on the cry of "reds to the rescue", some one of Bryant's party was always found "there". Honourable mention is particularly due to Mr. May, who gave a splendid kick, and, following the ball, out-paced his pursuers, and delivered another accelerator, when he came down a burster, his heels rebounding from the ground. It was thought by many of the spectators that he was seriously hurt, and it was quite a relief to them when they saw him rise and pursue the flying sphere. Nor was he alone in his misfortune, for we saw three other gentlemen down at the same time, and within a few yards of him. The ball at one period of the game was kicked into a gutter, and afterwards kicked, mud and all, flush in the face of a blue. These little *contretemps*, however, only served to add to the fun of the game, and we are happy to record that the greatest good humour prevailed throughout. As darkness came on, and failing to make a goal, "time" was called, and the game resulted in a tie.

THE FIRST GRAND MATCH OF THE SEASON

Bell's Life, May 25, 1861.

Melbourne v Richmond—The first grand match of the season was played last Saturday, between the abovenamed clubs, on the Richmond ground; Mr. R. Wardell having the command of the Melbourne Club, and Mr. H. C. Harrison marshalling the forces of the Richmondites. The Melbourne players appeared in their new magenta uniform, which, however, was not worn so generally as was expected, while the majority of their opponents adopted the light blue. The contrast was pleasing, but the effect would have·been greatly increased had there been fewer white shirts and more of the coloured flannel. The ball was kicked all over the field, mostly, however, in the vicinity of the Melbourne goal which was ultimately stormed by Mr. Nichols. Neither side had succeeded in getting another goal when darkness put an end to the game.

Melbourne v Geelong—The match between the representatives of the pivot and of the metropolis was played yesterday, on the Melbourne Cricket Ground, in the presence of about 600 spectators. The Geelongese were under the command of Mr. Rennie; Mr. H. C. Harrison being the captain of the Melbournites, who on this occasion, without a single exception, appeared in their magenta uniform, their opponents being distinguished by red caps. The ball was kept moving with great spirit till the signal was given for luncheon, when the rival forces agreed to a truce. Soon after a renewal of hostilities the first goal was kicked by Mr. Nichols, for Melbourne. On changing ends the metropolitans were again fortunate, Mr. Lucas gaining the credit of kicking the leather sphere through the barriers, and thus terminating the match. To finish the afternoon, a scratch match was played, in which Messrs. Harrison and Gregg joined the visitors from Geelong, and Mr. Baker, on the part of Melbourne, gained two goals.

THE SILVER CUP

Bell's Life, May 24, 1862.

The Silver Cup—The match between the Melbourne Club and the University, announced for last Saturday did not come off, owing to the absence of two of the best kickers of the University. The match was agreed to be played by fifteen a side, and when thirteen of the representatives of the University were mustered, the captain of the Melbournites volunteered to play an equal number on his side. This was not agreed to, and the Melbourne club claim the trophy which they intend to hold as a "challenge cup", to be open for competition by all clubs. At the termination of the discussion by the rival captains, a scratch match was played, and one goal kicked. The ball was kept continually moving, till the approach of darkness warned them to desist.

I HAVE NOT HAD THE PLEASURE OF KNOCKING DOWN A MELBOURNE MAN

"Lone Star" in *Bell's Life*, May 24, 1862.

Geelong v Melbourne—Dear Bell,—As one of the members of the Geelong Football Club, who intended playing against the Melbourne Club on the 24th inst., I must say I am surprised to meet so little courtesy on the part of our Melbourne antagonists, and if I did not know that it is with one or two members of the M.F.C. the disagreement arises, I should feel inclined to say that they "funked" playing the Geelong team, and to make such a mean evasion was paltry and despicable on their part. The dispute arises from a difference in the rules of the two clubs, the Geelong rules allow the ball to be picked up at any time, and the Melbourne rules only allow the ball to be taken in hand by a catch, or on the first hop—a fertile source of dispute. Now all players are aware that the Melbourne rules are a "farce", and are only put in force when the club finds a likelihood of an opposing team kicking goal; then they cry "Free kick!" "He has broken the rules!" The Geelong Club played six matches last season against the metropolitan clubs, and with the single exception of one match they played according to their own rules—allowing the ball in hand any time. The match played by the Melbourne rules was a series of disputes as to infringements against their rules. Players in favor of not picking up the ball will say it is not football if you do so. An Irishman would say it was not football if you did not allow hacking and tripping; so, if you alter one rule you can alter another. The Geelong Club made arrangements to play the Melbourne Club on the 24th inst, and are astonished that a mere subterfuge on the part of the Melbourne men should prevent the game. Disappointed that I have not the pleasure of knocking down, or being knocked down, by some of the Melbourne men on the 24th, I remain, Lone Star.

THE 1866 RULES

Bell's Life, May 12, 1866.

At a meeting of delegates held at the Freemasons' Hotel on Tuesday evening, . present—Messrs. Harrison, Wardill, O'Mullane, Murray, Clarke, James, and Chadwick, the following rules were adopted:—

1. The distance between the goals shall not be more than 200 yards; and the width of playing space, to be measured equally on each side of a line drawn through the centre of the goals, not more than 150 yards. The goal posts shall be seven yards apart, of unlimited height.

2. The captains on each side shall toss for choice of goal, the side losing the toss, or a goal, has the kick off from the centre point between the goals. After a goal is kicked the sides shall change ends.

3. A goal must be kicked fairly between the posts without touching either of them, or any portion of the person of one of the opposite side. In case of the ball being forced (except with the hands or arms) between the goal posts in a scrummage, a goal shall be awarded.

4. Two posts, to be called the "kick-off" posts, shall be erected at a distance of twenty yards on each side of the goal posts, and in a straight line with them.

5. In case the ball is kicked behind goal, anyone of the side behind whose goal it is kicked may bring it twenty yards in front of any portion of the space between the "kick-off" posts, and shall kick it towards the opposite goal.

6. Any player catching the ball directly from the foot or leg may call "Mark"; he then has a free kick from any spot in a line with his mark and the centre of his opponents' goal posts;

no player being allowed to come inside the spot marked, or within five yards in any other direction.

7. Tripping and hacking are strictly prohibited. Pushing with the hands or body is allowed when any player is in rapid motion. Holding is only allowed while a player has the ball in hand, except in the case provided in Rule 6.

8. The ball may be taken in hand at any time, but not carried further than is necessary for a kick, and no player shall run with the ball unless he strikes it against the ground in every five or six yards.

9. When a ball goes out of bounds (the same being indicated by a row of posts), it shall be brought back to the point where it crossed the boundary-line, and thrown in at right angles with that line.

10. The ball while in play may under no circumstances be thrown.

11. In case of deliberate infringement of any of the above rules, the captain of the opposite side may claim that any one of his party may have a free kick from the place where the breach of rule was made.

12. Before the commencement of a match each side shall appoint an umpire, and they shall be the sole judges of goals and breaches of rules. The nearest umpire shall be appealed to in every case of dispute.

Carlton Club—The opening match of the season took place on Saturday last, in the Princess Park, between sides chosen by the president and vice-president, and after a very well contested game victory was declared in favor of the latter, they having obtained two goals, which were splendidly kicked by J. E. Clarke. The play of Hillsden, Guy, T. Gorman, W. Gorman, M'Farland, O'Brien, Barfoot, and Lock, for their respective sides, was also exceedingly good. Mr. George Coppin, the president of the club, was on the ground, and opened the proceedings by kicking off the ball. The match will be continued to-day at half-past two p.m.

CARLTON v SOUTH YARRA

Bell's Life, September 15, 1866.

The Challenge Cup. Last Saturday these clubs met at South Yarra, for the third time this season, to contend for the trophy.

At a quarter-past two p.m. the Carlton team took the field (under the captaincy of J. Conway), and their opponents found it necessary to do likewise or else forfeit the Cup. H. Budd having been chosen to command South Yarra, won the toss, and elected to defend the western goal. At half-past two Conway started the match by a fine place kick from the centre of the ground, and soon the battle became exceedingly well contested. Morrell, Murray, J. Ogilvy, and Birkmyre worked like Trojans, and Budd's goal-keeping was as good as usual. For Carlton, the Gormans, Williams, Guy, Hiladen, and Byrne were especially active, and at half-past three the latter, by a fine running kick, succeeded in securing the first goal for his club. With very little delay the ball was again kicked off, and the game continued, with alternate prospects of success, until, at a quarter to four, H. Murray dexterously scored a goal for South Yarra. After this, until time was called, at a quarter to six, some very fine play was exhibited by both sides, but as neither managed to obtain a second goal the match ended in a draw. During the afternoon a numerous assemblage of spectators (including many of the fair sex) honored the game by their presence, and the players were much interfered with by a number of the ''lords of the creation'', who were continually getting in the way, in spite of many urgent requests to ''keep outside the bounds''.

The Royal Park Club, which everybody imagined was defunct, has suddenly come to life, and has had the temerity to challenge the South Yarra Club to play for the Cup. The challenge has been accepted, and the match will take place on the ground of the holders (S.Y.) to-day.

3
The 1870s: 'The game is getting hot'

After the successful, but ad hoc system of playing under Challenge Cup rules, the Victorian Football Association was formed in 1877 to regularise competition. It was an instant success, and the game prospered.

BILL NEWING'S POEM

Australasian, 1873.

Around the boundaries hundreds of spectators stand,
The scene presented to us is strikingly beautiful and grand,
Our men are as tough as trees with deeply earthed roots
    And the ladies quite mutually pronounced them really
    "Killing" in their new knickerbocker suits;
Conversing gaily the time has flown—the clock strikes three,
Each combatant is at his post you see
With determined eye and cap pulled on tight,
With body and soul eager for the fight.
Simultaneously every player for the ball has started,
While each man his adversary is tripping and shoving
    One has leapt up and caught it,
    It's nimble Bill Newing,
Though all make frantic efforts the ball can't be got
And spectators surmise the game is getting hot.

MELBOURNE PLAYER
LOSES KNICKERBOCKERS

Argus, May 23, 1877.

Melbourne (20) v North Fitzroy (25). The new football rules came into force on Saturday, but no very remarkable diminution

At the football match—a scene from the Australian Sketcher of July 1877, showing a well dressed crowd at the Melbourne Football Ground.

of the roughness they are designed to check was perceptible in the above match. The naughty hands forbidden to clutch an opponent's neck in order to pull him off his feet went thither not unfrequently in the course of the play. No doubt experts have got so skilful in the practice of suddenly bringing a foe to the ground that it will take them some time to learn enough self-denial to undergo the pleasure it affords them. Between 2,000 and 3,000 spectators were present. Though Fitzroy had the advantage in numbers, the men, as a rule, lacked weight and reach—the latter a quality of great service when "marks" have to be taken off high kicks.

Their slowness showed itself principally at the commencement. They got the choice of ends, and decided to kick with the wind from the west. Melbourne thus obtained the kick-off, and they had the ball up to the Fitzroy goal in three or four kicks, and might have sent it between the posts had the advanced guard only been in readiness to snatch the opportunity thus quickly offered to them. Fitzroy returned the ball from the kick-off spot—which was distant a strangely long 10 yards from the goal—into the middle of the field, and there it stayed for a short time. The activity of the Melbourne 20, shown in many ways, told with great effect.

Sometimes as two or three Fitzroy men stood with uplifted hands to take the ball from the air, a smart opponent would snatch it from them with a cat-like spring, and astonish them with the cry of "mark", which, of course, entitled him to kick the ball deliberately over their heads. Then, again, when, partly through luck, partly through sharp play—for they were not all novices—the Fitzroy middle division carried the battle forward, the crowd would see the ball snatched up by a nimble-footed red cap, and brought back swiftly along the edge of the ground, past all the hands outstretched to stop him. Then arose a hue and cry—"Pitch him over", "Hold him", &c.—until the whole field seemed to be thrown in his way, and the blockaded runner had to finish up with a hasty kick.

Though the advanced men to whom he had intended to fetch the ball were seldom reached, the play was brought dangerously close to the Fitzroy goal, and the attack, from which the defenders had obtained temporary relief by their abovementioned rally, was renewed with an energy which called for most desperate resistance. Fitzroy had some efficient men, especially one sturdy fellow, dressed in a uniform of his own, not the club's, whose dexterously achieved marks many times afforded his side relief, and transferred the play to the middle ground. But Melbourne could never long be beaten off, and at last F. Baker, who is supposed to be able to make dead certain of a goal whenever he gets a mark within 60 yards of it, secured a catch scarcely 20 yards from the posts.

The Fitzroy team backed quickly to the threatened goal, which became crowded like the entrance to an attacked beehive, and the crowd waited with impatience for the result. The result was *nil*, for Baker completely missed his aim. Every time Fitzroy got a kick off from the front of the goal they sent the ball down into the middle ground, and sometimes they even took it to the opposite end of the field; but Melbourne soon fetched it back, and eventually one of the well-trained twenty had the presence of mind, in the midst of a *melée*, to place the ball gently into the hands of Langdon, one of his own side, about 25 yards from the Fitzroy posts, and the goal was made with a clean straight kick.

When the game was started afresh from the middle of the field, much better play was shown by the Fitzroy team; they got less frequently collected into useless knots at a safe distance from the ball. At the close of half the time allotted for the match the teams changed ends. The public changed ends too, for they correctly foresaw that, now Melbourne had the wind, the forces would be concentrated immediately in front of the eastern goal.

Plenty of amusement was afforded to the onlookers. Combatants hurled one another over with vicious energy, "marks" were claimed and disputed, and captains and lieutenants shouted out encouragement until they were hoarse. Time after time, the well-managed Melbourne team were called upon to make the final charge, and their middle division zealously responded.

At rare intervals some speedy Fitzroy player got the ball through them and carried it half-way up the rise, on the top of which the Melbourne goal posts stood, but before he had recovered breath the ball was brought back to bound about in front of the Fitzroy goal, or to be lost in the crowd behind it. Melbourne, however, in spite of all their exertions, could not get a second goal. They had several sure men close up to the enemy's posts, but the enemy hung on to them so persistently that they never had the chance to make a leisured kick, and all the kicks made hurriedly went widely astray. Finally, when Fitzroy had become tired of the monotony of kicking off the ball from before their posts, and when the light had so faded that players were hardly to be distinguished from the crowd mixed freely in with them, time was called, and Melbourne were declared the victors with one goal. A ludicrous incident occured just before the termination of the game. One of the Melbourne twenty had his woollen knickerbockers plucked clean off him, and he suddenly found himself (with only his shirt and his stockings and his boots to protect him from the cold) the object of universal attention. Somebody generously lent him a coat—an indifferent substitute for a pair of trousers, and 500 delighted boys broke from the ranks and escorted him to the M.C.C. pavilion gate. All through the match the players were greatly hampered by the spectators, and in the last quarter of an hour there were as many onlookers amongst them as there were outside the lines.

FOOTBALL HOSPITAL SATURDAY

By Peter Pindar, *Australian*, August 9, 1879.

> And some, with many a merry shout,
> 'Mid riot, revelry, and rout,
> Pursue the football play.—SCOTT.

The matches for the charities realised about £120, and though the sum is not so large as I expected, it is, nevertheless, a fair contribution from football, and will doubtless be very considerably augmented by the collections at the last Carlton and Melbourne match this season on the Prince's Oval, as these will be handed over to the Melbourne Hospital. As misleading paragraphs have appeared in various places regarding the origin of Football Hospital Saturday, it may just be as well to state once for all that the article on "Sporting and Our Public Charities", which appeared in this paper, was at the root of the matter; this without intending to lessen the credit due to the Melbourne and Carlton clubs for their liberality to the charities in days gone by.

The match by electric light was a great success in point of financial result and attendance, the latter numbering about 8,000 paying members, and about 10,000 to 12,000 outside on the free list—but from a light point of view—and football, too, for that matter—it was not so good, the illuminating power being scarcely sufficient, and its distribution hardly so judicious as it might have been. It is intended to remedy all defects arising through want of experience, and in the machines themselves, and to get another light equal to 7,000 candles—I believe the one used on the Gipps Land railway works—by which the light will be increased about 50 per cent., and to have a match between Carlton and Melbourne, on Tuesday evening next. The admission fee will also be reduced, and I expect to see the Melbourne Cricket-ground filled to its utmost holding capacity.

A match between the past and present players of the Melbourne Football Club, on behalf of the Hospital for Sick Children, will take place on the Melbourne ground on the 16th inst. Mr. H. C. A. Harrison is getting the old players together, and some formidable names are among them, but as it is hardly likely in their present condition they can be very fit, it would, perhaps, be better if they accepted a handicap of a man or two, so as to make a good fight of it.

4
Respectable Opinions
"A DISGRACE TO OUR CIVILISATION"

It hadn't taken long. Visitor and native alike soon became appalled at the enthusiasm spectators showed at football matches, and pondered on what it all meant. Luckily, like all good Victorian writers, they were diligent observers, and wrote down what they saw as well.

The Vagabond *was the* nom de plume *of Julian Thomas, an English reporter who spent the 1870's investigating Melbourne's low life for the* Argus. *He died in Melbourne in 1896.* `

Henry Cornish was an Anglo-Indian, recuperating from illness in Australia in the late 1870's. His book, Under The Southern Cross, *was first published in Madras in 1879.*

Richard Twopeny came to Australia from England aged 8, in 1865. He was editor of a New Zealand paper by the time his remarkable bok, Town Life In Australia, *was published in 1883. He died in 1915.*

'ONE OF THE SIGHTS OF THE WORLD'

Richard Twopeny, *Town Life in Australia*, 1883.

Chiefly owing to the impossibility of bringing about an international football match, the popularity of football is more local than that of cricket; but in Melbourne I think it is more intense. Patriotism cannot, of course, be roused when no national interests are at stake, but club rivalry is decidedly stronger. Some measure of the popularity of the game may be gathered from the fact, that the member who has sat in the last three parliaments for the most important working-man's constituency, owes his seat entirely to his prowess on behalf of the local football club. In no other way has he, or does he pretend to have the slightest qualifications.

Of course there are numbers of people amongst the upper and middle classes who still have a holy horror of football as a dangerous game, and the want of unanimity in rules prevents the two principal colonies from meeting on equal terms. In the older colony the Rugby Union rules are played. Victoria has invented a set of rules for herself—a kind of compound between the Rugby Union and Association. South Australia plays the Victorian game.

I suppose it is a heresy for an old Marlburian to own it, but after having played all three games, Rugby, Association and Victorian—the first several hundred times, the second a few dozen times, and the third a couple of score of times—I feel bound to say that the Victorian game is by far the most scientific, the most amusing both to players and onlookers, and altogether the best; and I believe I may say that on this point my opinion is worth having. Of course, men who are accustomed to the English games, and have not played the Victorian, will hold it ridiculous that the solution of the best game of football problem should be found, as I believe it has been found, in Melbourne. But I would ask them to remember that the Victorian game was founded by rival public school men, who, finding that neither party was strong enough to form a club of its own, devised it—of course not in its present elaborate state—as a compromise between the two.

In corroboration of my opinion I would point to the facts that, while Sydney is at least as good at cricket as Melbourne, there are not a dozen football clubs in Sydney (where they play Rugby Union), as against about a hundred in Melbourne; that the attendance at the best matches in Sydney is not one-third of what it is in Melbourne; that the average number of people who go to see football matches on a Saturday afternoon in Sydney is not one-tenth of that in Melbourne; and that in Sydney people will not pay to see the game, while in Melbourne the receipts from football matches are larger than they are from cricket matches.

The quality of the attendance, also, in Melbourne is something remarkable; but of some 10,000 people, perhaps, who pay their sixpences to see the Melbourne and Carlton Clubs play of an afternoon, there are not a thousand who are not intensely interested in the match, and who do not watch its every turn with the same intentness which characterizes the boys at Lord's during the Eton and Harrow match.

A good football match in Melbourne is one of the sights of the world. Old men and young get equally excited. The quality of the play, too, is much superior to anything the best English clubs can produce. Of course it is not easy to judge of this when the games played are different, but on such points as drop-kicking, dodging, and catching, comparison can be made with the Rugby game; and every 'footballer' (the word, if not coined, has become commonly current here) knows what I mean when I say, that there is much more 'style' about the play of at least half a dozen clubs in Victoria, than about the 'Old Etonians' or the 'Blackheath', which are the two best clubs I have seen play in England.

'A SAVAGE SORT OF DELIGHT'

Henry Cornish, *Under The Southern Cross*, 1879.

There are notices of half a dozen different football matches, in which the features of the game are rather minutely described. A champion team from New South Wales has been over to play the champion team of Victoria. The players on both sides were fine active young men, good specimens of the youth of Australia, but, on the whole, hardly equal in physique to the young fellows who compete in the Oxford and Cambridge sports. The reporter continually refers to them as athletes, and is evidently a muscle-worshipper. One very objectionable feature in the public games here is that the decisions of the umpire are treated with little respect.

An English gentleman whose opinion was openly challenged by players on both sides, as well as by violent partisans among the spectators, would leave the ground in disgust, and probably not without expressing a strong opinion of the conduct of both players and spectators. But the umpire has to submit to this kind of thing, and his office is therefore not an enviable one.

It does not seem quite the right thing either to see the spectators of a foot-ball match behaving as if they were watching a dog-fight. "Go it, Charley", "Round the waist, Smith", "Down with him, Watkins", are specimens of the criticism made on the players by admiring acquaintances in the crowd, during exciting and critical points in the game.

A neat trip-up, or a violent fall, is greeted with applause and laughter, as though the crowd took a savage sort of delight in the discomfiture of the players, amongst whom the behaviour of the spectators encourages bad temper. The captain of a local club had to retire from the field the other day with a broken leg, while another player was put *hors de combat*. In both cases, the newspapers assured us that the mishaps were accidental, and might have happened in the best regulated game. Having witnessed some of the play, my surprise is these accidents are not more frequent.

Altogether there is room for reform in the matches that are played in public. The Victorian game is different to the Rugby one: it has no "scrimmages", and no running away with the ball under the arm; in fact it is played principally with the foot. There is nothing, however, to be said against the form of the game: it is only the behaviour of the players and spectators which is open to objection.

'UMPIRE HAS A HARD TIME OF IT'

Julian Thomas, 'The Vagabond',
from *The Vagabond Papers*, Third Series, 1877.

Football, as it is carried out here, is a new study, and it has given me some curious ideas as to the civilization and humanity of the coming Victorian race.

I am not going to indulge in a tirade against athletic sports, although I have a suspicion that the tendency of the age here, as in England, is to the excessive cultivation of the bodily powers to the neglect of the mental. It is, no doubt, a good thing to be able to jump a five-barred gate, to run a mile in five minutes, and throw fifty-sixes over your head until further notice. But all virtue does not consist in training, and the country will not be saved by such gifts. Mr. Wilkie Collins has shown the danger of muscle usurping the place of brains. *Mens sana in corpore sano* I believe to be generally true, but the principle may be carried to excess, and a healthy mind certainly does not exist where cruel and brutal sports are indulged in. Football, as now carried on here, is not only often rough and brutal between the combatants, but seems to me to have a decided moral lowering and brutalizing effect upon the spectators. The records of the past season show that several promising young men have been crippled for life in this "manly sport"; others have received serious temporary injuries, and laid the foundations of future ill-health, the luckiest getting off with scars which they will bear with them to their graves. Now, is the general good derived from the encouragement of physical endurance in the players, and the amusement given to the spectators, worth all this? I think not, and hold that the evil does not stop here, but that society is demoralized by such public exhibitions as the "last match of the season" between the Melbourne and Carlton Football Clubs, which I witnessed. I arrived early at the spacious piece of ground which has been given to our Catholic friends for religious purposes, and has been let by them for the highly religious performances of Blondin, football matches, &c. The Church of England reserve is adjoining, but that body has been foolish enough to erect a building thereon, the purpose of which is a mystery to most people. I was told that it was a school, a college, a theological seminary, a home for distressed persons, and the house of the care-taker. Now, it is a small building, and could not be all these, so I give it up. The full account of this match, of the goals, marks, free kicks, and individual play of the members, are they not written in the columns of the *Argus*? I deal not with these, but with the moral aspect of football, chronicling, perchance, some items which never appear in newspaper reports, but which I, as a "Vagabond", am privileged to, and do, shall, and will refer to at all times and seasons. The six or seven thousand spectators comprised representatives of nearly all classes. It was a truly democratic crowd. Ex-Cabinet Ministers and their families, members of Parliament, professional and tradesmen, free selectors and squatters, clerks, shopmen, bagmen, mechanics, larrikins, betting men, publicans, barmaids (very strongly represented), working-girls, and the half world, all were there. From the want of reserved seats, or any special accommodation for ladies, the mixture all round the ground was as heterogeneous as well might be. I mingled with the throng everywhere, and had a good chance of arriving at the popular verdict respecting football, as at present played. The Carlton Club were playing on their own ground, and the feeling of the majority was in their favor, and from the commencement was so expressed rather offensively towards the Melbourne Club, which is considered, I believe, to be a little more high-toned, and consequently antagonistic to democratic Carlton. At the commencement I got a position at the rails between a seedy but highly respectable-looking old gentleman, a commercial traveller, and several hardy sons of toil. The old gentleman was my principal study, and opened out on very little encouragement.

"This is a very fine sport," said he. "Yes," I dubiously assented. "It takes you back to old times—the Greeks, you know, and the Romans. You know the Romans?" I said I had met some Rum 'uns in my life. "Ah! you doubtless mean organ players: but I refer to the great men of ancient history, who had their sports in the—in the *Parthenon*," said my friend. "Indeed, sir." "Yes, chariot races in the arena, you know—fights with wild beasts, and Christian martyrs." I got very interested, and begged for more information, and one of the working men wanted to know if "them martyrs" were Catholics? "No, sir," said the old man; "how could that be, when they were killed at Rome. They were Protestants." The son of toil intimated his opinion that it was "all—lies, or else it served 'em right". My friend said that the ignorance of the masses on great religious and historical questions was lamentable, and further proceeded to enlighten me on the sports of the ancients. "The Greeks, you know, had boxing in the amphitheatre, but they had leather things on their hands; not boxing-gloves, but—but—" "Knuckle-dusters," I suggested. "Something of that sort," said the old man, "very brutal, indeed, you know. All the sports were cruel in those days. Now, the young men, here, I believe, are quite as strong and active, and no harm is done to any one. This is a tournament, but a bloodless one, and it perpetuates that love for physical sport which has made our race the most famous in the world, and England the most powerful of nations"; and, like Colonel Starbottle, my old friend swelled and expanded with the pride of race. "Bravo, guv'nor", cried a mechanic, and at that moment the play commenced. If an intelligent foreigner had been present, watching these young men clad in parti-coloured garments, running after an inflated piece of leather, kicking it and wrestling for it, receiving and giving hard blows and falls, he must have thought it the amusement of madmen. The spectators, who howled, and shrieked, and applauded, he would have thought equally mad. It is true that, as a spectacle of bodily activity and endurance, the show was a fine one, but the cruelty and brutality intermixed with it, and which the crowd loudly applauded, and appeared to consider the principal attraction, was anything but a promising evidence of a high civilization. I was told by several that it would be a pretty rough game, and they gloated in the fact. As the play went on, and men got heavy falls, and rose limping or bleeding, the applause was immense. "Well played, sir," always greeted a successful throw. "That's the way to smash 'em," said one of my neighbours. "Pitch him over!" and such cries were frequent, and the whole interest and applause seem centred in such work. It was no fair conflict either; a man running after another who has the ball, seizing him by the neck, and throwing him down, does not, to my mind, do a particularly manly thing. It inculcates bad blood, as the victim is sure to spot his oppressor, and be down on him when occasion offers. Early in the game it was apparent that a bad feeling existed between the players. There was a dispute as to the first goal kicked by the Melbourne club: Was it a "free kick" or not? The umpire's decision was loudly canvassed, and angry players congregated in the middle of the ground. "There's going to be a scrap," said a Carltonite, delightedly, and called out to one of the players, "Go into the—, Jim." Indeed, it seemed to me as if hostilities had already commenced. There was a squaring of shoulders, and the central mass heaved and surged for a minute, and then the would-be combatants were separated. Shortly after this, the umpire took up his stick, and walked off the ground, and the game was suddenly stopped. I asked this gentleman what was the matter, and he said the Carlton players used such blackguard language to him that he would not stand it; and in this, I think, he was right. One friend said, however, that he was wrong. "The umpire always has a hard time of it," said he; "the only thing he can do is to wear several brass rings, if he hasn't got gold ones, and let the first man who disputes his decision have it straight." This idea was received with great favor by the crowd, and is an instance of the good feeling generally engendered by this "manly sport".

After a fresh umpire was procured, the game became as rough as it well could be, without absolute fighting. Luckily the Rugby game, in which a man who holds the ball can be kicked until he releases it, is not played here. Still "hacking" was sometimes indulged in under cover of play, and I was not at all surprised to hear that a man had his eye kicked out at this very ground a short time back. The "scrimmages" were frequent, and altogether the violence used was often totally unnecessary and gratuitous. I watched several individual players. One man would throw or push another down after he had kicked the ball, and without, as far as the play was concerned, any excuse or provocation. The aggrieved one would "spot" his antagonist and repay in like manner. This system of aggression was altogether, to my mind, cowardly and uncalled for, and yet was loudly applauded by the spectators. Towards the end of the game one man fainted; several must be lame for weeks, and every man must have been bleeding or scarred. The gentleman who played in spectacles was plucky, but I would advise him to relinquish the game before he receives further injuries. The victory of the Melbourne Club proved unpopular with the larrikins, who commenced stoning the players outside the gates. One offender, however, received a good thrashing for his pains. I consider that football, as played at this match, is a disgrace to our civilization.

5
The 1880s: 'One of our most brilliant football campaigns'

Football was now well and truly entrenched in Melbourne. The VFA acquired new teams—Essendon, Richmond, Williamstown, Fitzroy, Footscray and Port Melbourne. Fanatical suburban crowds followed their teams, and in 1888, as if to celebrate Australia's (white) centenary, an English football team arrived. They played Rugby against New South Wales, and Australian Football against Victorian teams. It was a great amusement—but one that has never been repeated.

The Melbourne Football Ground, 1883. Early football was played on an irregularly shaped oval beside the cricket ground.

BUYING A PLAYER

By Peter Pindar, *Australasian*, May 6, 1882.

The published lists of players on Saturday last disclosed one very peculiar and interesting circumstance, namely, that a number of prominent men were expected to play in two matches at once, the result, no doubt, of the excessive eagerness of clubs, with the premiership in view, of "running in" any one who may be halting between two opinions, or looking out for the best market for his produce.

And in this connexion a very good joke came recently under my notice in relation to a rising Northern player, who was regarded with longing looks by a rival concern over the river, and who, moreover, was fully determined his wares should bring their highest market value. The club with which he was identified, and in which he had become known to fame, went out of its way to find him constant employment last season, and "all went merry as a marriage bell" until the preliminary canters this year, when the enticing rival decided to "go one

A goal scored at the Melbourne Ground 1881.

better", and therefore not only found him work, but also a house, rent free, and a reasonable prospect of a fair fee per match.

The bargain then was struck, and he shifted his camp, but whether he was dissatisfied with his surroundings, or whether he felt himself "a stranger in a strange land", or whether his old club agreed to improve his condition, history does not disclose; at any rate, he resolved on abandoning his new quarters, and the other night a number of his former comrades, to make sure of him, hired a van, and carted him, bag and baggage, household goods and belongings, back to where he came from, to the great disgust of his more recent friends.

Now, though this case has a decidedly comical side, it also has a decidedly serious one, as indicating how far clubs are prepared to go, even to the length of introducing the thin end of the wedge of professionalism, for the purpose of securing a desirable man; and there is no doubt, if this idea of beggar-your-neighbour goes on much longer, football will soon be confined to two or three clubs whose financial resources enable them to monopolise the best talent; and what is now a mere manly recreation, will speedily become but a money-making game, with all its attendant evils.

I suppose it does not require a very brilliant discernment to trace the present tendency to the rate-money business, and I think it about high time the better class of clubs should band themselves together and endeavour to stamp out this semi professional phase which is coming to the front, or before long we shall see such items as these in the annual balance-sheets—"Fees! for professionals, first 20, so much; special services of A. and B., so much," which specially would bring in the beginning of the end of football as it has been in the past, and as its truest votaries wish it may ever remain.

The "rain which gladdeneth the heart of man" came down in rather too copious profusion on Saturday last during the time appointed for play to make on-looking a particulars agreeable occupation. The players, however, were too eager for the fray to let a searching "Scotch mist" effectually damp their ardour, and they went through their engagements to a man, although "the earth beneath", as well as "the heaven above", was very wet, and playing a matter of great difficulty, and of very little effect.

Melbourne buckled to as usual with 25 of the public schools—
five each from the Church of England Grammar School, Geelong
Grammar School, Geelong College, Scotch College, and St.
Patrick's College—and managed to put them through by two
goals to none. Some of the youngsters displayed very good form,
or at least as good form as could be displayed on a wet and
"greasy" turf, which saw a very considerable proportion of
sitting as well as standing and running exercise. The old members of the senior club were also "all there", and the new ones
proved themselves, especially in one or two instances, decided
acquisitions.

Carlton tried conclusions with 23 of the Star of the same
name, to the discomfiture of the latter, who made a very good
show in the first half, but fell off when the pinch came in the
second. Some of the new men, and especially Baker, an old
Pivotonian, played in excellent style, and I hear that another
who did almost as well, i.e., Tankard, has changed his quarters
to the other side of the Sydney road. The old members also
showed up well, and conclusively proved that their right foot
had not forgot its canning. Of course the match, as an exposition
of the game, in the language of the poets was "not up to much";
a condition of things it did not take a very keen judge to decide
was owing to the state of the ground and not to that of the men.

South Melbourne also played 23 Emerald Hill Juniors, and,
of course, defeated them. And this leads me to remark that I
scarcely remember an instance of the defeat of a senior team
by juniors when the handicap was five men, and it has often
puzzled me why it was reduced to three. I suppose it was "to
make assurance doubly sure", but I really don't see much use
in handicaps at all unless they equalise the chances of a contest,
and this 23-men business certainly doesn't do that—it is always
a guinea to a gooseberry, especially against combinations, on
the seniors. Certainly, the South, in their match, scarcely came
off as well as they might have wished in results, but that was the
fault of their goal-sneaks, and not of their men generally.

Hotham were more successful in their 23 match, as they
defeated that number of the Royal-park with comparative ease,
principally owing to their excellent following play, which completely nonplussed the juniors, and kept them out of the game.

Essendon were the most successful in the matter of goals of all
the seniors in the matches of last Saturday, as they secured four

35

to none against 23 of the Powlett, and considering they were playing a club and not a combination, the outcome is all the more creditable to them, and speaks volumes for the existing playing strength of the club. Long may it continue as good.

I notice in the lists of matches furnished me some rather inconvenient discrepancies—such as two clubs playing one on the same day, two or three clubs playing on the same ground at once, and other little playful eccentricities. To save wrangling immediately before or at a match, I would suggest that the secretaries meet for half an hour some evening to compare programmes and adjust any differences, as there is nothing like settling matters while they will permit of a settlement, and the course suggested might save considerable heartburnings when the time for playing arrives.

THE 'NUMBER ONE' LINE OF BUSINESS

By Peter Pindar, *Australasian*, July 29, 1882.

The old names apparently are not shorn of their interest, for there were at least twice the number of onlookers present at the Carlton and Melbourne match that there were witnessing that between Essendon and Hotham, despite the fact that both the old clubs have had to haul down their colours this season to the youthful aspirants—Carlton to Essendon, and Melbourne to Hotham. Moreover, the contest proved very attractive, as it was well fought out from start to finish, and if the Carlton men have the credit of the win, it is very doubtful if they have the flattering consciousness of meriting it. Before the match the odds were held to be much in favor of Carlton, but after it a very different opinion prevailed, as the Melbourne men undoubtedly played the better football of the two.

Perhaps the individual efforts of the Carlton men rather surpassed those of their opponents, but the latter played together infinitely better, and, as a whole, displayed much superior discipline; the inevitable conclusion of a spectator being that a complete revolution had taken place in the play of the two teams, for Melbourne, once the home of individual glory, had

Carlton versus Melbourne 1881.

evidently become a well-organised, play-together kind of team; and Carlton, once the abode of little marks, shepherding and subordination of self to the general weal, had gone in for the "number one" line of business. I do not know if the experience of Saturday last will alter the tactics of the latter, but if it does not then a speedy farewell to former greatness appears very imminent.

Taking the ball out of bounds and in scrimmages was where the defect was most apparent, for whereas a Melbourne man usually solved the difficulty successfully by a little mark to a comrade, a Carlton man would invariably come to grief by wishing to shine alone—at least, he appeared to think the game depended on his individual efforts, and altogether ignored any assistance from a friend in the shape of a little mark to the latter. The match, as an exposition of the game, though it evoked great enthusiasm from the respective partisans, was scarcely up to first-class form, the kicking for goals being among the lamest I have ever seen, and most of the players were supremely indifferent to the fact that they had a particular place assigned them.

The Essendon men found Hotham a tougher nut to crack than they anticipated, though I understand the latter were very confident of the outcome, on what grounds it would be difficult to imagine—surely not on the result of the last match, after the Essendon and Carlton business. Essendon, at the start and against the wind, looked as if they were going to carry all before them, as they kicked a couple of goals in a few minutes, but after the Hotham men adjusted themselves, and calmly kicked three goals at comfortable intervals, the red and black found themselves, at the end of the first half, with a goal to rub out.

This, however, they managed to accomplish easily, and at "the conclusion of the whole matter", were decided winners by six to three—an outcome well earned on the merits of the play throughout.

South Melbourne had a bad time time of it at Geelong, as they were honestly and thoroughly drubbed by five goals to two. They certainly had hard luck in having their best follower disabled at the start, but they had nothing in the shape of a questionable umpire to contend against, that gentleman on this occasion giving complete satisfaction to visitors and locals.

I suppose the Pivotonians are decidedly elated over this victory, and they certainly have far more cause for jubilation than over the incidents of their Sydney trip, which aroused the enthusiasm of their fellow-townsmen to the pitch of the conquering hero business. Conquering heroes, indeed! Over a parcel of clubs a year or two old, on about the same level as a good metropolitan junior twenty.

East Melbourne added another victory to their rather scanty list, the victims in this instance being the Powlett, who made a decidedly better show than they did on the previous occasion, when they suffered defeat by five goals to none.

WINTER SPORTS

Australasian Sketcher, July 3, 1880.

Of all out-door sports that are played during the winter months football stands at the head of the list; indeed, it may be placed first, and the rest—as far as drawing a big crowd is concerned—nowhere. Cricket, the chief summer game, draws its thousands, but football draws its ten thousands. The wielder of the willow isn't a "circumstance" in comparison with the kicker of the leathern sphere.

At the first match this season between the Melbourne and Carlton clubs, it is stated that 13,000 persons paid at the gates, and the gross takings amounted to £400. And the excitement displayed over the match amongst spectators and players was really something wonderful to an outsider. Indeed, the struggles at times were quite gladiatorial, and suggested to my mind a group in marble for our Public Library, to be placed by the side of that unfortunate gentleman who was "butchered to make a Roman holiday". The group I have the honour to suggest to our rising sculptors might be called "*Playing* Football", or "Where's the Umpire?" It would be a most popular subject, and if Mr. Gardiner would consent to stand as a model for the Carlton athlete the thing would be the greatest success since the tinted Venus.

Youth and beauty are always well represented at the meetings of these rival clubs, and so deep is the interest taken in the struggle of the respective clubs by the ladies of Melbourne and Carlton that it is not difficult to tell from the expression of their countenance which side is winning. Five goals to one, and the damsels of Carlton fairly bristled with smiles, while, on the other hand, the brows of the Melbourne ladies were wreathed with frowns. "Peter Pindar" of the *Australasian*, in reference to the match under notice says:— "Coming to the match itself, I never saw so much excitement displayed over one. From first to last there was a constant hum of voices, which ever and anon as opportunity called, rose into a perfect storm of applause, and made the welkin ring again. The play which evoked it has frequently been surpassed, and we must look, therefore, for its cause in the increased enthusiasm of the partisans of the two clubs". These are the words of wisdom, and it is this same enthusiasm, I am told by regular football lookers-on, that keeps them warm, and helps them to enjoy the icy-cold weather.

A GREAT FOOTBALL MATCH

Australasian, June 23, 1888.

The Melbourne Cricket-ground this afternoon is something of a great octopus stretching out its arms to gather in its thousands. There is a stream of people passing along Flinders-street and down past Jolimont, another through the Fitzroy-gardens and out at the south-eastern gate, a third from the end of Bridge-road, and others almost as large from the direction of the Richmond railway station and down through the park from Powlett-street.

Passengers cling upon the trams from Melbourne anyhow, like a newly-swarmed hive of bees upon a bough. On one tram we counted 93 passengers, which is just about double as many as the licence permits, not only two of the number went further than the cricket-ground gates. What a struggle at the pigeon-holes for tickets! The Rugby "scrimmager" would be invaluable here. The turnstiles groan as though weary of registering the passage of so many people.

Inside the rink the Ragamuffin Troupe of acrobats and tumblers are giving the customary performance—not for mere honor and glory, since one member of the company is occupied nearly the whole of the time in taking up a collection in a ragged cap. An enthusiastic policeman, who has not yet been laughed at by the crowd for his folly in "achivvyin" the bounding wonder of the Yarrapark or the Punt-road phenomenon, enters the ground and attempts to evict the company, but he might as well try to corner rabbits. They decoy him over to the farther side of the ground, then stream back again and continue the performance. All these things are the signs of a great football match. The lode-stone that draws the multitude together is a large blue-lettered announcement on the hoardings "Carlton v. Geelong".

A few words about the clubs, chiefly historic. Although Carlton is known as the "old club", Geelong is really much the elder of the two, for it was first organised in 1859, while Carlton did not come into existence until 1864. Their first colours were orange and blue caps, the rest of the uniform being a matter of individual choice.

Melbourne, oldest of all the senior clubs, were distinctive in this respect, for as all their players were accustomed to wear white pants they became known in the field as the "invincible whites". A significance in the colours outside mere club considerations was sought. One club, for instance, wore green caps with a scarlet band, for, as there were a great many Irishmen in the team, an international blend was desired, and it was held that the blue jersey sufficiently represented Scotland. Someone suggested that this might indicate a resolve to hoist "the green above the red", so, to prevent misunderstanding, the cap was crowned with a large red button.

The soldiers under Lieutenant Noyes played in forage caps and grey jerseys, and it was of them that a poet of the period wrote in this pessimistic strain:—

> Woe to the chap with a narrow chest
> Who meets a 14th with lance in rest.
> A charge, a punch, a sudden crunch—
> Take him away till his wounds are dressed.

Carlton first went down to Geelong to play football in 1869— very nearly 20 years ago—and they were soundly beaten, but it was not until the Geelong and Barwon teams buried their local feuds and turned their united strength against the common enemy that Geelong footballers made a reputation.

They came up to Melbourne shortly afterwards, and a tremendous crowd followed them to the Royal Park, where they met Carlton in the open, won the match, and fairly started their since brilliant career. The poet sung their praises in the following issue of the *Australasian*, the commencement of the battle being thus described:—

"Now, boys, to your places!" Each forward man races,
And almost outpaces the ball as it rolls,
And ere half a minute the Pivot are in it,
And go with a rush for the enemy's goals.

So, after many battles, they meet again today.

Much of the colour and character of the game is foreshadowed in the dressing-rooms, although all that goes on here is something beyond the public ken. The thousands know the players only as they see them afield, but if they are ignorant of what goes on in the dressing-room it is not for want of any lack of energy in trying to find out.

The doorkeeper is constantly pestered with applicants for admission, and reiterates again and again the explanation, "Players and trainers only". A card from Mr. Atkinson brings us under either of these headings, but we are not sure which. Even then one finds that he has pierced merely the line of out-posts, for there is an inner cordon of camp sentries, who all, however, respect the M.C.C. countersign.

THE CARLTON TEAM

First to the Carlton dressing-room. Here are "the boys in blue" all in the bustle of perspiration. The first impression is an over-powering odour of eucalyptus oil, with which several players are generously anointing themselves. They are patriotic in their choice of unguents at any rate, and the room smells like a dense gum forest on one of those dull dewy mornings when the sun has not begun the work of distillation. The players say that this oil takes all the stiffness out of old bruises and generally makes one feel pliant and elastic—a fine physical merit in a footballer.

The little man who has the honor to be trainer of the Carlton team—and therefore to be the envy of all the youth of the north-ern suburb—flits about the room, stumbling over boots and entangling himself amongst uniforms, now with a pair of hard flesh-gloves laboriously rubbing down a player, next handing round a red-labelled bottle and giving to each player a wine-glassful of its contents. It is a cordial—a herbal mixture intended

42

to keep the player's mouth moist during the exertions of the game. It is a brown, bilious-looking mixture, but each player takes his medicine with a good grace, as though his physician had ordered it.

There are no intoxicants used in this room. Nothing but restoratives and "revivers", the latter being the name given by the trainer to his brown mixture. There are constant calls for "Bonnor". This was clearly not the name given to the little man in baptism, but his thrifty physique has provoked another christening from some of the facetious members of the team. Indeed, it strikes one that liberties have been more or less taken with the Christian names of nearly every member of the team. By way of endearment, perhaps, a termination has been added, so that the players have become variously Mickey, Geordie, or Wally.

At one end of a form the club shoemaker is fitting to the boots of the players small leather blocks to prevent their slipping upon the greasy turf. These are big or little, in proportion to the state of the ground, for the use of iron spikes is not permitted. Here is literally the old note of preparation from "Henry V"—"With busy hammer closing rivets up."

At the other end of the form is a heap of glistening yellow dust—the powdered resin into which each player as he leaves the room for the field rubs his hands, so that he may not at a critical moment lose his hold of an opponent. Amongst the uniforms of the players is as great a harmony as in their physique. Several wear small blue skullcaps, but the majority play bare-headed. Every man has the shoulders of his jacket—for it is no longer the jersey of olden times—strapped with chamois leather. Once these might be pulled over the head, and were often torn to ribbons in a match, but the sleeveless dungaree jacket is now tight-laced, and opposing hands glance over it without finding a hold.

It is the battle of ships and guns over again. The player puts on a jacket which he claims cannot be held, and rubs upon his hands a preparation warranted to hold anything. The Carlton team are wonderfully alike in build. There is no tall man amongst them, and but two to whom the descriptions small or slight may apply. They may be correctly described as little-big men. Indeed, as long as one can remember almost, width has been a characteristic of Carlton footballers, and perhaps the dark uniform, as giving the team a solid appearance, may have something to do with it.

Proportionately, most of the teams are models for a sculptor. One cannot look upon them and admit the Anglo-Saxon race is becoming physically degenerate. How safe we might feel on the lee side of a row of bayonets held in such sturdy arms as these, and what a corps either for fighting or a forced march might be organised in an emergency from our footballers. The discipline of a football team is so strict that they have already learned the best lessons of the soldier. The family resemblance in the Carlton team extends largely to the face as well as the frame, and apart from physical considerations the type might be said to lack character.

The profile of this club face is almost a straight line, the forehead hardly as expansive, perhaps, as Mr. Ruskin would have liked it, but the chin dominant, wonderfully square and eloquent in its expression of determination. Altogether not a team to be beaten half-way through a game. Here in the corner is a brawny follower with a skin brown and healthy-looking, carrying that ruddy tint which we noticed so strikingly in the arms of the ex-champion, Edward Hanlan, as he stepped into his boat on the Nepean River for his first race upon Australian waters. Everywhere is muscle and sinew, but no spare flesh. Everywhere the perfection of health and condition.

THE GEELONG TEAM

Now for a peep at the Geelong twenty ere they are summoned to the field by the voice of the impatient thousands outside. The Geelong mentor is quite another type of man to "Bonnor" of Carlton. An old gentleman, brown in complexion, and with his grey "bell-topper" pushed well to the back of his head. Like the prospects of the club this season it seems somewhat out of sorts with the world. Possibly the owner won it when Geelong were last premiers, and the chance of a new one at the end of the season seems poor at present.

Geelong methods are not exactly those of Carlton. Each player, for example, after coating his hands with the powdered resin, pours upon it a few drops of liquid from a small vial which smells strongly of ammonia. It makes the resin stick, and apparently has the effect desired, for the team have the reputation of being holders. Not that the Geelong men are lacking in respect for the rules, but their trainer's "hold-fast" is too strong for them, and they cannot always let go even when they wish to do so.

Before going out each player in turn stands erect, with his arms extended aloft, at an angle of 45 deg. between the line of the head and shoulders. Then, standing in front of him, the trainer drums on the player's chest pretty vigorously with his open palm, just as a doctor might in seeking for a possible weak spot in his patient's lung. This, no doubt, is intended to clear away all cobwebs and keep the breathing pipes clean, for during the next couple of hours they will be fully occupied. Then the trainer stands, towel in hand, watching the players go out, very much as you may have seen the horse trainer in the birdcage at Flemington send away his Cup horse with a last flick of the towel at an imaginary speck of dust upon its glossy skin. The Geelong boys have no chamois leather on their shoulders, and they wear hose of a distinct pattern, the stripes being narrow instead of the regulation inch band. They are, as a team, less muscular than Carlton, and the type of face is more intellectual all through, as might be expected of a team whose recruits are drawn largely from public schools, in contradistinction to Carlton, whose nursery is junior football. The Geelong Club claims the credit of having long ago taught metropolitan teams the benefit of a temperate training for football, and the latter, it seems, have benefited by the lesson. They showed that the footballer must be temperate, regular, and orderly in all things— that he must avoid public-houses as a local optionist would, and observe, at least, the first part of the advice, "Early to bed and early to rise", even if he be not too particular in his devotion to the latter half of it. It is told of a certain senior team that on the night it was founded the members determined to drink success to it, and the order given to the waiter was "Thirty pints of beer and one ginger-ale", the player ordering the latter remarking that he would preserve the harmony in colour, at any rate. The performances of the team in the field are just what the baptism of beer might have indicated. The Geelong team, at the height of their fame, were credited with doing a great deal of their training in the sea-water.

IN THE CROWD

Outside there is no lack of colour. At every step almost one meets some of the champions who followed the bounding ball in the days when the first two goals settled the match, even if they were got inside five minutes—an unsatisfactory arrangement as compared with the spirited two hours' struggle of to-day. These old footballers are wonderfully loyal. Having once worn the colours, they must perforce cheer them on for the term of their natural lives.

Foremost amongst them is the honourable member for the district, a dashing player in his day and a terrible charger. Who that saw it will ever forget the way in which he spread out "Big" Watson on the Corio ground, when that good-tempered giant from very force of circumstances was accustomed to play nine-pins with his opponents?

The pleasant face close by, with the "strawberry blonde" moustache, is clearly that of Lanty, "the famed punt kick". Not far away is a noted follower of the blues, who in the days when condition was a less important point than it is now, we have seen search about for a couple of pebbles to keep his mouth from catching fire, for there were no herbal mixtures then.

He seems to fit the family motto, "*Virtutis Gloria Merces*". Another equally old "Blue" is the honorary secretary of the association—one of the founders of the club. It is said that some of the keenest critics in the world are the crowds who gather to see Yorkshire or Notts play their county matches, and of this crowd of 20,000 people gathered here to-day it may be said with equal truth that, excluding the ladies, not five per cent can be taught a new point in the game. The game is too often described by those who know nothing about it as a mere vehicle for the release of passions otherwise dangerously conserved. Brain force is put down as the first and last requirement in the footballer. A player must necessarily have a good constitution to stand the strain put upon it, but unless he has, in addition to strength of arm and limb, a cool head, he soon learns that he has no business on the football field.

Even the suspicion of rough or unfair play will bring a thunder of groans from the crowd, and thus the very influences that urge the footballer to do his best prevent him doing that best in any other than a manly and generous spirit. He must be pretty thick in the skin who can disregard the censure as conveyed in characteristic manner by such a gathering as this.

The fascination of the game can only be realised in moving thus amongst the crowd. Here is a youth of 14, perhaps, hanging half over the front of the grand stand. His face is a mirror, in which every change of the game is faithfully reflected. Watching it, you may turn your back to the players, and yet know how the game goes.

In the one instant there is gloom—Geelong are forcing it up the ground—then a spasm of joy, Carlton has turned the attack. No comedian on the stage ever forced his face to express so many feelings as this boy unconsciously portrays. Now, again, facial expression cannot rise to the situation, and he screams out a word of approval or advice to a player on the further side of the ground, which distance, even it not the din of the crowd, would prevent his hearing.

All the badges worn are blue and white to-day, only of Geelong it may be said, something in the words of Ophelia, "You wear your blue with a difference." The "hon. member", hesitating between the claims of birth and residence, has compromised the matter in a necktie which pledges him definitely to neither team. The colours displayed in hat, scarf, or button-hole are of three styles. First, the sixpenny badge of superfine silk, then the threepenny favor, hardly so good in quality, and, last, the penny cardboard, generally worn by a boy in the band of his hat. Had it cost a guinea, it could not be the symbol of a keener partisan.

A delicate-looking boy, not more than eight years old, is talking football to a friend. "I've been a supporter of Melbourne for three years," he says in a melancholy tone, as though venturing the hope that such devotion must some day have its reward in seeing the club premiers. "The South Melbourne push", we learn, are pretty good; and a third team are described as "nearly all butchers", but whether by occupation or inclination is not made clear. For the time being, indeed, all the onlookers are but boys of large growth. The highest official of the Carlton club is even more illogical than the rest and all through the play continues to assert things just as firmly in the one instant as he denies them in the next. A Carlton player has the ball now, and the president applauds vociferously. "Well played Johnnie. Well played Johnnie. The best man in the team," he continues in a tone that challenges contradiction. Then the player bungles it sadly, and all the praise is taken back again with an indignant "Pooh! he's not fit for the second twenty." Space forbids one telling of all the funny things he sees and hears amongst the crowd at a football match.

COMING OUT

A cheer taken up all round the ground announces the appearance, just as you see them in the sketch, coming through the gate way. "The foremost Tartar in the gap" is the captain of the Geelong twenty. Close behind him is the umpire in white cricketing flannels and Cambridge-blue cap—the hardest-worked man, perhaps, of the whole forty. He is generally an old player, who acquired his stamina in playing the game, and now by reason of his coolness and judgment is chosen to see fair play. A still wilder cheer announces the Carlton team. Not many years ago the captain would have moved about, paper in hand, placing his men and instructing them. "You play back and watch the goal-sneak. You keep just outside the ruck. You go forward on the right and play to Dedman."

Such were the orders given by Carlton skippers of old. Now every man knows his place, and experiments in the way of changing are rarely made in a big match unless there is good reason for it. Even the coin is spun in the dressing-rooms. The losing side places the ball in the centre of the ground, the partisans of both sides unite their voices in a swelling roar of excited encouragement, and the game has commenced.

FROM THE PLAY

Now to single out a few of the leading players from the bulk as the game proceeds. M'Lean and Baker, two of the manliest and most generous of footballers, may appropriately be named together, for each stands at present a unique example of loyalty and devotion to one club. The former, though he carries on his business in Collins-street, does not permit distance to separate him from the team with whom he has so long and creditably played, while Baker has for years past been resident near Geelong, and has travelled down to Melbourne Saturday after Saturday, season after season, to play for Carlton.

And for this reason, not less than for their merit as players, the two, it is certain, are held in higher estimation by the 20,000 people round about them than any dozen of footballers of the "sundowner" type, of which there are one or two in blue a-field to-day. Here is a neatly-built footballer who has played the game with Carlton for, I should think, 15 years, played it manfully and well, and yet it seems to have hurt him but slightly, for, as one of the onlookers puts it, "He's a bit of a Goer still." The name links us in a sense with some of the worthies of the past.

HALF-TIME

In the dressing-rooms preparation is being made for half-time. The janitor at the door fills his bat with oranges from the club bag, while "Bonnor" wrestles with a carpet bag in which are nicely-sliced lemons. A half-dozen enthusiasts—champions of a bygone time—file into the room, pull off their coats, and roll up their sleeves, preparatory to giving the team a rub down.

The players are a long time forcing their way through the crush in front of the grand stand, and hundreds of hands are stretched out to pat them upon the back as they pass. Inside they have little else to do than wash away some of the mud from their faces and suck their lemons—enthusiastic followers see to everything else. Half the players are talking at one time about incidents of the play. The follower with the muscular arms looks upon them with some concern, for there are red weals across where opposing hands, coated with resin, have glanced, across. "Yes," he says, "they do hold you." At three quarter time there is a final and hurried distribution of lemons as the players change ends for the last time.

CARLTON V ENGLAND

By Markwell, *Australasian*, June 23, 1888.

Saturday last will, in time to come, be looked upon as a landmark in Victorian football, since it was the day upon which, for the first time in our history, a team of footballers imported from the mother country tested the quality of the native article. The first appearance amongst us of Lillywhite and Shrewsbury's

The English football team 1888.

combination was looked forward to with exceeding interest, and the fact that they were to be pitted against Carlton, the premier club of the colony, lent an additional attraction to the meeting, which took place on the Melbourne cricket-ground. The afternoon was beautifully fine, the turf was in perfect order, and the crowd that assembled was gigantic in its proportions.

The splendid attendance of the previous Saturday, when every available point of vantage appeared to be thronged with occupants, was improved upon, and the wonder was, not that so many were brought together by the novelty of the entertainment, but that they were able to cram themselves into the allotted space. There were fully 25,000 people in solid phalanx surrounding the arena, when, at 3 o'clock, the Englishmen, following close upon the heels of Carlton, filed out through the grandstand gates amidst applause that was as hearty as it was deafening.

The visitors were hard to please if they were not more than satisfied with their reception, as well as with the generous recognition accorded throughout the game to individual acts of smartness on their part. The doings of the local heroes, no matter how meritorious they were, received only scant attention and moderate cheering, but in no single instance was good play on the part of England's representatives permitted to go unrewarded. This was exactly as it should be, and it is to be hoped that the day is very far distant when exponents of any branch of sport shall come amongst us from the old land—or, for that matter, from any land outside of our own boundaries—and be treated less generously.

The formidable appearance of the visitors, their splendid physique, the neatness of their costume, and the appropriateness of their colours (the red, white, and blue of old England) formed themes of favorable comment on every side, and, indeed, it must be admitted that our men suffered by comparison, for they were neither so massive in stature, not genteelly equipped in the matter of attire. Their sombre dark blue, in many cases rendered more than naturally murky by contact with muddy soil in previous encounters, found no admirers amongst the unusually numerous gathering of well-dressed ladies who graced the scene.

But "the play's the thing". The handsomely-accoutred Englishmen had had only very moderate experience in the game under our rules, and perfection at it was not expected from them under the circumstances. It was thought that they would exhibit no aptitude whatever for our style of play, but this was the opinion of only the extremists amongst our native population, and it was more than counterbalanced by the absurd idea entertained in quarters where everything Australian is despised, namely, that the visitors would have no difficulty in putting our men through.

Neither prediction was verified in the encounter, which displayed great aptitude amongst the members of the team for accommodating themselves to the exigencies of their novel situation, and which showed beyond a doubt that, with a month or two's practice most of them would become adepts at the game. The task they undertook when they decided to meet Carlton in their first match in the colony was one which a less courageous band would not have had the pluck to tackle.

The Carlton representatives, headed by Leydin, first appeared upon the scene, and were received with loud cheering, which was increased tenfo'd as the stalwart forms of the Englishmen passed through the wicket-gate into the arena. Three hearty cheers were accorded the visitors by the wearers of the dark blue, and the compliment was vigorously reciprocated by Captain Seddon and his men.

After this teams took up positions for the start, and Carlton, who had lost the toss, kicked off against the wind in the direction of the grand stand end. The ball was returned in the orthodox fashion by the English backs, and T. M'Inerney, having secured a mark, sent the leather to White, who quickly passed it to Strickland. The last-named drove it well forward, where a free kick was awarded Anderton for having been pushed from behind by a Carlton man. The former kicked to Paul, who brought the house down by securing the first mark obtained up to this by the visitors. Shortly afterwards Bailey did a smart run on the wing, and Moloney obtained a mark which resulted in Stoddart (back) displaying some cleverness in repelling the attack, but Moloney once more drove the ball forward, and Cook ably seconding his efforts, succeeded in giving M. M'Inerney a chance of scoring, which produced the first behind for Carlton. Chapman kicked off, and Goer to Coulson caused the contest to be still continued in the neighbourhood of the English citadel. Haslem, however, came in grand style to the rescue, and with a good run down the wing, raised the siege. The little marking of Carlton soon again placed them in a forward position, and Green notched their second behind, which was followed by a third kicked by Bailey. M. M'Inerney also had a try for goal, but his effort lacked power, and Eagles, Stoddart, and Paul, in succession, were applauded for their determined efforts to drive back the assailants.

The visitors, owing to the fact that they seldom attempted to mark the ball, made no headway against their clever opponents, whom they permitted time after time to best them in this respect. Gellatley, by a smart exhibition of dodging, gave Hutchinson a chance in front of goal, but the ball hit the post, and a behind only was telegraphed. A neat little run by Dr. Brooks followed the kick-off, and was responded to by Bailey, through whose agency Coulson was enabled to give Gellatley a mark in front, which added another behind. Eventually, A. Coulson sent the ball through, and secured first goal for his side. The kick-off from the centre by Paul was a long one, and his side followed up with so much dexterity that Carlton's backs were taken unawares, and Scarborough kicked the visitors' first behind. The ball was next rushed up to the Englishmen's territory, and Chapman and

Stoddart repulsed the attack, only to have it renewed a moment later by Berry and M'Inerney. Again the English defenders warded off the danger, and by neat dribbling transferred the play to the other end of the ground, where Leydin showed to advantage, and the oval was passed to Hutchinson, who sent it along to Smith. The latter's attempt was spoiled cleverly by Haslam, and a good rally succeeded, in which the visitors displayed good pace and great determination, but, as before, they failed to mark when they had opportunities, and their opponents in a few minutes had them again under the whip. Batters gave Goer a mark in front of goal at an easy distance, and the veteran did not fail to put on second goal for Carlton. Stewart and Paul were busy after the kick-off, and the leather was forced out at Carlton's end, where Nolan and Anderton put in good work, which was responded to by Leydin and White, and Coulson marked to Berry, from whom Green came into possession. The last-named sent the ball to M'Inerney, who added a behind just before the first bell sounded. The visitors had up to this scored only one behind to Carlton's 2 goals 5 behinds. Anderton and Thomas were conspicuous for England after the change of ends, but their efforts were neutralised by a splendid run of Moloney's, which caused the play to be carried on at the visitors' goal, and Cook taking advantage of a very easy opportunity, put up third goal for the locals. Paul kicked off, and through the efforts of Scarborough England had a slight advantage, which White's grand marking and Strickland's brilliant running quickly deprived them of, and Berry piloted the leather neatly through for Carlton's fourth goal. Bumby, Seddon, and Nolan kept themselves meritoriously employed after the ball had again been set in motion, but Baker and Cook were well on the ball, and the former had a shot which was stopped by Banks. Nolan displayed great fleetness in taking the ball down the wing, but Baker to Bailey returned it at once, and Berry having obtained a mark from Whelan was again successful, and the fifth goal was recorded. Haslem, Stoddart, Bumby, and Seddon worked hard to keep the score of their antagonists from mounting, but in vain, for Gellatley and Baker each contributed a goal before half time, when the board showed Carlton 7 goals 7 behinds, England a solitary behind.

Up to this point the visitors had played spiritedly, and their forwards had had numerous opportunities which, through their inability to mark, had been useless to them. They appeared to think of nothing but dribbling the ball through, and the smartness of their opponents invariably upset their calculations in this direction. In the third quarter they showed to much greater advantage, and made a number of good marks. Their first successful attempt at a little mark, which was effected by Williams to Paul, evoked an outburst of applause from the assembled multitude, who all through liberally acknowledged any meritorious display on the part of the visitors. Indeed, everybody seemed delighted, and all cheered loudly, when Thomas gained their first goal, notwithstanding that it would probably not have been recorded if the dark sides had been in earnest at that particular incident. Carlton's tendency, added to the improved causing of the Englishmen, in which Eagles. Laing and Chapmen were most noticeable, kept the play during the greater part of the quarter at the locals' end and after Chapman had with a good shot hit the post, Dr. Smith obtained a mark from Eagles, and from an easy distance punted the ball through for their second goal. These successes seemed to rouse them to more strenuous exertions, and in all parts of the field they did good work. Their third goal was gained by Banks with a well-directed kick from a little to the side at 40 yards distance. Carlton had in the meantime added a goal, for which M. M'Inerney was responsible, and the quarter closed with the scores at 8 goals 10 behinds for them, and 3 goals 7 behinds for the Englishmen. No quarter was given by the dark blues during the concluding stages of the game, and they put on 6 more goals and 7 behinds to England's nothing. The latter were, however, on the point of scoring on their merits when the final bell sounded and deprived them of the honor. The totals were—

Carlton, 14 goals 17 behinds.
England, 3 goals 7 behinds.

Baker, Bailey, White, Cook, Green, and Leydin did excellent work for the local team, and amongst the visitors Bumby was conspicuous with many a really fine run, Paul marked and kicked well, Anderton did a lot of useful work in his place, and Eagles, Stoddart, Seddon, Haslam, Nolan, Burnett, Banks, and others displayed qualities which, if properly directed, would have given Carlton quite as much trouble as they would have relished, and perhaps a little more.

SOME PLAYERS

CHARLES BROWNLOW

Sportsman, July 2, 1884.

Mr. Brownlow is a footballer well and favourably known through out the colony. His success in the football field dates as far back as 1875, when he first donned football colours to do battle for the North Geelong club, which was then in its infancy. He stuck to the club for five years, and in 1880 had the honor of being grouped with nineteen others as the champion junior team of Geelong and Western District, W. Bates being the Captain. In 1881 Brownlow joined the Geelong ranks and played in different places in the field under the captaincy of 'Tommy' Austin, who had the honour of piloting the champion team that year.

In 1882 Brownlow played under Jim Wilson and in his place on the right wing (back) he 'was a hard nut to crack' and gave forward men some trouble. In 1883 he was unanimously elected Captain of the Geelong team, which was very weak. Indeed, it was feared that they would render a very poor account of themselves, but Brownlow was by no means discouraged, and what with careful attention to training and other means, he had the high honor at the end of the season of being placed in the centre of a group of portraits representing the Champion Teams of 1883.

At the beginning of the present season he was re-elected Captain of the team, but in consequence of having to closely attend to a business of his own he was unable to attend to practice. This precluded him from showing anything like his true form, and, after the Essendon match, he determined to resign his position. As a skipper Brownlow was a great acquisition to the team, and he was a great favorite with the general public. At present he holds the position of Captain of the Corio Bay Rowing Club, and in the athletic arena he has distinguished himself by winning the Geelong Football Club Handicap at the Corio Bay Rowing Club's sports on the 9th November, 1883.

PETER BURNS

Sportsman, September 23, 1885.

Peter Burns is a comparatively recent acquisition to the ranks of Melbourne footballers. Playing with the club which has the best record this season and which includes some of the best men playing, Burns, more popularly known by the Hillites as Peter, has shown up to great advantage. He is quite a young fellow, having been born at Steiglitz in 1866 and is therefore only 19 years old. This is his first Melbourne season, but he played with the Ballarat Imperials for two seasons, when, with McKenzie, another South Melbourne crack, he rendered great service for that club.

He is principally known as a follower, and in that position has few superiors, while as a goal kicker he has also won his spurs in this branch of the game. He is powerfully built fellow, his work at the boiler making trade making him hard as nails. Although possessed of unusual strength, he, unlike some other burly players does not use it in an offensive way, and he is about one of the most even tempered players who appear on the field.

He is a great favorite with the other players and all the supporters of the club, and if the red and white go through without defeat, as there is every probability of their doing, Burns will have the satisfaction of knowing that he has contributed his full share to the success of the club.

HARRY STEEDMAN

Sportsman, July 2, 1884.

Mr. Harry Steedman, the present Captain of the Geelong football team, is the youngest skipper that the team has ever played under. 'Steedo' as he is familiarly termed, first graduated with the Wanderers Club, which, in the year 1879, was distinguished for its fine play as a junior team. In 1880 he went over to Geelong and for the first half of the season played with the second twenty, where he gained great distinction for his play as a follower.

Later in the season he played as an emergency man against an Essendon team with the first twenty. His maiden appearance in the senior team was a great success and he has remained in the Geelong team ever since. In 1881 he played again with the Geelong team and was chosen as one of the Victorian team to proceed to Sydney for the purpose of playing against the Sydney clubs.

The match was won by Victoria 9 goals to 1, and out of this number Steedman kicked three.

Later on he played with the Victorian twenty against a South Australian team on the East Melbourne ground. In the season 1881 he kicked 11 goals for Geelong and in 1882 14 goals. Altogether he has played in three premier teams hailing from Geelong. At the beginning of this season he was elected vice captain of the Geelong team, and when Brownlow resigned, the team elected him to the captaincy.

His first appearance in his new role was against Melbourne, when he won the toss, kicked two goals, and the match ended in a decisive victory for Geelong. Steedman is in every way the essence of a genuine footballer; he never attempts to take a mean advantage and, if we had a few more Steedmans in the football field, there would be very few accidents, or ill feeling. He is a great favorite in Geelong, both in social and sporting circles, and his elevation to the position of captain has been received with great favor by the townspeople.

NED POWELL

Sportsman, August 26, 1885.

Mr. E. Powell is one of the best known and popular among Victorian footballers. It is now 9 years since Mr. E. Powell joined the ranks of Essendon, then one of the most promising junior clubs in the vicinity of Melbourne, and which some six years ago blossomed forth as a senior club.

A couple of years after this Mr. Powell was elected their captain, a position he has since held, except in 1883 and a portion of last season when he was suffering from ill health. As a skipper he has all the requisite qualifications, being cool, clear headed, and very much liked by his team, to whom he has always shown a good example on the field. Although not a brilliant player, he is yet a very safe one, and in his favorite position as centre-man has very few to equal him.

6
The Split: the 1890s

Collingwood won a premiership in its last year in the VFA in 1896, before the Victorian Football League of six clubs broke away from the Association. This split was fundamentally over what should be done with the gate money, professionalism, and the perennial problem of the powerful and successful clubs wanting to maintain control. The 1890s also saw an Essendon team which barely lost a game and which had in it the best player yet seen: Albert Thurgood.

MELBOURNE V. ESSENDON—
A GREAT GAME

By 'Observer', *Argus*, July 3, 1893.

To call Saturday's match a great one is neither an exaggeration in words nor an outburst of cheap enthusiasm, for, though we may see many good games yet this season, we shall not see such another. One of that sort in a season is a rarity, two almost an impossibility. Played under all the conditions that ordinarily make a match a failure, the importance of the issue, the splendid determination of the teams, and the sensationalism which was the one other thing wanting to make a great game memorable, lifted it above the commonplace, and one forgot the mud and all other disadvantages.

I doubt whether a football crowd has ever been worked up to such a pitch of excitement before as during the last half of the game, for however great may be the appreciation of such meteoric play as that of Melbourne at the outset, everything else must rank below the splendid determination and never-say-die spirit of Essendon towards the end, when they changed defeat— apparently as implacable and hopeless a defeat as ever faced any team—into a moral victory. Essendon has many fine things in its calendar of victories, but nothing finer than this game, which they did not win. I am not going to weigh points, phases, and chances in order to come to a valueless decision as to which

The 'novel spectacle' of a costume football match staged by members of the theatrical community at the East Melbourne Cricket Club on behalf of the widow and family of the writer Marcus Clarke.

should have won—that is a point that may be left to barrackers and partisans to argue and argue again until the 5th of August, when the teams meet again on the Melbourne Cricket Ground—but one cannot help feeling that it was a good thing for the game that neither side won, and that ahead we have the certainty of their meeting again and the chance that it may be on a dry day and a sound turf.

Those who care not a straw which team wins will, by a great majority, say that the balance of honors at any rate was with Essendon, for the dogged pluck that neither sees nor accepts defeat is, we are pleased to consider, one of the attributes of Anglo-Saxon blood, and we like to get the proof of it occasionally just to show that it is no mere worthless conceit. Again, Essendon at the finish were fighting for the win, and Melbourne obviously content with the draw—but here again comes in the sense of satisfaction, for if Essendon's play was fine then, so also was the courage and thoroughness of the Melbourne backs when overwhelmed again and again, and some of them almost dropping in their tracks from exhaustion, they fought bitterly against the threatened defeat. "Good boys, all", was the verdict, and I should not like to say which team the crowd has most in mind when they cheered both at the finish of the game.

Passing on to the different phases of the game there was a strong impression that, whichever team got the wind to begin with would gain a great advantage, and that bit of good luck fell to Melbourne. For the wind was strong enough to keep most of the play with anything like evenly-matched teams in the ground of the twenty fighting against it, and here was the other side's chance to kick goals before the ball got so wet and heavy as to make goal-kicking difficult. And for a little while it looked as though Melbounre were going to waste the opportunity in missing the goal, while literally running over Essendon in the general play.

It was not so much the record of 4 goals 7 behinds to nothing that dazed the Essendon men and threw a funereal gloom over the usually chirrupy right-hand corner of the grand-stand, but the fact that the Essendon team were being beaten so decisively in every point of play, that while Melbourne played like a machine, marking, passing, and kicking the wet ball as quickly as surely, Essendon fumbled, missed, hesitated, and were, to all appearances, hopelessly lost. Never have I seen so bad a beginning to so superb an ending, for the one point that cannot be overlooked is that Melbourne got their lead with a comparatively dry ball, and Essendon wiped it off with a wet and heavy ball. Essendon, as the beaten team of the first half, still got 1 goal 7 behinds; Melbourne, as the vanquished in the second half, scored 1 behind.

It was the manner in which Melbourne kept on against the wind when ends were changed that frightened Essendon, if anything did, for the early half of this quarter, when Melbourne got another goal, had a show touched in going through, and a third marked in the goal, made it look as though, wind or no wind, Essendon had met their masters. Some of the Melbourne men think that their team played themselves out in the first 40 minutes, but their superiority was only partly accounted for in Herculean effort and partly by the fact that Essendon had not yet begun to play.

When they did they had things so much their own way that a better record should have been achieved at half-time, three of

Off to the Essendon v South Melbourne match.

their misses especially being ridiculously easy ones. At half-time Dick sent two extra men into the ruck, and Fox, it is held, should have done the same, but he took the justifiable view that a disposition of the field that had given his side a lead of five to one was worth keeping on, and a captain, it will be remembered, has to form his judgment before the event, but his critics after it—conditions which are all in favor of the critic. Personally, I am inclined to think that it was more Alick Dick's superior team than his superior tactics that pulled the colours through.

The game was played in a fine spirit though the credit in this respect lies chiefly with Melbourne, for Essendon at the outset broke the rules constantly, and although some of the thoughtless amongst their supporters think that Trait was then unnecessarily severe upon them, that strictness, for it was not severity, was really the best thing that could have happened them, for it did what the repeated appeals of their captain and cooler players could not do, caused them to knock off wrestling and play football. Had Trait not punished them as he did, Melbourne would certainly have retaliated, and had the game deteriorated into mere spiteful rough and tumble, it is doubtful whether Essendon would have made up its leeway. My own conviction is that Trait's judgment and fairness had an effect on the game which those who take the umpiring as merely a detail quite fail to appreciate, and if Essendon have any feeling over the matter it should be one of gratitude.

Passing on to comment upon the individual play, it was decidedly bad luck for Essendon that so valuable a ruck man as Forbes should have wrenched the back sinew of his leg in the first few minutes, so that he had to go forward instead of being the power he usually is in close play. That fact adds still more to the credit of Essendon's recovery, for what one really good man means to a team has been illustrated of late in the accidents to such players as Banks and Peter Williams. Usually opinions do not differ widely as to who is the player of the forty, but in this instance I don't care to attempt the task, and prefer to think that Essendon were almost equally indebted to Campbell, Crebbin, Gus Kearney, and Vautin for their success. Campbell was certainly the lion of the third quarter, and the splendid dashes of that pleasant-faced, mud-bespattered pocket Hercules roused everybody to enthusiasm.

In addition to getting a goal, one of his shots for goal, too, it was said, touched the post, and two others were remarkably close. Crebbin's play was of an all-round character. It may be urged that a centre-man who is playing back into his own goal one minute and down to within goal-kicking distance of his enemy's posts the next instant is not keeping his place, but the amount of work he did covered every objection, for nothing succeeds like success. The two goals he got too—one of them a beauty—came when Essendon needed goals and the hope they bring with them very badly. Between these two—Crebbin and Campbell—the pride of place for the day certainly lay. Gus Kearney worked away untiringly in the ruck as usual, where both he and his brother were valuable men, not merely because of the persistency with which they got the ball themselves, but for the way in which they spoiled the ruck play of their opponents, more especially in the last half of the game. Vautin started slowly, like all the rest of his side—and their Fitzroy, Carlton, and Melbourne matches would seem to say that they are bad beginners—but later on he had his share of the glory of the occasion.

Of the place men on the Essendon side the most consistently useful was young Grecian, and many complimentary things were said of his skill, his sureness, and his coolness; but admitting all that, his efforts are in my opinion not to be mentioned in the same day as the four already named. He wisely kept out of the ruck, unwisely, on the Melbourne part, had scarcely any opposition, since his opponent was always somewhere else, and so, having little difficulty in getting the ball often, always took care to do something useful with it. G. Stuckey, the other centre man, did very well, and having a man of very much his own height, weight, and pace against him in O'Dea, their tussles were clever and interesting, the Essendon man having the best of it at first and the Melbourne later on. In a comparison of the backs the credit lies all with Melbourne, who were much the strongest in that quarter of the field. Essendon certainly made a mistake in substituting Young for Prentice, for the former was not himself and of little value to the side. Chadwick was under notice a good deal for three things—his rattling good back play, the disregard he showed for all rules about holding, and the persistency with which he watched Smith, the Melbourne goal sneak. Alick Dick, like Grecian, was always cool and collected, and always in the right place in an emergency.

Finlay's high marking was always clever, and once or twice superb, but otherwise there was nothing in the defence to rave about, and it was not the Essendon backs who kept the play in Melbourne ground in the last half. Going right forward again the comparison in smartness was all with Melbourne, though perhaps in long-kicking Essendon were superior, Sykes and Thurgood covering a great deal of ground in that way. The latter only saved himself from a failure, however, by one magnificent goal, and some other excuse than over-anxiety to get the ball was required for his slinging Fox as he did on one or two occasions after the Melbourne captain had marked. He had the distinction of being about the only man in the forty hooted for rough play. Watson was the only other man on the side, perhaps, who could be named as a notability, his play being quite up to its ordinarily high standard.

Turning to the Melbourne twenty, their forwards were distinctly better than those of Essendon, their exchanges being rapid and sure, and some of the shots from which they did not score remarkably close. Smith was undoubtedly brilliant here, for he got three of the five goals, was remarkably clever in playing to his own side, and showed no trace of selfishness—all under the disadvantage of being much more closely watched than Thurgood, and not spared when hands could be laid upon him. Roche got few chances, but his quick passing was useful, and Dick Kelly, though less valuable than on a dry day, was very useful.

It was thought that M'Kenzie was of little use on a wet ground, but this view of his abilities had no support on Saturday, for he played as well as he has ever played, and that is saying a good deal. At any rate, he was about the best man on the Melbourne side. Christey has not played a poor game this year, but that of Saturday was not quite his best, though the goal that he punted undoubtedly was, and the same thing may be said of Wiseman, who was a much better man in the ruck than out of it.

The centre line of the Reds was a strong one. At first it looked as though Lewis were going to give Crebbin a very bad time of it in purely centre play, but they drifted apart after a while and then the little man got his chance and took it. Fred Sheehan almost invariably beat his men to the ball and played a fine game, but his quick clever play wants sound ground underfoot

Players contest the hit-out in a St. Kilda–Carlton game.

to bring out its finest points. The Melbourne defence was strong and determined, Moore, although far from well the night before, handling the ball more frequently than any other man back. O'Halloran's high marking was very fine and his strong aggressive play always telling. Two men who did much for Melbourne during the crisis of the game were O'Loghlen and Fox.

The former, whose clever ruck work was a big factor in Melbourne's success at the outset, was yet a more valuable half-back on the left wing in the last quarter, where he turned many a dangerous rush. In one instance the effect of an irresistible body striking an immovable object was illustrated, or nearly so, in the meeting of Fox and Forbes. Both started the same distance from the ball, both reached it at the same instant, neither flinched, and both kicked together. The result was that each turned a double somersault and sat in the mud looking at the other in a dazed sort of way, and neither quite realising what had happend. That the battle is not always to the strong was illustrated in the experience of the Melbourne captain in this match, for every man's hand was against him, and one could not help reflecting that had he used his strength as strength was used against him something must have gone. Joe Wilson was another first-class Red man, his back play—though he made one very bad mistake—being the best part of his performance.

THE BEAVER AND THE DOG

By 'Observer', *Argus*, May 28, 1894.

FOOTSCRAY v SOUTH MELBOURNE

The old story of the remarkable beaver and the equally remarkable dog illustrates the positions of Footscray and South Melbourne on Saturday. "It was nip and tuck whether the beaver would get to the tree, and tuck and nip whether the dog would get to the beaver and the beaver just climbed up the tree in time." "But," said a critical listener, "beavers can't climb trees." "Snakes!" retorted the storyteller, "he had to climb, the dog was crowdin' him to." The South had to climb. Footscray's play, as compared with Thursday, was as complete a reversal of form as I have ever seen in racing, and were they racing instead of footballing they would be up before the stewards for an explanation. The fact is that good football makes good football, and the football at Footscray was as good as anyone would wish to see—as good, indeed, as I have seen for years past. Footscray rose to the occasion.

On Thursday they fumbled and tumbled, and got in each other's way; on Saturday they got very much in the way of South Melbourne. In the first five minutes the South started playing to each other, as everyone expected they would, and soon got a goal. For those few minutes only it looked like a walk-over. Then Footscray remembered its instructions, "Break up their ruck whenever you can, and keep it open at all hazards", and they played to order so splendidly that thence on to the last quarter South Melbourne never had a chance with them.

It was superb football too—very little of it on the ground but any quantity high in the air, Footscray could not play with the South in the ruck, but could spoil them there, and as soon as ever the Southerners began to pack on the ball one of the heavy tricolours went through the crush with something of the effect of a locomotive through a flock of sheep. Time and time again the South's efforts at concentration were thus baulked, and when they got it open Footscray showed some of the football that was in them.

At the last change, with scores of 4–11 to 2–3, it appeared to be only a matter of condition, and though it seemed to me unlikely that Footscray would last it out at the pace, their own people never had a doubt about it. As a matter of fact, they did not quite last, and this, coupled with the splendid courage which enabled the South to bear up against that four goals lead by Essendon on Thursday, helped them now to snatch the equalising goal when all their side were fearing that the next second would bring the clang of the bell. It was a splendid thing, though, to see the team which claimed to have morally beaten the champions in turn morally beaten by Footscray, for with a little more tact and organisation forward they must have won it handsomely.

The effect of such a performance on the crowd, which was the greatest seen on the ground, was electrical. Men and women alike went wild with excitement, and from a similar bulk I have never heard such cheering as there was in the third quarter when Footscray were getting their lead. It was such as can only happen when people have worked and waited for years, and see their hour of triumph at hand. The suspense when the South drew up level was almost painful. The yell that rose when Thompson kicked the last local goal must have been heard across the river, and the shouts of the strong visiting contingent when Allan Barn's splendid effort just saved them were not less joyous.

At one stage the excitement was so great that about a chain of fence fell in with the crowd on top of it, and one of the small boys who will trespass had his leg broken. Another youngster forgot that he was in a tree top when Chadwick kicked a long goal, and in his enthusiasm fell and was injured. If Footscray keep winnng, the juvenile population of the town will be on crutches. Mr. J. Williams, the secretary of the Footscray club, is to be congratulated in that years of hard untiring work in keeping his twenty together have been so well crowned, and he at any rate will have no sympathy with those who either through ignorance or in a spirit of meddlesome interference would undo all the good that has been done. No later than Friday last the secretary of a leading club told me that with a system of go-as-you-please he could have had the cream of Footscray's players his season.

THURGOOD'S MATCH

By 'Observer', August 13, 1894.

Once again Essendon have been completely, soundly, and scientifically thrashed—up to half time. When the resting-time came on Saturday Fitzroy had five goals to one, and though Essendon's followers said afterwards, "We must give them a bit of encouragement to begin with", they were none the less in a state of painful anxiety during the whole of that first hour. For Fitzroy had done everything in the game immeasurably better than their rivals, and simply walked round Essendon with the superiority of their little-marking. Then came Essendon's pet term, and with it Fitzroy's complete discomfiture. One ineffectual rush by Fitzroy and then Essendon simply took possession of their goal—and stuck to it as pertinaciously as a sheriff's officer. Wright was the first to score, and then Thurgood, the invincible, played a lone hand that simply drove the spectators frantic with admiration. He had played back, forward, and on the ball everywhere with infinite credit; but the four successive goals in a few minutes was the coping-stone—and one of those special feats of which Thurgood alone seems capable. Three of his four goals were splendid ones, and he had a couple of shots in addition quite 80 yards out that covered the whole distance, and were only a trifle out in direction. Unquestionably we have never had such a goal-kicker as Thurgood—save and excepting always a number of those pioneer marvels to whom we gladly give the distinction of being all that they claimed to be. It saves argument. At all events Fitzroy saw their well-earned lead disappear in a few minutes before the remarkable capacity of one man, and by this time they were so exhausted by their tremendous efforts in the first half that all chance of a recovery had gone too. Though the game was interesting to the close, Essendon having once got the lead kept it. The goal to Forbes should, I think, have been a free kick to Banks, but it did not affect the main issue. While one never expects an umpire to do all that the unreasoning barracker asks him—such a thing is not within the range of poor human ability—Schaefer's umpiring in this match was by no means his best performance.

Essendon's triumph is summed up in one word—Thurgood. He may not boast, "Alone I did it"—in fact, he is not one of the boasting type—but none the less it would not have been done without him. Captain Dick now fully realises that he has command not merely of a phenomenal goal-kicker, but a fine all-round footballer, and when Essendon were playing against the wind he did not waste him forward, but sent him to more responsible posts. Early in the game Banks undertook to watch him, but seemed to tire of his task and wisely assumed that he could do better for his side elsewhere. Essendon's defence was particularly well looked after by that fine, manly footballer, George Stuckey—Officer being given an outlet for some of his energy in the ruck. Further out Finlay and Grecian were a most capable pair. In the early stages it seemed that George Moriarty would hold his own with Finlay, but later on the dashing Essendon centre-man defied all opposition. In the skirmishing line Wright was, next to Thurgood, the most valuable man to the side—his high-marking and clever passing being especially noticeable. Ball, Kearney, and Watson did splendid work in the ruck—the last-named a bit better than his average form for the season. Of course there were many other Essendon men prominent in the game, but those named should be thanked for special services.

For Fitzroy Banks once again not merely told his men what to do, but showed them how to do it. His high-marking was superb, and his desperate rushes through the ruck such as only men of Banks's physique dare attempt. The umpire was at times a little kind to him, yet Fitzroy, as a whole, were far from satisfied with him. They were similarly dissatisfied with Trait last Saturday, but, of course, it is not to be assumed that umpires are in league against Fitzroy; it rather shows that umpiring for a losing team is always difficult—umpiring for winners correspondingly easy. I don't consider Fitzroy a team of grumblers by any means—on the other hand they must not expect many others than their ardent supporters to side with them in the theory that umpires, who are quite as anxious to excel as are players, lay themselves out to thwart a particular team, and sacrifice their own reputation in their own sphere—the thing is absurd. Next to Banks, in what has become almost a regular order of merit with Fitzroy, was Clenry, who in the first hour was ubiquitous. Melling's football had the merit of being consistent right through, and one rarely sees Stoane to quite as much advantage as in the first hour of this game. Hickey got one mark that he would willingly have parted with to any player on the ground. It was a greenish-blue mark around one eye. M'Michael and Weir were a useful pair of backs, the former's *forte* being hard work, the latter's trickiness. Few, if any, of the place men pleased friendly critics as much as Whelan. Fitzroy's forward disposition was nice and even, but once again, with considerable gain to the side, they put Grace as much as possible into the ruck.

HOW FOOTBALLERS TRAIN

Argus, July 1, 1893.

One of the chief points of difference between the old and new football speaking, of course, solely of the Australian game—is

Essendon footballers in training in the 1890s.

the greater pace at which the game is now played, an outcome, no doubt, of the more thorough training which club executives demand from their players. "A good man, but he won't train," is an every-day criticism in connection with football, and it is significant that however good the man may be he is not good enough unless he is prepared to spend at least some time in the gymnasium. Those who have seen both games will, I think, agree with me that if it were possible to put one of the old-time twenties into the field against a trained team of 1893 the latter would have it all their own way in everything but physique, and, perhaps, running with the ball.

Even in rough and tumble the short, thick-set modern player, with every muscle finely developed, would probably hold his own against the giants of the past, for weight, as we have seen lately in boxing, will not always overwhelm cleverness. I once saw that point illustrated in a game between country and town teams, in which the former, badly beaten in scientific play, chafed under the restrictions of modern rules, and thought— with an old Essendon player who has just returned from some years' residence in London—that the umpire had altogether too much to do with the game. So they demanded old rules for the last half, and were perhaps surprised to find how readily the suggestion was accepted. The weight was all on the side of the country team, but its only effect was to make their falls the heavier, for the city players, sharpened by their experience with strict umpires, knew a dozen means of effectually, but undemonstratively, bringing a man down where the rustic Hercules had but one—his weight. It was the familiar spectacle of the scientific feather weight and the unskilled "chopping-block" over again.

Two nights a week in the gymnasium is the general course for the footballer of today, with as much practice at running with the ball, little marking, and kicking in the open as circumstances will permit him to take. But many of the manual labourers who play get very little daylight practice on the grass, and, doing most of their work in the gymnasium, become exponents of that heavy plugging ruck work which is a feature of the modern game, but has added nothing to its attractiveness. A night with the Melbourne team in their gymnasium, when putting on the final polish for the big match to-day, fairly illustrates the general method.

Their trainer has the undemonstrative methods of all boxing instructors, but in his quiet way is none the less an autocrat, and talks to his boys as a schoolmaster and with just as complete authority. The player may have a preference for practising high marking, but when the trainer sends him to a corner to skip, he skips promptly. The players are more or less in uniform—the trainer lightly clad in white knickers, a thin singlet, and slippers, for though the night is cold the rubbing down of a score of players, for which work there are a couple of assistants, keeps the blood in circulation. One of the team has so little reverence for winning colours, and so little regard for mementoes, that he has converted his blue-and-gold intercolonial costume into a gymnasium dress.

The Melbourne trainer, known to all footballers as Jim Mitchell, started for love of the thing with the Britannia, a junior club, and got them in such fettle that they soon became premiers in their class, and, finally, seniors under the title of the Collingwood Club. Then he helped the Fitzroy Imperials a few rungs up the ladder of fame and started football training in real earnest as the mentor of the Fitzroy twenty. Thence he went over to Melbourne and took his luck with him, for the team has been going up steadily until it stands to-day unbeaten for the season and on an even eminence with Essendon—where there is, however, only room for one and this afternoon will decide which one.

Practice at high marking seems to be most popular with the players. The ball hangs from the ceiling by a long elastic band in its natural state at just about the height the best of the high markers take a ball in play. Beneath it are stretched wrestling mattresses to ease the jar of landing on the cement floor, and so the players, starting in turn from the end of the gymnasium, jump for marks. Each as he gets the ball brings it down with him through the elastic stretching, and, released, it travels on a rapid and most eccentric course, so that no two players in turn get it at exactly the same height or coming in the same direction. Seeing this practice continued for some time one begins to understand whence that skill in high marking which is so prominent a feature in the play of O'Halloran, Forbes, Banks, or Ramsden, and others comes. The element of humor is provided in the Melbourne gymnasium by the perseverance with which ground players in the ruck like Wiseman and

Stranger try for these high marks as compared with the few rare occasions on which they get them. Apart from marking the exercise is, of course, a good one.

Punching the ball, the prize-fighter's favorite practice, is another exercise which players take in turn, and the stand is rarely vacant, but it seems work peculiarly suited to the development of the arms and the hitting muscles, and, therefore, better for prize-fighters than footballers, whom the association think should keep their hitting muscles dormant. In the ruck, however, there is naturally a good deal of arm work, and strength is useful. Being in a manner a variation of boxing, the exercise has also its effect upon every part of the body, and for that purpose few branches of athletics are better than boxing, as those may realise who have either boxed themselves or noted the difficulty with which a couple of partly trained men get through an exhibition four rounds when the weight of the hitting has nothing to do with exhaustion. In fact, the trainer admits that boxing would be a first-class exercise for football, and his fear is not of fighting in the field, but fighting amongst the team. The spirit of emulation always induces men to try and be a little better than each other at any game, and with boxing that sort of feeling leads up to trouble. "It would never do," he continues, "to lose our matches in the training-room."

This swinging ball, simple as it looks, is to the novice full of guile. I have seen a leading barrister, on a big night at the Melbourne Athletic Club, walk up to this appliance, and hit it hard just for fun. The harder it is hit the quicker the rebound—and in this instance the unexpected counter drove his cigar into his mouth and eyes, knocked his silk hat flying along the floor, and generally wrought a complete transformation in less than a second. The simple ball had hit back with a vengeance. But when an old footballer or experienced boxer punches the ball the exercise is really pretty and spirited, the quickness and certainty of the hitting being remarkable.

The use of the skipping-ropes, it need hardly be explained, is for the development of the leg muscles, and to vary the monotony of the exercise the players occasionally form four square and dance an improvised and competitive quadrille. The "flying horse" and springboard are also in use—the players, as those familiar with gymnasium work know, taking a running jump on to the spring-board and then over the horse, generally touching it lightly with the hands as they go. After each player has marked, hit, vaulted, and skipped, he has a shower bath, and is industriously rubbed down. There is a stock of Indian clubs and dumb-bells in the training-room, but though much affected by a former trainer they are rarely used now.

The Melbourne trainer takes his men in hand not as a team but as individuals, and now and again quietly orders a player to keep on at a particular exercise, when the player himself thinks he has had enough of it. Every trainer has his own peculiar oils and ointments, but there can be no mistaking the popularity of eucalyptus oil. It takes permanent possession of training and dressing rooms alike, and seems to pervade everything connected with football, though its enemies of course say that palm oil is much more essential to success at the game. Tuesday is the big training night with the Melbourne team, and, like most other twenties, they may now be considered as fairly wound up for the season, and only require to be kept going. There can be little doubt that whatever may be the effect on the general health of severe training, such exercise as footballers take can hardly be otherwise than stimulating, and the elasticity of frame thus obtained reduces to a mere trifle the effect of the shock and strain of a hard game, which would leave rather unpleasant effects upon an untrained footballer.

COLLINGWOOD PREMIERS, 1896

Age, October 6, 1896.

The much discussed play-off for the season's premiership between Collingwood and South Melbourne, who had tied for first place, was settled on the East Melbourne Cricket Ground on Saturday, and resulted in Collingwood gaining the coveted distinction, after a hard fought and splendidly contested game. Despite the increased charge for admission the match was witnessed by at least 10,000 spectators, who were treated to a display of football well worth the extra money. The special appointment of J. J. Trait to umpire the match, although it naturally offended the umpires officiating in premiership matches, who recognised in it an implied doubt as to their fitness for

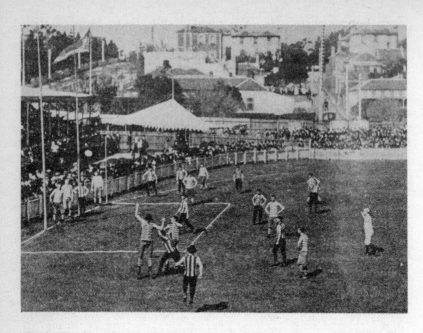

Collingwood's 'first try for goal' in the premiership match of 1896 against South Melbourne.

the position, gave general satisfaction, and his appearance on the ground was the signal for a hearty cheer of welcome. Arnutt, who had injured himself at practice during the week, was unable to play for Collingwood, but otherwise each club put its full strength into the field. Experience has shown the play in these matches of special importance to be generally disappointing, owing probably to over anxiety, but this proved to be an exception, the play from first to last being hard, fast, exciting and skilful, and as the result was in doubt up to the last minute, the most intense interest was sustained until the ring of the final bell proclaimed Collingwood the premiers of 1896. As indicated in a review of the season's play last Monday, the honor has been well and worthily won, and there was probably no prouder man in Melbourne last Saturday night—there certainly was not in Collingwood—than the veteran captain W. Strickland, who fully maintained his excellent form, even after having the skin removed from his right knee in one piece during the game. It was a beautiful afternoon for spectators, but much too hot for the players, who on the hard ground and slippery turf frequently found it difficult to keep on their feet when playing at high pressure.

The South Melbourne captain won the toss, and evidently considered it of more importance to have the wind's assistance at the finish than at the commencement, as he started against it, which can hardly be said to have proved successful, as Collingwood, who only won by one goal, gained a lead of two in the first quarter. It was a fluctuating match, Collingwood playing the stronger game in the first quarter (though not nearly so much better as the scores appear to indicate), and being badly beaten in both the second and third quarters. They not only lost their lead of two goals, but started the last quarter a goal in arrear, having at the end of the third quarter distinctly presented the appearance of a beaten team. Collingwood's finish, however, was a treat to witness, as they pulled themselves together for a final effort, and made it in the grandest style and with complete success, kicking 2.3 to 0.1 after the last change of ends.

That the team had taken no liberties in training during the idle fortnight was apparent, as they were certainly fresher at the finish than their opponents, or perhaps it would be more strictly correct to say they were not so much distressed. The Collingwood trainers certainly deserve a bonus out of the winners' share of the substantial gate, as the men were turned out as fit as hands could make them. Collingwood decidedly won the match by making good use of their chances in the first quarter, and South as distinctly lost it by failing wretchedly in that respect in the second quarter. The opinion which I expressed long before the match commenced, that "it was not guineas to pounds on either team", was fully justified by the result, and it would be almost impossible to find two sides more evenly matched. On Saturday, as shown by the scores, each side passed the other's goal line 15 times, each hit a post, and the previous match had resulted in a draw. By way of still further showing the evenness of the game, it may be added that when 10 minutes remained available for play each side had scored 5 goals and 9 behinds.

The feature of the finish was the magnificent marking of Monahan, who was in quick succession successful in three splendid efforts, but each time failed to kick a goal, though within easy range. Collingwood's winning goal was the result of a free kick awarded to Flaherty for being slung, and it is a singular fact that time after time for years past this player had, through various mishaps, been unable to take part in matches against South Melbourne. Although Trait allowed great latitude all through the match it was only abused on few occasions, the worst instances being when Williams most unjustifiably slung Minahan, and when Burns charged Monahan as he was going for a mark, which in this respect made "honors divided".

On the winning side excellent work was done by Strickland, Monahan, Pannam, Condon, Dowdell, Stock, Calleson, Proudfoot, Smith, Gillard, M'Donald and Flaherty. For South Melbourne, the veteran M'Kay, who played brilliantly, was second to none on either side, and Fraser all through showed fine form. As usual, the ruck, consisting of Gibson, Pleasa, Purdy and M'Arthur, with Windley roving, was powerful; and others who worked well to avert defeat were D. Adamson, M'Cartney, Williamson, Howson and J. Adamson. Collingwood's goals were kicked by Gregory, Hall, Condon, Dowdell, Hailwood and Flaherty; and South Melbourne's by M'Kay (2), Pleasa, J. Adamson and Windley.

THE DEED THAT WON THE UMPIRE

By 'Follower', *Age*, June 20, 1896.

Encouraged in the belief that one Englishman is a match for any three foreigners that can be pitted against him, the rising generation is apt to overestimate the power of British arms— and fists, and to undervalue the important part that strategy has borne in establishing the supremacy of the nation. It may safely be assumed that in the eyes of the average youth the Iron Duke was "small pumpkins" compared with Shaw the Life Guardsman, that Gladstone and Salisbury "are not in it" with W. G. Grace and Tom Richardson, and that to talk of George Higinbotham alongside "Tracker" Forbes is to proclaim yourself "a mug". There is not the slightest doubt that the characteristic weakness of the British nation is adulation of brawn and a contemptuous disregard for brain power.

When, therefore, instances are forthcoming of cool calculating diplomacy winning the day for an inferior force against the superior muscular power of an opposing combination it becomes the solemn duty of those in authority to miss no opportunity of impressing the greatness of such achievements upon the youthful mind in order to demonstrate that subtle intellectuality is no less a power in effecting the accomplishment of great deeds than a strong right arm, a cannon ball or a battering ram. Such a triumph of keen intellect, judgment of character and strategic negotiation over brute force unbacked by the help of brainy briskness, as is exemplified in the history of the famous contest narrated below, should, for instance, be written in characters of gold and placed within the grasp of young Australia throughout the length and breadth of the land.

Perhaps to guard against as unlooked for and undesirable contingency which might arise to the detriment of the youth whose moral elevation is sought to be accomplished, should he happen to discover that the gold by a little manipulation will "come off", it would be better still to have the moral lesson printed in plain black ink at the expense of the Government and incorporated in the text books used in State schools for teaching the young idea and moulding its future.

The shades of evening had fallen over the mining township of Streaky Gully, and in the bar parlor of the Reefers' Arms sat three local celebrities in earnest conclave. The subject under discussion was, next to the race for the Streaky Gully Cup, which had been won a fortnight before by the equine champion of Blanket Flat, the event of the year—the annual match between the first twenties of the two once-flourishing Eldorados. Twelve months ago the Streaky Gully main reef had "petered out", and in consequence Streaky Gully was down on its luck, and rapidly approaching the unenviable financial position known as "pebbly". The defeat of the local butcher's skewbald gelding Cleaver by the Blanket Flat crack Hazard in the cup had pretty nearly cleaned out the Gully, and the problem which was racking the brains of the trio abovementioned was how to get a recovery over the football match.

There was a distinct individuality amongst the three men. Bladen, the butcher, was a stout man of about 45, with bull neck and a face that shone like a whole string of newly made sausages, and of about the same complexion. Frisby, the landlord of the Reefers' Arms, at least 10 years older than the knight of the cleaver, had established a reputation as one of the leading "sports" in the Gully, but the most superficial observer could hardly fail to discern in the imperturbable expression on the face of the third man the index to a mind capable of "buying and selling" the other two. Streaky Gully viewed "Cooney the Nark" with mingled feelings of fear and admiration. If a blathering bully emboldened by the influence of bad liquor ventured to "take him on", Cooney never lost his temper, but always managed to come out "on top", and at the finish to drink at the other's expense.

If an opponent holding "two pair" "called him" it was odds on The Nark producing "a straight", and although he admitted to having "fallen in" over the defeat of Cleaver, he had got it all back on the Selling Hurdle Race through taking the wise precaution of walking round the course at 1 o'clock on the morning of the race with a small saw borrowed from Bladen, and at 2.15 leaving the hurdles in a much more favorable condition for negotiation by his grey mare Donah, who was a clumsy jumper, but "had a bit of toe", than before they had received his attention. Cooney might have been anything between 30 and 40, but his clean shaven face probably made him look some years younger than he really was.

Just as Bladen, knocking the ashes out of his pipe, had suggested to the landlord that he might as well "fill 'em up again 't any rate", a young fellow of about four and twenty, carrying a small black handbag walked into the room, and seeing the landlord steering for the bar ordered "a small beer", and with a "Good evening, gentlemen", in almost the same breath, sat down on the sofa. A scarcely perceptible gleam of intelligence shot from Cooney's grey eyes as he responded to the stranger's salutation, and added, quite careless of the fact that it was the butcher's shout, "Join us, won't you?" The cordial invitation being accepted, it soon transpired that the new arrival (Cooney afterwards explained that he had "placed him in once" by his bag) was the professional central umpire sent specially over from Reefton at the request of both teams to officiate in the big match.

During the conversation which occupied the next couple of hours, Harry Trott's introduction to the Prince of Wales, the prospects of the first test match, Sam Allen's cable message, and similar affairs affecting the welfare of the State had been discussed, finishing with Essendon's chance of regaining the premiership. Finally the subject of the morrow's match came on the board, and after the landlord had made feeling reference to the handicap Streaky Gully would suffer through Chris the Crumpet, who worked for the local baker, having nearly chewed off the thumb of the Gully's famous follower, Gouger Glubbett, in a "muss" over a game of devil's pool, the butcher left, the landlord threw out a couple of drunks and locked up, and the new arrival falling in with Cooney's suggestion that it was about time to "perch", the two, whose rooms adjoined, went to bed. Six or seven rounds of drinks had been served during the evening, Cooney and the butcher doing all the shouting, and as Cooney opened his bedroom door, he said, "How would a good cigar go? Those cabbage leaves of old Frisby's are enough to poison yer. Come in!"

The distance between Blanket Flat and Streaky Gully was about nine miles, and shortly after midway the appearance of two coaches, a dozen carts of various descriptions, and a score or so of horsemen thundering along Main-street, proclaimed that the Flatites and their barrackers had arrived. All the Gully seemed to have congregated in the vicinity of the Reefers' Arms, and when Gouger Glubbett appeared with downcast visage, and his arm in a sling, it was agreed that the absence of the dreaded follower who invariably "laid out" two or three opponents in the course of a match, and who in last season's contest had made a Cyclops of Blanket Flat's champion goal sneak, made it "a monte" for the visitors.

The disconsolate looks of the local barrackers mutely strengthened the assumption, and when Barney Boko, the Blanket Flat leviathan penciller, emerged from the door of the Reefers' Arms, diamond decked, and removing a huge cigar from his mouth, exclaimed, "Well! the Flat wins, a pony", there were no takers. Bullocky Biffen—who, having 10 years before played half back for a crack junior team near Melbourne, was recognised as the best judge of the game on the Gully, and who, although "tanglefoot" had long since incapacitated him from active service, always gave the Gully captain a hint at half time respecting the placing of his team—had thrown a wet blanket over the local barrackers by pronouncing emphatically that "Without Gouger we 'aven't got a bloomin' dog's chance!"

At that same moment Cooney entered the shop of Blades, who, having scraped the block, was just preparing to "clean himself" for the match, and with a silent jerk of the head, motioned the butcher to follow him into the latter's sittingroom, adjoining the shop. "See here", said The Nark, producing a roll of notes and handing them to Bladen, "There's a century. All the Blanket push is over at Frisby's with 'Boko' and 'The Squelcher' and 'Dick the Crook', and the rest of the talent all flush with their Hazard stuff. None of our crowd'll back The Gully with The Gouger cronk, and before the start you'll get 6 to 4 like water. Plank the dollop, and if you take my advice you'll have a bit yourself!"

"But we haven't—" began Bladen; but Cooney cut him short with "I said plank the lot, didn't I? Hundred's don't grow on the tops o' trees, and I don't chuck stuff away as a rule, do I? You put the stuff on, 'oof' up, mind that's all you've got to do; and if you don't want to be in it, why stand out, but don't be a goat if you ask me!"

Before the teams took to the field the professional umpire, who in white knickers and blue cap, and with a plated whistle slung round his wrist by a new leather boot lace, was voted "a toff" by the admiring spectators, had informed both sides that he wouldn't stand any "funny business" with little marks. While this functionary pursing the ball was waiting for the players to strip—the luxury of eucalyptus anointment was unknown to those brawny battlers—Cooney had been playing his cards with characteristic skill. Known as the biggest bettor on the Gully, he had been the special object of attention from "Boko", "The Squelcher" and "Dick the Crook", but to every offer of a "level pony", or even 5 to 4, he had merely replied with a quiet smile, "What d'yer take me for? Try the mugs!" The very fact of "The Nark" not "coming at it", was enough to satisfy everybody that The Gully wasn't in it, and when Charley the coach driver rang Frisby's dinner bell—lent for the occasion—to summon the players to the field, offers of 6 to 4 on The Flat were as numerous as threepenny bits at a fashionable church collection.

When, however, "Boko", in a louder voice than ever, yelled defiantly as he glared at the disconsolate Gullyites, "Well! 'Ere 70 to 40 on The Flat!" and "The Squelcher" and "Dick the Crook," emulating the Leviathan, roared in chorus, "Yes! And 35 to 20 me!" a sensation was caused by old Frisby, who had apparently "had a few", taking all three wagers and "putting up the ready"! Cooney was heard to mutter in a stage whisper something about fools and their money, repealling some similar expression every time the burly butcher took 7 to 4 from a Blanket Flat enthusiast, the parties to these smaller wagers invariably making Mat Martin, the well-known manager of the Monte Christo Extended, stake holder.

The metropolitan custom of splitting the game into four quarters was ignored, the old fashioned half-time interval, with a swig at "black jack", taking the place of three changes and cut lemons. Acting on the advice of Bullocky Biffen, the Gully captain, Scorcher Simmons, who having won the toss with a coin lent him by Cooney, had the advantage of a strong wind blowing dead into the Blanket Flat goal, massed his men on the ball at the bounce, and before the visitors grasped the situation Ginger Griffin had scored first goal for The Gully. One of the Blanket Flat backs had also gone for the mark, and held up both hands for a free kick as he dived head foremost into the ground impelled by the united efforts of two of Ginger's shepherders; but the appeal was disallowed. The wind increasing, it was generally agreed that nothing short of 4 goals in the first half would give The Gully a good show, and, therefore, when at half time the socres were 2 goals 5 behinds against The Flat's 2 behinds, the visiting barrackers offered to bet evens "till the cows came home!"

Surely enough the Flatites, who had been reserving themselves for the change of ends, went off with a dash at the opening of the second half, and although The Gully captain, realising that forcing it against the wind was out of the question, had brought four or five extra men back, it was not five minutes before a mighty "roost" from the 13-inch foot of Smasher Smart.

The Flat's crack follower, sent it through, but so close to one side that the spectators waited breathlessly before the majority burst into a roar of local satisfaction at the hoisting of *one* flag, the goal umpire's decision being that "it had just touched". Five minutes afterwards Smasher with a regular "Monaghan" effort rose high above the crowd of Gully backs, who tried in vain to "crab" him, but simultaneously with a roar of admiration from the cluster of Blanket Flat barrackers, the umpire's whistle blew out a shrill bias. A Gully player who had not gone as high as Smasher by a foot had been pushed, and his free kick towards the left wing temporarily averted the threatened disaster.

The wind had slightly shifted, and though still blowing hard was no longer in a dead line between goals, and as Biffen energetically waved a red handkerchief the Gully captain "took the office", and every time a local player got on the ball it was sent wingwards to leeward, frequently by hand play, as the Flatites, now fairly roused, were rushing it at an awful pace. A dozen times it seemed inevitable that the visitors must score, but with nearly every little mark came the shrill sound of the umpire's whistle, the free kicks being in favor of The Gully except when the ball was on the left wing and out of range. Then the award was always made to the other side, and this apparent impartiality elicited the opinion that although the umpire was "terrible strict, he seemed to be doin' his best in a jolly rough game".

It was not until within six or seven minutes of "time" that the Flat's first goal was scored, a beautiful long placer, which raised the two flags. The remainder of the game was marked by uninterrupted possession of Gully territory by the Flatites, but three more good chances were lost through the superior knowledge of the professional umpire, whose keen and practised eye discerned breaches of the rules which to the ordinary observer were not noticeable. With only three minutes to go the disappointed visitors were fighting hard for a draw, and a yell from the group of horsemen and others assembled in the vicinity of the Gully goal announced the coveted consummation. But Oh, what beastly luck!

As the goal umpire grasped the two flags, up went the umpire's hand! What had happened? Touched in transit! Only one flag hoisted! A behind! And just as Smasher Smart, after the kick on, had come a thumping whack on the ground, which raised a lump like a billiard ball on his intellectual forehead, the bell rang out on the local victory by 2 goals 5 behinds to 1 goal 9 behinds, and Streaky Gully went loyally mad with delight.

As many of the visiting "supporters of the game" remained to dine at Frisby's, it need hardly be said that the ceremony of fighting the battle over again was marked by as much vehemence as the actual contest had been, and before the last of the Blanket Flatites left broken heads were as numerous as broken tumblers.

Cooney, apparently unable to stand the chaff showered upon him at missing a good thing, cleared out early, having as "Boko" (who to do him justice was a good loser) declared "got the spur", but before retiring from the atmosphere of beer and blasphemy he had, in anticipation of the ructions which experience had taught him were inevitable, made the umpire aware that he too would "vamoose" if he were wise.

The latter was staying at the Reefers' all night to catch the Reefton coach at 7 o'clock the next morning. Before these two newly-made acquaintances separated in Cooney's bedroom the latter pressed into the other's hand a couple of "fivers", quietly remarking, "And here, here's a couple o' thick 'uns extra. You worked it well, but what price my hint about them free kicks to the other side when it was out of danger! If it hadn't been for that they might ha' tumbled!"

A month afterwards Cooney and Boko, who were both in Melbourne for the Grand National meeting, met at dinner one evening, when, with the cool effrontery characteristic of men of his class, Cooney told the other with a chuckle over a big bottle the whole story of how he had taken him and the other boys down. "It was a bit of odds on Simmons winning the toss with my 'grey,'" he said, "so I knew the first half was all right, but *you* know, Barney, it don't do to throw away chances at our game, so in case of accidents I had that joker with the flags on my side in the second half."

"How was it?" laconically responded Boko. "Oh! After slinging a fair 'com.' to old Frisby and the butcher, twelve quid to young whitelegs and a 'fin' to the flag faker, it panned out about four fifties!" "Good biz," was the quiet rejoinder. "Do you know, I had a sort of suspicion that old Frisby wasn't quite so shikker as he kidded, directly after he took that 70 to 40. There's no mistake, old pal, you take a bit o' doin'!"

Never was there a more pronounced instance of the triumph of brain over brawn. Dependant only upon the latter, Streaky Gully would have suffered inevitable and humiliating defeat, but thanks to the intellectual resources, quick perception, judgment of character and persuasive eloquence of "Cooney the Nark", impending defeat was turned into overwhelming triumph. Many a time since that famous day of Blanket Flat's defeat have the "sports" of Streaky Gully been entertained by old Frisby's narrative of how Cooney, in the quiet privacy of his bedroom on the night before the battle, did "The Deed that Won the Umpire!"

THE OPENING BALL, ANON

Comic Australian Verse, Lehmann

Up rouse ye then my merry men,
And kick the leathern cone,
We'll rush it along through the middle of the throng,
For the game is all our own—
'Forward Carlton!' is now the cry,
And we rush it like the wind,
A roar from ten thousand throats go up,
For we've kicked another behind.

MELBOURNE GRAMMAR GAMES SONG

Innocent Austral Verse, Barry Humphries, *Sun Books*

By Ambrose Wilson
(To the tune 'Men of Harlech')

Play together, dark blue twenty,
Long and little marks in plenty;
   Get your kick, let none prevent ye,
   Make the leather roll.
Mark your men, keen effort straining,
On the ball and show your training;
Still though short the time remaining,
   Get another goal.

Chorus:
None of our ranks shall sunder,
Who will shirk or blunder?
   If all are true
   To our Dark Blue
Our foemen must go under,
Honour ye the old School's story,
Those who played and won before ye,
Bear the Dark Blue flag to glory,
   'Grammar' to the fore.

HARRY FURNISS'S IMPRESSIONS
OF FOOTBALL

Australasian, May, 1897.

I am quite prepared to be told that these caricatures of Australian footballers, my first impressions after seeing an hour's play, are libels on the famous athletes of the country. Out of the many thousands who go to sports of this kind, probably not 20 go with the object of seeing the humorous side of it. All are terribly serious. Their thick-necked, long-bodied, bandy-legged Herculean cousin is, in their eyes, a perfect Adonis. Their long, lanky, favorite, all bone and sinew, is, in their eyes, an Apollo Belvidere.

In fact, in every case they merely look through the glasses of sportsmen, admiring the speed and cleverness of their favourites, not thinking of onlooking for the artistic effect; and when they see their champion depicted, as seen through the microscope of the caricaturist, they are naturally surprised and incredulous. I do not expect Australians to be different in this respect from other nationalities.

An exception, by the way, I found, strange to say, among the sensitive Americans, when I gave my first impressions of their football, a game in which there is more science than in all other football systems in the world put together; a game in which fatalities are numerous, and is played with a seriousness and intenseness unsurpassed in any game I have ever seen. The players I have seen depicted in pictures compared with gladiators in the Roman amphitheatre.

Yet a more ridiculous, grotesque, pantomimic crowd on the field it has never been one's lot to see. Long massive hair, falling all over the head; huge indiarubber shields on the noses; extraordinary shapeless garments padded all over; shields on the legs, on the fingers; pads on the heads; protections on the ears— nothing could be more absurd: yet to their public they are Adonises and Apollos. There is as much difference between the Victorian and the American game of football as there is in the costumes worn by the players.

I notice the Victorians are attired above the waist as scullers in a boat race, and from that down they have loose kind of garments cut below the knee; stockings and boots, seemingly not protected in any way. When I saw the game, some of these stockings slipped down, and the players wore wide-awake hats, and other caps, which fell off in the scrimmage, although most of the players are bareheaded, with short-cropped hair.

As regards the game itself, I can only say that I was too busy in picking out the most ludicrous on the field—the duty of the caricaturist—rather than in watching the play. But what I saw of it struck me as the fastest game I have ever seen. Hands are used, legs, heads, everything, in breaking down all the rules of other football systems, with the one object of speed. Science must therefore to a great extent suffer. Every man seems to play his best individually. The combination is nothing compared with the combination in any other football I have seen; although, no doubt, it exists.

However, I shall pay another visit to watch the play more than the men, and perhaps on a second visit, I may give the more serious side, and show the athletes without so much caricature, and understand the science of the Victorian game of football, which is too quick for a stranger to grasp at first sight, or an artist to depict with justice.

A.J. THURGOOD, CHAMPION
OF CHAMPIONS

C. C. Mullen (1958)

In the 100 years of Australian football there have been numerous famous players, many of them being stars, and a number who reached championship class. Admittedly it is difficult to compare present-day stars with those of the past owing to the many changes the game has gone through in 100 years. In its infancy players were only feeling their way into a strange code, and it was thought that brute strength and brawn were the first essentials. These gave way to skill and cleverness and enabled the good small player to be just as prominent as the big heavyweight. Play then became faster and still faster with more rapid exchanges and handball, and the old-time "catching" became higher marking and developed into the more spectacular air work we see today. Present-day critics would claim the old-timers would never stand up to the pace the game is played today, but men of past years would have just as strong an argument and say the present-day pampered footballer would never have been able to see out the hard, rugged style of a game of years ago. Old players would also have it on the moderns that footballers of 40, 50 and 60 years back could kick drop, place and punt kicks long distances, even up to 100 yards, while teams now use mostly short punt kicks. And so you could carry such arguments on indefinitely and get nowhere.

Those of us who have seen all the star players in the past 60 years and many changes in the game's progress can form a good idea of champions through the ages, and taking all aspects of the game into consideration, everything would point to Albert John Thurgood (Essendon, Vic., and Fremantle, W.A.), (1891–1906) as the greatest all-round footballer the Australian game has produced. A champion must be a reasonably good high mark, he should be able to kick well, with either foot if possible, and if he can kick the drop, place or punt, so much the better. He should be fast in ground play, an accurate pass to team mates, able to turn and dodge with ease, and hold down at least one of the key positions. Most important of all he should be able to go on the ball when his side is up against it and "take hold" of the game at the critical stage and turn what appeared to be defeat into a victory.

Albert Thurgood could answer all these tests. He was the most spectacular high mark of his time, indeed, he was the man who developed the present style of high marking from another Essendon player (Charlie Pearson, 1882–1892), and if we were doing the right thing we would be calling the high mark the "Pearson" or "Thurgood" mark. Thurgood was an artist in ball control and balance. Being a brilliant runner, able to cover 100 yards in under 11 seconds, made him fast in ground play; he could get rid of the ball with either foot and was a magnificent kick, covering 80, 90 and even 100 yards, and could use the drop, place or punt whenever the occasion demanded it. He dominated the most difficult position on the field during the whole of his career—centre half-forward—a position in which he has never had an equal either before or since. That alone would make a man a champion, as there have been less star centre half-forwards than any other position player.

Thurgood was without the slightest doubt the greatest forward and goalkicker the game has known. In 1892 he scored 56 goals, in 1893 he had 64, and totalled 63 in 1894 and topped the list of goalkickers every full season he played. With all the pace and streamlined football today there is not a centre half-forward in Australia who has equalled his records. On the Richmond ground in 1893 he kicked 12 goals out of 14, and the following Saturday at North Melbourne he registered 9 out of 10, and in scoring 21 goals out of his team's 24 he made another record that has not been equalled. His versatility in goal kicking was shown in scoring from a left foot angle shot from the boundary one minute, while the next he would thread his way through the field and score with a lovely drop kick on the run from 60 yards out, and the next minute a goal would come from a long place kick from the cricket pitch or out on the boundary. According to the *Australian Footballers Almanac* of 1951 Thurgood holds the West Australian record in having kicked 99 yards at Fremantle in July, 1895, the South Australian record with a kick of 95 yards on the Adelaide Oval in 1894, and having recorded place kicks of 107 yards and 104 yards at East Melbourne ground in 1899 and 1893 and scoring a drop kick goal from 90 yards out on the Melbourne ground in 1893. Although he missed easy shots now and then like any other forward, he was never thrown to miss when the fate of the game rested on his kick—and that is the hallmark of a champion.

Thurgood, however, was more than a goalkicker. He frequently had to take the centre half-back position when the defence needed strengthening; he was rushed into the centre at times or on to the wing to check a speedy opponent, he could play in the full back post in an emergency and above all he was the ideal man to throw on the ball at the critical stage of the game where he would immediately dominate the rucks with his pace and high marking and kick the goals needed for victory. On many occasions Essendon were three or four goals behind with only five minutes to play and every time Thurgood won the game for them. One of those memorable occasions was on the Melbourne ground in 1893, when the Dons wanted four goals to win and only a few minutes to play. An old-time newspaper report states that "As a last resort Thurgood was sent on to the ball and immediately won the game. He marked over everyone, ran half the length of the ground when it suited him, got the four goals needed for victory, and covered himself with glory, as it was not thought possible for one man to win a game in such a manner".

Thurgood went to West Australia in 1895 and played with the Fremantle Club for three seasons, and he was the man who put West Australian football on the map. His team were premiers, he topped the goalkicking list and created a sensation with his marking, running and long distance kicking, and was classed as the "greatest footballer of all time". Returning to Victoria, he was refused a clearance by the Victorian League, which had been formed in his absence, on the grounds that he was an Intercolonial player, and he had to stand out for twelve months. No doubt had Thurgood decided to play with any other League club he would have been granted permission, but he was a splendid club man and announced: "No, I have come back to play with the 'Same Old' Essendon. I play with Essendon or no one". And he kept his word. There was, however, such an outcry from the daily and weekly press against "keeping Australia's greatest footballer looking over the fence" that the League had to let him resume with his old team.

His winning of the 1901 premiership for Essendon was a classic. An injury kept him out of the game for five or six weeks, during which the Dons, who had made a good start, fell down to the bottom of the list and did not look to have a ghost's chance of making the finals. But when Thurgood came back he lifted the team which won every game remaining, ran into the finals and won the premiership comfortably. In the semi-final against Fitzroy he was the outstanding player afield, kicking five of Essendon's six goals from centre half-forward, three of them from 80 yards out and then in the third quarter he had to take the centre half-back position owing to another player being injured, and in the last term played in the ruck and defence to save the game in the end by three points. The following Saturday, mainly by his brilliant play in kicking three goals in the first half, Essendon had the premiership easily won at half time against Collingwood. In 1905, when living in the Fairfield district, he applied for a clearance to Collingwood, as he was on the eve of retiring and it was thought his experience would have been of value to the younger Collingwood club, but Essendon did not let him go. He announced his retirement from the game after being injured in the Essendon and Carlton game at Princes Oval in 1906, but the Dons brought him back for the semi-final match against Fitzroy. After scoring first goal of the day with a running shot he broke down again and finally retired. In 1924 he organised an old players' carnival on the Melbourne ground, which was played on week days to assist the Lord Mayor's fund, and when he took the field he amazed the crowd, many of whom had never seen him play, and an outburst of applause followed when he picked up the ball and drop-kicked it sixty yards down the field and immediately snapped a goal with his left foot.

Although six feet and thirteen stone, he looked bigger on the field. Those who saw him in action with Essendon will remember his lordly appearance with head and shoulders thrown back and he looked more like a drum major in front of a band or a big military general at the head of a regiment when taking control of a game.

Albert Thurgood was born in North Melbourne and, according to John Worrall, the well-known critic and authority on the game, his parents came from America. Perhaps the most remarkable thing about his career was that the only football club that did not chase him for his services—Essendon—secured him. He attended Brighton Grammar School at Middle Brighton, and Geelong and Melbourne fought for his services until all other clubs joined in. St. Kilda actually selected him to play in one match in 1891 but he did not leave the Brighton junior team until the start of 1892 season, when he unexpectedly turned up at East Melbourne to play with Essendon. No doubt he had been influenced by the large number of public school boys who went to Essendon, as the Dons were the "school tie" club in their East Melbourne days. He scored two goals in his first game, but Essendon officials were not over-impressed with his play and Alex. Dick, the captain, had to fight hard to keep him in the side, but after a few weeks the Dons realised they had gained a champion. He played in the Victorian Intercolonial and Interstate teams of his time and New South Wales, South Australia and Tasmanian people saw him when he toured those places with Essendon, who played many games outside Victoria in those days. Thurgood was also an excellent cricketer but gave up the summer game, as he considered it too slow. Taking up golf he became one of the best drivers on the links. After retiring from football he was well known in racing circles. He played 209 games with Essendon and 53 with Fremantle, besides Interstate matches, and during his career kicked 714 'goals, an extraordinary performance seeing that goals in his time were much harder to get than they are today.

7
1900s: 'Oh, a bonzer, a bonzer, a boshter, a bontoshter!'

A golden era. Carlton won three flags in a row, Fitzroy and Collingwood two; great players like Vic Cumberland, Dave McNamara, Dookie McKenzie and Bill Busbridge showed their skills, and issues like payment of players, bribery and transfers simmered. Teams developed different styles, and Carlton obtained the first recognised coach in John Worrall from Fitzroy. The game seemed as violent (and entertaining) as ever. Edward Dyson's account of Benno Dickson's stay in the outer of a South Melbourne and St Kilda game is from the great larrikin novel 'Benno and Some of the Push'.

AN ENORMOUS ASSEMBLAGE, COLLINGWOOD'S PREMIERSHIP

By 'Old Boy', *Argus*, September 22, 1902.

The detractors of the scheme under which the premiership has been decided this year cannot say that public interest has been in any way lessened in our great winter game after the enormous assemblage which thronged the Melbourne Cricket Ground on Saturday; 24,880 people paid for admission, and, with members of the cricket club, of the opposing teams, and others who had complimentary tickets, the estimated total attendance was barely short of 35,000. The takings amounted to £901, and thus all previous records were beaten. The highest takings previously were £860, at the match between South Melbourne and Carlton on the M.C.C. ground in August, 1890, when the estimated attendance was 32,000.

Collingwood at the last moment decided to leave out their brilliant back man Monohan, the injury to his leg making it doubtful whether he could stand a hard tussle, and Incoll went

Essendon v Fitzroy—the first match of the season.

94

in in his stead. Baxter was away from Essendon, and O'Loghlen took the vacant place. Mr. T. Sherrin had manufactured two balls specially for the game, and if the long kicking which was shown during the day was any criterion no fault could be found with the ball used. As soon as the teams came out the crowd, which was excited, began to shout and yell, and they kept it up until the end. Collingwood, kicking towards the grand-stand, had first use of the wind, and they attacked at once. It was an eager, rushing game, with the players all crowding into the centre.

The first item of note besides the eagerness of the players was a beautiful pass from Pears to E. Lockwood, which the latter failed to take. Pannam and Hailwood were forcing Essendon back, but Gavin relieved grandly, and 10 minutes had gone before A. Leach punted the first point—a behind. Then M'Kenzie from a free kick failed to raise the ball, and it hit the man facing him, and as it bounced away Rowell dashed in, and a mighty roar told that he had scored a goal with a running shot. So far Collingwood had been doing everything, but Essendon charged forward from the bounce, and M'Kenzie, working like a tiger to retrieve his error, got a behind. Proudfoot's kick-in was a mighty one, but Thurgood skirting round the crowd shot for goal, but his kick went wide. Before Collingwood could relieve the pressure Griffiths had a shot, which Proudfoot stopped one hand lying down. It was a dramatic incident—the first of many in the day.

Thurgood kicked another behind, and then some fine concerted work between Robinson, Hastings, Vollugi, Hiskens, and Kinnear brought another point. Hailwood was working like a Trojan, and as he forced the ball up two 'Woodsmen went for the mark. They spoilt each other, and Anderson chipped in and passed to Hutchens, from whom Thurgood got it. The big man was playing finely, but shooting wildly. Hiskens, however, from a free kick made amends with a beautiful place kick. Proudfoot was minding his goal grandly, and turned many a rush. In the closing moments of the quarter Tulloch passed to E. Lockwood, and as the bell rang he hit the post, and they crossed over. Essendon, 1–3; Collingwood, 1–2. It was a grand struggle, in which both sides spared neither themselves nor their opponents, and the man standing back had the best of it, for in their eagerness the men often overran the ball.

As soon as they began again a clever run by Fell got the ball to Condon to E. Lockwood to Pears, who, with a nice shot, scored the goal. This was an instance of that clever passing with which the Magpies have been so dangerous. Essendon were passing well, too, but with long kicks Robinson and Hutchens gave Thurgood a chance, but again he kicked badly. Though Monohan was not playing, his advice was valuable, and it was at his suggestion that F. Leach and M'Cormack changed places, the former taking up the burden of Thurgood's watcher. Anderson saved Essendon in a hot scrimmage, and Mann, Martin, Vollugi, and Hiskens carried it on, and Thurgood, marking in the crowd, with a mighty punt made the scores even; but Collingwood got the lead at once again, Incoll and Condon sending the ball in front of goal, where Allan easily scored. The game was being played at a tremendous pace, and when Dummett slipped down as he kicked he had not time to get off his knees before the ball was back to him, and he marked it kneeling. The Essendon wing men had beaten their Fitzroy opponents badly the previous week, but the Magpies' wings were too good, and Pannam and Allan were invincible. Dummett was marking grandly in defence, and the Essendon forwards, shooting wildly, could not get the goal for which Robinson, M'Kenzie, Hutchens, Hastings, and Martin were working so hard, and at half-time the scores were:—

Collingwood, 3 goals 2 behinds (20 points).

Essendon, 2 goals 7 behinds (19 points).

Up to this it had been a grand struggle, not the best football perhaps, but still forceful and exciting, and there did not seem to be a point between the teams. They began again at the same tremendous pace, and a peanut man was mind to scamper for the boundary. He had been crossing the ground, but there was no room for anyone but the players and the umpire in that oval when such rushing and tearing was going on. For a while the game hung in the balance, and after Pears had hit the post, Rowell ran in and scored, Geggie dashing into the goal post in his endeavour to stop the goal. Essendon looked like faltering, so overwhelming was the Magpies' rush, and though Gavin marked grandly in defence.

Essendon could not get the ball away, Anderson and Hastings broke through once, and when Hiskens marked splendidly and passed to Thurgood right in front, Essendon seemed to have a chance. He missed an easy mark, however, and Essendon's hopes were shattered as A. Leach relieved, and Rowell, after a grand mark, passed to Angus, who ran on and scored. Essendon were fighting for their lives, and in the closing moments of the quarter they managed to score their only point, a goal, O'Loghlen punting it. The bell rang with the scores:—

Collingwood, 5 goals 5 behinds (35 points).

Essendon, 3 goals 7 behinds (25 points).

Essendon had the wind in the final quarter, and there were many who still hoped for victory. Ten points was the difference in the scores, and they dashed on to get them. They attacked strongly, but seven minutes' play brought only a behind by Robinson, and then came the turning point. Kennedy, who had been having the worst of his bout with Allan on the wing, beat his man badly by very clever play. He turned and ran like a hare, but, alas for Essendon's hopes, he kicked straight into Fell, who passed to Hailwood to A. Leach in front.

He quickly passed to E. Lockwood, and Collingwood's sixth goal came easily. It was another of the dramatic incidents. Essendon were failing slowly, but still dying hard, and Rush, defending grandly, beat them back, and Rowell was awarded a free kick. He placed the ball, and as it soared in mid air it looked as though it would just fail to bridge the distance against the wind. It was a moment of suspense, and as the ball flew toward the goal the Collingwood supporter in the press-box yelled "It's there! It's there! By Heavens it's there!" and as the Collingwood team rushed to Rowell to grasp his hand, the excited barracker sank back into his seat, "That settles it," he gasped. "They can't catch us now." It did settle it, for with victory and the premiership in view, the Magpies kept up the attack, and though Essendon, struggling bravely and with defeat staring them in the face, threw themselves into it; it was no use, and twice again the Collingwood system having full play resulted in goals, E. Lockwood, standing out by himself, getting the ball, first from Angus and then from Condon, and though Thurgood made a splendid try the game ended—

Collingwood, 9 goals 6 behinds (60 points).

Essendon, 3 goals 9 behinds (27 points).

The Collingwood men rushed to one another and to their dressingroom, and were met at the gate by their hon. secretary (Mr. E. Copeland) with open arms. There was an excited scene in the dressingroom, and in the midst of it appeared the Essendon captain, H. Gavin, dripping with perspiration. He had fought for his colours like a hero, and had been beaten. With the uniform he had worn so gallantly and all the evidence of the fray still on him he jumped on a form and congratulated his victors, giving them sincere praise. The better side had won, he said, and that was all. They cheered him, and away he went to his own room, to be cheered by his own men as well.

Crapp umpired the game magnificently. He did not use his whistle too much, but never failed to notice breaches of the rules. There was no doubt about the superiority of the winners after half-time, and no one was more ready to acknowledge it than the Essendon men themselves. The winners take the medals presented by Mr. Alex. M'Cracken (president of the league) to the premier team. In addition the team get the league caps, and from the Victoria-park flagpole next winter will fly the pennant bearing the inscription:

"COLLINGWOOD, PREMIERS 1902".

It was a game in which individuality had to give way to combination, and it is safe to say that every man on the winning side did his share. But there are some who must be singled out. Pannam, by reason of his wonderful dashing wing play; Hailwood, for his untiring following and his high-marking; F. Leach, for his splendid work up to Thurgood; Allan, for his brilliance and pertinacity on the wing; M'Cormack, for his brilliant work; Rush, for his fine defence; Proudfoot, for his mighty kicking and goal-keeping; Rowell, for his pace and dash; and the others for their splendid play all round.

Essendon, though beaten, were not disgraced, and every man did well. Gavin was a marvellous back, where Mann, Anderson, and Hastings worked brilliantly. Wright was clever in the centre, and Kennedy and Vollugi, though beaten on the wings, never gave in. Hutchens, Thurgood, Larkin, and Hiskens worked hard forward, and in the ruck M'Kenzie, Martin, Griffith, O'Loghlen, Robinson, and Kinnear all did well at various times.

The following were the teams:—

Collingwood—Allan, Angus, Condon, Dummett, Fell, Hailwood, Incoll, Leach (two), Lockwood (two), M'Cormack, Proudfoot, Pears, Pannam, Rush, Rowell, Tulloch (captain).

Essendon—Robinson, Geggie, Mann, Hastings, Gavin

(captain), Anderson, Kennedy, Wright, Vollugi, Hiskens, Thurgood, Hutchens, Larkin, Kinnear, O'Loghlen, Martin, M'Kenzie, Griffiths.

CARLTON WIN THREE IN A ROW

By 'Follower', *Age*, October, 1908.

The football season terminated on Saturday, when on the Melbourne Cricket Ground Carlton defeated Essendon by 9 points—5.5 to 3.8—and won the League premiership for the third consecutive year. The match attracted an immense gathering of spectators, 49,371 persons passing through the turnstiles, and the gate receipts amounting to £1789, which eclipsed all previous records. At the corresponding match of last year 40,505 were present, and the gate money amounted to £1471. On Saturday all the stands were densely packed, and the ground presented a splendid appearance. On two occasions part of the iron railing surrounding the playing enclosure succumbed to the pressure of the crowd. Spectators were perched in the branches of the elms on the railway side of the ground, and numbers of people who had paid for admission to the big grand stand, being unable to obtain sitting accommodation under cover, sought and found it on the roof. In the vicinity of the western goal some of the over exuberant onlookers came to blows, and some excitement was caused by a woman fainting and being carried on to the playing ground, where, after being fanned and attended to, she recovered. On the whole, however, the crowd was well behaved, and when the railing gave way spectators who were pushed on to the turf quietly seated themselves round the boundary and continued to watch the play. The match was witnessed by his Excellency the State Governor, who arrived early, and was received by the M.C.C. committee. Notwithstanding the immense attendance, most of the spectators were able to view the game in comfort, an advantage which, however, was not enjoyed by representatives of the press. The inconveniently situated press box on the M.C.C. ground is a disgrace to the club, whose other appointments are irreproachable. In the compartment set apart for them the pressmen have their view intercepted by numerous iron pillars; one portion of the playing enclosure they cannot see, and on such an occasion as that under notice they are annoyed by a constant stream of people passing in front of them or invading their compartment. This state of things is quite inexcusable, as the misplacing of the press box was pointed out when its present ridiculous position was first decided upon, and attention has since been frequently called to it without any alteration being made.

In view of the interest attached to Saturday's match, two special balls were manufactured by Mr. T. W. Sherrin, of Collingwood, whose footballs, cricket balls and boxing gloves have been pronounced by visiting champion athletes to be equal to any produced in England or America. Mr. Sherrin made the balls for Saturday's match similar in shape to those which he manufactured for the recent jubilee carnival games, the ends being rounded, and experts agreed that the innovation was a decided improvement.

Carlton were again without Gillespie and Caine, and their famous follower, Johnson, who had bruised his hip in the match against St. Kilda, was disposed to stand out, but at the request of his comrades was stripped, and proved as useful as usual, being one of the most prominent players on the field. Caine, who was recently prostrated by very severe illness, has so far recovered as to be able to get about again, and was one of the most interested spectators on Saturday. Essendon were handicapped by the absence (through injury) of L. Armstrong, one of their most brilliant players, and of M. Londerigan, whose father had died on the previous day. The Essendon players wore mourning armbands as a mark of condolence with their bereaved comrade. The Essendon executive, after long and careful consideration, decided to leave out Parkinson and Landmann, and it was not at all surprising to find that the latter's omission proved to be a disastrous mistake. On several occasions this season Landmann's cleverness and accuracy in shooting for goal have been of considerable service to Essendon, whose greatest weakness on Saturday was in attack, and when the game had been won by Carlton by the narrow majority of 9 points, the Essendon committee must have been forced to the unsatisfactory reflection that by the omission of Landmann the match had possibly been thrown away. Daykin, who played in place of Armstrong, thoroughly justified his selection, and M. Shea, who took Londerigan's place, did excellent work; but

Legge, until late in the game, was seldom prominent, and his substitution for Landmann certainly weakened the team. Heaphy, from Tatura, however, did well, and though Prout, the Wesley College crack, was lost in the first half, he played a great game on the wing subsequently.

On the whole it was a decidedly disappointing game, Essendon all through the first half quite failing to play up to their best form, and from the interval to the finish Carlton directed their efforts solely to kicking across the ground in order to prevent Essendon making up their leeway, in consequence of which Carlton only added 1 behind to their record of 5.4, put up before half time. In the early stages of the game Essendon seemed to be over impressed by the importance of the occasion, lacked system, fumbled the ball, failed to watch their men and left their places, while Carlton played a fine, cool, systematic game, with judgment and skill. In the last two quarters Essendon showed to much greater advantage, adding 1.4 to 0.1, and might have pulled the game out of the fire but for the lamentable failures of their forwards, who missed several easy chances; but, as above indicated, Carlton were then satisfied not to attempt the aggressive as long as they were able to keep Essendon from scoring. The better team on the day won the match, and on its conclusion the winners were heartily congratulated by Mr. Alex. M'Cracken, president of the Victorian Football League; by Mr. H. C. Harrison, and by Mr. Mat Wilson, of the Essendon club. The victory of the Carlton club for the third consecutive season roused intense enthusiasm, and as the players were leaving the ground several of them were seized and carried on the shoulders of their delighted supporters.

BENNO THE BARRACKER

BY EDWARD DYSON

From *Benno and Some of the Push*, 1908

Goudy, the town traveller, examined the clerk curiously. Benno was perched on his high stool like a monkey on an organ. He crouched at his work, hiding his face with his left arm, writing laboriously. He only pretended to be oblivious of the Scotchman's scrutiny. As a matter of fact, he wrote at random, setting down meaningless figures. His small intellectual capacity was occupied in framing bitter and biting abuse of Goudy, whose cursed inquisitiveness was very unwelcome at that moment.

Benno consumed his splendid invectives, however, and was silent under the scrutiny. Goudy moved in a semi-circle, peering under and over with an air of grave concern, and the clerk manoeuvred adroitly to hide his injuries.

"It's never my old friend, Benjamin," said the town traveller with affected concern; "never our Mr. Dickson! It's not possible. Man, man, but you've changed. Tut, tut, tut, poor laddie, the moths have been at you."

"Garn, scratch!" grumbled Benno.

"But you have a black eye, Benjamin; your ear is a ruin; you have a split lip. You are ashamed, my boy, you are covered with contrition. Your effort to hid your disgrace implies a lingering remnant of decency, but it advertises your fall, Benno. The beaten bantam creeps under the barn, but the conqueror crows from the housetops. Open your heart to me, laddie. Weep on my bosom. It will ease you."

"Some'n 'll get a belt in the whiskers if he don't behave," said Benno, reaching for a glass paper-weight.

"That face outrages the proprieties," Goudy continued. "It ought to be brought under the notice of the Executive. Bless my soul, it's enough to lose us all our Wesleyan trade."

"Come erway," interposed the packer, taking Goudy by the arm. "Respect a strong man's sorrer."

Feathers led Goudy to the packing bench, and he resumed the handling of a ream of printed tea wraps.

"There was a game iv footy, Saturdee," said Feathers.

The town traveller whistled a gust eloquent of enlightenment.

"Our Mr. Dickson was there. Benno's bin bestowin' his vote 'n' patronage on St. Kilda fer some time past. He's bin recitin' bits 'n' expressin' loud 'n' large opinions t' th' effect that St. Kilda is the dazzlin' P., the bonzers, the boshters, the pink, the pride, 'n' the pick iv th' earth at the noble game iv footy. Jimmy Jee! T' hear him flute you'd think he'd discovered th' whole team on a doorstep, 'n' 'ad brought 'em up by 'and on the bottle with much patience 'n' self-sacrifice."

"You know Dickson has a splendid public spirit," said Goudy. "He'll be city dog-catcher one of these days."

Benno crouched lower, and the figures swarmed over his

page. He knew the ignominious story would be told, and, knowing *how*, felt his inwards curdling with hate for G. Mills.

"Benno don't live at St. Kilda," said the packer, turning in the end of his parcel with movements graceful and adept, "but he 'as 'igh notions. He lives on the fag end iv one iv them cheap, weatherboard subbubs what's all sloppy rightaways 'n' battered rubbish tins, 'n' what's inhabited mainly by bottle-ohs, deserted wives 'n' soured cats. But he's a peacock fer style, 'n' he hadopted St. Kilda 'cause it goes well with his two-'n'-six-penny helephant's breath gloves 'n' his pinch-back overcoat.

"I have t' report that our Mr. Dickinson went t' the match, Saints versus South, Saturdee. Me 'n' the Don was privileged to accompany his nibs, 'n' his chinnin' aboard the train was th' chatter iv th' man what ain't mistaken, never was, 'n' never will be. In one iv his proud moments he offered t' wager a forty horse-power 'igh-grade, nickle-plated motorcar agin the poor but honest belltopper iv the ginger gent opposite that Saints 'd win, 'n' he threw a goal in. His magnernimity was terrivle t' behold.

"The ginger bloke declined t' bet, mentionin' how he was a preacher iv th' Gorspel, a hanti-gambler, 'n' a Society fer the Prevention iv Vice.

"'Then don't talk so much,' sez Benno with some severity. 'Don't get eloquent iv yeh ain't prepared t' put yer oof down with a firm hand.' Which was scaldin' hot, seein' the ginger gent 'adn't said a word. But you can't stop little Benjamin once he gets flutterin' his rag in public. Afore we reached St. Kilda he'd got th' people in the nex' compartments peepin' over th' partitions in the belief he was the prodigal son iv a rich old family; 'n' the perfect lady, with the brazen head of 'air 'n' the beautiful set iv new china teeth, lookin' like a glazed tile stair-case, told th' Don she knew Benno well. He had mountains iv gold, she said, but he was crool t' women."

Benno screwed his head around, and snarled at them like a teased dog. "Yar-r-r-, get work," he said. "Who's polin' on th' 'ouse now? Strike me dilly, they's blokes 'ere don't earn enough t' keep a canary in corf drops."

"But Benny was at th' height iv his splendour on the field iv battle," continued Feathers remorselessly. "He got an early camp, 'n' screwed in t' th' fence, 'n' gave th' general public some advanced opinions on a lacrosse game what was pervided ez a sort iv preliminary canter. Our Mr. Dickson always selects a confidant on occasions iv this kind—someone t' sort o' play 'Oratio t' his 'Amlet—someone t' lean up agen 'n' address hisself to. By this means he lets information about hisself leak out, 'n' 'elps t' edjikate the masses. Ez a matter o' fact, his niblets don't know th' game iv lacrosse from tiggie-tiggie-touchwood, but that didn't diminish the flow ev Benny's helo-quence nothin'. He told the silent bloke next him all about it, trustin' to his own common-sense t' pick up points ez he went along.

"Benny's always trustin' to his own common-sense, dis-regardless iv th' fact that he ain't got none. Presently the crowd sort iv glued itself round Mr. Dickson 'n' the silent lad, 'n' bekan t' pass the blurt. Then 'Oratio bestirred himself. He shouldered 'Amlet off.

"'Gar-r-rn,' sez he, 'this ain't a game iv hi-spy-hi, Cuthbert, this is quoits. Turn yer vice th' other way. It's givin' me the sleepin' sickness.'

"'P'raps I don't know lacrosse?' said Benno bravely. 'Yeh think yeh can gi' me instructions, don't yeh? Let me tell yeh I was playin' the game when you was sucking milk through a tube.'

"'Any'ow, Ned, don't talk all over me. I got me Sunday things on. 'Sides everybody's lookin'. They'll be thinkin' we're out o' th' same cage.'

"'There's someone in th' himmediate vicinity infested with rats,' says Benno in his 'appiest style.

"At this th' lad got the flat iv his juke agin Mr. Dickson's chiv, 'n' shoved it 'ard t' th' off. 'If yer turn it on me again, Ned,' sez he, 'I'll hurt it.'

"Benjamin the cop-out was dooly impressed, 'n' suffered a long spasm iv silent reflection. Then he shifted his bunk, 'n' wormed in lower down. When the Saints ambled out, he was ready 'n' waitin'. The yell he let loose caused er fat peeler t' shy, 'n' turned er lady's umbreller inside out.

"'Git at 'em Saints!' he howled. 'Now fer th' sacrifice. No beg-pardons, 'n' no mercy. Give 'em a bump. Stand 'em on their necks. You can do it, you beauts!'

"Little Benny's frenzy when the game got goin' would freeze yer blood. He was that angry with the South piebiters, he didn't care what 'appened to 'em, 'n' the way he screamed at the doomed wretches would mind you iv Mrs. Canty tellin' Mrs. Bill Higgins candidly what she thinks iv her 'n' hers over the right-o'-way after a sisterly spree and a dispute 'bout a stew-pan.

"'Wade into 'em Saints!' he yelled. 'Swing him on his ear, Cumby. Snatch th' 'air off him! Bring 'em down, you boshters! Jump 'em in the mud. Good man, Barwick! That shifted 'im. Give 'im another fer his mother!'

"Benno's 'appiest moments was when a S'melbin' player got busted, or took the boot in er tender place, 'n' curled up on the field, wrigglin' like a lamed worm. These affectin' incidents stirred th' clerk deeply.

"'Oh, a bonzer, a bonzer, a boshter, a bontoshter!' screamed our Christian brother. 'Fair in the baloon, 'n' good enough for him! That's the way to tease 'em, the blighters! They're lookin' fer it, so let 'em have it wet 'n' heavy! Lay 'em out! Stiffen 'em. You can get better players fer old bottles anywhere!'

"There was on'y one thing our Mr. Dickson was undecided erbout, 'n' that was th' humpire. He couldn't quite make up his mind whether he should get a presentation gold watch 'n' a gran' banquet, 'r be tethered t' the field with a stake driven through his gizzard. Yer see, when he gave a free kick t' Saints he was a noble soul 'n' a bright 'n' shinin' example iv all th' virtues; but when he gave a free kick t' South he was a despicable 'n' disgustin' object what orter 'ave been smothered in mud. Th' humpire blew his toot, 'n' passed the leather on t' Ginger Stewart, representin' Saints, 'n' iv course, the South Barrackers took it in bad part, 'n' put up the yell iv hate. Sez Benno:

"'Yah-h-h! get work. What's er matter with that? Want the blanky humpire t' put the Saints t' bed, 'n' let yer lame hens play it on their own, do yer? Good man, Tulloch! You're a blitherer!' 'N' the nice boy 'd put his 'ands t'gether 'n' exalt Mr. Tulloch with prayer 'n' praise.

"By'm-bye, Tulloch blows his horn again, 'n' Hughie Callan, representin' South, is allowed a free-'n'-easy, coz one iv the Saints bit him in a burst iv affection, 'r somethin', 'n' Benno's disgust almost stiffens him.

"'Lorblime!' 'e wails, 'wot sort! Jimmy Jee, it's murder—

gory murder, 'n' blanky robbery, tha's what it is!' Then he lets his whole himpassioned soul loose, 'n' blasts th' humpire with abuse, coverin' his family with shame, 'n' degradin' his name for ever.

"But 'twas when someone was shootin' fer goal that little Benjy worked 'is 'ead t' the best effect. 'Twas et sich tryin' moments that his nibs ducked in, 'n' went it blind, hangin' on ter the railin', his mince pies stickin' out like warts on a horse, 'n' all his henergies 'n' his surprisin' intellec' screwed up to the breakin' point, 'n' his young emotions fair seethin' 'n' blubblin' out iv him. 'Twas et a moment like this Benno hachieved his splendid effort iv diplomacy."

"Don' be fergettin' what yer got frim the three-card sparrer at Flemington that Saturdee, Mills," said Benno from his desk, with sudden ferocity. "'N' by the holy, you'll get it again if you give me too much iv yer gibber. Jist you be careful, tha's all."

Mr. Dickson actually looked as if on the point of coming down from his stool, and indulging in manslaughter, but the packer paid no attention.

"Scotty," he said, "you don't do justice t' the keen 'n' brilliant mind iv our Mr. Dickson. Yiv no idear iv his power t' grasp a situation, 'n' his great promptness 'n' resource in a hemergency. The game was at a critical stage, 'n' Benno was bumpin' the Saints up all he knew 'ow.

"'Lay 'em out,' sez he. 'Tear 'em down, 'n' walk over 'em. Jerk him on his chin, Scotty. Bust up the gander-neck. Fracture his back. Lorblime, Saints, you got 'em goin'. Rush it along there, Harwick! Oh, the cripples, they're dead t' the world! Welt their 'ead in! *Stiffen 'em.* KILL 'EM! Buck in, S—.'

"There Benny's eloquence was shut off. Yeh never struck anythin' suddener in yer natural. 'Buck in, Sus—', sez he, 'n' stuck there, with his north-'n'-south wide open, 'n' his eyes fair glarin'. ''N' why?' sez you. Fact is, Benjamin's splendid powers iv persuasion 'ad bin attractin' a good deal iv public attention lately, 'n' slowly but surely a lot iv South barrackers had been percolatin' through the crowd, 'n' gatherin' round Benno, 'n' Ben discovered 'em at that tragic moment when his head was wide ajar in his best burst iv horatory. The push had blood in its eyes, 'n' its fists was ready. 'Twas jist th' toughest bunch, 'n' carried a banner made iv a old white shirt with the legend: 'Deth or Victry'. For ten terrible seconds Benno glared, chokin' on them vital words, 'Buck in, S—'. Then his bright

106

mind got t' work, 'n' the squeel he put up split the blouse iv a fat lady on his left.

"'Buck in *South*!' sez he. 'Lay 'em out *South*! Tear 'em down! Waltz over 'em. Whooroo, Souths! Oh, you beauts, you bonzers! South'll do 'em! South's the pride, the boshters! I'll lay a dollar to a dump on South Melbin!'"

"'Twas a masterpiece of strategy," said Goudy gravely.

"'Twas an instance iv phenomenal presence iv mind," continued Feathers, "'n' it saved Benno's life. The push suspended 'ostilities, 'n' fer twenty minutes 'r so Bennie was very subdoo'd, puttin' in on'y a half-earted word fer South now 'n' agin. 'N' when he got his chance he backed out, 'n' shifted his pitch. He shoved in further round, where the toms was thickest, 'n' where he reckoned it'd he safe t' have some hopinions iv his own.

"We had some trouble in findin' him agin, but when we did he was hittin' up St. Kilda once more, 'n' givin' South samples iv slum language that'd demoralize a navvy's cow. But Benno had made another mistook. The toms erbout was ingrained South barrackers to a woman, fact'ry rats from the Port 'n' the river mills, ez willin' ez cats, 'n' 'ard in th' face ez fish-plates. We 'eard Benno's yell, 'n' then somethin' fizzed like pullin' the cork out iv a soder-water foundry, 'n' out iv the throng comes a push iv bright girls fighting round somethin' like a pack iv greyhounds on a starved cat. There was no noise 'cept a sort iv buzzin' 'n' tearin', 'n' then the toms opened out, leavin' their prey on the ground. 'Twas Benno. 'Twas th' immortal cop-out, 'n' he sat up in the mud ermong his rags, blinkin', a monimint iv human sorrer. His eye was black, 'n' his nose was bleedin' free, but the look on his face was not anger. 'Twas a look iv sad perplexity. He thort th' earth had bin hit with a comet.

"He went 'ome at once, not bein' fit fer publication. He rode in the guard's van, hidin' from the crool world under a 'orse rug, 'n' he never spoke iv his troubles.

"This, Scotty, accounts fer them evidences iv a bad past what our Mr. Dickson is displayin' fer th' edification iv the vulgar, 'n' which he tells the junyer partner was obtained in a 'eroic effort t' save a sick policeman from a ill-mannered gang up in Little Lon. Poor Benno; his luck's disgustin,' but he's the backbone iv our national winter game. I wouldn't give peanuts for a play iv footy without him as leadin' comedian."

THE VIC CUMBERLAND POEM

By JCD, *Sport*, June 26, 1908.

His height is just on five foot ten, his weight is 13 stone,
And on every football field as champion he is known;
But I think the greatest game that we have ever seen him play
Was against South Melbourne, on the 16th day of May.

A good man, yes; against good men he made them all look
small,
For every time that I could see it was 'Cumby' on the ball.
A better player than this man so far has not been found
For the critics always class him as 'the best man on the ground'.

The finest player of them all, we've seen what he can do;
He's the greatest champion on the ball St. Kilda ever knew.
When from the ruck he brings it out, or taps it with his hand,
You'll hear the old familiar shout of 'Good boy, Cumberland!'

ROOKIE NOLAN'S POEM

By Billy T., from *100 Years of Football*—E.C.H. Taylor.

Melbourne may have lacked something in skill, but there was
always found a sufficient supply of those duly qualified "to mix
it" if the occasion demanded retaliatory action. Such a game
between Melbourne and Essendon this year was certainly
colourful. Immediately the ball was bounced, for some reason
never revealed, a prominent Essendonian felled Jack Gardiner,
the Melbourne rover. "Rookie" Nolan, the powerful Demon
follower, let it be known that he disapproved of this method of
attack, and promptly put the Essendon offender out of action.
In a twinkling a dozen players were punching one another, and
this "friendly" spirit continued until three-quarter time. At this
juncture Nolan called his troops together and suggested a truce.
The "war cabinet" agreed, and peace having been restored the
game finished in a somewhat quieter atmosphere.

The result of it all was that only two players were reported by
the umpire, though they all feared a lengthy sentence. A few
beers in the local hostelry after the match calmed the ruffled

tempers of both sides. However, a certain bard of the time, under the *nom de plume* of "Billy T.", was inspired to pen the following lines, which in quality and expression almost rival the inimitable C. J. Dennis. His hero was undoubtedly the redoubtable Bernard Nolan.

Begob, it was a lovely game, a game iv blood an' hair,
Wid a thrifle iv torn whiskers an' an eyelid here an'
  there,
And iv all th' darlin' bla'guards that was afther raisin'
  Cain
There was niver one like Nolan. Whoop for Oireland
  once again!
    Yer a jooel, Mister Nolan,
    Yer a bhoy there's no conthrollin',
And when Erin wants a Saviour sure we'll send our
  noble Nolan.

When the foight was at its hottest how he charged th'
  writhin' mob,
He whirled his fists, and yelled "Whooroo!" and punched
  'em in the gob.
The riots Home in Belfast they was nothin' worth a
  word
To the lovely dose of throuble that on Saturday occurred,
    When the splendid hero, Nolan,
    Sent the other divils rollin',
And all Essendon was crippled by our lovely fightin'
  Nolan.

Poor Parkinson was waitin', an' he got it in th' jaw.
And for anything that followed, sor, he didn't give a
  sthraw.
On the ground th' bye was lyin', wid his eyes up to the
  sun,
While his conqueror was layin' out the others one by
  one—
    Was the dashin' Misther Nolan;
    It was bowls, an' he was bowlin,'
Wid th' bodies of his rivals, was th' harum scarum Nolan.

He jammed th' ball down Martin's throat, he did, upon
  me soul,

And then he shwore the umpire blind he thought it was
the goal.
He whirled the players 'cross th' field like feathers in th'
breeze.
He punched them wid his bunch of fives, he dug 'em
wid his knees,
Did that playful divil Nolan,
Och! His style is so cajolin',
Ye must have a heart of iron if ye're not in love wid
Nolan.

At th' finish he was thereabout, his heart so full of fun,
That th' umpire couldn't shtop him wid a poleaxe or a
gun.
An' when he'd filled th' Hos-pit-al wid players that was
there,
He yelled: "Bring in all Essendon, its Council and its
'Mare'."
He's a bhoy there's no conthrollin',
And when Ireland's wantin' Home Rule, begob! we'll
send her fightin' Nolan!

8
1910s: 'The Call of Stoush'

What C. J. Dennis dubbed 'the call of stoush' was as evident on the football field as it was at Gallipoli, and the argument over where a young man's duty lay was not settled by the conscription referenda, or war-time football. St. Kilda got very close in 1913, Carlton, Essendon and Fitzroy won two Premierships each, but the game, with arguments over professionalism and on-field violence, staggered through the Great War. Many players did not return.

ST. KILDA'S GREAT VICTORY

By 'Observer', *Argus*, September 22, 1913.

The meeting of Fitzroy and St. Kilda, on the Melbourne Cricket Ground on Saturday, furnished a desperate game. It was a final, but not a grand final. That will be played next Saturday. Had Fitzroy won, the season was over, but for the second time this season, and after victory had swung in the balance for the greater part of the game, Fitzroy in the end found themselves overmastered by St. Kilda. As details given below show, it was the greatest crowd that had ever gathered inside the Melbourne Cricket Ground, and the biggest gate for a football match, the takings being over £2,000.

Owing, unfortunately, to his father's illness, McLennan, the dashing centre man of Fitzroy, and a great unit in their organisation of this season, was absent. Otherwise the teams were strong, and the game was as strong as the players. From the start there was such dash, vim, and at times recklessness, that it looked like developing into bitterness. But Elder, the umpire, who always rises to the big strain of these finals, kept control of the players admirably, and was rewarded in the round of cheers which the more generously-minded of the crowd gave him at the finish of the match—as well as one groan, conspicuous in its isolation.

At the start the football was rather more earnest than skilful, and for a time it seemed that St. Kilda were playing Fitzroy's game in throwing themselves into crushes, in wasting themselves against superior weight. St. Kilda got to work at once. Schmidt and Cumberland played it up to Woodcock, who, with one of his fine shots, placed it in front of goal. Jory marked, but, not being quite sure of it, took the risks in a rush through, and scored first goal. In a series of exciting crushes, Walker and Heron kept St. Kilda off for a time, and the free kicks which punctuated the game were not an evil, because they gave players breathing and thinking time, which already was rather badly needed.

Willoughby got close to goal with a shot, and when Heaney's bulky figure was seen soaring over a crush, but he failed to mark, Millhouse and Schmidt took it out of danger. Toohey was conspicuous in high-marking for Fitzroy; Schmidt, on the other side, played up to his great reputation, and gave Morrissey a rare chance to score another goal. He carried his run to the last instant—just a moment too late, for a Fitzroy charge found him just upon the point of kicking, spoiled his aim, and nothing was scored. Although St. Kilda were chiefly attacking, the ball went from end to end in the way that always means good football. Lenne, the Fitzroy full-back, had to do his finest in defence, and his finest is always of a high standard.

In a Fitzroy interlude Parratt and Shaw, who worked together all day with beautiful effect, got it in front of St. Kilda's goal, but Lever came out with one of his streaming rushes and gave them temporary relief. It came back; instantly there was a crush in front, and active little Freake, who needs very little help as a forward, went very close with a hurried shot.

A moment later Shaw and Buisst gave him a second try, and this time he scored a goal. Again Buisst, with a beautiful kick, dropped it in front of the Saints' goal, where a crush was for a time terrific, Jory, Bowden and Schmidt finally bringing it away. The attack had eased for a moment only, for Parratt and Shaw were conspicuous in the Fitzroy rush that carried it back. Bamford backed them up, sent the ball well within range, but Harris was a cool defender for St. Kilda in the emergency. The game seemed to be swinging a bit in favor of Fitzroy, for, with excitement and overeagerness, it was the crowded game that suited the maroons.

Heron passed to Norris, who made a very fine mark, from which Fitzroy got no gain. The game was roughening up all the time, and onlookers agreed that it was going to be eventful. There was far more charging than necessary, especially after players had taken their kick. On this fault both sides should be censured.

Lynch, who brought down some rare high marks during the day, passed the ball to Schmidt. It seemed out of range, but Schmidt on occasions is equal to anything, and there were roaring cheers when, with a magnificent place kick, he got second goal for St. Kilda. In a minute Schmidt, Cumberland, and Lynch had it up to Morrissey again, and third goal was scored. This is where St. Kilda shines—in the sudden passing dashes.

All their finest achievements this season have come in that way. They were attacking again, when Johnson stopped them, but only for a moment, for immediately afterwards the ball was with Sellars right in front. He took all the risks, bluffed for a free kick, got it, and missed the goal. Next Jory was cheered for a fine mark, and anything that excited special notice in high marking in that game had to be very fine indeed, for it was a feature of the match all through. He passed to Millhouse, who, as usual, looked for Cumberland and placed the ball with him, and the big fellow, taking it very deliberately, got fourth goal. Fitzroy were anxious. Willoughby lodged it amongst a crush in front of St. Kilda's goal. The ball, hit by hand, was rolling through, when Toohey made a desperate effort to get up to it, and just failed, so that a goal was lost and a point won. Martin had a shot just on the finish, but as they changed ends St. Kilda had the better of the scores by 3 goals.

As in their game against South Melbourne St. Kilda had changed their ruck constantly. Sometimes the captain did it; mostly it was left to the players' own discretion. When they felt the strain too great they called a substitute in. Thus far it was not football of the highest character, though very exciting, and unquestionably earnest.

The early pace was altogether too hot to last, but on the wide area of the Melbourne Cricket Ground players soon discover that for themselves. From this stage discretion and judgment took the place of impulse. Changing ends Fitzroy slowly became aggressive, Lethbridge making some fine dashes from their back line whenever St. Kilda approached.

It was Parratt and Toohey who next got the ball to scoring range, where Shaw, having a clear opening, kicked second goal for Fitzroy. A minute afterwards Heaney gave him a second chance, but this one he missed. Then Eicke and Bowden, who were always prominent on the wing, took it around the fence till they met Johnson on Fitzroy's half-back line, and their progress stopped.

Lethbridge was his best assistant, but Eicke from a fine mark had it into Fitzroy's ground again, where Sellars very nearly got it through. Before that attack eased Lynch had a shot—a very fine one—which hit the goal-post. From the kick-off Lynch got it again, and Cazaly, marking in front, got fifth goal. It seemed to sharpen up Fitzroy, and for a time the game swung in their favor.

Parratt scored their third goal. Martin and Freake had chances soon afterwards, which added nothing material, and Dangerfield twice had to do his best to keep Fitzroy out of the danger zone. All through it was a grand exhibition of high marking—a great, striving match. Willoughby was giving St. Kilda rather many free kicks. Holden and Shaw were able to play brilliant football for Fitzroy without incurring any penalties, and the maroons at that stage were apparently taking the upper hand.

Then a St. Kilda blunder gave Fitzroy their fourth goal. Lever, finding an opening, tried to run with the ball, lost it, and Freake like a flash had it through the goal. It seemed to me that St. Kilda were getting a bit rattled, though Eicke, Bowden, Sellars, and Lynch shone in one of those dazzling approaches which are the spectacular feature of their football.

Morrissey got a free kick, and missed. Cazaly made a fine long shot, also faulty in direction, and not until the rules were broken did Fitzroy find relief. Then in a dash quite worthy of their rivals Parratt, Walker, and Toohey took it up, but a foul charge—and there were many of those during the day—stopped their progress, with the consequent free kick. Just on half-time, and out of a terrific crush on St. Kilda goal front, Toohey scored the fifth goal, and for a period that lasted perhaps two minutes in actual playing space Fitzroy were 2 points ahead. They got that lead just on half-time, enjoyed it during the interval, and lost it immediately afterwards.

Recommencing the struggle, Cumberland came to his best for the second half. He placed it in a nice position for Morrissey,

Dave McNamara takes a saving mark for St. Kilda.

who missed his mark, but Schmidt snapped a behind. Fitzroy were helped out by a free kick to Shaw, and Heron aided a further approach.

In a rush of the Saints Cumberland again shone, and Cazaly taking a big risk in overrunning his distance without a bounce got sixth goal. It might just as well have been a free kick against him. A fine mark by Lynch, who brought down some beauties during the match, gave Cumberland a shot, and a miss. Just afterwards St. Kilda had a rare show to score an easy goal, but their forwards were all so eager to take it that a bungle spoiled the opportunity, and at that stage every mistake was a matter for mourning amongst their followers.

Fitzroy shone in an attack, which began with Lethbridge, ended with Norris and Martin. St. Kilda still needed judgment in their passing, but they were coming surely to their own, and Cumberland and Dangerfield were two men who conspicuously kept their heads at a critical stage of the match.

Next Willoughby from a free kick within range, but on the angle, had a chance for Fitzroy, and failed. Heron in a fine passing effort placed it, with Martin, who got a free shot within easy distance, but kicked badly, as his try went out of bounds. At that stage the balance was swinging again. It seemed to be just a question of which side would crack up first, and St. Kilda were straggling a bit. From a Fitzroy attack, in which Heron was the central figure, he got two shots in quick succession, and missed them both.

Then came the turning point. A dazzling St. Kilda rush began with Dangerfield, was carried on by Schmidt and Cumberland, and ended with Morrissey, who scored their seventh goal, a fine demonstration of the tri-colours' scoring rush.

A mark by Dangerfield staved off trouble an instant later. Then Parratt, Shaw, and Martin shone for the maroons, and in the midst of this tussle, an outbreak of hostilities was threatened till Walker dashed in between two men who had lost their tempers. St. Kilda were being threatened again, when Lever brought it out. Schmidt marked a fine long kick, passed it to Cumberland, who took it high in the air, but was not straight in his shot for goal.

Once Lethbridge took a mark for Fitzroy in such an awkward position that he stood on his head as he brought it down. Again it seemed for an instant as if the blow which means investigation and trouble would not be long delayed, for players were much excited. Heron was not one of them. He played splendidly for Fitzroy all through, and was giving them relief which they badly needed, when Bowden carried it right up to Fitzroy's goal front, took all the risks in dodging players, ran within easy range, and missed by a few feet.

In that quarter, St. Kilda did well everywhere except in shooting for goal. It seemed possible that the defect would lose them the match. Just on the finish of the quarter there was a bad case of charging, in which Heaney, who so far had done little else, came in for censure. At three-quarter time St. Kilda were leading by two goals, and there was a feeling that it was not yet enough, because all through the game the goals had been scored at the railway end, to which Fitzroy would kick in the closing quarter.

In the last stage the game was not long in suspense. Half-way through one would have said that St. Kilda were a tiring team. But before things had gone far in the last quarter, it was quite obvious that they were going to outlast Fitzroy. The pace had told upon the heavier men. The first incident was a beautiful mark by Heaney, without anything of advantage to Fitzroy. Then Lynch and Eicke passed it to Morrissey, who was crossed by an opponent just as he took his kick at a close open goal. The ball was turned outside the post. There was a great crush around Fitzroy's goal for a while, and Lenne made one fine effort to give them relief. Then Cazaly got a free kick—he would have marked the ball in any case—and scored eighth goal for St. Kilda. In an instant Bowden had it with Collins, who was sent flying from a bad charge. He got a free kick and earned it. He also got ninth goal for St. Kilda and that was practically the end of the match.

Fitzroy were beaten. As they died out St. Kilda came on, and we saw the streaming rushes in which the cross pass is so effective. The first of them by Bowden, Lynch, Dangerfield, and Jory failed to bring anything material. Then Millhouse and Schmidt had it with Cazaly, who missed the goal. Jory next placed it with Sellars again, but Fitzroy were equal to the strain.

Their defence was always sound. Right in front of the stand there was a crush, and Willoughby, swinging his elbow with terrific force, caught Jory full in the face, and knocked him out. It looked worse than it really was. Willoughby, who is an

117

awkward, but not an unfair, footballer, swung his elbow recklessly, but he was not looking behind, and did not see Jory's face so close to him. It was chance, and not intention, which made the consequences so serious. There was simply a roar of indignation from the crowd thereabout, and calls of "Come off, 25", that being Willoughby's number. The demonstration had one effect. It stopped Willoughby's football. He realised the possible consequences.

Yet Fitzroy played on with splendid pluck. Freake, who was always conspicuous, always active, scored their sixth goal, and the game roughened a bit again. Sellars passed the ball to Cazaly, who had an open goal, and no one near him. He did everything that he should not have done, but it was all accident. First, he fell down in turning, then he failed to pick up the ball, then, when he did get it with Fitzroy charging on him from every point, he took a four yards deliberate shot, and hit the goal-post for the second time.

One of the prettiest things of the day was seen with Lever streaming out of St. Kilda's goal, and Freake always, yet never quite, catching him. Just as Freake seemed to have his hands on the St. Kilda man there was a slight swerve, not more than a foot, and Freake had to catch up again. A roar of cheers greeted the cool and showy bit of football.

Then Lenne swept the ball in front of him with hand and foot, putting it half way round the wing for Fitzroy. But it was all over as far as the maroons were concerned. In St. Kilda's next rush Hattam, Baird, and Millhouse placed the ball with Morrissey, and he got their tenth and last goal. Freake, who was playing very cleverly indeed, had a couple of chances towards the finish, but was off the mark, and Dangerfield on the half-back line carried his fine form to the end in checking most of the Fitzroy advances. On the further side of the ground one heard a great roar of censure from the crowd, and Martin apparently cautioned. But a crowd sees offences in Martin that would pass notice with other players. He is, I think, one of their scapegoats.

There was great cheering when the bell rang, and St. Kilda had won a strong, troubled, but wonderfully dashing game by 25 points. That they earned their victory there could not be a doubt, but the way in which Fitzroy played it through to the finish raises the highest expectations for the grand final on Saturday next.

I think there were no two better men in the St. Kilda ranks on Saturday than Lever and Dangerfield, the last-named great indeed on the half-back line. Next to them Lynch's high-marking was really very fine. In the brilliant things Schmidt and Eicke chiefly figured. Woodcock was one of the lions of the ruck, and Cumberland was at his finest, especially in the last half. These two stalwarts are a great power for the tricolours. Jory, too, was much in evidence. Cazaly came to his best about goal, and there were others.

All things considered, the smallest man in the Fitzroy team, Shaw, was their champion. He got it often, made few, if any, mistakes, and played wonderfully good football. His combination with Parratt was particularly effective. Next to them came Heron, who was a game little worker all day. On the defence lines Lethbridge, Lenne, and Johnson were at their best. Holden again played a great game in the centre. Norris, although an awkward player, was a valuable one, and one might add half-a-dozen more names without giving any man more than his due.

Further trouble for Fitzroy came after the match. Willoughby was reported for rough play by both the field umpire and the steward, while the steward and boundary umpire laid a similar charge against Heaney.

The scores were:—

	1st Q'ter.	2nd Q'ter.	3rd Q'ter.	Final.	Points.
St. Kilda	4–2	5–4	7–8	10–10	70
Fitzroy	1–2	5–6	5–8	6–9	45

The great ruckman Roy Cazaly pictured here in his South Melbourne days, was a star for St. Kilda in the Fitzroy-St. Kilda final of 1913.

CORRAWALLOP V POSSUM BEND

By H. McDuffie, *Sport*, 1911.

Dan had been diligently studying the newspaper one evening.

"Fine game, football," at length he remarked casually.

Father glared hard at him over the top of his "specs" and sniffed. There was a wealth of hidden meaning in one of father's sniffs.

"Lot of fools that play it," he said decisively. "We never went in for such nonsense when I was a young chap."

"Strikes me you never did anything a bit foolish in your young days, according to you," snapped Dan, with a baleful look at father.

"It's rather a rough game," chipped in mother conciliatingly, scenting a row. "Lots of young men get hurt at it."

"They're just as likely to get hurt at work," answered Dan. "There's a risk in everything."

Father laid down his paper very deliberately, and, taking off his "specs", glared hard at Dan. "What's that you say?" he asked.

Dan repeated his observations for the patriarch's benefit.

"Work!" spluttered father. "Work! There's no comparison between the two things."

"It's jolly hard work playing football," asserted Dan.

"Well, a man shouldn't waste his time at it," replied father. "And, furthermore, none of my crowd are going to play it. Remember that, young feller, me lad. A nice chance we'd have of getting the work done if everybody started wasting half a day a week playing football."

"Why shouldn't we?" retaliated Dan. "They do it in town. And they're talking of forming a football club here in Corrawallop, and the fellers want me to be sec'et'ry. And—"

"Oh! do they?" interrupted father, with a snort. "Well, you can tell the fellers you're not going to be their darned sec'et'ry, so that's the end of it."

The "Leigh Creek Chronicle", which, to quote itself, circulated widely in Leigh Creek, Corrawallop, 'Possum Bend and other districts, was published every Saturday, and in the issue following the night on which the above conversation took place an announcement appeared in large print, which informed all and sundry that on the Tuesday night following Mr. Boundry Field, organising sec. of the Australian Football Association, would visit Corrawallop, and in the Mechanics' Institute there deliver a lecture on "Football and Its Relation to Work".

Dan and all the young chaps of Corrawallop were jubilant.

Father sniffed scornfully, but remarked that he'd go just to hear what the darned fool from town had got to talk about.

Tuesday night found the institute packed full long before the lecture was timed to start.

Mr. Boundry Field was greeted vociferously by the young bloods on his appearance.

Then he started to explain things.

Father and a lot of the old cockies listened sceptically and endeavoured to appear bored. But the lecturer had a persuasive way with him, and before it was half over father began to get interested, and remarked to old Jerry Briggs, next him, that there was p'raps something in what the chap was saying.

The lecturer explained how too much work and no play makes Jack a dull boy, and went on to show how much more work a man would be able to do if he had a bit of recreation now and again.

Then the old chap got really interested, and asked several questions bearing on the subject. "Did he really think they'd get more work out of the young fellers if they started playing football?" was one of them.

Mr. Boundry Field said he was sure they would. It would make the young chaps so much quicker and smarter in their movements also, he added.

"Strikes me Peter ought to go in for football a bit," father was heard to remark. Peter was the bringer-in of the cows at our place, and father wasn't very favourably impressed with Peter's ideas of locomotion.

Then Mr. Boundry Field intimated that he was making a tour through the country lecturing on football, and was desirous of seeing the game tried and fostered in every place he called at. "You've no idea how much pleasure and profit you would derive from it," he assured his audience. "It would start a spirit of friendly rivalry between the young fellows in each district, and they would in the end try to excel each other, not only on the football field, but in their everyday work as well." Then he sat down, while the elders digested this assertion.

The young chaps cheered, and the old ones put their heads together and talked the matter over. After a bit Mr. Boundry Field rose and, intimating that the hour was getting late, asked them if they were in favour of starting a football club in Corrawallop.

A lot of the young chaps glanced apprehensively at their fathers and answered, "Yes, they were." Presently there was a stir amongst the elders, and father, who always took the lead in everything, stood up and made a speech.

He said that "they were glad to have had the pleasure of hearing Mr. Boundry Field that evening, and that if only half of what he had said about football and its beneficial effects on the young chaps was true, then football was the one thing most needed in Corrawallop, and the sooner it was started the better. He for one would give it his support, and he thought that most of the fathers present would be glad to see the game started and fostered in their midst."

Great applause greeted this speech, and Mr. Boundry Field, striking while the iron was hot, proposed that they should form a committee and appoint officials there and then.

He stayed long enough to give a bit of advice, and assured us that the Australian Football Association, of which he had the honour of being secretary—(ahem!)—would watch the development of football in Corrawallop with interest.

Father got himself elected president of the new club; Skinny Jenkins, One-armed Grogan and several others formed themselves into a committee and appointed Dan secretary.

The committee didn't let any grass grow under its collective feet, and Dan, at a meeting held a couple of nights after Mr. Boundry Field's visit, was instructed to write to the secretary of the 'Possum Bend club, which, mushroom-like, had sprung into existence since Mr. Field's visit, and arrange a match for the following Saturday week.

The local store sold out its entire stock of eucalyptus and embrocation in one night, and every night a crowd of half-naked men was to be seen in our barn (which father had given the use of as a training room) careering wildly up and down, skipping with leg-ropes, and slogging at a sugarbag filled with straw hanging from a rafter on a rope in lieu of a punching-ball.

The old chaps paid visits of an evening, and remarked to each other that things were likely to boom in the labour line in

Corrawallop that winter. Most of them were surprised at the unusual display of activity and energy on the part of their sons. They'd never witnessed such before.

We heard that the residents of 'Possum Bend were just as enthusiastic over their team.

Dan went about our place wearing a look of importance, and spent hours of an evening figuring out things with the aid of an arithmetic book when he ought to have been in bed. He offered Peter, the only scholar in our family, an unofficial position as assistant secretary.

Peter, bitten with the football mania, accepted eagerly and unconditionally. Peter was usually a great bargain driver when his efforts were requisitioned. He did all the work, and Dan got all the credit for it. Father wasted hours, hanging over slip-rails, discussing Corrawallop's chances with neighbours. As the eventful day approached local excitement became intense, and on the morning of the match father and Dan were absolutely unapproachable. The match was to be played in one of our paddocks, which was bounded on one side by the river. For a week all the neighbours had helped to clear away legs and stumps and stones, and father, as he surveyed several acres of cleared land, remarked to Dan that there was something in football after all.

Dan, with a look at the cleared land and then at father's face, replied that it wasn't a bad game—one derived pleasure and profit from it at one and the same time.

Father agreed heartily, and so far forgot himself as to promise Dan a new saddle as a reward for his arduous duties as secretary.

At one o'clock on the eventful day most of our team was assembled and putting in a bit of practice.

At a quarter to three the 'Possum Bend team arrived, followed by a great crowd of supporters.

The uniforms of the players on both sides were varied and wonderful. A few had become possessed of coloured jerseys, hardly any two alike, and knickers of various hues and stages of preservation. Most, however, rolled their trousers up to their knees and turned their waistcoats inside out, whilst others played in their singlets. Several sported new boots for the occasion—huge, heavy things, with rows of aggressive-looking hobnails in the bottoms of them.

An umpire had been sent up from town to referee the match, and seemed none too pleased at his selection as he surveyed the assembled players. However, with a few words of advice, he set things going. The whistle blew, and the great match started. The crowd of supporters cheered, and Corrawallop made play towards their opponents' goal.

Ten minutes after the start Corrawallop got a mark ten yards in front of goal, and with a very wobbly gait the ball sailed between the uprights. Corrawallop barrackers cheered wildly, but a few minutes afterwards 'Possum Bend equalised matters by scoring a "sixer".

The play thus early was remarkable for the strenuousness of the players. They bumped and pushed and pulled, they kicked and swore at each other, and outraged every known rule appertaining to the game.

Free kicks became as plentiful as flowers in springtime, and the umpire worked harder than any man ever seen in Corrawallop. When not employed blowing his whistle and awarding free kicks, he was engaged in stopping fights and threatening to report players. The players, for the most part, told him politely to report to the devil if he liked, and continued to embrace each other's heads and limbs. One exasperated Corrawallopian offered to fight him one hand kneeling, and likened him to a wonderful breed of bovine.

Father became greatly excited, and so far forgot himself as to offer to bet anyone a pound that Corrawallop would win.

A still more excited man from 'Possum Bend took up the bet.

The game continued strenuously through three quarters, and at the last change of ends the teams were dead level in points, and also players. Three on each side had been carried off—too upset to continue for a time.

It took some forceful eloquence to convince the umpire that it was a highly desirable thing that he should stay and see the game through; but after father had promised to use influence with the players and spectators at the termination of the match the umpire reluctantly consented to stay.

The whistle blew, and they started off for the last quarter.

Then father's hardly-restrained emotion broke forth, and he let himself go properly. His excitement became contagious, and all the old chaps began to follow the president's lead. Round and round the ground they ran, wherever the play chanced to be, cheering madly, and giving the players heaps of encouragement and the umpire quantities of advice, until they were red-faced and scant of breath.

Each side was playing (or running amok would be nearer the truth) as for a kingdom, and utterly ignored the umpire's presence and decisions.

Father went mad, and offered to bet anyone £5 that Corrawallop would win.

A madder man from 'Possum Bend took the bet. Father stopped to breathe, and hauled five sovereigns, which represented his last weekly payment for cream and which he had received that morning, from his pocket. The 'Possum Bend man did the same.

Mother, who chanced to be standing near, sought to remonstrate with father, and reminded him that he was a president of the local Band of Hope and a great supporter of the Church; but he pushed her roughly to one side and told her to mind her own dashed business. The 'Possum Bend man's wife was treated similarly when she sought to interfere with her liege lord.

The gamblers looked around for someone to hold the stakes, and their gaze fell simultaneously on "Props", a one-legged derelict who frequently visited the district. He looked surprised when ten sovereigns were thrust into his hand, and glanced regretfully at his wooden leg.

But father and the man from 'Possum Bend took no chances with him. They stood, one on each side of him, each grasping an arm, and in their excitement pinching those unfortunate members. "Props" apparently did not know what to do with so much wealth, and so stood holding it firmly in his hand. Then, as each side kicked a goal in rapid succession, father and the other gambler started to yell again, and dragged "Props" first this way, then the other.

"Ki—ki—kick, you dashed fool!" father would shriek at a struggling Corrawallopian.

"Stop him! stop him!" would yell the man from 'Possum Bend to one of his team.

Dan got a shot straight in front of goal and kicked out of bounds. Then father's language was something awful to listen to.

All around the ground angry and excited men were yelling and fighting and shaking horny fists in front of each other's noses.

126

Women were shrieking out at each other and making insulting remarks about each other's personal appearances and pedigrees. Friendships of years' standing were shattered that afternoon. Five minutes to time, and each team still level on points and nearly done.

The six injured men limped back on to the field to help in the work of demolition. The ball came bounding towards where father and the man from 'Possum Bend were standing with "Props" between them, with the whole thirty-six blood and dirt covered players charging madly after it.

Dan caught it and spun around, and with a lucky kick popped it between the goal and the behind posts.

A minute to go and Corrawallop one point in the lead. Father went raving mad and offered to lay £10 to £1; but the 'Possum Bend man looked worried and heedless. Father then shrieked in his ear £20 to a shilling; but the 'Possum Bend man was stone deaf. The back man kicked off and the ball landed in front of "Props" and rolled on till it rested against his wooden leg. A 'Possum Bend player with the light of madness in his eyes hurled himself at the ball. He grabbed it, but the impetus sent him crashing into "Props". With a wild cry "Props" fell backwards, and as the final bell rang out he rolled down the bank of the river, dragging father and the other gambler with him towards 20 feet of water. The hand that held the sovereigns opened to grasp at a tree root, and for a second or two the rays of the setting sun gleamed on a shower of gold diving beneath the water.

Father scrambled back on to the top of the bank, and "Props" coat caught in a root, and he hung there with his wooden limb dangling in the water.

Up on the bank the 'Possum Bend player was being murdered by father.

"Ten quid gone, you—you thief!" gasped father at a loss for words, and sitting on top of the struggling, exhausted player and trying to knock his brains out on the ground.

We got Father home at last. That was the last and only football match played at Corrawallop. Half the players and numbers of the spectators lost several weeks' work through injuries sustained in the Homeric encounter, and the umpire, who managed to escape with his life, handed in to the Australian Football Association such a scathing and unpromising report of football

as played at Corrawallop that the association positively refused
to allow any of its umpires to officiate again up our way, and
straight away withdrew its patronage and interest.

And after that the old chaps failed to see how it made the
young ones work harder. Only father winked his eye at times at
the cleared paddock, and remarked in his family circle that after
all it had been cleared dirt cheap at £10.

THE VOICES FROM THE CROWD

Argus, September 30, 1912.

An intelligent foreigner of an inquiring and philosophic turn
would have found much to interest him in the psychology of the
crowd, 54,000 strong, which watched the final League football
match on Saturday. To the cold, unbiassed mind of what the
Americans call the "highbrow", the enthusiasm and expendi-
ture of energy exhibited by a football crowd must be absolutely
incomprehensible. And, at all events, here were the facts,
54,000 people stood—or, at any rate, 40,000 of them stood—
laying the foundations of varicose veins and bad tempers, for
fully three hours, packed so close that movement was well nigh
impossible. As the ball went to and fro their heads turned,
obedient, as the glowing faces of the sunflowers turn towards
the sun. They cheered, they clapped their hands, they growled,
and they swore. If they had had brothers or even relatives
further removed playing, if they had had large sums of money
on the result of the match, this enthusiasm would have been
explicable. But to hear a man, who was totally unrelated and
unknown to any of the players, incite a red and black player to
kill a red and white one, and to appear quite willing to climb
over the fence and help in the slaughter, certainly seems unrea-
sonable to that dull soul whose be-all and end-all is not the
watching of football.

"One touch of nature", says a rather well-known writer,
"makes the whole world kin." He must have been thinking
of football. There were three classes of spectators, broadly considered—young men, other men, and that bright and beautiful
sex without which the world would be so peaceful and so dull.
The young men, who formed the larger portion of the vast

crowd, ranged from the beautiful young gentleman who wore the very latest thing in clothes, the latest shade of perfumed socks, and shoes with pretty laces tied in a large bow, to the strident hoodlum from Moray-street, where the Flying Angels once inhabited. This futile person wore a red and white ticket in his hat, and his ferocious delight in the game was, to the languid interest of the other, "as sunlight is to moonlight, or as wine is to water", if one may reverse the well-known line. Then there were the many boys who had dodged their drill. What was compulsory service, the defence of one's country, to a football final?

In a car on the St. Kilda line two lads in uniform chatted about the great affair with another lad. The other lad began.

"Goin' t' compulsory?" he asked.

"Yair," replied one of the soldiers; "ain't you?"

"No fear; I'm goin' t' the match."

"Wot about you for gettin' copped?" reminded the soldier.

"Well, me old man has to pay it," said the other.

He was a nice, thoughtful boy, and his father, who is perhaps a socialist, should be very proud of him.

South Melbourne emigrated en bloc to the Melbourne Cricket Ground. The red and white supporters came down like the wolf on the fold. Every cab, every dealer's barrow, pierced the long stream of dust, and small boys hung out the banner over the tailboard and sang. Many South Melbourne residents so far forgot themselves as to walk from the Flinders-street station (the tram service having, as usual, gasped and died) with champions of Essendon. These road-mates would argue fiercely as to who would win. They were not content to wait until the deities which watch over the game decided. And so they came to the ground, still arguing, and pledged to the extent of at least 2/ or so on their opinions.

A crowd is a wonderfully suggestive thing. Each little dot of pink in that mosaic of black and flesh-colour represents a point of view. It looks nothing, but it is different, really, from every other dot of pink in the vast ribbon. It represents the thoughts and emotions and, schemes and affections of a man. And half these dots are wishing for one result, and half for the other. The concentrated wish in that gaze of 100,000 eyes or so, were it all one way, must be almost overwhelming, one would imagine. In the shadow of the ladies' stand one observes that cornflower blue and, that newer, more artistic, cobalt shade, toned with grey, are going to be fashionable this spring. A chrome-yellow bunch of feathers "carries" from the blue symphony like the french-horn from amongst the violins. There are ladies, too, in the enclosure, where the patient "bobite" shifts from foot to foot. One faints and is taken out by a constable. The ladies do not seem very interested in the game. Their attention wanders. They talk to each other and ask maddening questions of their brothers and other male victims. They want to know "what side is that man in white playing for?" According as their escort is South Melbourne or Essendon, comes the bitterly satirical answer "Essendon", or "South Melbourne". The umpire is like the Athenian sculptor who placed his masterpiece in the market-place and invited the Athenians to express their opinions by marking the places they did not like with charcoal. In the morning the statue looked like a Nubian slave. So the citizens were bidden to express their appreciation in a similar manner, and next morning the statue was as black as ever. And so, while thousands who will shortly be abusing the umpire, applaud a decision, a yell of hatred and contempt rises from the throats of other thousands, who will shortly be applauding him. He is an Ishmael, with every man's voice against him.

Essendon forges ahead and the sun drops slowly down, lengthening the shadows of the tall pavilions on the turf. Hope slowly fades out of the South Melbourne supporters; their cries become tinged with rancour. They advise violence and death, and the umpire endures very much. There are two reasons given for the forging ahead of Essendon—firstly, that the Essendon team is at the top of its form; secondly, that the South Melbourne team never played a worse game. It all depends. If one is an Essendonian, the former is the reason. The South Melbourne partisan, however, chooses the latter reason. And, the last bell rings, and the little stream of provident and far-sighted souls who moved out during the last quarter so as to get seats in the trams or trains suddenly becomes a great flood. An Essendon man and a South Melbourne man walk together. "Well, a great game!" says one, and "A rotten game", says another; and it is not difficult to pick them out. The cabs fling dust over the pedestrains, but the concertinas are silent now in the South Melbourne barrows and carts and buggies, and the flags are furled, as the crestfallen hordes of Emerald Hill go back, explaining how it all happened, and to hang crepe upon their door-knockers.

9

The Twenties: "invincible dash and determination"

Although Melbourne won its first Premiership for 26 years, and Geelong and Richmond for the first time, in the VFL, the twenties belong to Collingwood and Jock McHale, the Coventries, the Colliers—and Roy Cazaly.

JOHN WORRALL ON THE 1925 SEASON

Australasian, May 9, 1925.

The great day has arrived, and with weather conditions favorable dense crowds rushed to all the ground where the Victorian football premiership was being ushered in. The cable cars, particularly those proceeding to Fitzroy and South Melbourne, were so crowded that they toiled along more painfully than ever, with the human freight clinging on like bees in a swarm, all anxious to arrive in time to hear or join in the full-throated yell of "they're off", as the bell clanged the signal that the ball was in motion. The hold which the game has on the multitude is ,astounding.

We hear that football has been commercialised and is being ruined; people who affect a milder form of athletics assure us that the game is falling into disrepute, and that really respectable people would rather be seen at a dog-fight; visitors who have never seen Essendon or Richmond "down" their old rivals on their own grounds after a fierce struggle leave our shores and declare that Australians worship the horse and care for nothing but horseracing; but the great fact remains that the popularity of the Australian game of football is increasing and appeals to the great mass of the people in a manner in which no other sport affects them.

The spectators there must have been 150,000 people watching the games on Saturday—comprise all classes, from the grey-headed old lady who clenches her umbrella or her husband's arm as she feels the thrill of conflict, to the care-free "flapper" who, with a girl's hero worship, regards every action of her favorite player, even a nasty "bump" to an opponent, as an act of great moral beauty.

The sedate professional gentleman, who thirty years ago played for Hotham or Essendon, goes and lives his football battles over again, and cheers the son of his old opponent when the name strikes a chord in his memory. And then there are the "Ginger Micks", who in their anxiety to get there, are prepared to climb on the roofs of our ancient cable-cars, and when they get to the ground are prepared to make a personal matter of any argument that may happen to arise, until—

A stern "John"

Serloots me with a cold, unfeeling eye.

THE OPENING DAY, 1920

John Worrall, *Australasian*, May 1, 1920.

After many weeks of preparation and wide publicity the great winter game "King Football" commences its arduous season to-day. The optimism pervading the atmosphere of football is truly remarkable. All ranks become saturated with it. There are 12 clubs in the competition, and every club has already won the premiership by word of mouth in its own opinion before a ball has been kicked in deadly earnest. It is really a disease, and an incurable one. It has been in existence for years, gaining strength as the seasons advance, until in the present year of grace it has developed into an epidemic.

It was not my fortune to witness many matches last year, so I cannot write with certainty as to whether the game had assumed its pre-war eminence. Yet in the final game of all Geelong imparted the impression that they were a combination worthy to be classed with some of the great teams of the past, as they possessed weight, dash, cleverness, and determination—essentials that carried them through.

There is no apparent reason why football should not recover its pre-war glories, and the wish of all its devotees is to see an all-round improvement that will compare favorably with the past. Admittedly a great deal depends upon the management of the game in general, both as regards the controlling body and the clubs.

It is a grand game properly played, a code that has almost become perfect through the years, even though anomalies still exist. It is simply a waste of time impressing upon all those concerned in the management the necessity of playing the game, for never mind how brutal a man may be in his intentions to opponents he is regarded as a hero by the rabid supporters of his club, and loses nothing by his disqualification except a bit of personal glory.

There are some things that are ineradicable in the season's preparations, notably the number of recruits upon which valuable time and oil are wasted. A side may require but four places to fill to make it worthy of being a team, yet there are 100 applicants, with perhaps none of them capable of adequately filling any of the vacant positions, for they may be considered vacancies so far as efficiency is concerned. In March and April all grounds are flooded with embryo champions.

They can all run 100 yards in even time, can kick straighter than Thurgood, can mark better than McNamara, are cleverer than Dick Lee, can play anywhere on the field, yet while many are called few are chosen. The further afield they come the greater the stars they are supposed to be, and so the farce goes on.

But this apparent comedy serves a useful purpose after all. The barrackers are pleased beyond measure, proudly pointing out what an energetic body of men are the committee. Certain players are boomed, interest is aroused, committeemen are applauded, and, the best thing of all, tickets galore are sold.

So it will be seen that there is method in the seeming madness. And it is almost safe to predict that after the first four rounds have been played no difficulty will be caused by sifting the sheep from the goats. That has been the history of the past, and in all probability will be repeated this season.

Building up a football team to possess premiership pretensions is not so easy as it looks, for players to excel in certain positions must possess certain characteristics. No team is any good without stout defenders, the centre-line should be speedy and clever, and the forwards men of marked ability. And even if all the 18 players are athletes and footballers of ability, they will be unsuccessful unless selfishness is eliminated and all play with a set purpose.

Defence, granted the right class of men are available, is about the easiest part in the field to play. Dash, marking ability, and going straight through are essentials, so solid men are needed. Wing men should be speedy and clever, and should be two-footed artists. In fact, all footballers should be able to kick with either foot, as it means getting out of many a difficulty.

Usually a serious fault of flankers is that they cannot drive a ball any distance. The ideal centre should be a sturdy man, one that comes straight down the ground, like Greeves, of Geelong. A fine centre player is always causing trouble, as he keeps continually driving the ball to the half-forwards.

Perhaps the most difficult position on the field to fill is centre half-forward. He should be a splendid high mark and a long kick—place for preference. Place kicking has gone out of vogue, but the centre half-forward should possess the art. Half-forwards and full forwards on the wings should of all things be clever at turning, and resourceful. Weight should be well distributed, for while brawn is necessary in such a fast and strenuous game as ours a team of big men would never win a premiership. And the reason is obvious, for little men possess those terrier-like qualities in ground play that but few big men possess. So the weight must be well blended if proper results are to be shown.

Our game really has grown out of nothing in particular to the greatest winter game in the world. Red-shirted miners and others were eager to kick a ball in their spare moments, and out of the medley arose the Australian game, through the agency of Messrs. H. C. A. Harrison (the father of the game) and T. M. Wills, his cousin. Rugby at the time was played in the schools in England; yet one would imagine that the code could not have been in any way universally adopted, otherwise we might have had Rugby foisted upon us.

Whether we would have remained under its restrictions one cannot say with any degree of certainty, but that we escaped such a fate is something to be thankful for. At the time when our game was in its infancy and struggling for the light, Rugby found a footing in Sydney and flourished exceedingly. There are now four codes of football played in this country. First comes the Australian, then soccer, followed by the two Rugby styles. It must not be supposed that in the placings above they have been chosen in order of merit.

Between the two imported games the migrants can settle the

order of merit among themselves, as the game we are interested in is our own game—a home product—Australian in name and character. It is racy of the soil, the only game played in this wide land of ours of local origin. Truly, it is the national pastime.

The qualities that Australians were noted for at the war are all existent in our game. Dash—glorious dash—resource, determination, a never-say-die spirit, lasting power, gameness and "help your neighbour" are essentials in our game that permeated the breasts of all our Australian boys at the war.

Therefore, the game is not only national in origin, but intensely national in the characteristics of the true Australian. And all those who love and admire the greatest spectacular game of football on earth should raise their hats in admiration and respect to the grand old man of the game, Mr. H. C. A. Harrison, who, by the irony of fate, was born in New South Wales, as was also his cousin, Mr. T. Wills.

While there is room for all the different codes of football, as it is better to be playing than looking on at others disporting themselves, it is a thousand pities that the game is not universal and predominant in all the cities of the Commonwealth. In Sydney and Brisbane the soil has been unyielding and unreceptive.

But if once Sydney were captured, Brisbane of necessity would have to capitulate. Nevertheless, the game is steadily progressing. In Victoria, South Australia, Western Australia, and Tasmania it is the game of the people, who take a proper pride and delight in the fact that the home product is the greatest game of all. Right through the Riverina the Australian game also holds sway, and, like the whales, goes ever northward; and it thrives also at Broken Hill.

In other sports Australians are patriotic, yet in football their interests are divided. Of course, games such as cricket, tennis, and golf are played the world over under practically the same set of laws. It has been argued in many quarters in Australia that there should be a universal game of football. A grand idea, if workable. It is a farce seeing a Rugby match between England and New South Wales termed England v. Australia.

It can never be Australia with the greater part of the continent unrepresented. So far as Rugby and the Australian game are concerned, it would be like the fusion of oil and water, they can never mix without destroying the outstanding features of either. And while it is to be regretted that international matches between

Australia and England are practically impossible under existing conditions, the fact remains that the public are splendidly catered for in those States where nationalism is triumphant.

All Australians, irrespective of State should take an inordinate pride in the fact that we have evolved a game of football that is pre-eminent. Just think of it: every other game we play is imported. The appeal of our own game—especially as it is such a grand one—should stir the blood and pride of all Australians. Let those from overseas play their own games by all means. They are good in their way; but all Australians should patronise the home product, which is pure and unadultered as a pastime, and made for the native born.

'A bunch of fuschias'—some of the stars of Melbourne in the '20s.

THE BARRACKER

By 'Den', *Herald*, 13 May, 1929.

"Demonstrations by angry crowds against football umpires and individual players were made on three Melbourne grounds on Saturday."

Large mouth and little head,
Loud voice and idle brain,
Reason, judgement, caution shed.
"Pull 'im down! Yah! Crook again!"

A crook day Saturdee. Say was you there?
I never seen a football match so tame,
The bloomin umpire acted strictly fair!
Why, strike a light! You don't call that a game!
'E never done a thing to nark the crowd.
Them spoil sports 'adn't ought to be allowed.

'Ow can a decent bloke enjoy a match
Unless there's somethin' 'e can 'oot about?
A dead crook game. There wasn't one bright patch
Where we could tell 'im off or count 'im out.
'E done 'is best to please both sides. The coot!
We 'ad no chance of puttin' in the boot!

One eyed and partisan,
Folly loose and fairness fled,
A sorry semblance of a man.
"Crack 'im! Yah! Knock off 'is 'ead!

Gimme the days when umpires makes mistakes—
Somethin' to put some ginger in the game,
When reason's chucked aside and passion wakes,
An 'owls ran round the benches like a flame,
When blokes gits reel worked up and yell fer blood.
And even ladies take to chuckin' mud.

Give me the days with langwidge flowin' free
'At pins and pickets an' a all-in fight,
An broken fences. That's the stuff for me.
It's better than the Stajim of a night.
A bloke's reel naycher then gets dinkum play.
But ideal umpires? Wot? Aw, fade away!

137

Wild eye and drooping fag.
Futile, silly and inane.
Coarse lips that loosely say—
"Yah! Kill 'im! Crook again!"

WEIRD COUNTRY GAMES

Argus, August 8, 1924.

The best football story of the season comes from Port Fairy, where, the train being two hours late, the Terang team were not able to take the field before half-past 4 o'clock. The last part of the game was played in the dark, or rather, lamplight; the large number of motor-cars parked around the oval displayed their headlights on the playing ground. This caused a weird scene, watching the shadows flitting across the ground in the pale light. Port Fairy, who were leading before dark, were unable to adapt themselves to the altered conditions, and were beaten.

THOSE WERE THE DAYS!

FOOTBALL UMPIRING IN THE 80'S

By 'Old Timer', *Herald*, 13 May, 1929.

The 'riot' at St. Kilda Cricket Ground on Saturday would have caused any seasoned barracker of the spacious days of '88 to yawn and ponder on the degeneracy of the game.

An umpire was hooted and counted out. A crowd gathered around his dressing room to subject him to further forms of the Lower Criticism on his emergence. That was all. Not a rock was cast not a fist swung, not a boot raised. Lovely woman did not pull one hat pin from her hair to signify her disapproval of the manner in which her favorite team had been disciplined. The barracker of the sober days of Mid-Victorianism would wonder whether he was not attending a Toorak croquet tournament.

In the Eighties and early Nineties, the football barracker was a red blooded he-man, as red blooded as any of the bad men who roamed Old Arizona during the same days, when the world was wide. It was he who was responsible for the presence of those mounted troopers to provide an escort at the final bell—an escort now merely ornamental.

It was his unerring marksmanship which led to the wire netting avenues through which the latter day umpires still march to and from the arena.

Today the umpire leaves the ground as he likes. Thirty years ago he was hustled to the sanctuary of neutral ground by an armored wagonette—that is a wagonette protected against sticks and stones and putrid bananas. And it was only the owners of decrepit and battered vehicles who could be persuaded to carry an umpire from a match except at exhorbitant rates or watertight guarantees against possible damage.

On some more virile grounds it was said that the umpires always brought a spare bag containing a disguise, and that they made their escapes wearing long white whiskers.

Whether football is played better or worse is a disputed point and always will be as long as men continue to grow old and grow up but there can be no question that the vigor of the barracker is a weak and failing thing as compared with what it was. There is no loyal supporter of a club of the eighties who did not proudly flaunt his colours in the band if his hat *throughout* the week.

ROY CAZALY

Daily Mirror, June 9, 1978.

In the sunbaked North African desert, in the steamy tropical jungles of the Pacific war theatre, wherever Australian troops fought and died in World War II, the battle-cry "Up there Cazaly" was certain to revive flagging spirits.

After the war when the Australian play *Summer of the Seventeenth Doll* was produced in London, New York and other overseas cities, theatregoers were puzzled when the same three words were repeated in a telegram read out on the stage.

To many Australians the words "Up there Cazaly" have a special meaning as a form of greeting and a sign of recognition between fellow countrymen.

A cowardly attack on an umpire brings this reaction from a contemporary cartoonist.

But not all Australians know that the words, which will live on for ever in local idiom, originated more than half a century ago as a call of encouragement to a South Melbourne footballer player.

One of the greatest players Australian Rules has ever known, the lean and wiry Roy Cazaly, specialised in spectacular leaps enabling him to mark over taller opponents.

Rover Skeeter Fleiter first yelled "Up there Cazaly" in a 1921 game when spurring his teammate on during a tense battle for possession of the ball.

Fleiter and other South Melbourne players continued to use the cry. Before long not only South Melbourne followers but whole crowds were yelling "Up there Cazaly" as the little ruck-man went up for a high mark.

Cazaly played with such dash and sparkle that his football deeds over more than 30 years became almost legendary. He was called the Babe Ruth and the Don Bradman of Australian Rules.

He became the toast of Melbourne and his name was a household word throughout Australia.

By the 1930s the term "Up there Cazaly" was being heard and used all round Australia and beyond by people who had never seen a game of Rules in their lives.

Born in Melbourne in 1893, Roy Cazaly spent his boyhood in the suburb of Albert Park and at 10 was playing Australian Rules for the local State School.

"I was in everything bar a wash," Cazaly once recalled those years in later life. "I was a bundle of energy and always looking for something to do to get rid of it."

One way was to accompany his mate Frank Beaurepaire, the later Olympic swimmer who liked to swim far out in the choppy waters of Port Phillip with Cazaly rowing behind in a small boat.

When not out with Beaurepaire he could generally be found running full tilt at trees in Albert Park reserve, sidestepping at the last possible moment to avoid them.

From that youthful game came Cazaly's later uncanny ability to evade oncoming opponents on the football field.

News of the schoolboy's football skill spread and at 14 he was snapped up by the St. Kilda Club.

At 15 Roy Cazaly played his first A grade game for St. Kilda (scoring four goals against Carlton) which made him one of the youngest players ever to wear a jersey in the Victorian Football League.

But that was not enough for Cazaly and he also played in midweek games for a wharf laborers' team. Actually it was with the wharfies he learned how to look after himself when tangling with bigger and tougher players.

Cazaly collected more than his share of cuts and bruises but also perfected a smart forehand jab that served him in good stead for protection in later years in big football.

He first showed he knew how to handle himself in a rough match early in his VFL career when playing against Carlton.

The opposing skipper, veteran Pompey Elliott, kept picking on young Cazaly who was still a bit shy about hitting back.

But eventually Elliott went too far and the next time he tried to get Cazaly the target neatly side-stepped and retaliated with a stinging punch to the jaw.

To Cazaly's surprise Elliott grabbed his arm and said: "Good on you son. Don't take all they give you."

And in later years as a coach Cazaly used to pass on the same advice to young players: "Don't take a punch lying down. Let them know you'll have them and they'll leave you alone."

For 13 years Cazaly played for St. Kilda, carefully honing the football skills that were to make him famous. He neither smoked nor drank and was a training and physical fitness fanatic.

He developed his renowned leap for a high mark by jumping for a ball strung up in a shed at home. And by control of breathing as he went up he eventually added about 60 cm to his natural upward leap.

But extra leaping height was not all that made Cazaly different from other players.

While in the air when he threw his slight frame above a pack to pull down a fingertip mark, he could turn a complete circle, land and keep running without missing a step.

In 1921 Cazaly transferred to South Melbourne club and his career there until 1926 saw him at the peak of his ability and fame.

That first year with Souths the cry "Up there Cazaly" was coined as, with Mark (Napper) Tandy and Fred (Skeeter) Fleiter, he formed one of the best ruck combinations of all time.

Skeeter Fleiter was the first to call "Up there Cazaly" to encourage him as he went up with one of his prodigious springs.

Soon both Tandy and Fleiter were calling out and before long every South Melbourne supporter was screaming "Up there Cazaly" at the top of his voice whenever the player prepared himself to fly for the ball.

South Melbourne's success with Cazaly naturally brought retaliation although Tandy and Fleiter usually managed to protect him.

Before a 1921 match against Fitzroy, Cazaly had received an anonymous letter warning that his opponents would "get him" that day.

It was no idle threat for as soon as Cazaly stepped on to the ground players came at him from all directions.

That Cazaly finished the match unscathed was due to the gallant Skeeter Fleiter who took the knocks for him.

"They voted me the best man on the ground", Cazaly remembered years later. "But the honor was really Skeeter's. He cleared the way for me and I just followed him up to collect the laurels."

For all that it was one of the roughest games Cazaly ever played and repeatedly only luck saved him from serious injury.

There was an occasion for instance in the first quarter when he leapt up for a mark and got his fingers on the ball.

Intuition warned of danger and instinctively Cazaly let himself drop to the ground on top of the ball.

At that instant there was a jarring clash of bodies above him from a collision between two Fitzroy players as they attempted to "sandwich" him.

When they regained their senses one of them staggered up to Cazaly and abused him for not standing still.

He did not always escape injury. In 1923 South Melbourne met St. Kilda in a match for a place in the final four. Actually Cazaly was not supposed to play because he still had stitches in his eye from an accident the previous Saturday.

But Souths had little chance without him and ignoring protests from his doctor who refused to treat him ever again Cazaly went out to play.

Heavily bandaged he gave one of the best performances of his career—only to collapse on the ground at the end as the 49,000 spectators were wildly cheering him.

Cazaly probably gave his greatest exhibition in the famous "rough-house" match between Victoria and Western Australia in Hobart in 1924.

A long-standing Australian Rules feud between the two States reached its peak that day with the game turning into a slugging match.

At one stage Cazaly sensed the opposing skipper Fat McDiarmid was just about to let go a punch at him.

He ducked and as the blow whistled past his chin swung a haymaker of his own that caught McDiarmid on the jaw and knocked him flat on the ground.

Despite the brawling both sides were playing brilliant

football although heavy rain turned the field into a quagmire.

McDiarmid got his own back when he shouldered Cazaly so hard that he slithered 20m through the wet and crashed heavily into the fence.

Victoria won narrowly and when they returned to the dressing room the team went out to get some victory beer—leaving tee-totaller Cazaly behind.

Then from outside the door came a shout from Fat McDiarmid: "Come out Cazaly."

One of the trainers took a look outside and told Cazaly the whole West Australian team were there.

They continued to call him so Cazaly went out and faced them. Whereupon Fat McDiarmid grinned and said: "We've come to drink our beer with you."

All the team trooped into the dressing room and when the rest of the Victorians returned a party developed that continued at their hotel until 5 am next day.

In later life when discussing that game Cazaly always used to argue that the conviviality afterwards proved that "bad feelings never leave the ground".

But they were on hand once more when in 1926 the two States met again in Perth and it was open knowledge in the city before the match that the locals were out to "get Cazaly".

They did it too with a vicious knock 10 minutes after the start of the Saturday game. Cazaly was carried off unconscious.

He was in hospital until Monday but came out still sick and sore to play in the return match on the Tuesday.

Victoria lost the game but they always claimed they won the fight that day.

The groggy Cazaly was only a shadow of his usual self in play but escaped further injury because he was followed throughout by rover Jackie Millen of Fitzroy who had been nominated as his bodyguard.

All afternoon he kept close to Cazaly and called reassuringly: "Right Roy, I'm behind you. Right close."

Cazaly felt he needed a change after the 1926 season and left South Melbourne to become player-coach with the Launceston City team in Tasmania.

Thereafter he became a wanderer, for years playing and coaching with various teams in both Victoria and Tasmania.

Already a legend in his own time, he played his last game for Camberwell in Melbourne in 1941 at the age of 48.

But in 1951 he was still coaching in Tasmania and late that season played in a benefit match in Hobart.

He turned out first in the curtain-raiser between two teams of veterans. Then when the main match came on his own team was a man short.

So Cazaly played in his place through the full four quarters kicking a goal and having a hand in three others.

That was Roy Cazaly's swansong. The following year he turned to training greyhounds and trotters and ran a gymnasium in Hobart.

He died in October 1963 and although perhaps his deeds are now fading from memory his name will never die while there are Australians to yell: "Up there Cazaly".

10
The Thirties: "Victoria's Winter Industry"

South Melbourne's Foreign Legion achieved their one Premiership, in 1933 and three seconds in the next three seasons. Football was a way, during the Depression, for a player could earn enough to survive. The Depression had hardly any effect on attendances, such was the game's hold on the city. It was the time of Haydn Bunton and Dick Reynolds, Laurie Nash and Bob Pratt, Jack Dyer and 'Skinny' Titus.

THAT WAS THE SEASON

John Worrall, *Australasian*, October 8, 1932.

Loud cheers greeted the bouncing of the ball. The men were worked up to concert pitch, and though there was a good deal of fumbling there was no finesse. It was "woe to the man with the narrow chest", and the players dashed into each other without fear or favor. How they stood it was wonderful, as men were sent flying unmercifully in all directions.

There was some fine high-marking, and an utter disregard of danger, with strength the main consideration. It was an even first quarter, Richmond leading by 3–3 to 2–2. It was instinctively felt that Richmond's strength was in defence, its weakness in attack. While those gallant defenders were meeting the ball full-chestedly, the cleverness of Richmond's attack took Carlton by surprise. D. Strang, full-forward, was the man to be dreaded; but Richmond attacked by the wing, through the agency of Geddes and Titus, a move that was worrying the Blues.

The same style of play prevailed in the second quarter. It was too hard, too fierce, too intense to be scientific, and Scott, the umpire, should have checked it. It speaks volumes for those concerned that the breaches of the laws were so few. To the surprise of the experts Richmond was the faster and smarter side, which, added to its dominance in the air, made it look the prospective premier team. Still one side could not get a break on the other.

A montage of pictures from the clash between Collingwood and South Melbourne in 1930.

They were too evenly matched, and were playing the game that made a break almost impossible. At the interval Richmond led by 7–9 to 5–6. It was a handy margin in such a fierce battling game.

If Carlton had to do anything of a great nature the third term was the one in which it had to be done, the slight breeze being of some assistance. Still the character of the play never changed. McCormack, playing his best game for the season, was holding the clever and elusive Shea, who, however, had a sore heel, while Baggott was carrying out his job splendidly in looking after Crisp. In keeping these players comparatively quiet they interfered with the spearhead of Carlton's attack, and as Richmond led by 8–12 to 7–11 at the last change its stocks were still fancied, though neither side was showing any marked superiority.

An old player near me remarked, as they changed over for the last time, "It will be old rules this quarter", and he was not wide of the mark. For excitement and variation in fortunes— first one side and then the other leading—that last 25 minutes will never be effaced from the memories of those privileged to see it. Men were bumped to the ground, but they re-entered the fray as if the match depended upon their exertions.

It was marvellous how they stood it. One expected to see players carried off the field in dozens, but the only one who had to retire was Hunter, though Geddes played all the second half with a fractured bone in his jaw, and he was about the best man on the ground. To the consternation of Richmond supporters it was seen that Carlton was finishing better, and that their big men were tiring. As the big men became less virile, so the smaller men became more in evidence.

Carlton was now coming along in those streaming dashes that are such a feature of their play, and with about five minutes to go held the lead.

Richmond was palpably defeated when it received an inspiration. It might have been the marking of Gordon Strang or the beautiful passing of Zschech, or O'Neill's wonderful relieving dash, or a combination of circumstances, but in the final five minutes the desperate Richmond men, seeing victory slipping from their grasp, literally hurled themselves into the fray and carried all before them to gain the day amid wild cheering. It was a gallant effort and a worthy finish to a remarkable game and season. The final scores were:— Richard, 13–14; Carlton,

12–11. Scott had control of the game, an admittedly hard one to handle, and made many mistakes.

THE MAN WITH THE WHISTLE

By R. G. Jennings, *Argus*, September 14, 1935.

In private life the umpire is just like you and me—a perfectly reasonable and normal member of society. No doubt he has a wife and family, and is an eminently respectable person who follows his hazardous calling for the sole purpose of supplementing his income. It appears to the casual onlooker that he deserves every penny he earns.

In his professional capacity he ceases to be entirely human, and assumes the guise of an animated robot, which runs about in white from one region of the field to another with a whistle poised within easy reach of his lips. He leans forward between his bursts of speed in an attitude of studied concentration and gives wind to his whistle whenever he detects the slightest indication of any infringement of the rules.

He has no book of reference, unless he secretes it adroitly in the palm of his hand, and even then the traditions of the game would not permit of a temporary lull for any verification of the rights or wrongs of the decision. He is entirely dependent upon his momentary judgment, and if he decides later in the game that he has erred he must restrain his natural inclination to balance matters by awarding a free kick to the other side. He is conscious as the game proceeds that his decisions are not giving general satisfaction. The combined volume of voices of the huge crowd so densely packed around the pickets carries no friendly note. In fact the voices are distinctly hostile, and he harbours the secret hope that the dividing fence will hold out against the pressure of the surging mass until the final bell gives him an opportunity of making an honorable if hurried escape. He steals a furtive glance occasionally toward the wire-netted exit through which he will be escorted by friendly constables if the feeling at the end of the game shows any tendency to run too high.

Yet he succeeds in disguising any outward show of these disconcerting fears. He is admirable in his isolation and inspiring in his apparent lack of concern, for the wild, full volume of lung

149

Percy Leason's brilliant football cartoons appeared in Table Talk in the 1930s—'Football umpire about to take the field, bidding goodbye to friends and relatives'.

150

power, which swells and lulls and swells again, is alarming in the extreme—a confused, unrestrained babel of sound, devoid of any definite note, except that of hostility. It is only when he is near the boundary that he is able to discern any clear meaning in the conflicting words of advice which the raucous voices hurl at him. As far as he can gather they are not complimentary.

The estimate which he might once have placed on his own value is now rudely shattered. The strength and vigour of the language make it appear that he is not only a deep-dyed scoundrel but an individual of sub-normal mentality, who has no right whatever to be at large. In the opinion of these excited people he is there for the sole purpose of blowing his whistle at the wrong moment and thus punishing an innocent man. He is naturally relieved when the ball moves along towards the members' reserve. He wishes that he could confine the scope of the game within that locality, for the voices are not half so bitter in their invective. The aristocracy of onlookers are here, fenced within their own preserve. He is now able to pick out quite easily individual voices, and he is aware that even the aristocracy ane not of one mind. Their sentiments are far from unanimous.

He is informed above the clamour that he is one-eyed and in need of immediate ocular treatment, in fact a kind of diabolical Cyclops. This critic is evidently of the classical school. The allusion is obvious. Another shrill-voiced aristocrat, who regards the umpire as a partisan disporting himself in the arena with the base object of giving the game to the other side, wants to know whether the committee has put drugs in his beer—a further subtle reference, no doubt, to the questionable exploits of Ulysses' men in the palace of Circe. A red-faced man, who is unquestionably an enthusiastic supporter of the home team, wishes to ascertain quite politely and not without a note of sympathy whether the umpire has inadvertently swallowed the whistle—a feat by the way which was once accomplished without any ill-effects by a certain Charlie Chaplin, who whistled each time he hiccoughed.

Ah! A cheer rings out above the turmoil. The umpire is really grateful to the aristocrats for this encouraging outburst, for he has succeeded in detecting the slight elevation of an elbow which has found its way to a tender spot on an opponent's rib. The whistle acclaims a free kick to the writhing man, and the umpire is shaking a warning finger at the offender. This is definitely a case for the tribunal, when both players will swear that they are unaware of any unseemly incident.

The ball has now travelled towards the forward lines, and has gone out of bounds just where the less cultured barrackers are at work. They were too far away to detect the little incident of the elbow, and they are under the impression that the big fellow who had done the damage had been the recipient of the cheers from the pavilion. They lose no time in letting the umpire know their sentiments, and when a warning finger is again shaken at their champion a great quiver of hoots reverberates along the pickets, to be drowned by wild cheers, for their idol has got the ball and is dashing through a gap, while the goal-umpire in the long white coat is busy taking the line of the ball, which now floats high towards the posts. All eyes are on it.

The white-coated figure has stumbled, but he rights himself. He makes a mystical sign to the field umpire and then proceeds to rush from one goal post to the other to procure two flags, which he waves in a series of complex curves and angles, to be answered with the same varied exercise by a similarly clad figure who is officiating at the goal posts at the other end of the ground. The crowd roars itself into a very frenzy of excitement.

Meanwhile the ball has been retrieved from the crowd, and still another functionary, who has been unceasingly careering up and down the boundary all the afternoon, seizes it, and after a sprint of about fifty yards he transfers the ball to the hands of another runner, who dashes on to the centre of the field, where the field-umpire takes delivery. When this ritual is complete, the ball is bounced, and off they go again to the accompaniment of the mingled shouts and groans and cheers of a fully roused crowd.

At this stage a slight diversion is caused among the dense throng in the outer circle as the result of two over-heated onlookers, who have suddenly decided to settle a minor difference of opinion concerning the umpire by resorting to the use of their fists in lieu of their brains. They are hard at it, urged on by a delighted gallery, which is determined, above all else, to get its money's worth; but word is passed round that two uniformed figures are approaching.

The contestants, hot and a little bloody, disappear in opposite directions, to be lost in the crowd. A shrill whistle from the near proximity of the field recalls them to the main object of their afternoon's recreation. A prostrate figure is rolling on the grass in considerable discomfort, while men with towels round their necks and a varied assortment of handbags, are rushing from the direction of the boundary to render first aid. Their ministrations are of a vigorous nature, and very soon restore their victim, who suddenly dashes from their grasp to take a brilliant high mark.

The game is close and the crowd is thoroughly warmed up. It has come to get its thrills and it is getting them in full store. The enthusiasm is infectious. Even the stout lady with the remnants of an ostrich feather in her hat has not failed to respond to the appeal of that high mark. She has come early to gain a place of vantage in the front row, and her shrill voice joins in the clamour for redress on behalf of her limping hero. She shakes her tasselled umbrella at the umpire, who has deliberately failed to raise a warning finger at the base fellow who had, for a few moments, put her muscular friend out of action. The luck of the game, the vigour of the contest, weigh nothing with her. It is justice she wants—plain, unvarnished justice and unsparing retribution. She has caught the fever of the moment and is carried away by the sway and shouts of the great crowd.

And these are our fellow beings in the mass, and "What fools these mortals be," says Puck. But, as individuals, detached in units from this seething gathering of humanity, none would dare to show this wild exuberance in a public place, lest the arm of the law embrace them. But humanity in the mass . . . ! The world forgives it much. It is merged into one great, unthinking whole, bereft of individuality, except that which it has cast into the common pool. It is swayed, roused, inspired, or dispirited, acting as one in response to some emotion or at the dictation of others. It is the great compelling force in the world that has no power of itself except that which it has absorbed from its neighbour. It is fever-stricken. The man who controls the mass is the superman who holds within himself the power to frame the destiny of nations.

FIFTY YEARS OF FOOTBALL

By John Worrall, *Argus*, October 3, 1936.

One sees many changes in the growth of a young country, and
in its sporting proclivities, even in the short space of 50 years.
Evolution is all round us, working insidiously, slowly, but
surely. We may not be able to grasp its significance without an
intense backward study, though, of course, everything changes,
if not necessarily for the better. It is astonishing to contemplate
that in this broad land of ours the only sport of Australian origin
is the aptly named Australian game of football. The idea was
evolved 78 years ago, and apparently no man living is capable
of establishing a new game suitable to local colour and taste.
This game of ours, truly national in design and character, and
played all over the Commonwealth, differs entirely from any
other code of football. Its high marking, long kicking, cohesion,
and wonderful dash have made it a game apart, and as one who
played it since the days of his youth, and with the virus of the
game in his blood, I trust that it be kept free from foreign
impurities, and that whatever changes may be considered
necessary will be on truly Australian lines.

Victorians—and I am sorry indeed that I cannot use the
better and broader name, Australians—have two obsessions
apart from racing—and the Melbourne Cup is near at hand.
They are the football finals—a wonderful pageant, pleasing to
the eye and senses—and Test cricket, against England for preference. But as this is the final period of the football season one's
thoughts are turned upon the winter game—King's Football—
though I think he is more a dictator than a king, as he demands
abject allegiance from all his subjects. And what a vista opens
up before one's vision when in his mind's eye he sees again
the great figures of the gladiators who strove in the arena for
mastery, and the kaleidoscopic effects that marked the final
series of every season. To the writer, at any rate, it is a soul-
stirring sight to see 60,000 or 70,000 people strung up to concert
pitch, thrilled to the marrow in watching their own game played
by experts. It is their own product, evolved especially to suit the
temperament of the people, who desire life and action, and that
those grand old pioneers builded in a national sense has been
verified by results.

When I came to Melbourne from Maryborough, by way of

Ballarat, the only clubs in the senior competition were Melbourne, Geelong, Carlton, South Melbourne, Richmond, Essendon, Hotham, Port Melbourne, St. Kilda, Williamstown, and Fitzroy. And there were many great players in those far-off days, and even before that period, though it was really an era of development. It is an established fact that owing to the introduction of boundary umpires, followed by the out-of-bounds law, the game has greatly increased in speed, and many consider that it has become more scientific. I concede that the pace has increased beyond all knowledge, but that the play is more scientific than say 30 years ago is strictly at variance with fact. One of the chief faults of modern football is the number of errors that are perpetrated in every match. It is a decided blot on the game, as evidently the pace has outstripped necessary first and guiding principles. In my day, and after, we were judged on our mistakes, though if that procedure were in vogue at the present time it would be subversive to the game itself, as it bristles with errors.

In my time, and in the interval, the individual players were equally as dashing and as quick off the mark as are those of to-day, though the play has been speeded up greatly. Players laugh to-day when told of the little marks that disfigured the game in its early history; and they were the negation of football, which went out of date during my playing period. They produced a certain type of player almost as inimical to the game's progress as the bullocker of later days, and were about on a par for ineffectiveness with the futile 10-yards pass now in vogue. They are blood brothers, mere excrescences on an otherwise sturdy growth—passing phases only, let it be hoped.

The game was cleaner in my day, and more robust and manly. There were no half-arm jolts in the crushes, or the unfair use of the elbow, and one could tackle an opponent fairly and bring him down without penalty if he had the ball when collared. The interpretations, however, have become a little too technical in many instances, and as a preventive against being met by the shoulder when coming through the elbow licence has been brought to a fine art. I would allow tackling from below the shoulder and above the knee to a man in possession, which would be a foil to elbowing.

Players in my day were just as skilful as any of the present day, and certainly equal in knowledge. About the only player

155

to-day whom I would include among the giants of the game is Nash, of South Melbourne, and he would not be a member of the leading bunch. The high marking is no better than 50 years ago, though there are more artists in that branch at the moment. Drop and place kicking have degenerated badly, with the standard of play in 1936 a long way below the Carlton brand of 30 years ago. In expert manipulation on wet days, however, the modern player is supreme. Thus, while some aspects of the game have improved, others have declined, with the spirit of sportsmanship on a decidedly lower level. There were many old heroes who would have been lost in the modern conditions of play. Others, too numerous to mention, would have been stars. It all depends on the style of play of the individual.

The art of adjudication may be more difficult than in the days of Jack Trait, Ivo Crapp, and Jack Elder. Yet there is no umpire in this year of grace the equal of the famous trio mentioned. It may be that the men of old were easier to handle than the present generation of players, as they possessed in the main a higher standard of sportsmanship. In leadership also the quality has declined, though it varies with the years.

How many great and stirring games has one seen in the finals, and what recollections are brought vividly to mind? The roar of the crowd, the hanging of the games in the balance; the mighty deeds of the players, the wild excitement at the end of the match, the quiet and orderly melting away of the thousands are all phases of a climax to a grand national sport, once seen never to be forgotten, and of yearly occurrence. It is rather remarkable that since the formation of the League in 1897, a period in which 39 premierships have been won, the highest prize of the football world has been shared by eight clubs only, almost an average of five times each, the successful clubs being Collingwood, Fitzroy, Carlton, Essendon, Richmond, Geelong, South Melbourne, and Melbourne.

The finals that remain most vividly in my memory are those in which Carlton and Essendon were engaged when under my jurisdiction. One final in particular I will never forget. Essendon was playing Carlton, there being no 19th man in those days. A minute after play began, Fred Shea, Essendon's talented flanker, was carried off the field owing to an injured leg, and Essendon was in sore straits. I have never been a believer in playing injured men, and set my face against Shea's reappearance after half-time. Like all footballers of mettle Shea was anxious to reappear, feeling that he had let his side down. It was left for me to decide, and I reluctantly agreed upon his re-entry, on the distinct understanding that he was not to move away from the goal-mouth. It was not that anything was expected of him, but that his mere presence on the field would prevent our opponents from having a loose man. In the dying moments Ernie Cameron broke his leg, and as the game hung in the balance it appeared as if Essendon was doomed. Cameron was a champion, expert in any position, though it was as a rover that he stood head and shoulders above his confreres. As he lay helpless on the ground he exhorted his comrades to see it out and leave him alone, and his advice acted like a tonic, as his mates made one despairing effort for victory. In the stress the Carlton full-back left his post, being sick to death of minding a wounded man, and at the psychological moment the ball was marked by Shea on his own a few yards in front. He steadied himself, gave pressure on his wounded leg to see whether it would stand the strain, kicked the ball, staggered, and fell. The bell rang, and Essendon won the day by a few points. It was his only kick in the match, and it won the premiership. Injured and all, he felt he had redeemed himself. Neither Cameron nor Shea ever played again.

And who will forget that wonderful second half played in six inches of ice between Carlton and Richmond in 1921? Dan Minogue, who led Richmond on that memorable occasion, solemnly assured me the other day that his men did not wear special stops on their boots on that occasion. But both teams played wonderful football in that sea of ice.

WHY DO THEY PLAY THIS FOOTBALL?

Percy Taylor, *Argus*, April 23, 1938.

Footballers are human beings. As they are regarded in some quarters as merely chattels and just pawns in the game, one may be pardoned today when the League football season opens in emphasising this fact.

Unfortunately some footballers endeavour to make the game their life's work, and they are perfectly content to live in the present, for that is their nature. They are short-sighted, for the average life of a player is not more than about five years, and few play as long as 10 years.

Among those who played League football last year only 25 had such a period of activity. They were Gilby, Vallence, and Davey (Carlton); A. and H. Collier, Bowyer, G. Coventry, Rumney, and L. Murphy (Collingwood); Webster, Baggott, and Forbes (Essendon); T. Williams (Fitzroy); Morrison (Footscray); Hickey and H. Hardiman (Geelong); Lonsdale and Pool (Hawthorn); Ogden (Melbourne); Gaudion (North Melbourne); Titus and Bentley (Richmond); W. Roberts (St. Kilda); Robertson and Thomas (South Melbourne). Of these 11 at least will not be seen in their League colours this season.

The thinking footballer—and they are many—endeavours to use his skill as a player as a stepping-stone to a position that will enable him to take his place in the community as a citizen. Constant work and prospects of advancement have a greater attraction to him than the Coulter law payment of £3 a week. Frequently players in the more successful clubs receive a bonus at the end of the season, and practically every club has a provident fund, from which the players receive a substantial amount when they retire from the club.

There are many old players now far removed from the adulation that was theirs in the heyday of their prowess who are still doing casual work and who now have no tangible assets as the result of their ability in the game. On the other hand, there is a surprising number of men who received their opportunities in life because of their football skill, and have reason to bless the day when they joined a League club. They were found employment that gave them their chances, and, in addition, they still enjoy the respect and friendship of old players, officials, and supporters alike.

Many leaders in the professional and industrial life of Melbourne were leading footballers in their youth. With some of them the game was only a hobby, and they would have advanced in life just as rapidly and just as surely had they been "Z grade" sportsmen. It is safe to say, however, that they are better citizens and probably better able to handle men because of their association with the game.

Others, again, received their chances solely because of their football ability. There are many examples. One boy, working on the roads in the country at only shillings a week, was brought to a Melbourne League club. He was found employment in a large firm as a labourer and gradually became a champion player. Just as gradually he worked his way up the ladder in his firm. He was found to have an aptitude for figures, was taken into the office, studied as an accountant, and is now almost the head of his department.

Then there is the story of the Melbourne youngster who went to another State, where he was engaged in farming. He gained fame in the district as a player and was brought back to Melbourne, being found employment by his club. No player had finer performances in the last 20 years in the League, but he worked as hard as he played, and now is in charge of a big department and is just as highly regarded by his employers as he was by his League club.

These are only two instances, but football executives could tell of many similar cases. It all goes to show that, in addition to being human beings, real footballers are among our finest citizens.

FANS IN A FERMENT

Argus, September 10, 1932.

Fifty thousand people are ready today for their weekly pilgrimage, to make another Saturday safe for Victoria's thriving winter industry. If its patrons abandoned football as a national winter sport and took up yo-yo, £250,000 a year would be diverted to other pockets, many people would lose employment, and hero-worshipping would slump.

A surprising number of people benefit materially by this popular "industry". Some of them have never seen a football match, and they have no desire to do so. The giants who will take the field at the M.C.C. ground this afternoon for the first League semi-final and the 50,000 people who will roar from bounce to bell make the stage-show of football, but there are many behind the scenes. Behind the players—who receive thousands of pounds a year in a season—are coaches, trainers, rubbers-down, groundsmen, turnstile men, laundry-men, football-makers, uniform-makers, doctors, insurance agents, and others. Each club may pay more than £100 in a season to doctors, £500 to coaches and trainers, £40 for footballs, £1,200 a year to players, and £30 for laundry. Throughout Victoria about 50,000 footballs are required a year, and these cost about £4,000. It has been estimated that more than £40,000 is spent on players' outfits; and that for the "big games" £5,000 a year is expended on trainers and masseurs.

About 100,000 people attend League and Association games each Saturday. Transport for these enthusiasts puts £55,000 into the coffers of the Railways Commissioners each season. The liquor trade also takes its share. Barracking is thirsty work, and those who cheer loudly and drink deeply believe that 500,000 pints of beer are consumed by the "fans" each Saturday.

As the season approaches an end, the tempo of enthusiasm— and the thirsts—increase. Exhaustion point is reached with the final, when chemists enjoy a mild harvest by way of relaxed throats. With today excitement will reach "summer heat". Fever and danger points come later. For at least 50,000 people today the world is only a football ground.

BATTLE SONGS FOR FOOTSCRAY

Argus, January 19, 1935.

Supporters of the Footscray Football Club will co-operate for brighter and better football next season if certain suggestions which have been made are adopted by the committee of the club. The committee has already made a move in this direction by its decision to conduct community singing at matches on the Footscray ground. Gramaphone records suitable for amplifying through loud speakers will be bought. The committee is seeking club songs for the supporters to sing on these occasions. It is claimed that such songs would arouse enthusiasm among the spectators and inspire the team. A suggestion has also been made that a "cheer leader" should be appointed so that the best results from the club's "battle" songs may be obtained. The committee will consider the suggestion.

A FOOTBALL TALE OF TWO CITIES

Hugh Buggy, *Herald*, May 12, 1932.

Here is a modern tale of two cities!

Above each of them grey winter clouds drag their tattered

fringes. Leaves of the Yarra Park elms rustle before a wind that smells of icebergs. Fronds of the Moore Park palms bow before a bitter blast that often whips noses with the same lack of mercy.

You struggle in the racing rapids of rivers of felt hats eddying, twisting and converging into a great bowl of agitated headwear, a bowl that will simmer and rumble and smoke and rock and shriek for two hours. Into that wild fantasy of felt you plunge as the river surges over the green lawns of Moore Park to the Sydney Cricket Ground or down the leaf-crusted aisles of Yarra Park to the M.C.C. ground.

You march with those hosts of fellow-Australians who are both bent on seeing football.

Yet if you hail from Carlton you are as detached as remote from the spirit of that Moore Park throng as you would be on a peak in the Andes.

Should your home suburb be Marrickville, you trudge along a lonely soul in Yarra Park as far from the thoughts of your fellows as a Laplander would be from the ideals of a Parsee.

When winter comes, Sydney and Melbourne are two worlds, poles apart.

They are two cities whose aspirations always more or less take different paths, but in football an abysmal gulf separates them. Mingle in the two football crowds and note the divergence. Should you be from Carlton, a strange race of men on a Sydney Saturday afternoon will chatter excitedly about such mystic terms as "five-eighths" and "wing three-quarters".

What may a five-eighth be or a wing three-quarter? You have not the faintest idea.

Likewise if you hail from Marrickville you will stalk gloomily among strange men on a Melbourne Saturday afternoon who babble in frenzy about "marks" and "back pockets".

What is a back pocket unless it be a hip pocket? You from Marrickville are completely in the dark.

Around the stranger from Carlton in the football jungle of Moore Park an army sways and responds to electric waves of enthusiasm, now lifted to its toes with made hope, now sagging limply in the pit of despair. Why? If you are from Carlton you do not know.

Somewhere out in that vital Rugby League match a man in a blue jersey has grabbed the ball, shoved it under his arm, and

161

has dashed off with it. A surging pack races after him. They clutch at his legs, they tear at his knickers; they clamp wild arms about his waist. Down he goes!

"How's that, Umpire!" you in your Carlton innocence feel like shouting. But you are not at Princes Oval now. The crowd cheers.

The gentleman whom you thought had aimed at taking the ball home has been floored—or rather grassed—in a flying tackle. There is no free kick for this playful pleasantry. This habit of players falling on one another, you say meekly, must tend to slow down the game.

Say so at Moore Park at your peril!

You will be told with almost ferocity that Rugby League is the fastest game played, and that Australian Rules (the Sydney football fan expectorates here in disgust) is only a parlor game— a game for young ladies from a refined seminary.

You reflect on the hobbling, battered champions you have seen cheered as they are helped to the pavilion in a rugged Melbourne match. It's no use! The man from Newtown or Dulwich Hill laughs in your face.

Memories come to you of a dazzling wind burst or a centre attack, which in three magnificent kicks takes the ball from end to end of the ground. Then you watch again a scrum, a locked jumble of players, heads down, feet stamping, crowd cheering. Somewhere underneath the tangle is the ball. Somctimc, something will happen to it. You again venture an heroic opinion about respective pace. You are again talked down. You give it up in despair.

"Did you get that?" someone shouts in your ear. "Get what?" Somewhere at the corner of the ridiculously tiny playing square a player who has survived the mauling of a cohort of tacklers pats the ball on the ground in triumph. The crowd, or at least half of it, goes wild with joy. A Try! A Try!

"Try what?" you ask. Thunder bursts round your head. You escape to the bar. There later you are told that Easts downed Wests by three to nil. Three to nil! What puny scores, you from Carlton reflect with your memories of bounteous goal kicking. Again angry men glare at you.

North is north and south is south and never the twain shall meet in football harmony. To the man from Carlton "a try" is quite a needless excrescence on the game. To the man from

162

Marrickville "a behind" is utter futility—a reward for a miss. And so we remain poles apart.

THE HUMOURS OF FOOTBALL

R. W. E. Wilmot, *Argus*, September 9, 1939.

With the League finals so near, football is growing harder on both the players and the spectators. But the game never loses its humours. In this article Mr. R. W. E. Wilmot ("Old Boy") recalls some of the incidents which have lightened matches for him in recent and not so recent years.

The merits of big men and little men are often argued. I recall many small men, who looked like terriers barking at the heels of mastiffs in the shape of ruckmen. The big fellows have much to put up with from these midgets, who as a rule revel in the opportunities afforded by the clash of giants in the heavy work.

I remember seeing "Curley" Jones—now Councillor E. L. Jones, of the Melbourne City Council—playing for St. Kilda against Essendon at East Melbourne, when in the Essendon ruck there were four giants. "Curley" was bumping them and daring them regardless of his inches. The ball had been kicked over the fence into Jolimont road, and as the rucks were waiting for it "Curley" was challenging his opponents to mortal combat and threatening personal violence, when suddenly "Tracker" Forbes, the tallest man in Essendon, picked him up by the collar of his jersey and depositing him on a seat outside the fence, among the spectators, said, "Get out of this, you little pest."

Another time Forbes was running with the ball when "Curley" jumped on his back, and with his arms round Tracker's neck, hung on without impeding the progress of his rival. The umpire was so astonished that he did not know whether to award a free kick to Forbes for "round the neck" or against him for "holding the ball".

Stewart McLatchie, the Carlton rover, was under 5ft. 9in., and when it was found that he was to oppose Dave McNamara, of St. Kilda, who, in addition to standing 6ft. 4in., in his stockings, had abnormally long arms, Stewart was advised that the only way to stop McNamara was to tickle him. "Just get in

Famous Victorian cartoonist Percy Leason captured the spirit of the times and the humour of football in a brilliant series of cartoons—some of them set in the mythical country region of Wiregrass.

How Wiregrass Won the Premiership.

Unfortunate scene at the unfurling of the Wiregrass pennant in the presence of the opposing team.

Economy—owing to the financial depression Wiregrass sportsmen have agreed to the letting of the oval for grazing.

Out of action.

Her husband's.

front of him," he was told, "and when he puts his arms up for a mark tickle him under the arm pits."

After the match he was asked how he had fared. "How did I get on?" he replied. "Why he dashed near killed me. It was a long while before I had a chance. Then it came. Dave was in a crush and I was just in front of him. The ball came and up went his arms. By standing on tiptoe I could just reach his arm pit, and in went my fingers. As soon as I touched him down came his arms, and his two elbows hit me on the shoulder and almost knocked me out. Dave was ropeable when to his amazement the umpire gave me a free kick, and threatened to report Dave for elbowing, and I think he would have done so, but at three-quarter time I told the umpire what had happened."

And talking about tickling, I never saw anyone so ticklish as Bill Crebbin, the Essendon centre man. He would jump out of his skin if you touched him in the ribs. One day, on the old East Melbourne ground, Bill was waiting just outside the pack when Joe Shaw, the umpire, was about to bounce the ball. One of his own side tickled Crebbin. He jumped forward, more than a yard, head down, and butted the umpire, knocking him over. Crebbin apologised profusely, but it took a lot of explanation to mollify Shaw.

"Joker" Cameron, the South Melbourne follower, was one of those of whom it is said: "He takes it and gives it and never squeals." In a match between South Melbourne and Fitzroy "Boxer" Milne was in a crush when he received a blow on the ear. Looking round he realised that it could be only Cameron, with whom he was on particularly friendly terms, and expostulated, "What's up Joker?" only to receive the reply, "It's all right, Boxer, someone hit me and I am passing it on."

Playing at Geelong, for South Melbourne, on the opening day of the season Joker was throwing his weight about to some effect. There was only juniors in the Geelong pack, but that mattered not to Joker. Henry Young, the Geelong captain, called one of his juniors and went into the ruck in his stead. Getting beside Cameron he said, "Steady up Joker, these are only kids." Cameron looked at him in blank amazement and replied, "Blow me, Henry, I'm breaking them in for you."

Perhaps the most famous story about Joker Cameron was told once when as vice-captain he had to lead the side. In the first half Essendon played all over South, who were disjointed. At half-time the South Melbourne officials demanded that Joker should address the team and urge them to play up. Joker had never made a speech in his life, but mounting a form and hanging on to a hat rack with one hand, he said: "Blokes, we're in the blooming soup and we've got to get out of it. Come on." He walked out of the room at the head of his team, who, playing as one man, won easily.

A very different style of speech to a team that was playing very badly was that by Sydney Barker, captain of North Melbourne. Brunswick had a long lead at half-time, and North, playing very badly, seemed sure of defeat. In the North Melbourne dressing-room there was dismay. Everyone in the dressing-room seemed to realise that there was a crisis, and everyone looked at the captain. "When are you going to speak to them?" whispered an agitated committee-man, and Barker replied: "All right; in a minute."

The atmosphere became tense with anticipation. The players felt they were in for a lecture such as only Barker could give, and again the whistle blew. Without a word Barker rose, gave a hitch to his shorts, brushed his hair, and strode in silence to the door, the players making way for him. Just as he reached the door he turned, and, facing the players, said: "There are 17 of you, all experienced footballers. You know what is wrong without me telling you. I would not insult your intelligence by telling you what to do", and out he walked. His team, who had expected a sound rating, flattered by their captain's confidence, rose to the occasion, and from that moment the game changed, and North Melbourne gained the upper hand, and won easily. Who will say that psychology does not enter into football?

Perhaps the greatest comedian the game ever knew was Charles ("Tracker") Forbes, of Essendon. He was a great player, and enjoyed every moment of the game. In all his long career, although he played the game as hard as anyone, he never incurred the displeasure of the umpire.

In his final appearance for Essendon one man at least thought he should have been reported. That was Jim Sharp, who was playing his first game for Fitzroy. "Tracker" was pressed into the Essendon team at the last moment, owing to someone being absent, and he was placed full back. Jim Sharp was full forward, and had to mind Forbes. After a while the ball came their way, and both ran for it. As they did Sharp felt a fist on his jaw, and Forbes marked the ball and kicked it away. As he returned to his place he said to Jim Sharp: "I'm sorry, lad; but when you've been playing as long as I have you'd have to do that if you want a kick." Jim Sharp appreciated the explanation.

BERT CHADWICK'S FIRST GAME

Sporting Globe, September 7, 1935.

Bert Chadwick's story of his introduction to senior football is worth recording.

'So you think the play's poor, do you? Do you think you could do better?' The speaker had turned sharply on me, a challenge in his eyes and satire in his tone.

'Well, possibly I could,' I replied quietly. 'Good!' he retorted ironically. 'You're the very man we want. We want barrackers like you to show the players how to play. Come and have a run on Tuesday. See me, I'm the Prahran Secretary.' Rather nettled, I watched him move away through the crowd. Those around me laughed. The laugh seemed on me. It was in 1919. I was just home from the war. Out of curiosity I had strolled across to Toorak Park to see an Association match. I had played both Australian Rules and Rugby on active service in Palestine, and although I never professed to be a champion at either I was disappointed with the play that day, and said so to a man standing alongside of me. He happened to be the Prahran Football Club Secretary.

That chance remark was to lift me swiftly into senior football, though at the time I had not the faintest notion of ever playing in Melbourne.

As I walked home the Secretary's satire rankled in my mind. Perhaps I could not do any better—perhaps I could. So ran my thoughts. Finally I decided more for a joke than anything else to take him at his word. Wearing my heavy military boots, and without any preparation, I went to Toorak Park on the Tuesday afternoon. Training was in full swing. Throwing off my coat and donning shorts, I joined a group of players unnoticed. I had a few marks and kicks and quite enjoyed myself. Somebody asked my name and address. I told him and clean forgot all about it. In fact, I clean forgot about football altogether, and began to wonder where I would spend the following Saturday afternoon.

To my great surprise, however, the Prahran Secretary arrived at my home in the morning and wanted me to play that afternoon. His invitation fired my football blood again. There was evidently no difficulty with permits, for a few hours later I was playing in the Prahran uniform and getting a tremendous kick out of it. Occasionally I wondered whether the spectators were saying the same thing about me as I had said when a spectator a short week before.

That was how I began to play senior football in Melbourne. After a season with Prahran I transferred to the Melbourne Club without a clearance, and played for them for nine happy years.

CARJI GREEVES

Table Talk, May 29, 1930.

"Who will be premiers this year?" That is a question very popular these days. Though to the stranger in Victoria this query may verge upon the cryptic, to those residing in the southern State it is readily understood, for during the winter months "premiers" can only refer to the football team that is to finish head of the list at the conclusion of the season.

"Carlton are a sure thing," comes a thunderous reply from the Dark Blue hordes: "Melbourne's the cleverest team in the game," is the not so loud but equally as confident answer from the Fuchsia followers; "Collingwood will be there, as usual," rises from the Magpie ranks; "Fitzroy", "Footscray", and even "Hawthorn" are added to the collection. So we are none the wiser than before, and then, to cap it all, "Carji" Greeves tells me that, despite their lapse against Melbourne, this season's Geelong side is the best with which he has ever taken the field. After this tip from headquarters, who knows that the boys from the Pivot might not be the pennant-winners for 1930.

"Carji" has been unfortunate this year, for a knock on the leg received in the first game against North Melbourne has kept him out of the Geelong side ever since. I say "Carji" is unfortunate, but it is really the team itself that one should feel sorry for, for without Greeves giving his customary brilliant display in the centre it is far from being a representative Geelong combination. "Carji" must, I think, be classed as one of the greatest footballers that has ever stripped for the Pivotonians, and also as one of the really great centre men of all time.

If one were to give "Carji" his correct Christian name it would be "Edward", and it was in 1904 that Edward Greeves saw the light in Warragul. He continued looking at the Warragul light until he reached the age of three years, when he was taken by his parents to New South Wales, and resided in Lismore, on the Richmond River. The name "Lismore" must have been popular with the Greeves family, for when young Edward was seven they collected together their belongings and moved down to Lismore in Victoria, where "Carji" attended the Struan State school.

It was in 1916 that "Carji" (a nickname, by the way, that has stuck to him ever since a small baby, when a friend of the family's so rechristened him) began an association with Geelong which has brought much pleasure to the good people dwelling by Corio Bay, for in that year—a lad of 12—he was enrolled as a scholar at Geelong College.

Whether "Carji" staggered the masters of this famous public school with his remarkable grip of all languages and his uncanny knowledge of vulgar fractions we do not know, but what does interest us is the fact that the Warragul lad quickly began to prove his abilities as an all-round sportsman, and in a short space of time had secured his colours for football, cricket, and rowing. As a rower "Carji" enjoyed the role of the boat-race week flappers' matinee-idol—stroke of his crew in the Head of the River races—while in 1922 he further enhanced his claims to being a "star" all-rounder by annexing the school's tennis championship.

In 1923 he returned to college merely to take part in the Head of the River, and then, after all this excitement, he said "Goodbye" to school days, and wended his way homewards to the comparative quietness of Cressy—the latest abode of his nomadic parents. Here he was permitted to blush unseen for but one short month, after which Geelong—having tasted the Greeves' ability, and loth to let one who promised such good advertisement for the town slip through their fingers—invited him to come down and play with their football team.

Nothing loth, "Carji" accepted, and that year played his first game in League football with the Pivotonian eighteen against Essendon, at Essendon. In this match Greeves was stationed on the forward line, in the hope that he might take some of the strain of goal-kicking off the shoulders of Lloyd Hagger and Cliff Rankin, but during the tussle with the Same Olds, Geelong's clever little rover, "Jockey" Jones, unfortunately broke his collarbone, so "Carji" had to take on the job of following the pack.

At the end of the season the famous quarrel—Geelong executive versus the Rankin brothers—cropped up, and with Bert having been dropped out of the centre position, Greeves was called upon to take the pivot, and there he has played ever since. So well, indeed, did "Carji" perform in the centre that at the end of the following year he received the umpires' vote as the best and fairest player in the League, and was the first to receive the medal to perpetuate the memory of Charles Brownlow.

"Carji" continued to be recognised as one of the State's leading footballers in 1927 and 1928, and it was then that he was singled out to be the recipient of a very great honor. Over in America the University of Southern California decided that their football team would do much better if they could kick further, so Mr. Andrew Chaffey (then in America) told them that he would secure an Australian footballer to come across to give them instruction in the art. The agreement was that if the Australian succeeded in improving the University team's kicking powers, the University would pay the expenses, but if he failed Mr. Chaffey was to foot the bill.

By communicating with Mr. Alexander, of the *Sporting Globe*, it was decided that "Carji" Greeves was the man for the job, and so on August 4, 1928 "Carji" left our shores to become resident at the University of Southern California as kicking instructor—and that the University were subsequently only too glad to sign the cheque for expenses speaks volumes for Greeves' success with the team.

"Carji" explained that the trouble with the American men was that they drop-kicked off their toes instead of their insteps—thus getting height but no distance—and it was on correcting this that he concentrated, with such good results that the team won the championship of U.S.A. under his guidance.

As the University of Southern California had scored but one field goal in the season previous to "Carji's" advent, and 21 out of 23 shots after they had received the Greeves tuition, the

Geelong footballer must have felt indeed pleased with his work when he returned to Australia on March 30, 1929, to take up his old position in the centre with the Pivotonians. He had certainly been a great advertisement for not only Geelong, but also Australia.

"Carji's" most brilliant form was shown in 1924, in which year he earned a place in the Victorian Carnival team in Tasmania, while in 1925 he played against South Australia in Adelaide and Melbourne. In 1926 he went with the Victorians to the West.

As a cricketer he has also earned some recognition, playing with the Melbourne team in 1924, and with the Colts against South Australia in 1925. He was in the Geelong XI, in 1926 in Country Week cricket, and out of the 48 teams competing he secured the best aggregate score, highest individual score, and the batting average. In 1923 "Carji" rowed with the Barwon crew in the Henley and V.R.A. Senior Eights; and as a tennis-player he won the Northern Districts Singles Championship at Bendigo in 1928.

HAYDN BUNTON'S AMAZING STATISTICS

Star, September 11, 1935.

Haydn Bunton has at least two particularly staunch supporters, for they have forwarded a detailed list of, among other things, how often he has handled the ball in the last two seasons, the

Haydn Bunton.

means by which he gained possession, and to what use he put the ball.

They found that Bunton had possession of the ball 380 times this season, took 147 marks, and received 71 free kicks. Thus he had possession of the ball 598 times, and disposed of it as follows:—

| | Score | | Passes | | Shots | | Other kicks |
	Gls	Bhds	Foot	Hand	Missed	Marked or cleared	
In general play	24	15	79	109	9	33	111
From marks	11	10	36	7	..	10	73
From free-kicks	6	4	16	..	..	4	41
Totals	41	29	131	116	9	47	225

Foot passes to team mates amounted to 131, hand passes 116, and scoring shots were 70. Thus Fitzroy benefited 317 times out of the 598 times Bunton had possession.

Bunton played in 17 games and averaged 28 kicks in each game. He averaged 35 times in possession in each game.

An analysis has also been prepared of Bunton's kicks in each game this season. His best were 45 against Footscray, 44 against North Melbourne, 43 against St. Kilda, and 42 in the second match against Footscray.

Last year he had possession 592 times, kicked 33 goals and 39 behinds (72 scoring shots), passed to team mates 104 times, and hand passed 98 times.

Bunton won "The Star Cup" for the best and fairest player in the League, and his club's handsome trophy, presented by Mr. Cyril Steele, for best and fairest.

HAYDN BUNTON, GLAMOUR BOY

By Jack Dyer, from *Captain Blood*, 1965.

Bamm . . ! A jet-propelled fist slammed against my nose as I lay sprawled on the Richmond turf. I couldn't believe it. The shock hurt more than the punch.

Because on the other end of that punch was the great Haydn Bunton, not only the best player in the game but said to be the fairest and already a triple Brownlow Medal winner. I couldn't believe he would throw a punch.

Not that I blame him for throwing caution to the wind, I'd been giving him some pretty rough treatment during the day. I'd been instructed to niggle him off his game and that's just what I was doing. I'd been pulling and pushing at him. In fact every player in our side who got near him had a go. That was the tragedy of Bunton. He had every side gunning for him and developing elaborate plans to get him out of the game, just as they do today with Farmer. Probably for this reason and because Richmond could counter, I haven't as great an impression of him as I have of players like Laurie Nash who had the help of a great side.

Bunton still showed me enough ability to make a lasting impression. He was the elusive Pimpernel of football. You couldn't catch him with a fishing net, but the day he punched me at Fitzroy I had managed to catch him and gave him a hard ride to the ground and for good measure I rubbed his nose in the mud. His reserve burst and so did my nose. He didn't give me time to crack back, but was up and off again. I wouldn't have hit him. I appreciate when I deserve a bit back for my corner.

You can imagine how tough it must have been for Bunton when every Saturday a coach opened his address: 'Only one player can beat you, Bunton. I want him stopped'.

But Bunton brought immortality to Fitzroy when they had nothing. They were as weak then as they are now.

He was the glamour boy of football and had more girls chasing him than Valentino. He was a floor-walker at a city store, a handsome, debonair fellow with tremendous personality. The store filled daily with beautiful heart-thumping females just clamouring for a glance. And his football was pretty too.

A lot of critics have argued that Haydn Bunton junior, his son and current idol of the West, is even better than his father. Anybody who says this never saw Bunton senior in action. I laugh and yawn whenever I hear the suggestion made. His father was bigger, stronger, faster, a better ball-handler, better mark, better balk, better talker and a better footballer. Bunton junior would be struggling to get a game in Victoria, let alone win three Brownlows. Bunton senior also won Margery Medals in South Australia and Sandover Medals in West Australia.

JACK DYER'S FIRST GAMES

From *Captain Blood*, 1965.

The Metropolitan Junior League was the breeding ground for the roughest, toughest assortment of players football has ever seen. It also produced some of the greatest and most colourful players and clashes. It was depression football at its grimmest.

Alan 'Killer' Killigrew, who has coached St. Kilda and North Melbourne as well as in South Australia, was a member of my team known as the Richmond Hill mob. He was a weeper even then. He couldn't get a game and used to come crying round to my home on a Friday night when he missed selection. I don't know why he was so upset, there were times when I wished to heaven I wasn't playing.

We were in a lot of trouble. We had a brilliant side but no fighters and the football in that League was grim, serious business. We were up against all the toughs the industrial suburbs could muster. Every match was followed by a fight. You had to win both to stay in business.

We met every side twice and it was always better to meet the tough teams on their home ground first. If they dished out the treatment they knew what to expect in the return match on our home ground. It was foolhardy not to carry a knuckle-duster against these fellows. At Richmond we used to engage the local toughs to hang around the boundaries yelling out threats.

Some of the toughest sides were Brunswick Laurels, Yarra-ville Stars, Mernic (Fitzroy), Moray Stars (South Melbourne).

It was football mayhem.

You weren't supposed to do it, but it was possible to ring-in star V.F.L. players. It was nothing to be on top and playing the weakest side and get a terrible hiding.

At one stage we were going like bombs on top of the ladder and met Mernic, who hadn't won a match. They killed us. Later we found they had 10 Fitzroy players in the side.

Things became so bad we had to hire police protection at our games. We always needed them when we played Brunswick Laurels, who had a string of six-round fighters in their team. They couldn't play football, but threw punches wild and plentiful. It used to get a bit disconcerting.

The opposition hated to lose and their supporters were dangerous. In a game against Mernic we snatched the lead right on the bell. An opposition supporter stood over the timekeeper, Jerry O'Callaghan, with a bottle and threatened, 'If you ring the bell before we score again I'll dong you.' The match dragged on and we clung to our lead. At an exciting moment Jerry rang the old cow-bell and set off like the devil with the bloke and bottle after him. But we'd won, and Jerry escaped unscathed.

The most riotous clash was the final against Yarraville Stars. We gave them a nice doing on the North Melbourne ground. That was the first half of the battle as far as they were concerned. We knew the fight was going to be on straight after the game, so without changing we headed, jet-propelled, for the North Melbourne railway station. They anticipated our move and as we turned the corner of the station we spotted the whole Yarraville team and their band of toughs waiting for us. Being all church-going young fellows, we were not accustomed to fisticuffs, but, worse, we were outnumbered. So we took to our heels in various directions.

Most of us headed for an old cable tram. As we piled on the other fellows were gaining. The tram-driver only had one of two levers to pull, but the way he fumbled and grabbed you'd have thought he had 70. Naturally he pulled the wrong one and he couldn't get it going again. With the women and ourselves screaming the attackers piled on.

One of our chaps, Snifter McConville, jumped from the tram, ran into a garage and locked himself inside. Another was hit over the head with an iron bar, some defended themselves and the rest of us just ran. The rioters broke every window on the tram before the driver eventually got it rolling again. It pulled away with bodies writhing everywhere, in the tram, on the roads and at odd spots throughout the district. We forgot all about the bloke in the garage. I'm not quite sure if he ever got out. In spite of the cuts and bruises the victory still tasted sweet, and they were teaching us how to fight.

We had another tough match to face up to against Richmond South. Collingwood player Frank Meahan decided to play with us under an alias and asked me about our chances. 'We're the better side but they're the better fighters. They'll probably bluff us out of it,' I told him.

'Don't worry, china,' he said, 'just play football, I'll look after the rest.'

He had 11 brothers and four of them were fighting at the stadium. He phoned all 11 and told them to be at the Royal Park oval for the match. They obeyed. Just before the game Frank gave us a pep-talk in the hearing of the opposition. Then like a general he sent his brothers to vantage points around the ground, saying, 'As soon as the blue starts, knock down anybody without a red and black guernsey.' You can imagine the lift it gave us. Our full-forward kicked six goals in the first quarter and we romped in, and, needless to say, there was no serious fight. I often wonder at the result had the Meahan brothers not turned up.

Our most bitter rivals were the Moray Stars at South Melbourne. They looked so ominous one of our chaps once took fright and tried to leave. 'I forgot my boots,' he stammered, but we made him face up. We were just as scared, but you don't win being a shirker. My brother Vin played with us against them that day. He was a six-round fighter and his opponent gave him the needle all day, calling him a four-round stumble-bum. So I started to needle Vin too. 'How long are you going to cop that?'

Finally Vin said, 'Well, what will I do?'

'Drop the ratbag,' I answered.

Crash . . . and down went the needler. But I'll say this for Vin. He only threw one punch, he's a very placid bloke.

I handed out a few punches myself and Vin and I were heckled all day. We were officially notified we were scheduled to be dumped in the Albert Park lake directly after the game.

Just before it finished Brother Peter sneaked off and came back with two policemen. They came on to the ground and walked me off, one either side. Just for good measure I gave my hecklers a real Australian gesture to indicate my thoughts about them. They turned ugly and the police said, 'Right, do that again and we'll leave you.' I went like a lamb. They put me on a bus and it drove off under a hail of rocks.

In between the fights and the foot races my football was improving, but I still hadn't given any serious thought to breaking into the big time. Names like Leeta Collier and George Rudolph struck a bit of awe into me and I doubted if I could make the grade.

My attitude changed one day when I found myself on a ring-in against Yarraville Stars. I went like a bomb and massacred him. He turned to me and said: 'You must be a ring-in. I'm Buckley, full-forward for Yarraville, and you won't give me a kick.' He was a top boy and when I told him I was a fair-dinkum Richmond Hill boy he invited me to play with Yarraville for £1 a game. That was big dough to me. I didn't take up the offer but I did change my attitude and decided to have a crack at my favorite club, Richmond.

It was to prove a hard job. There were good reports about me, but Richmond didn't seem to know I existed. They didn't send an invitation, so I continued with Richmond Hill.

I was picking up a few pounds on the side playing in the Wednesday League with Yellow Cabs. They were just as tough as the Richmond Hill games. The teams were full of cut-throats and criminals. You could pick a more honest team at Pentridge Gaol than some of the teams in that competition.

Playing at centre half-forward in one of the fieriest matches, I came up against a human mountain of muscle and I wasn't feeling too fit. When the customary fight broke out every other player on the ground and a couple score of spectators joined in. My opponent stood in silence for a few moments and then glared across at me and snapped:

'Do you want to be in it?'

I took one look at the bulge of muscle and let out a big and very definite 'NOOO!'

'O.K., then let's have a kick to kick until it's finished.'

The ball had been lying forgotten on the ground and we kicked it to each other for a good 20 minutes while the brawl raged on. They were a sick and sorry group when they got back to the game.

One of the meanest and toughest bunches I ever played against was the Watersiders. Each side had to appoint their own goal umpire. The wharfies had a beauty. We had to put the goal straight through the middle or he would signal a point. You can imagine how we felt.

With only a few points separating us in a crucial game a policeman named Hanrahan slapped a perfect six-pointer right between the big sticks. It could not have been a clearer goal.

The umpire quietly picked up one flag, ignored the gaping Hanrahan, and began signalling a point.

Hanrahan exploded, 'That should have been two flags, you—'

The umpire coolly pointed to the umpire at the other end returning his signal, 'There's the other one.'

After that the League decided to appoint and pay goal umpires.

Things became so tough in the Wednesday League with so many toughies and crims out to square accounts that the police teams and the fire brigade had to pull out of the competition.

Still, as far as I was concerned it was preparing me for the task ahead, and I loved football no matter how hard it was played.

I always had a bit of an edge on other young footballers. I was a pro right from the start. The win was everything, a hatred of losing. That attitude is the makings of a footballer. You can be the slickest player on two legs, with bewildering pace and long kicking, but you won't reach the top without that fierce desire to go in and win.

I was breaking my heart trying to get a crack at Richmond. Every night after training I went to Richmond ground and watched the champs in action. I wanted to play with them more than anything I had ever wanted but it was just as hard to get an invitation to train as it was to get into the senior team, and that was harder than winning a lottery.

Meantime Collingwood were taking a bit of interest. My father had written to them, my old stand-by Frank Meahan kept telling them what a champion I was and another Collingwood player Snowy Barr tried to get them to invite me to train. I decided on a desperate gamble to make Richmond aware of me. I asked for a clearance to Collingwood even though the Magpies didn't want me. It worked.

Richmond hated Collingwood. No sooner had I applied for

the clearance than Checker Hughes, then Richmond coach, came to watch me play in the Metropolitan League final. I won the best and fairest for the season and I played at my peak in that final.

Our colours were black with a red 'V' on the chest. Checker approached me and told me I had no hope of getting the clearance to Collingwood. 'But don't worry, son, I'll turn that red 'V' into a white 'V' inside two seasons.' He meant he would have me in the interstate side. He was to fulfil his prediction.

Not knowing the future, my problems were far from over. Although Checker said I would get an invite to train, the invitation didn't arrive, and I had to go chasing them. I asked so often I think they finally sent it to me out of sheer exasperation; besides, it wasn't costing them anything. I was a local, and they didn't have to pay board or travelling expenses.

About this time one of the Metropolitan Junior League officials disappeared with all the assets and the League was abandoned—which might have been a good thing. The way the game was played it looked certain to develop into killings. However, the experience had done a lot for my football. It was in those games I learned to play rough, tough football and most important of all that you have to give punishment as well as take it. I doubt if we will ever see the same toughness in football again, but I never regret that era. There was little of the present-day spite and cowardly behind-the-play viciousness, simply he-man encounters, straight-out fights and no beg pardons.

When I talk of tough football I admit I played hard, but I was not vicious. The ball was my object and if somebody was in the path of it I went through. I didn't set out to maim a man or knock him deliberately out of the game. That's the difference these days.

The night Checker invited me to train with Richmond I went home to my parents with my stomach in knots. 'I'm going to train with Richmond,' I told my father.

He didn't bother to look up from his food as he answered, 'You'll be killed.' There was no further discussion.

That was hardly the reaction I anticipated, but my stomach was still twisting when I went to bed.

I was on the way.

The ball floated down to me. It was a simple mark. I had it

well covered, but suddenly it was plucked from my fingers. I blushed all over and could have hidden my six foot in a stop mark.

That was my first attempt at a mark when training with Richmond for the first time. I thought I was the boy wonder. I was going to kill them. Instead I was being killed.

As the practice game continued I tried everything to get a touch of the ball, but my opponent Joe Murdoch beat me every time. Joe was to become one of my closest football friends, but he couldn't be a friend on the field. He went right into orbit. He concentrated so deeply that at the end of the practice my tally was no marks, no kicks, no touches. He'd eaten me. He showed me I was far from a champion. He had me off balance all day and when I was given a free kick I was so flustered I couldn't kick. I walked from the ground friendless, almost in tears of frustration, and as Checker strolled over I knew he was going to tell me to get back with the hicks at Yarra Junction—any other coach would have.

It was then he showed what a great psychologist he really was. He was the best in the game, take Killigrew, Norm Smith and all of them. He simply said, 'You didn't go so well, eh?' I had to admit he was right. Checker answered: 'I wasn't worried about that. I just wanted to know if you had what it takes. If you can stand up to that fellow you can stand up to anyone. That was a try-out. You were on trial for guts, to see if you could keep coming back.' I didn't feel friendless any more, Checker was my new idol.

All recruits feel friendless, but at times you can't blame the clubs for not being too open-armed about them. Most recruits who turn up for a run think they are Haydn Buntons and you can't get rid of them. We had one at Richmond called Dutchy. As a footballer he was a good billiards player and no matter what I told him he wouldn't stop turning up to training.

'You're not worth a bumper,' I told him a thousand times.

He was hurt, but would say, 'All right, I won't come again Jack.'

Next training night there he was again, sprinting up and down the field, getting in the way of everyone. Finally we found out he came from South Melbourne district, so I phoned the South secretary. 'We want a clearance for a chap in your district, Dutchy—. He's just an Indian as far as football goes.

He'll never make a chief; still, we think he might come in handy as a reserve.'

I knew after a spiel like that South wouldn't clear him. Sure enough the secretary bluffed. 'No, Jack, we won't clear him. We've been watching him for some time.' They'd never seen him or they would never have blocked his clearance.

Next training night Dutchy came to me waving a letter. 'I can't train with you any more, Jack. South have sent me an invitation to train and told me not to train here any more.'

He went to South and a few weeks later the South secretary phoned. 'You no good—, Dyer. We can't get rid of that cow.' I wouldn't be surprised if Dutchy is still there training.

It is a terrible experience for a young recruit when he first trains. On my terrifying first day I knew only one fellow.

That is the hardest moment in any footballer's career. All the others know each other and call out their personal nicknames, I was running around like a rabbit calling: 'Hey, mister. Here.' The regulars do not deliberately ignore the recruit, but years of training and playing together results in their making instinctive passes to the calls they know.

On that first day I ran round and round the ground warming up. Checker was watching and I couldn't get a touch. In the end he called to me. 'What do you think you are, a prize bull at the Royal Show?'

It was an awe-inspiring introduction. I was surrounded by the big names of football. Columns and columns of newspaper stories had been written about them. I was supposed to be a ruckman but how could I make the grade? They already had 10 good ones on their lists and six of them couldn't get a game. I was a raw no-hoping kid.

However, hope dies slowly and I wouldn't stop trying. It was enough to mix with the champions. I was soon to have my first big thrill in football.

To me it was unheard of to be able to talk to a star footballer, let alone have a bath with the great George Rudolph.

I have no doubt he was the greatest big man ever to play football.

One Sunday I went to the Richmond club rooms for a rub-down and the only two present were George Rudolph and the club masseur, Mark Noble. Rudolph was a strange character, capable of doing any extraordinary thing. During a match he was just as likely to curl up on the ground or walk off in disgust. Yet he could turn the tide of a game with his brilliant play. The crowd hated him, but the more he was hooted the better he played.

So I was a bit awestruck at finally meeting my idol face to face. He asked my name and who I played for. I said, 'Richmond, I'm hoping.'

He was in the bath and just said, 'Hop into the bath and we'll have a talk.' He was 6 ft. 2 in. and over 15 stone. I was a tick over 6 foot and I couldn't see how I could fit in, but nothing in the world would have kept me out. It was a tight squeeze, but we made it. We talked there for an hour on football with a not very pleased Mark Noble working on Rudolph. I think Mark could cheerfully have drowned me, only there wasn't room. Little did he know at that stage he would be rubbing me down for the next 15 years and looking after me like a baby.

Rudolph was the one man I would have loved to have teamed with, but he was to leave Richmond the next year and play with Oakleigh. As a footballer, he was like an antelope. He could turn on a trey bit and despite his bulk could rove and play wing if necessary.

With Rudolph's encouragement and Checker's coaching my form improved as I continued to practise, but I was also learning the meaning of the Tiger war-cry 'Eat 'em Alive'. They played it just as hard on the training track as they did when the real thing came up. They were ferocious and they were fearless and I knew before I played my first game that a V.F.L. football ground would be no place for weakies. It's a man's game, and never forget it.

My heart was thumping when the Richmond 1931 training lists were posted. I couldn't be sure I had made the grade. But there it was, 'J. Dyer'. I felt like running 10 laps of the oval. I had myself a guernsey. Whether I would ever wear it with the senior side was yet to be decided.

Richmond's first game was to be played against Collingwood, their most bitter rivals. I was half hoping I wouldn't make the team. The thought of facing up to the awe-inspiring Rumley, the Colliers and the Coventrys was a frightening prospect. The Collingwood champions were tearing through the packs and the opposition players regardless of the consequences. When the selectors met and announced the team I was 19th man, and that is even more terrifying than being named in the side.

Sitting shivering on the bench alongside Checker Hughes was a never-to-be-forgotten experience. I knew I would be on with the first injury. What a baptism to League football, to be thrown in against the mightiest Magpie combination ever assembled.

I trembled at every bump and whenever a Richmond player hit the turf my spine crawled. It was a grudge match out of the ordinary. I was frightened and praying not to have to go on.

In those days players were not allowed off a ground except on a stretcher. They took a very dim view of it if you walked off—they figured if you could walk you could play. They hated sending the 19th man on, one reason being they had to pay him if they did.

As luck had it my prayers were answered and Richmond finished with all players intact and myself still on the bench and we'd won. Next week I was relegated to the seconds and my chances of making the seniors that season appeared very slim. They had a ruck combination which has seen few peers. I thought so little of my chances I even gave my much prized guernsey to my brother Vin.

Halfway through the season Richmond had a walkover match scheduled against North Melbourne and Jack Bissett decided to give me a chance to play with the seniors. He 'developed' a hand injury and I was selected in his place. They weren't happy about giving me another guernsey.

The big day came.

I ran on to the ground with butterflies fluttering about my stomach. The roars of 'Eat 'em Alive', 'Carn the Tigers' almost caused me to double-back off the field again. This was the game to decide my future. The Shinboners, as they were known in those days, were a pretty ruthless mob and no doubt planned to give me the acid test. You needed shin-guards against that mob, they preferred to kick a player than the ball. I was calculating without my team-mates.

Before the ball was bounced my Richmond protectors had given the Shinboners the warning. 'Lay off the kid. Touch him and they'll carry you off—in pieces.' It was an ominous warning and the North players knew it was no bluff. They didn't have the muscle to buck the Richmond machine, so they gave me a clear go. With the help of that armchair ride I played at my peak and was named best on the ground. A tremendous boost in your first game.

My form was so hot the selectors couldn't drop me the next week, and Bissett had to spend another week on the sidelines. 'It's the last time I'll ever help a kid out,' he growled at me, being depression days it must have hurt and it was a poor reward for his decency. But what could I do?

He wasn't on the sidelines long. My next game was one of my worst. It was tough football against Footscray and my teammates had their own hands full and unable to give me all the protection I needed. I was slammed into the fence twice by Bullet Lamb and couldn't get into a gallop. I was in more trouble than the early settlers and Bissett was in the side next game and I was back in the seconds in disgrace.

The Richmond seconds were loaded with older players struggling to hold their position and keep the extra bit of depression day money coming in. I don't know whether they ganged up on me because I was a newcomer and threatening their security but I couldn't get a kick. They didn't play to me or through me.

I got fed-up and quit the club. My Richmond career and V.F.L. career could have finished right there.

The Richmond Hill mob welcomed me back with open arms and I played a few games with them before Richmond secretary Perc Page suddenly realized I was missing. He came looking for me.

'I'm not playing with a team that won't play with me,' I told him.

He was surprised to learn there was a clique at Richmond, but he wasn't a man to mince matters. He went back and gave the seconds a complete shake-up. A number of players were given open clearances to any League club. One of them even managed to make the state team.

With new enemies scattered everywhere I went back to the newlook Richmond. Now the seconds were a young side and Fritz Hefner was put with me in the ruck to develop understanding with me. Against Collingwood I was to meet one of the sacked Richmond players, Porridge Langdon.

The message came along the grapevine that he was out to get me. Soon after the ball bounced he made an almighty charge at me. He had me right in his sights and I couldn't get out of the road. I did the next-best thing and brought my knee up and sent him crashing to the ground. When he regained his breath he snarled, 'I'll have you after the match.'

It was a soaking wet day and I was pretty worried about the formidable Porridge, but I knew I'd have to face him or be branded a coward. While all the others dressed I sat in my togs waiting for him, shivering with cold and fright.

Twenty minutes later he walked in, freshly showered, fully dressed. He came over to me. 'Nice to see you're not a squib, anyway, hop off and have a shower.' I was never so happy to get under a shower.

My hopes of playing with the seniors again in 1931 were pretty faint, but in the last game before the finals Perc Bentley broke his hand and was out for the finals. It was my big chance and I was keyed up all week knowing I was a certainty to play in Bentley's position.

I had to play a Wednesday match for Yellow Cabs and I was scared stiff of being injured. It was my chance to play in a V.F.L. final and I didn't want it spoiled. The worst happened. I wasn't injured—I was reported.

There were 13 other players reported from that match and I was certain I would be rubbed out because I knew I was guilty.

It was my first visit to the tribunal, although there were to be many more such visits in subsequent years.

Richmond were far from happy about the business, but they couldn't very well forbid me to play mid-week. I was employed by Yellow Cabs and it wasn't easy to get a job in depression days. So when Yellow Cabs told me to play, I played.

The charge against me was hacking. A nice word for kicking. During the Wednesday match I had been kicked 16 times by this fellow, a real football desperado. Eventually he made a mistake in going for the ball as I was running head on into him. I gave a tremendous kick at the ball and tried to send it, my boot and everything else right through him. The central umpire missed the incident but the goal umpire picked it up from 60 yards away. It was a nice rugged match and it was lucky only 14 of us were reported.

We all faced the tribunal, which was held in a dungeon at Eastern Hill, three days before the final. They used to administer justice pretty ruthlessly in those days and I was the last to be granted audience.

One after the other the accused came out, 'Two weeks', 'four weeks', 'six weeks', 'eight weeks', 'twelve weeks'. It kept going up. By the time I went in I was preparing for a life sentence. Fortunately Richmond needed me badly on the Saturday and the president of the tribunal was also president of Richmond with the result I was the only one of the 14 to be cleared.

It was the unwritten law that a player never squealed on another player at a tribunal hearing. If he did the whisper went around the clubs and he was dealt with very seriously in future matches. So it was usually the players v. umpires, and you had to be a good talker or have a good mouthpiece, because they gave the umpires a good hearing.

After the tribunal let-off I was automatically selected to play in the 1931 final series. We played Geelong in the first semi-final and I was alight. We won easily and I kicked three goals. The reason I did so well was that we had 17 stars in the side and the Geelong players were told to concentrate on the stars and not to worry about a kid playing his third game.

The story was vastly different in the Grand Final when we met again. Geelong's Bull Coghlan was my opponent, a nice tough guy if I have ever seen one. His opening gambit, 'Hello, has Mother let you out today, Sonny?'

He followed this pleasantry up with a backhander while the umpire was going about his business at the other end of the ground. After that I was a nervous wreck and played accordingly. So did the rest of the team and we were soundly beaten.

During the game I was switched to Geelong's Reg Hickey and that was my first big lesson in football. Hickey was very strong and very fair. I thank God for that. I stood on his toes, pulled his guernsey and did everything to put him off his game. The more treatment he got, the better he played. He handled me like a baby. He taught me a football lesson in concentration.

After the match I was petrified about what he would do to me. He came to me asking, 'What's your name, Sonny?' I answered 'Dyer, Mr. Hickey'. The only time I have called a man Mister on the football field. 'Stick to it and you will be a pretty good footballer one day. I think you'll be all right, son,' Hickey said and then trotted off.

My baptism year into League football had been one of mixed fortunes, but I was becoming confident I would make the grade.

11
The Forties: 'the smell of eucalyptus oil again'

The 1945 Bloodbath Grand Final between Carlton and South Melbourne seemed to be an expression of the violence and horror of World War Two—which had ended the previous month. The 1940s were marred by an acceptance of physical football unseen this century. Fitzroy won their last forties flag in 1944, but the forties belonged to Jack Dyer, Mopsy Fraser, Basher Williams and Soapy Vallence.

ADVICE TO FOOTBALL BARRACKERS

By P. F., April 29, 1944.

The football season is kicking in again, and barrackers should have a little brisk training. What about a short refresher course—a quick run through?

I need not remind you, intelligent barracker, that in the first place the umpire is never on your side, and while a good solid elbow to the ribs administered by one of your chaps is an artistic delight, a similar blow, aimed at the beloved bones of your man, is an offence against decency, the act of a fiend not fit to associate with humans.

... Simple points like this you will remember instinctively. Right? Sure, you remember. You'll hit top form in no time. Let's make it a super-season. Get the will to win. Remember, the enemy is never right. Opposition barrackers are just not made that way.

Be courageous this year, don't be soft with them. Be fierce—belligerent. Don't forget—the tougher you are the less likely that anyone will want to fight you.

And be warned against the insidious fifth columnist. This is the quiet, subtle foe—the snake-in-the-grass who, with a pretence at friendliness, says "Ah, be fair now. See both sides."

Scorn him; cut him dead. Whenever was a good barracker built on such a theory? This is a new and scurrilous doctrine, designed to bruise the old traditions of the game.

Don't let any appeal to sentiment throw you out of your stride. If your own champion and favorite is off his day, be true to yourself! Don't pamper him. Abuse the mug. Curse him. He's out there to win for you. Tell him to get into it—to use his weight. Tell him to flatten Jack Dyer. Let him think you'd show 'em all what was what if you were out there. From the ground he can't see you're only five feet and as skinny as a swan's neck.

Here's another point—save your high-pressure abuse, your worst epithets for the biggest and toughest player in the enemy eighteen. It impresses the crowd and there is still no record of a footballer being game enough to leap the fence and attack a first-grade barracker.

THE WILD ONE

By Mopsy Fraser, from *Wild Men of Football* by Jack Dyer and Brian Hansen.

Collingwood! How we Richmond players hated them. And there they were, three of the mightiest Magpies of them all. The fabulous and feared Twomey brothers, all lined up against Richmond like wooden soldiers. Pat, Mick and Bill flexed their muscles, expanded their chests and smirked confidence as the umpire bounced the ball.

The leather shot straight to Bill and he sprinted towards me at full speed while I charged at maximum revs at him. There was a bone-jarring smack as my shoulder slapped him straight down the middle, and I'll always cherish his "EErraaagh" of agony as he hurtled to the turf. Off the ground went the No. 1 Magpie and then there were only two.

Brothers Pat and Mick were far from happy about his untimely departure and said some pretty choice things about me and I didn't take kindly to the expressions. Pat stuck his head out during a ball-up and again said things that no redhead could tolerate. As the ball moved in the vicinity of his head I let fly, accidentally missed the ball and smacked him a beauty and down he went.

Trainers escorted him from the ground and then there was only one ropeable Twomey. We came together near the boundary line and Mick went sailing into the fence. Then there were none, and the entire Twomey clan was wiped out for the day.

Boy, that Collingwood crowd! It wouldn't have been so bad if I had done the deed at Richmond. Probably they'd have made me mayor. At Victoria Park the atmosphere was decidedly ugly and, to cap it all, a Richmond official flattened the reserve umpire on the boundary. The crowd went wild. A soldier jumped the fence and ran at the Richmond official, but my timing was good and I added him to my list. The police were nice enough to supply me with an escort from the field.

Jack Dyer and I waited in the dressing-rooms for an hour after the match. Jack, too, had been up to a bit of mischief. Normally an hour is ample time for even the most irate fans to go home. We sent Roy Wright out to scout and he came back white-faced: "Don't go out there. There's a tremendous mob there and they'll kill you." They just wouldn't go, so finally we decided to brave the mob with our police escort. The Collingwood toughies milled around us, pushing, shoving and punching the backs of our heads.

I told a police trooper to stick close. I was frightened they were going to tip over my car. Suddenly I couldn't help laughing. Dyer growled: "What's there to laugh about?"

"Well, here I am worrying about the car being turned over. Why should I? It's yours."

We got into the car as they continued to try and overturn it, and they even held the back wheels off the ground so we couldn't drive away. Somehow we got it going and left under a hail of stone and debris.

Trouble seemed to follow me all my football days. Reports, tribunal hearings and suspensions became commonplace.

I was rubbed out for 84 weeks all told in a pretty turbulent period. I'm not proud of that record—but I'm not ashamed of it, either. It was my way of playing football—HARD.

Sometimes I was fitted for offences that didn't happen, plenty of times I got away with murder. So over all it evens out. But 84 weeks! That's six full playing years and must be some sort of a record when you consider I missed three years by serving in the Army.

I didn't start senior football until I was 22 and I'm not quite sure how I got into the business. My father was a one-time full-forward for the Richmond seniors, but he didn't try to persuade me to take up the game. Yet some of my wayward football traits must come from my father.

After topping Oakleigh's goal-kicking for three years straight, he fell foul of the umpire one day and sat on the ball and refused to give it up. Something must have upset him. He was suspended and immediately retired from football. That's where he was different from me. I wouldn't have lasted very long if I had retired because of a suspension.

I went to Yarra Park school and football was only an occasional game, so I didn't do anything to set the world on fire. I could get up high for a mark and wasn't a bad kick, but there was nothing to show I would make a mark as a footballer. Still that could have been the fault of Alan Strang, the captain of the side, who later played for South Melbourne.

There wasn't much of me in those days, but I suspect he knew I was a better footballer than he and he wouldn't let me near the ball. With little or no encouragement football was the last thought in my mind when I quit school and set about getting myself a crust.

When I was 19 my father intruded for the first time, grabbed me by the ear and marched me to Richmond. He probably thought I needed the exercise. That was 1940, the war years. To this stage I had kicked more paper footballs around Collingwood and Richmond streets than I had real footballs. That was my football background, hardly a background for League football.

Somehow I made the supplementary list at Richmond and managed to get a regular game with the seconds, either full-forward or centre half-forward. That competition was pretty strong.

The seniors and seconds were two different mobs, and I didn't have much to do with the Jack Dyer tribe. But I was a keen eavesdropper on Dyer because he was captain-coach of Richmond and the biggest name in football.

Finally he spoke to me: "Listen, you're as skinny as a rake. Your father was a real footballer, but you don't seem to be showing the right interest. Put on some weight and get into the game.'' He kept needling me, but I ended all discussion on my football future by joining the Army and that put me out of business until 1945. It was a drastic way of following Jack's order to put on weight.

My attitude was different when I rejoined the Tigers in '45. I was pushing 13 stone, but felt at my physical peak and believed I would now make the grade. The ball chased me in the practice games and I made a good impression on Captain Blood.

I made the senior side and clashed with Carlton in my first match. A tough initiation, because they won the flag that year in the bloodbath Grand Final against South Melbourne.

Captain Blood, in his pre-match address, warned me: ''Watch this fellow Bob Chitty on the forward flank. He'll do anything. Don't put your head out or he'll send it into the grandstand.''

Chitty was one of the roughest, toughest characters the game has produced. He was just luckier than me with tribunals.

There was more than ordinary fire in that first match. No love was lost between Carlton's coach, Perc. Bentley, and our Captain Blood. It stemmed from a row when Bentley was at Richmond.

Dyer started the game with a blast against Bentley: ''Don't let that renegade beat us. He'll send Chitty right at us, so be ready to give it back.''

The game wasn't long in progress when Chitty crashed a Richmond star and the Tiger was carried off with a broken leg.

Then I bent down to tie up a boot lace. There was a sudden squall of wind, but I didn't take much notice of it.

A Richmond player said: ''My God, you were lucky. Chitty threw a Sunday punch right from his toes. How did it miss? It should have sent your head out of the ground.'' That sudden squall had been a Chitty swish and the fact that he missed almost tore his arm out his socket.

They reckon he smirked as he threw it. Luckily for me, Chitty was on his way out then, and so was his timing. That was the one and only shot I gave him at me.

Dyer sent Les Jones after Chitty, just to dissuade the Carlton boy from going after our fellows. Jones was a big, strong type who could pick up a bag of spuds under each arm. He grabbed Chitty and hurled him round and around in an aeroplane spin, then tossed him 10 yards to the turf. But you couldn't hurt

Chitty. He got up laughing and went on crashing our boys until Carlton won by a point. Chitty may have been a bad boy, but he was as game as they come.

One week he sliced some fingers off in an accident and still fronted for the Saturday game, with his replaced fingers in a special guard. The game wasn't long under way when he tore off the guard, saying: "The damn thing gets in the road." He played on as though there was nothing wrong with his fingers.

My football days were almost numbered when the Army released me in 1945. That cagey Melbourne coach, Checker Hughes, claimed I had lived in Melbourne territory for three years and hadn't played football. He forced me to train with Melbourne. They wanted me to play with them, but I would never have joined that team. They weren't my type. I was a working man. It was only a Hughes bluff. Just as I was about to quit football I found the rules still made me a Richmond player.

In those early days of '45 I was a clean, ball-playing footballer with never an umpire looking crossly at me. How that changed.

I didn't have a clue about how to go into a pack and get the ball. The word filtered back to me that Dyer thought I was shirking the issue. "Having moments of fear", was the way he put it. Jack had brought a tradition of fearless and hard-hitting football to Richmond. But this tradition is a bit hard for a lightly framed youngster to follow, particularly when he didn't know the art of tough-man football. So I guess I played the fringes as often as I could. It was all right for Dyer. He knew all the tricks and he looked as though he was cast in iron. Still, from the start of my football career to the finish, he always had the power to lift my game.

His pre-match speech never failed to have us going out with a cold determination to win. In fairness to him, he wasn't trying to make me a basher. Often he told me to take things easy, that I could win a Brownlow Medal if I could control my temper. Some things are impossible. It wasn't that I was so nasty, but I can't blame Dyer for my becoming a football baddie.

It was in me all the time. If somebody mistreated me, I went mad. That probably brought about most of my trouble. Jack had plenty of control over himself and waited for the right moment before levelling a bloke out. I did it at the first opportunity. That's probably why I was spelled for 84 games during my career and Jack missed only four.

In the dressing-rooms he never told us to go out and get an opponent. He waited until we got on the field and then, as often as not, he did the job himself. He used to pick them well. Somebody would burst from a pack, head down, and he'd call: "Here's a chance!" CRASH! He wasn't often wrong.

Probably one of the main reasons he figured I was frightened stemmed from my first match, against Collingwood, his pet hate. He didn't know it, but I used to move around with the Collingwood fellows and lived almost within the shadows of the Collingwood ground. They were tough fellows and I knew they carried out their threats. They weren't pleased with me when I went to Richmond instead of Collingwood.

Before the ball bounced in that first game, the Uttings, Pannam and the Richards were giving me hell. "Traitor" . . . "We'll get you later" . . . "We'll knock your head off." Those are samples of their menaces. They meant it, too.

Dyer was running about the ground, talking to us and threatening the opposition as he yelled to me: "Don't take any notice of these mugs. We'll fix them for you." We had some tough players, but I was worried. "I've got to live over there," I said, and played pretty quietly that day.

Captain Blood hated Collingwood, and that hate became infectious and from that day on I never tried as hard against any side as I did against Collingwood.

During that first season I clashed with South Melbourne's Laurie Nash on his comeback trail. He took a mark and, in his usual fashion, smirked at me: "Which foot will I kick it with— left or right?"

"Kick it with your big head," I snarled back at him. So he left-footed it through the centre. For all his scoffing, he didn't have a kick after that and I guess I was lucky the old boy was coming down the other side of the hill. Trouncing Nash does a lot for your confidence, even an ageing Nash. It proved that it doesn't matter how good you are. When you're too old it's time to get out.

At the end of that season, Dyer took me aside: "It looks like you're a bit frightened. Get some weight on and come back next year with a bit of fight." I think he was harsh. I wasn't frightened. I just didn't have the knowhow.

But he did me a lot of good. I went timbercutting over the lay-off and it made a tremendous difference. Even in the '46 season I was still a ball player, but I knew a lot more about the finer points of retaliation. There were a lot of whacks, kicks and punches in the back of the head I had to repay.

Full-forward and centre half-forward were my key positions for most of the year. I did a few shabby things, and probably the worst was at Footscray.

They had a backman named Kelly, who had beautiful hair. It made me envious. Always looking for some means to upset an opponent, I seized on a couple of hair clips he had pinning back his locks. "You must be a sheila," I laughed at him and, for good measure, gave a tug.

What a shock! I thought I had scalped him, because his complete mop of hair came away in my hand and left nothing on his head but gleaming skin. Honestly, I didn't know it, otherwise I'd have pulled it off earlier. You should have seen that fellow fume. It had the desired effect and put him right off his game. But I'll tell you something about the fellow. He was tough, and there was nothing girlish about him. He was just self-conscious about his naked nut.

Not that I should scoff about a man's hair or lack of it. I had a thick crop and on wet days I had to use hairpins to keep it down. The well-known press cartoonist Sam Wells always depicted me as a long stick with a mop on top. From that came the nickname Mophead, later to become Mopsy.

In my second year, and, backed by extra weight, I started mixing a bit of rough stuff with my football.

One of my main attributes was the ability to fly high for a mark and hang in the air if I went a bit early. To do it I climbed the backs of other players. For laughs I did it at practice—which wasn't too well received by the Richmond players who were scraped by my stops. I went to the well once too often and soared up the back of Skinny Titus. I was in full flight above when he reached up, grabbed my leg and gave it a quick twist. "You're with old-timers now, son," he called above the crack of my leg.

I landed like a lame duck, took a couple of paces and my leg collapsed under me. They shoved the cartilage back into place and I limped off. Later it collapsed again as I walked across St. Kilda Junction. Luckily it was at the end of the season and I had time for an operation and was back in business for the opening game of the next season.

Marking and kicking, I was really burning, but I was in the

kicking horrors. Downfield I could pass the ball with deadly accuracy from 50 yards. I reckon I was a darned good kick, but near the goals I sprayed the ball everywhere and couldn't land a goal.

The turning point in my career came at St. Kilda. The Saints' centre half-back was Test cricketer Keith Miller—a pretty formidable sort of character on a football field. In the first quarter I was all over him. I marked them one-handed, sidewards, upside down. He started patting me on the back, and when they do that you've really got them licked.

I scored 14 times in that quarter. One goal and 13 behinds. The second quarter was no better. By half-time I'd taken more marks than I had taken in any match, but Dyer was fuming.

"Ratbags go to the backline," he roared across the room at me. "Aw, fair go, Jack," I begged. "Let me stay and I'll kick seven this quarter."

"I said ratbags to the backline," he hollered.

I got the message. So off I went to centre half-back, never to return. It made me. With the straight-through play of defence, my pace and marking gave me a tremendous edge. I was bulldozing through the packs, knocking them down like bowling pins.

Some critics of Dyer, although admitting he had great success as a playing coach, blast him as a non-playing coach. Well, there's a good reason why he didn't have as much success—a side can ill-afford to lose a player as great as Jack and he couldn't find a good enough player to fill his boots.

It was strange playing without him. Something vital in our machinery was missing.

Playing in defence, Jack and I often combined to unsettle the forwards. Against Melbourne we spied Lance Arnold tearing downfield with Jack and I converging from either side. What a beautiful sandwich. Two near 15-stoners hurtling in and a nice juicy Demon steak in the middle. Arnold was in real trouble.

Jack roared: "Now." At full pace we crashed in. But at the last minute Arnold took fright and I'll never know how he did it, but he jumped straight up in the air above us.

Boooomm! Dyer and I crashed together. And if you've ever been hit by Dyer at full pace you could still be in hospital while you are reading this.

We both flopped to the ground and a shaky, white-faced Arnold started to make himself scarce. "Chase the—," ordered Dyer. I couldn't get up. "Chase him yourself," I gasped. It was taking a risk, because Jack can get pretty hot. But he suddenly saw the humor of the situation and started laughing his head off.

The medical officers were kill-or-cure boys in those days. I went to the Richmond doctor one day with a large carbuncle on my wrist. He went to his kitchen and I heard him fossicking around. I thought he was getting needles, injections, pain killers and antiseptics. He emerged with a carving knife; it went flash, and I was minus a carbuncle. "You'll be right in a couple of hours," he said as the color drained from my face. No bandages, no nothing. I just walked out with a gaping wound. Two hours later all the pain was gone and I was as good as gold.

Another doctor was sent to Queensland for that infamous mudbath football carnival. We had to queue up for anti-tetanus injections. His needles must have been a family heirloom. I reckon they must have passed down through generations of horse doctors. He had to put the needle against your skin and then hammer it, to pierce the skin. For days the boys' arms were so sore they couldn't lift them over their heads.

When we played South Melbourne I always found myself on that great Brownlow Medallist, Ron Clegg. His wife, Billy, used to sit in the stand and watch our every move. She was his greatest fan. At the first opportunity I used to grab Smokey's footy nicks and rip them off him. Then I'd wave the remnants triumphantly at Billy in the stand. She used to cry with rage.

About that time I had a clash with Geoff McGivern, a star Melbourne player, and the newspapers gave me hell. Some even declared I should be rubbed out for life. None of them saw the incident. They haven't a clue what happened and I never bothered to tell them.

Dyer had given me a roast at half-time for playing in front of McGivern. It was a shocker of a blast and I went out seething. In the first few moments McGivern went up for the ball and left the trunk of his body completely unprotected. He was slightly built and I caught him with the shoulder, REPEAT, the shoulder, right under the heart. It was completely legitimate.

I thought I'd cut him in two. He looked dead and the crowd started howling as I looked down at his prostrate body. It was over in a flash and nobody knew what happened. The screaming from the crowd must have woken the goal umpire, because I saw him moving out towards me. I set off at top pace, only to run into Dyer, who moaned: "What have you done now?"

"Let me get going," I squealed and raced off with the umpire after me. I burned him off, but he did a pretty good job over the first couple of hundred yards. The roaring from the crowd was so tremendous the field umpire had to stop the game. Norm Smith, who didn't know what happened, said: "You shouldn't have done that." I hadn't done a thing, so I snarled back: "You're the next."

Then the dailies started their howl and I thought I would get life. There were screaming headlines for weeks after I beat the charge. That was the trouble, the crowd hated me so much they would squeal even at a legitimate charge, and there were plenty. There were times when I felt every spectator at the ground was after me. They could really yell the skies down. All the same, I loved the game. I enjoyed clashing with the champs of the time, and there was an abundance of them.

I had my share of success against the greats. It was always a picnic against Ron Clegg or Fred "Troubles" Flanagan, and there have been few greater players than these two. There were plenty of meetings with Troubles.

In the last game of one season, Troubles was leading in a big cash newspaper award. He was a point or two ahead of Essendon's Bill Hutchinson. The game was at Geelong and the Cat coach, Reg Hickey, who knew I had an edge on Flanagan, moaned: "Not you again, Mopsy. Couldn't you have missed the bus just this once?" I grinned.

As we took up our positions, I said to Troubles: "You can win that money today for half." Troubles complained: "Aw, cut it out, Mopsy, make it a tenner."

"No, I want half."

Flanagan countered: "Oh, well, in that case I'll just have to win it off my own boot." I scoffed: "You know you never get votes against me." We went at it. I got the votes for best afield. Hutchy got the best at Essendon and Troubles missed the cash.

A lot of work goes into beating a champion like Flanagan. I would phone him before a match and say: "Bad luck, Freddy—you're on me again." Or I'd send him a telegram: "It's me again. You needn't bother turning up."

On the ground, I'd say: "You'd better get down the backline, you won't get a kick here." Tossed in were other pleasantries, a couple of jerks on his nicks and I was off on a great day. Troubles would try to ignore me, but he couldn't fire when I was on him. Another tactic was to tell him he wasn't looking well and, sure enough, he'd start feeling ill.

IT'S A SIN TO LOSE

By Lou Richards, from *Boots and All*, 1963.

Just on every winter Saturday for thirty-seven years, an average-sized, fresh-faced man, invariably dressed in a blue single-breasted suit, and with a hat with its brim turned up, perched jauntily on his head, would walk out of the Collingwood dressing-room and amble down the enclosed 'race' to the coach's bench inside the arena.

As he made his entry before the crowd, the Collingwood supporters would call out: 'How many goals will we win by today?' ... 'Are the boys fit?' ... 'We'll kill 'em, won't we?' and all the usual enthusiastic chit-chat that flows from a crowd of expectant barrakcers.

Throughout the game he sat there, fighting out every kick by wrenching and twisting his hat in his hands, while every Collingwood player on the ground would have given more than a penny for his thoughts.

Because on what this grey-haired man thought rested the ambitions not only of the players but of the entire Collingwood Football Club. ... That is why they called Jock McHale 'The Prince of Coaches'.

When people ask: 'What is the Collingwood secret?' ... 'Why have they been so successful?' I feel the answer is extremely hard to pin-point, but, in finding the reason, one of the starting points must be Jock McHale.

Tradition is one of the foremost ingredients of the Magpie formula, and old Jock not only kept tradition going, he created it himself.

The club is steeped in tradition, which started in 1892 when Britannia merged into Collingwood. Five years later they won the V.F.A. Premiership, and then became one of the eight clubs that formed the V.F.L. in 1897.

Right from the early stages they were successful, and in the first fifteen years of the V.F.L. they were never out of the final four—and in 1962 their record during their sixty-six years in the League stood at forty-four final four appearances, during which they had won thirteen premierships . . . a record unequalled in the V.F.L.

This early success gave them tradition that grew and grew, to the extent that it became a sin to lose.

When you came off the field after being defeated you had a feeling of guilt, as if you had committed the greatest crime of all time. When some of the weaker clubs lose a match, after putting up a pretty good performance, everybody is happy, and they go around congratulating one another. At Collingwood you must win every game, even a Grand Final, by fifteen goals before everyone is happy. They're not satisfied to get into a Grand Final, they want you to win it . . . every Grand Final . . . every match you play you *must* win.

This ruthless outlook started with the first secretary, Mr. E. W. Copeland, after whom the club's best-and-fairest trophy is named. He was evidently a very strict disciplinarian who wouldn't stand any funny business from the players. If they got out of order at all he was the first to pull them into line.

When Jock McHale became coach of the side he adhered to the same policy. In the early days they never had a coach, the captain looked after the training, and Jock as captain was in charge from 1913 to 1920, but when he retired as a player in 1920 he became the first coach in the club's history—in fact they've only had three in the entire history of the club! Jock, Bevyn Woods (who lasted about a fortnight) and Phonse Kyne.

In 1961 they had a very poor season, and most clubs would have been content to make 1962 their year of rebuilding, but not Collingwood—they wanted to rebuild and be premiers in the one year—they were over-ambitious and finished seventh, but this was still a jump up the ladder. But perhaps this type of thinking is one of the reasons they are so successful.

Once a player joins the club he becomes imbued with this spirit, and he comes to automatically feel that he has let the side down when they lose . . . . McHale was one of the men who were instrumental in Collingwood adopting this attitude towards football.

One look at Jock was enough to tell how the team had fared. At the end of the game he would wait at the top of the player's race—if you won he would be all smiles, and his face would be lit up like Luna Park—but if you lost he would still be standing at the race all right—with his back to you and a look of utter disgust on his face. It was a folly to walk past him, a wiser tactic was to run past as quickly as you could, unless he turned round and said something to you.

I think one of the most typical examples of his 'after-game' mood happened to the famous Jack Regan. Although Jack was one of the greatest full-backs of all time, he first went to Collingwood as a half-forward. In a match against Fitzroy he took a mark when Collingwood were three points down, with 'time on' being played, and like a number of young players who have taken a mark when their side was in this position he became very nervous.

Jack didn't know what to do. He was in a dilemma, he couldn't make up his mind whether to punch it to Syd Coventry or kick it himself.

Finally, he appealed to Syd: "What will I do?"

'Kick the bloody thing, and make sure you put it through the bloody middle,' snapped Syd.

Jack was later to become renowned for his glorious kicking, but this day it went off the side of his boot and through for a point, and Collingwood lost the game!

He was down-hearted as he walked into the rooms after the game, he felt that he had lost the game. The first fellow he spotted sitting in the corner of the room with his hat all twisted up, and a face a mile long, was old Jock, so, being a young fellow, Regan tried to be the perfect gentleman, and he strode straight over to Jock and blurted out: 'Sorry, Mr. McHale.'

The old hands nearby shuddered in anticipation, as Jock reacted rather violently by yelling: 'Go and throw yourself in the bloody Yarra!'

This was his entire attitude towards the side and players when they lost, in fact he was a shocking loser, but by the Tuesday night when you turned up for practice he would have forgotten it, and he'd be back in harness, talking about how we would win the next game. Once Jock had this feeling about him it seemed to become contagious throughout the club. The committee, officials and players all caught it off Jock.

I don't know whether they were frightened to smile in front of him or whether they felt the same way; perhaps they were a bit scared of him and felt it was better to be in the same mood as him. This has caused considerable controversy with other clubs, because when Collingwood lost they developed a habit of not going into the opposition rooms, but, despite the bad feeling this sometimes costs, I still feel that this is one of the reasons why they have been so successful . . . they take their defeats seriously.

In my early days at Collingwood we were having a bad trot, so three players—Jack Burns, who is the present secretary; Mac Holten, now a Member of Federal Parliament, and I—decided that it would be a good idea if the players had a meeting. We felt it would help the players to get better acquainted, and we could thrash out why we were playing poorly.

It was highly secret, and only the players were supposed to know, but old Jock got to hear of it, and when we arrived on the Tuesday night to have the meeting he was there waiting for us. He accused the three of us of being Commos trying to cause a revolution in the club, and told us it had never happened in his forty years with the club, it wasn't likely to happen while he was still there.

He polished us off by saying: 'Now buzz off!', with which he kicked us out of the room, and there was no meeting. This was the way Jock worked. He ruled the club with an iron hand, and stood over the players, yet behind it all he was a very fair-minded chap.

Jock was a brewery foreman. If we won he'd take the players who he thought went well up to the brewery, where he would produce the keys to the brewery bar, and 'shout'. If we lost he would often still take some of the boys up, but he refused to talk to anyone until after he had had about six pots, and then he became a little more expansive and even managed a friendly word or two!

Up at Carlton they still talk about the 1945 Grand Final against South as being a rough match. There were plenty of players reported, and it was rough in this regard, but the match we played against the Blues the week before was just as rough and tough, only not as many players were reported. It often happens that way. Because players are reported it doesn't necessarily mean that a game is rough. It's more of a spiteful game when that happens.

However, this particular match was a real rough-and-tough affair. Carlton had Bob Chitty, who in my opinion was the toughest player who ever pulled on a boot, in their side, despite the fact that he had cut his finger off at work. When he turned up at training on the Tuesday the selectors naturally thought that he wouldn't be able to play, but he astounded them by announcing: 'I'll be able to play all right, I'm getting a metal guard to put over the top of it.'

Sure enough, he ran on to the ground on the Saturday with a special metal guard over his finger. When he came off at half-time the selectors asked how his finger was. He growled: 'No bloody good. This metal guard is getting in the way'. With that, he flicked the metal guard off, and when he came back at the half-time interval he was sporting his sawn-off finger in the raw!

Chitty was minding Des Fothergill, and doing everything but hit him with the grandstand and a goal-post. He was bumping him, pulling him by the hair and grabbing him by the athletic support, with the result that Fothergill was completely rattled and couldn't get a kick, and, to be perfectly honest, Des started to 'turn it up'.

I suppose he had a reason for it, but he wasn't a small chap by any means, he was about 5ft. 9in. and weight about 14½ stone—Chitty was a tough customer, but he certainly wasn't much bigger.

We were in a bad position at half-time, and when we went inside Jock McHale was sitting on a bench, looking very disgruntled. Fothergill went up to him and asked: 'What will I do, Mr. McHale?' . . . Jock looked up with despair, and quietly replied: 'You're a man . . . aren't you?' . . . and he let it go at that.

Was Jock's reputation as a coach justified? I think it was, because Collingwood's record while he was in charge of them was outstanding. He certainly didn't believe in the theory that you could learn something on the ground, irrespective of what age you were, which was a flaw in his make-up, in my opinion, because it doesn't matter what age you are in football you can always learn something.

He felt he couldn't teach you anything because you should have learned how to play before you arrived in senior football. He never ever tried to teach me anything; perhaps he thought I was a genius when I arrived, as he did with many other players. Whether this was the secret of his success I don't know, because he did allow players to learn for themselves by following the advice of the big names at the club.

He also had the reputation of being able to pick when a player was perfectly fit, and he had the happy knack of resting this player so that he would come up fresh for the Saturday.

During a game he often made some fantastic moves. The theory he worked on was that if a player was not going so well in a certain position then shift him somewhere else and he may do better there. There have been many, many examples of this.

At South one day Jack Hamilton wasn't getting a kick at fullback . . . he was being murdered, so Jock decided to shift him to a half-forward flank. Jack looked as much like a half-forward as I do a ruckman, but he kicked four goals, and we won the match.

These were the sort of changes Jock thrived on, they were unorthodox, but they paid off, and Collingwood have always followed Jock's lead in doing this. I feel that there is something to it, because if you move a player from a position where he isn't going too well, and put him somewhere else where another player also hasn't been going well, they can't do any worse than they were before, and I'm sure Jock always had this in mind. Collingwood, you must agree, have made more fantastic moves than any other side—and they usually get away with it.

Jock's first love after his family was Collingwood. He lived for the club, and I know that on many occasions he was offered fantastic sums of money to leave and coach other sides, but he always refused, and continued to take £3 a week, the same as the players.

Although he felt life wasn't worth living for the first hour or so after a defeat, he very rarely got a 'set' on players. This was very much in his favor, because even though a loss upset him far more than the average person, he was tremendously loyal to his players, and he always stuck up for them.

Most players feared Jock McHale, yet respected him. He would never let the players stand over him, but he was very kind, considerate and fair when it came to a serious decision as far as the player was concerned, particularly when a player wanted to leave the club. If he felt the player had a little more football left in him he would want him to stay, but if the player was still determined to go somewhere else Jock would make sure that wherever the player went he got the best of deals.

And that's what old Jock always strived to get Collingwood—the best of deals. He was as much Collingwood as Collingwood itself, and through his knowledge of the game, built up over a long period of years, he gave tremendous service to the club—and to football.

At the same time as the McHale era Collingwood also had a great patron, a man small in stature, who became one of the most famous men in Victoria . . . the late John Wren Snr.

A man who started from nothing, yet built up a fortune, Mr. Wren was an avid Magpie who idolized players who kicked goals. The chap that kicked a goal always got a 'little something' in the hand after the game, but the poor old back man who battled hard never seemed to crack it.

He was a tremendous patron of the club, and gave large amounts of money. I know that on many occasions players who were short of money during the week went to John and asked for a loan, and also I know that they have never paid him back to this day. They probably thought: 'He's got plenty, he won't miss it,' but I'm quite sure Wren knew they were doing this but didn't worry about it.

Many people have criticized him in the past, but I feel Collingwood owe him tremendous gratitude, and he most certainly won himself a big part in the club tradition.

When star full-forward Ron Todd left to go to Williamstown Wren offered to give him more money than he was going to get at Williamstown, but apparently Todd had signed a contract and couldn't do anything about it. These were the sort of things that John Wren did; he was always there with his hand in his pocket whenever the club needed money. In later years I know that he gave £1,000 each season to be divided up amongst the players in the way of best-and-fairest trophies.

North Melbourne was nearly always a happy hunting-ground for me, and one day after I kicked seven goals the first person I bumped into when I came off the ground was Mr. Wren.

'Good game, young Richards,' he said, as he thrust his hand deep in his trouser pocket. He then proffered his right hand, and as I gasped it to shake hands, I felt somehting slip into my palm. I didn't look until I walked back to my nail on the wall, and then I saw it was a pound note. I thought: 'Oh, well, the poor old devil must be going broke, we can't expect too much from him.' Later when I went outside to meet Edna, my fiancée, she asked: 'What did the kindly old gentleman give you?' When I told her a pound she said: 'What? Is he having a bad trot at the moment?' . . . It was typical of a woman, they always want more money.

I had forgotten about the incident the following week when we played St. Kilda, but the first man I bumped into after the game was again John Wren—I seemed to have the happy knack of bumping into him!

'How much did I give you last week, young Richards?' he enquired.

'A pound, Mr. Wren.'

He looked most perturbed, and immediately said: 'I made a terrible mistake, I meant to give you a fiver'.

I held my breath as he produced a huge wad of notes and peeled off a fiver. Once it was in my hand, I quickly regained my speech, and with all my natural innocence asked: 'Do you want your pound back?' . . . He told me I could keep it.

12
The Fifties: a decade of heroes

Perhaps because it is remote enough for the players to have retired, but close enough to remember some of them playing (or remember remembering), the 1950s are dominated by great players: John Coleman, Roy Wright, Bill Hutchison, Lou Richards, Bob Davis, and legendary coaches Dick Reynolds, Jack Dyer and Alan Killigrew. In part they reflect the dominance of Essendon, Geelong and Melbourne.

ROY WRIGHT—THE GENTLE GIANT

By John Dunn, *Herald*, April 1, 1955.

It is hard to imagine a footballer of the calibre of dual Brownlow Medallist Roy Wright ever being disheartened. But Wright was, very early in his career.

He was a follower, and at that time Richmond had a formidable line-up of big men, headed by Jack "Captain Blood" Dyer, Bill Morris and Les Jones.

Wright despaired of ever making the grade with the Tigers, and four times applied for a clearance to Hawthorn. He even went to the Glenferrie ground to look over the club rooms and meet the players.

But Richmond refused each application, so Wright had to stay. For five years he plugged on . . . playing this week, dropped the next . . . until he won a regular place with the firsts in 1951 . . . his sixth season with the club. He was then 22.

However, Wright's worries were not only centred on just getting into the team. Frequently when he "made it" an injury would put him out.

"I guess I just grew up too quickly", says Wright, looking back over those early years.

"It was a case of being too big too soon.

"I was 14½ stone in those days and a sitting shot for all the knocks in the game. I didn't have the experience to ride the bumps. There was too much of me to be looked after properly."

Altogether it was a dismal start to a career which was later to include two Brownlow Medals (1952 and 1954), the winning of Richmond's best and fairest award last season and selection in three Victorian sides—1952–53–54.

Actually Wright almost did not enter league football. He trained at Camberwell for four weeks before coming to Richmond.

But his great love for the Tigers and his hero worship of Jack Dyer prevailed—Wright's family were all great Richmond supporters, "although Dad did have a liking for Geelong because we lived at Portarlington, near there, for three years.

"But when Morrie Fleming and Pat Kennelly came out to see me I almost tripped over them to sign the form and get to Richmond," he explained.

Wright was born at North Kew on February 23, 1929, and was educated at Kew State School, East Kew Central School and Melbourne High School.

He did not play football until he stripped with a few of his mates for North Kew in the Eastern Suburban League in 1945.

He was more interested in cricket and was quite a handy player for Kew thirds.

One of Wright's opponents in his first league game was Australian Test all-rounder and vice-captain Keith Miller.

That, of course, was against St. Kilda, towards the end of 1946.

Wright started off in the ruck that day against Ernie McIntyre and Reg Garvin, and was later moved to full forward, where he opposed Miller.

"Miller was a good footballer, but they were all tough that day," Wright recalled.

Wright played the last six games with the firsts. He also won the best and fairest award in the junior league, even though he had played only eight games for North Kew.

Then came the long seasons of "ins and outs". In 1947 he had a leg injury and also hurt a bone at the base of his spine.

All this coming on top of sickness when a child—he had weak knees, necessitating splints at nine and rheumatic fever when 11—demanded tremendous courage.

But he answered every challenge and at the end of that season gained his biggest football thrill to that time—playing in a final on the M.C.G.

It was against Fitzroy and the Maroons won, but that did not dim Wright's appreciation of playing before a League semi-final crowd there.

The same year Wright played with Richmond Seconds in their grand final against North Melbourne. Once again Richmond lost, "but the thrill was still there".

Wright says he did not really start to settle down until the 1951 season. Richmond lost Bill Morris to Box Hill that year and a lot depended on Wright.

He rose to the task splendidly, became associated with first rover Bill Wilson, and never looked back.

"I didn't get 'cork' legs any more, and that season and the next were free from injuries," Wright said.

In that next season—1952—Wright won his first Brownlow Medal and tied ith Des Rowe for Richmond's best and fairest trophy.

But injury had not finished with Roy Wright. It struck him down the next season.

"I just couldn't take a trick," he said. "I broke my nose, thumb, split the webbing in my hand (four stitches), and had concussion three times, once having to get four stitches in the head."

However, Wright rose above adversity for his best season ever last year. He won the Brownlow Medal in a canter and also Richmond's best and fairest award.

Wright says his Brownlow wins have been his biggest football thrills. But not far behind is that semi-final appearance back in 1947. And he's living for the day when the Tigers will again make the finals.

"It could quite possibly be this year," he said. "We've now got the best bunch of footballers since I've been at Richmond and we'll be very hard to beat.

"Footscray will have a good side again, but I think there might be a big levelling out among the clubs.

"Last year you could never be sure who you'd beat and who you wouldn't and I think it will be the same—or more so—this year."

Wright names Jack Mueller as his hardest opponent. Not far behind are Arthur Olliver, Jack Graham, Bob Chitty, "Bluey"

212

McLure, Don Cordner and Phonse Kyne.

In a special category is Denis Cordner.

"He's really got me beat," Wright confessed. "He's a wonderful footballer and the best wet weather man I've seen.

"Just how he does it I don't know. He seems to put up those long arms and funnel the ball on to his chest."

Wright considers John Gill the best prospect in League football and forecasts a wonderful future for him.

The most complete footballer he has seen is Les Foote, with Bob Rose almost on terms with him.

"Foote has everything a footballer could wish for," he said. "Rose can be so destructive. He'll be as quiet as a church mouse, then all of a sudden he'll kick four or five goals, one after the other, enough to win a game."

Wright is learning the hotel trade—he is now a barman at Doug Elliot's Doutta Galla Hotel at Newmarket—but although he serves beer all day, he is a teetotaller.

He smokes only to keep his weight down. Just now he weighs 16st. 1lb. and is 6ft. 2in. tall.

He plays a lot of golf during the summer, but his main exercise—summer and winter—is walking.

"There's nothing like it to keep the muscles in trim," Wright says.

"If I'm stiff, I just walk and walk. At week-ends I go out rabbiting and walk for miles across the paddocks. It's wonderful."

Wright, who has played 125 games with Richmond, has found that the style of play has changed a lot during that time.

"There's no room in the game these days for anyone who hasn't got a bit of pace," he said.

"Collingwood and Geelong introduced the fast play-on game, and the other teams are following suit.

"I haven't got much toe, but I can usually keep going at a reasonable rate throughout a match.

"We had to change our style at Richmond. Alby Pannam had a hard job. He had to change tempo and pressure and adapt the men to it. He's succeeded, though, so watch out for the Tigers from now on."

Wright has only one misgiving about the coming season— he'll be without his partner Billy Wilson.

"I'm going to miss Billy", Wright said, with a touch of sadness.

"We had developed a fine understanding, and that takes some working up.

"There are no signals as some people might think. We just seem to know where each other will be.

"But I'll probably have young Ron Branton with me. He's an extra good rover.

"I'm quite happy about the coming season, and I hope to realise an ambition and play with Richmond in a grand final."

BOB DAVIS—THE GEELONG FLYER

By Alf Brown, *Herald*, April 10, 1981.

Soon after he started playing for Geelong in 1948, Bob Davis earned the name the Geelong Flyer.

At first he was fast around the packs. Later when he realised that his 15 stone (95 kg) propelled at speed was almost a lethal weapon, he was just as fast through them.

When Bob retired from football his friends continued to call him the Geelong Flyer. It was because of Bob's skilled, controlled, but frighteningly fast dashes to Melbourne.

His best time from Geelong to Melbourne by car, it's about 72 km (45 miles), was 27½ minutes.

Some friendly warnings by police did not slow up lead-foot Davis. But three suspensions of his driving licence and a belated maturity have combined to increase considerably 52-year-old Bob's travelling time to Melbourne.

"I used to drive good, big cars; now I drive good, little cars," says Bob, explaining how he has pushed aside the temptation to speed.

"I realise that my behavior was wrong. Being a footballer is all very glamorous. But the time comes when you have to return to reality; remember that the laws for footballers are the same as for everyone else.

"I wish I had today's head on my 1950 body. But the past few years have been good for me. I suddenly grew up. I reckon the fact that I did not drink saved me from a lot of trouble in the long years that it took me to settle down."

Bob always has been strong against alcohol.

I remember in 1963 when Bob coached Geelong to a premiership. A former champion from another club who was coherent but very wobbly claimed me near the Geelong bus outside the M.C.G. We had a yarn and then he tottered across the park towards Richmond Station.

Bob recognised the champion of the thirties and dived into the bus. Next second he was herding his players into the park.

"Look at it, look at it, that's what booze does to you," Bob yelled, pointing to the drunken star.

Bob does not smoke and the only time he drinks is at a Geelong premiership dinner. Which makes it a long time between glasses of champagne—which he does like.

Bob belies the adage that a proficiency at the billiard table denotes an ill-spent youth. Bob will back himself against almost anyone at Kelly pool and snooker. He grew up alongside a billiard table.

Bob was born in Golden Point in Ballarat. Later his family moved to Clunes, a small town in the Ballarat area. His father owned the Clunes barber shop, billiard saloon and was the local SP bookmaker. It was the focal point of the town. Bob's earliest memories are about billiards, snooker, racehorses and football.

Bob is literally a born gambler. His grandfather was a bookmaker. So was his father. All his life Bob has loved a punt.

The only thing that keeps Bob away from the races is his beloved football. Bob has been on many race-courses. He was even foolish enough to go to the races at Bangkok. He held his money in his hand, which was fortunate. When he came out of the betting ring every pocket had been sliced out with a razor blade.

He was more successful at Royal Ascot in 1979. His topper did not fall off once and he had the bookies cringing well before the last race.

Davis was a champion half-forward flanker. One of the best ever. He had everything—pace, skill, courage. He could mark and kick and although his mate, Lou Richards, has repeatedly stated that Davis can not think off the field, he had a quick, cool, calculating brain on it.

Late in his career, when Geelong was weak, Bob played everywhere. He starred in the centre, did well at centre half-back and played full-forward, full-back and ruck-rover.

Bob reckons one of his best games in defence was at centre half-back against Jack Collins, of Footscray.

"Jack got two kicks that day," recalls Bob. "One when I was down with cramp and the other when a teammate free-kicked him. But Jack goaled from both kicks."

Davis was in three great Geelong sides. It won premierships in 1951–52 but over confidence and inability to withstand Collingwood's ferocious 1953 grand final side cost it three flags in a row.

"Yes, I suppose we were lucky to win the 1951 flag from Essendon," Bob admits. "Essendon was without John Coleman who had been disqualified and we got in by 11 points. Coleman could have made the difference.

"Bernie Smith was magnificent that day, especially in the last quarter when Essendon attacked most of the time and kicked four goals to two."

(Bob does not mention that he was magnificent in that last quarter, too. But for them Essendon would have won).

"But we were on the verge of being a top side," says Bob. "We started an unbeaten run when we won the 12th game of the 1952 season. We were unbeaten until Collingwood defeated us at Geelong in the 14th round the following season.

"That gave us 23 consecutive wins. In that period we were invincible. That record never will be broken. Of course I'll bet on it; I'll lay you any odds you like.

"We should have won the premiership in 1953 but Collingwood knocked us off. We were too confident. No, I don't think the Magpies frightened us although they were fierce.

"I coached Geelong to a premiership in 1963 but overconfidence cost us games in the 1964–65 final series. We could have given the flag a fright in those years, too. The same thing happened last year. We finished at the top of the premiership list and lost both final games."

Bob will find plenty of people to disagree with him about those statements.

In 1964, Collingwood beat them in the preliminary final. Next year Essendon beat Geelong in the first semi-final to go on to win the premiership from fourth place.

As Richards often declares, maybe Bob does say the first thing which comes into his head.

Talking of Davis and Richards, they're an unlikely double. They are close friends despite the public verbal fights. Davis is straight man to Richards but is not the buffoon he portrays. He has a number of substantial assets to prove it.

Bob owns a motel which he has leased to former Richmond ruckman Michael Hammond. He built it years ago before property became an expensive hedge against inflation. He owes some of the motel-building idea to Richards.

"I stay at Louey's place on Thursday nights," explains Bob. "When he had the Phoenix Hotel I slept in a tiny room which was so small you could not close the door.

"I am better housed now that Lou is in Toorak.

"One night while we were watching the late, late movie Lou advised me to put any money I had into property. 'Even if you pay off only one brick a day, the property will eventually be yours,' he said. It's the best advice I've ever had."

Bob still can be, well, er, different. In 1979 he decided to take a year off from television and radio and get away from it all with his family.

Most people would have gone to Brisbane or farther north. But not Bob. He went to England.

"I had been in football since 1948 and I felt it necessary to get away from it all and live together as a family and not as Bob Davis, television stooge to Jack Dyer and Richards.

"It was to be a holiday but I got bored. I was fortunate to get a job with a progressive car group which had franchises for 11 different makes of cars. It worked so well I almost stayed in England.

"It gave me tremendous confidence. I found out I could do things without being Bob Davis, former Geelong captain and coach and football commentator.

"The car firm made me a generous offer to remain in England but I knocked it back. After all they don't play Australian Rules over there, do they?

"I was very lucky at the punt, too. I had a friend in England who owned horses and he had a big year. Yes, Royal Ascot in a topper was very, very nice."

As a footballer who played and excelled in most positions Bob met some great players. When he was a half-forward flanker the man who worried him most was Essendon Aboriginal defender, Norman McDonald.

"He was a great ballhandler and although he never seemed to

mind you he was always alongside you when it mattered," says Bob. "And he would whip the ball away from me, too.

"I was 15 stone (95 kg), McDonald was 12 stone (76 kg). Pound for pound he had to be the best defender I met."

I am delighted that Bob recalls McDonald. He was a great player and Melbourne rather than Essendon discovered him. Essendon played him on a wing but he did not click. Melbourne asked for permission to interview him; Essendon gave him a last chance in defence and he was sensational.

But back to footballer, punter, snooker player and shrewd businessman Davis. In the centre he met one opponent who stood out.

"Bill Twomey, of Collingwood, was magnificent," recalls Bob. "He had everything."

Bob has nightmares about playing at centre half-forward. A bloke named Ted Whitten was invariably horrible to him.

"Teddy had a nasty habit of breaking my cheekbones when he was standing alongside me," says Bob.

"I would be talking to Ted when the ball was at the other end of the ground and he would snap 'Shut up, Woofer' and let me have one. There had to be a more friendly way of shutting me up.

"Yes, I suppose Ron Barassi has to be the best ruck-rover although he did not have great talent. But as a sheer competitor he was tremendous. He rose to great heights by sheer guts and effort rather than ability.

"I remember in a game against Melbourne, it had a narrow lead. Norm Smith instructed Ron to keep the ball out of play. At boundary throw-ins Ron kept jumping over the big ruckmen and whacking the ball back to the boundary umpire. We could not get the ball away and Melbourne won.

"Sometimes John Coleman intrudes into my Whitten nightmares. He was unbeatable.

"In 1952, Essendon and Geelong played a game for premiership points in Brisbane. I started at full-back on Coleman. I could not get off him quick enough.

"He took one mark standing on my shoulder. Next time he stood on my head. He kicked two goals against me. He kicked 11 more on the four other players we tried on him.

"Coleman was a tremendous bloke. Because we did not drink we roomed together on State trips. Wherever we went John and

I were photographed. But mysteriously when the photos were published, poor old Bob Davis had been cut out. I was not even allowed to bask in the great man's shadow.

"Coleman was a great kick. I remember in Brisbane, John was taken to the Gabba Oval to demonstrate kicking to the rugby players. They stood back sneering. But when Coleman put it over the crossbar from all angles from 70 to 75 metres out their mouths dropped open.

"I used to dread Fred Flanagan having an off day against Richmond. That meant I was switched to centre half-forward where the terrible sight of Mopsy Fraser awaited me.

"Fraser scared hell out of me. He was no gentleman. He would come out with most of the front of his guernsey torn away to show a frightening collection of muscles.

"He had long hair years before it was fashionable; he would not have shaved for days and, honestly if you got a kick on him he would start to froth at the mouth.

"But Fraser was not just a rough player. He had great skill. I remember I did a shocking thing against him one day. He had marked all over me and I stood on the mark casually. Next second Fraser was off. He had three bounces and a long kick and the centre half-back had kicked a goal on me. It was very, very embarrassing.

"If it happened today the coach would whip you straight off the ground, then make you listen to him while he blew hell out of you on the phone from the coach's box."

Bob does not disagree when people tell him football is better than it used to be. But he wishes that the stars of his day could compete now with the much better training and discipline which clubs demand.

"There was a tremendous amount of undisciplined talent in the fifties," says Bob. "There is not so much today; there is a curtailment of natural talent.

"I would love to see players like Jarrard, Dynon and Foote, of North Melbourne; Bob McKenzie, Melbourne; Clegg, South Melbourne; Fraser, Sutton, Footscray; and Hutchison, Essendon; playing under today's conditions. They would be sensational.

"Run-on football is not something discovered in the seventies. I played it in 1957-58. I used to kick-off, come down the field for a handball if a teammate had marked and go on again. I had the pace to do it.

"When I watch David Dench of North Melbourne I can see myself. I regret we have few films of the game in my era. It is difficult to imagine what you looked like when you played.

"It must be a great thrill for today's players to see themselves in action. Remember that great run of Turner's last year that won a goal for Geelong? I would like to think that is how I looked when I played half-forward."

Bob has a new hobby. He collects memorabilia about football. Five times he interrupted our interview to give me such snippets as: "Who was the first footballer to mark over his head? Charlie Pearson of Essendon in 1890. A writer of the period said if he continued this practice he would ruin the game."

Bob would then break into paroxysms of crazy Davis laughter. When he subsided he would ask: "Well Alfred, where were we?" Generally I had no more idea than Bob.

I understand now why Teddy Whitten kept breaking Bob's cheekbones.

DICK REYNOLDS' OWN STORY

Argus, September 23, 1950.

After this afternoon's League grand final, Dick Reynolds, three times a Brownlow medallist, will retire. One of the greatest players of all time, he gave this message to Argus *readers.*

Today's grand final, barring a tie, will be my last game of League football.

I've played for Essendon for over half my lifetime, but I've lost that yard—the extra yard I used to have over the other fellow—and I know it's time for me to get out.

It was one of the hardest decisions I've ever made. Perhaps I could still squeeze out another year of League play, but if I tried I might have to give up half-way through the season. I'd hate that.

I've been told that my marking and kicking have improved during the last few years, but it's getting harder for me to keep up with the game.

Until now I've been able to pull my weight, but I'm not going out there, year after year, to let my mates do all the work.

I've weighed up the pros and cons, and its time to hang up my old football boots.

Those boots mean a lot to me. Often they've reminded me of how much of my football success I owed to my parents.

While my dad was alive he never allowed anyone else to touch my boots. Week after week he used to clean them and check the stops. He knew that balance was my greatest asset, and I never lost a stop while dad took care of those boots.

He did more than that. He was on night shift when I first started with Essendon, and he used to give up his sleep in the afternoons so that he could pick me up in the truck and run me across from my work to the ground.

He and my mother both kept a pretty strict watch on my diet. They made me eat plenty of fresh food. It's largely due to them that I don't drink or smoke.

My parents used to say that I'd been a football crank ever since I was a little boy. They told me that when I was very young I even took a football to bed with me.

What really started me on a football career was the trip I had to Perth in 1929 with the Victorian State Schools team. We didn't do very well, but it made me determined to become a good player.

I still remember my first game with Essendon. I was only 17 then, and I got a shock when the selectors picked me to play against Footscray.

I was put on the wing. I was tense and nervous. With about five minutes to play I kicked my first goal. I thought I'd get into trouble, but it put us ahead by a couple of points. Then after all we lost the match. Alby Morrison got the winning goal from right on the boundary line.

My best game was in 1937 against Collingwood. At centre half-forward I seemed to have the ball on a string. Everything came my way—even one-handed marks. It amazed me. I never knew a man could get so many kicks. I've never had another day like that.

And my ideal type of player? Jack Collins, from Geelong. I admired every phase of his play—the way he turned, his marking, everything. He was a player I loved to watch.

Garnet Campbell, captain and coach when I first came to Essendon, taught me a lot. Keith Forbes and Bill Hutchison were the greatest rovers we ever had; and Hughie Torney, my ruck, was a tower of strength. Wally Buttsworth was the team's greatest centre half-back.

Then there were the first unforgettable years as coach. I started as joint coach with Harry Hunter. If we lost, I'd worry so much that I wouldn't be able to eat tea on Saturday night.

The game itself has changed during the years. It's more scientific now, it's faster, and it's better. It's getting to a stage where every player must be able to stab-pass.

And it's harder for new players to break in. But youngsters with ability can make the grade if they take care of themselves and set out to learn.

It's no good a youngster saying: "I'm a natural footballer." You have to keep on learning. In my own last few years I've copied good players and tried to adapt their best points to my own style.

Essendon have won three premierships and have been runners-up five times during my 18 years with them. Those games will always stand out in my memory.

Crowds don't worry me, but it does something to a player when he runs out on to the ground in front of 90,000 people. When they roar the air seems electrified. There's something about it that you can't explain. . . .

During my time as captain and coach I've tried never to let anything but football ability influence me in judging players. I think my team mates know that.

I've won a lot of trophies, and been given many presents. But the one that touched me most was a New Testament. A lady who had followed Essendon for years gave me that—she even had my initials inscribed on the cover.

The people I've met, particularly the people of Essendon, have all been generous to me. My best friends are my football friends.

Football has given me confidence, too. I never dreamed that one day I'd be able to get up and lecture, or speak over the air. I had trouble when I started. I was almost frightened to say "Boo".

The going was even harder on Thursday night, when, for the last time, I talked to my team-mates as captain and coach. I was thinking of that, and, honestly, it took me about five minutes even to get started.

Even though I've finished my active football life as a player, I hope to stay on with Essendon—as coach, if they'll have me.

But that's looking forward to next year. Perhaps by then I'll have got used to the idea that I'm no longer a player—I just can't realise it yet.

JOHN COLEMAN

By R.S. Whitington, *The Champions*

No one player has caused more of the hysteria that surrounds Melbourne's Australian Rules Football than John Coleman, Essendon's near supernatural high-marker and goalkicker of the years 1949 to 1954.

Recruited from Hastings, a secluded coastal village on the Mornington Peninsula, Coleman kicked twelve goals in his first game for Essendon on Saturday, April 18, 1949. His last kick of that winter brought his hundredth goal, still a V.F.L. record total for a 'fresher'.

Coleman kicked 120 goals in 1950, 75 in 1951 and 103 in 1952, or 398 in his first four seasons. He topped the Victorian Football League goal-kicking list in all but the third of those years. Few doubt that he would have done so in 1951 but for his suspension from three final round matches for 'retaliation' when struck twice by a Carlton opponent in the last of the home and away games.

It was not the number of goals Coleman kicked, nor his unerring accuracy that created all the hysteria. It was the way in which he gained possession of the ball before he kicked them. Had he been a trapeze artist in a strolling circus, Coleman could have dispensed with the trapeze.

High-marking is the feature of Australian Rules Football which separates it from all other games, which elevates it, in the spectacular sense, above all other footballing codes. According to Melbourne football writer, Alf Brown, who has covered several decades of V.F.L. matches, Coleman 'as a high marker of the ball, was the greatest—was, indeed, the greatest of all the footballers I have seen'.

A glance at the accompanying picture of him soaring waist-high above his opponents' heads, of him rising erect and entirely unaided by the accepted, if often painful, use of their bodies as a ladder, helps to reveal why Brown formed and retained this opinion of Coleman.

His star quality, his grip on people's imagination, came not only from his foraging, marking and kicking ability, however. Coleman was the most colourful personality the Melbourne game produced after World War II, at least till the coming of Ron Barassi and Alex Jesaulenko.

He was an aggressive full-forward, no pampered paper-doll, and he aroused as much animosity among the footballing enemies of Essendon as he did idolatry among Essendon's supporters. Spectators hurled bottles and stones at him during and after play. They hooted and swore at him, even attacked and spat at him as he left the field.

As a forward Coleman was something of a hunter. He needed to be to gain possession of the ball from such full-backs as Jock McCorkell of North Melbourne, Ollie Grieves of Carlton, Shane McGrath of Melbourne, and Vic Chanter of Fitzroy.

When comparisons are made between Coleman and other great Victorian forwards, between him and Bob Pratt, Gordon Coventry, Ron Todd, Dickie Lee and Peter Hudson, it is emphasised that these other players had champions to deliver the ball to them, had protective, resting ruckmen next to them. Coleman seldom had a top-class centre half-forward to give him the ball straight, low and fast or an intelligent follower to shepherd him.

He also received far less protection from the umpires than was his due—or was beneficial for football as a spectacle. A strong psychological factor seems to influence the minds, maybe the hearts, of umpires when they are called upon to make decisions regarding breaches of the rules near goal.

Bob Pratt has claimed that Coleman 'was often crucified by lack of protection from his teammates'. This kicker of 150 goals himself, in one V.F.L. season has also said, 'If I was better than Coleman, I was twice as good as I thought myself'.

Like many champions in other sports, Coleman had no scientific explanation for his brilliance. To him 'it just came naturally'. Others have said he succeeded above others because of his ability to gain the vital break of a yard when leading out for the ball, his ability to leap higher than any other player and when doing so to retain the balance, and disregard of the ground way below him, necessary to grip the ball surely. They said Coleman baulked and rose for high marks when most players would have been off-balance, that he could swerve his body through packs, then snatch the ball from the finger tips of his opponents in breath-taking fashion.

A great goal-keeper of his day said, 'You thought you had him out of position, off-balance and completely covered yet, the next moment, he was rising above you for a spectacular mark'.

Coleman did not just take two spectacular marks a game. Often he would take ten or more such marks in one afternoon. He marked sensationally from in front of a pack as well as from the middle of, or behind one.

Alf Brown claimed in April 1973, the month of Coleman's death from a heart attack at the age of forty-four, that he drew more spectators to watch him than *any* other Victorian footballer of any era. And this means more than any Rules footballer of *any* era. He attracted crowds in such a way as to suggest the player, in his case, was greater than the game. Loyal supporters of other football clubs deserted them to watch Coleman.

John Coleman was born at Port Fairy in 1929. When he was still young his family moved to Flemington not far from the famous racecourse. He became 'an average pupil' at the Moonee Ponds Central School, one keen on football and cricket. At cricket he became school captain; at football he played in the ruck and at centre half-forward, learning to kick those prodigious punts. His father soon moved the family to Hastings and John joined the local football club, because his brother Albert was its star defender and he and Albert were always inseparable. John also entered Melbourne University as a commerce student and took a job in a big Melbourne firm. He learned enough accountancy to equip himself for his subsequent management of hotels.

Coleman was a friendly, extremely good-looking youngster, popular with both men and women. He grew to 6ft 1in. tall and weighed 12½ stone, when he came to Essendon at the beginning of the 1949 season. In 1947 he had kicked 136 goals for Hastings and followed this with 160 goals (twenty-three of them in one game) in 1948.

Umpires are apt to be laxer in country games than in V.F.L. ones. The full-backs who opposed the teenage Coleman began to hit him with everything they had, to test his courage and trim his sails. He realised he would have to learn to defend himself,

225

even resort to fisticuffs at times. This he did and was reported on one occasion.

The V.F.L. clubs who opposed Essendon in 1949 were aware that Coleman could be goaded into retaliation and their full-backs were instructed to treat him roughly. Despite this, he kicked those twelve goals against Hawthorn in his first game and it still is a record on debut.

Despite Coleman's freakish performances in front of goal, Essendon fared poorly in the autumn and early winter of 1949. But they won their last eight home and away games and were standing fourth at the start of the final rounds.

No team had won the V.F.L. premiership from fourth position since the introduction, in 1931, of the Page system of conducting the final rounds.

At this stage of the season Coleman had kicked eighty-five goals. Great interest existed as to whether he would reach his 'ton'. Essendon won its semi-final and then the preliminary final. It faced Carlton for the premiership and Carlton had one of the finest goal-keepers of any era in Ollie Grieves. Coleman still needed six goals to become the first player to kick 100 in his first winter of V.F.L. football.

Six goals is a lot to get in a hard-fought grand final. His opponents gave him some hard knocks in the first two quarters; Grieves appeared to have his measure. Looking listless, Coleman still needed four goals at half-time.

During the third quarter it became obvious Essendon would win. It was gaining the ascendancy in most parts of the field, almost everywhere except in front of goal. His team's supremacy brought more frequent opportunities to their fullforward, but even late in the last quarter he was two goals short of target. Knowing the game was won, his teammates began to feed him with the ball and in the dying moments of the game he kicked his ninety-ninth and hundredth goals. Essendon won by seventy-three points.

Grieves, as is the custom on such occasions (let's hope it doesn't spread to swimming), exchanged guernseys with the young hero. But Coleman lacked the time to slip into this souvenir of his triumph before the crowd mobbed him and bore him shoulder high, and shoulder bare, from the field.

Coleman was chosen to represent Victoria, to wear that formidable 'Big V', in that first season. He kicked seven goals against South Australia at the Melbourne Cricket Ground and four against it in Adelaide. Coleman won Essendon's best and fairest player award in 1949 and came fourth, with fifteen votes, in the competition for the Brownlow Medal.

Any chance Coleman had of winning that enviable honor in 1951 was destroyed by an incident towards the end of the last pre-final round game against Carlton. As usual, Coleman had received a considerable amount of what is euphemistically described as 'attention' from his immediate opponents.

During the third quarter, a Carlton supporter hurled a bottle at the Essendon champion. He was heckled continuously and, at half-time, hooted from the field. In the dressing-room Essendon's coach told one of his team's rovers, 'Spudda' Tate, to keep Coleman out of trouble. Essendon knew they needed Coleman in the finals if they were to win the flag.

But, when the trouble came, Tate was in midfield taking care of himself. Near the goal Carlton ruckman Harry Caspar struck Coleman twice. He then retaliated, as men are apt to do in bars and boxing rings.

The V.F.L. Tribunal conducted an inquiry during the week. A crowd gathered around the building. In their wisdom, the Tribunal suspended Coleman for four matches (three of them likely to be finals) and his assailant Caspar for an equal number of games.

Essendon supporters formed a cordon around Coleman as he made his way from the building to a car. Other members of the mob broke the cordon, knocked Coleman to the ground. He reached the car in a dazed condition. Essendon won its semi-final and preliminary final. It lost the grand final by two goals to Geelong.

Coleman's reaction to these events of late August 1951 was: 'They are evidence of the high degree of partisanship associated with the game I love. There have been times when I would have liked to have got hold of people who abuse me and hurl missiles at me. I spurn the idea of giving police protection to players, however, if these characters want to get you, they will. Generally, however, they are too cowardly to come out into the open.'

Magnanimous? No, idiotic and ingenuous, in my·view. The Melbourne Cricket Ground has been called a colosseum but we are living in the twentieth century, not in Nero's time.

Coleman's playing career ended after the eighth round of the

1954 season. He dislocated a knee in a game against North Melbourne. He was leading the V.F.L. goal-kicking list at the time. He coached Essendon to the 1962 and 1965 premierships.

His collapse and death from heart attack at his Dromana, Mornington Peninsula, hotel in early April of 1973 was shrouded in considerable mystery. So much, indeed, that the Victorian Minister for Health ordered an immediate inquiry into allegations that several doctors had refused calls to attend him in his last moments.

More than 1,000 mourners attended his funeral on April 9, less than twenty-four years after he kicked those twelve goals as a twenty-year-old in 1949. The mourners included many of the Essendon champions of his time and those of subsequent times.

Cricket champion and St. Kilda fullback Keith Miller was in Barbados watching a Test match between the West Indies and Australia when he heard of Coleman's death. A week later I received a letter from him, one almost entirely devoted to a tribute to Coleman as a footballer and friend.

BILL HUTCHISON—A GREAT ROVER

By Alf Brown, *Herald*, August 15, 1980.

Bad luck, a tendency to argue with umpires and always being in a top side with teammates stealing votes from him prevented Bill Hutchison joining the select group of champions who have won three Brownlows.

Hutchison was always amazingly fit. He could go all day. The fact that he did not smoke—and that was before smoking seriously was linked with cancer—nor drink contributed to his long run in top football.

Hutchison played in a premiership side in his first year and his last game was in a grand final. Fresh-faced and slim and looking younger than 57 he is still in football. He has been a Victorian selector for three years.

Hutchison, like many other Essendon players of his time, was influenced by non-smoking, non-drinking captain—coach Dick Reynolds.

Once Essendon secretary Bill Cookson, who died recently, told me that Essendon's bill for soft drinks was much higher than the club's account for beer.

Bill always barracked for Essendon. As a 12-year-old he used to admire the brilliance of top rovers Reynolds and Keith Forbes.

"I can still see Forbes running around the boundary at top pace and without a hitch in his stride, drop-kicking goals from the boundary in front of the wooden Dick Reynolds stand," he said this week.

Hutchy came to Essendon in 1942 from the local junior league. He was 19 but nobody would believe him. His age was given out as 17.

"I have heard much criticism of Dick Reynolds as a coach but I thought he was tops", Bill says.

"He allowed you to develop your own game. Players were allowed to use their initiative. I would have trouble playing today with coaches telling me what to do. This regimentation of players detracts a lot from the game."

Bill played for 16 seasons and was in a record 30 State sides. Later John Nicholls broke the record. Bill never made much out of football. Ten pounds for a final match was about the most he ever earned on a Saturday.

"I remember the £10 clearly," says Bill.

"We were coming off the M.C.G. in 1948 after playing a grand final draw against Melbourne and full back Cec Ruddell said: 'Is this any good? We'll get another £10 next week for the replay'.

"Essendon was always conservative and I realised other players were getting more. But there was nothing you could do about it. Once treasurer Harry Hunter told me: 'I look after Essendon's money as though it was my own'."

Hutchison played in a great Essendon period and including the 1948 grand final replay was in 10 grand finals. Essendon won four.

Jack Dyer was still a fine player when Hutchison came into football.

"Jack collected me in a final at Carlton in either 1942 or 1943. He hit me in the back and I took off like a rocket.

"Jack was tough, strong, fast, and colourful. He could mark and kick and was very, very tough. No, he just didn't dwell on the little men.

"He would have a go at anyone and he was always there if you felt like coming back at him.

"We won the 1946 grand final when we bolted in the third quarter and kicked 11 goals to Melbourne's one. Bad kicking cost us the next two premierships.

"In 1947 against Carlton we had 30 scoring shots to 21 and lost by a point when Fred Stafford kicked a goal seconds before the end.

"In 1948 we drew with Melbourne in the grand final. We kicked 7–27 to 10–9. Thirty four shots to 19 and we couldn't win it. In the replay on October 9 we lost easily.

"No I don't agree it was bad captaincy by coach Dick Reynolds in not shifting Bill Brittingham when he started to kick inaccurately.

"Bill was a great ball-getter. In one of those losing grand finals Bill had 15 kicks. We had no other forward who could win the ball like that. No, Dick was correct in persisting with him."

I always will remember Reynolds reply when in an article I criticised him for not making changes up forward. "I don't like hurting players' feelings", he said.

I bet North Melbourne players wish Ron Barassi had Reynolds' easy going philosophy.

When John Coleman reluctantly joined Essendon he changed all that. In his first year he kicked 100 goals, getting six in the 1949 grand final.

"The game was all over by three quarter time when we led Carlton by nine goals," recalls Bill.

"The main interest was whether Coleman would get his 1000. We were determined he would.

"Once Gordon Lane, who was 19th man chased the ball into goals and got it just near the line. He almost broke his back twisting around so he could kick the ball back into play to give Coleman a chance of getting it."

In the late forties and early fifties Essendon had plenty of rovers.

In the 1949 final series they had Hutchison, McEwin, Tate and Rawle with Reynolds roving and ruck roving. The next year they had Hutchison, Tate and McEwin.

"Perhaps rovers are scarce because they are not developed, not encouraged," suggests Bill.

"Nowadays, everyone plays like a rover. Everyone runs down the ground.

"For years Essendon always had at least two top rovers. I

used to watch Reynolds and Forbes as a kid and rovers just kept appearing.

"But the last two top rovers Essendon had were Jack Clarke and John Birt. Now we are struggling around the packs.

"But Essendon are not alone. Look at North Melbourne—the best recruiting side in the League and they have been struggling for rovers ever since Cable returned home.

"Kevin Bartlett of Richmond is 34 and he can still show most rovers how a really good rover goes about his job."

Talking about Bartlett brought us to the new holding the ball rule. Bill was happy with the old rule.

"Bartlett, Birt and Darrell Baldock used the old rule cleverly. They would hurl the ball out in front of them.

"Good players could use the rule; it was part of the game. If a player was smart enough to create a doubt in the umpires mind, good luck to him.

"The new rule has made the game less attractive. Once you could get the ball, throw it in front of you and away you would go. Nowadays you rarely see a breakaway. A pity, it was one of the thrills of football."

Bill is not one of the old-timers who can see nothing good in the game, although he thinks hand-passing is greatly overdone. As a State selector he sees a game every week and reckons football is as good as ever. It is some of the background stuff he dislikes.

"Some clubs insist that their players be at the ground before 12.30. It's crazy. They are taken into a small room and given motivational talks, pep talks and other gimmicks. Then they are shown films.

"Players lose their edge. They have too much time to think and worry about their game. When I was playing I used to like Saturday mornings. I would hate them now."

ALAN KILLIGREW

By Alf Brown, *Herald*, April 11, 1980.

Alan Killigrew, the little man with the stoop and the big heart, has just completed a round trip. It took him 42 years.

He started as a rover with St. Kilda in 1938, and had a short but brilliant football career.

This year Killigrew, a former Royal Australian Navy able seaman ("I was the least able of all time") returned to St. Kilda to help with recruiting, as a hobby.

On the voyage back to St. Kilda, Killigrew stopped over at a lot of ports and learned about football at each one—especially at North Melbourne.

"Killa" was nick-named the hot gospeller of football when he coached St. Kilda. He still preaches a colourful football sermon, full of sense, wisecracks and philosophy at 200 words a minute.

Unless you have a couple of days to spare, don't drop in to have a chat with "Killa".

As a player Killigrew did a lot in a short time. He started with St. Kilda in 1938. Was club champion in 1940 and made the Victorian side the same year. Next year he was in the Royal Australian Navy.

At 5 ft. 4 in., "Killa" was one of our smallest sailors. He says they used to tie a rope around his ankles and force him down gun barrels to clean them out.

In the Navy, Killigrew contracted tuberculosis of the lungs. It spread to his spine and he nearly died. He was operated on and was in bed, encased in plaster, for three years. That was the end of him as a footballer.

When he was discharged from hospital "Killa" was down; way down. "I loved football; not being able to play it any more hurt a lot", he recalled this week. "I could not face up to it; I did not even go to games.

"I bought a taxi and deliberately worked all Saturday to get away from football. Not being able to play it meant I couldn't bear to watch it.

"But every passenger talked about football. It started to drive me crazy. So I went into the hotel business in Ballarat to try to get away from it all.

"It sort of worked. Every Saturday afternoon the pub was deserted. They were all at the football.

"One day my wife Ida said, 'Why don't you go and watch a game. You're useless around here and making everyone else miserable'."

And that was the rebirth of Killigrew the footballer.

He watched Golden Point play Ballarat East. He went to the match under duress; looked for mistakes, found them and was back in the pub after the first quarter.

"Do you know," he reported to Ida, "I even saw two clowns who were not playing have a punch-up."

Mrs Killigrew was not impressed. "So what's new?" she asked. "It's better than fighting ON the field, like someone I know."

As a St. Kilda player "Killa" had football priors—three reports, two convictions. It got him thinking; got his blood pounding. Philosopher Killigrew came forward and held centre stage ever since.

"Those blokes fighting weren't clowns, they were just enjoying themselves," Killigrew explained to "Killa". "They were getting involved. That's the name of the game—involvement.

"So next year I was coaching in Ballarat. And I don't have to tell you the name of the clown who got into a fight in one of the early games!

"I coached Golden Point and Ballarat East to grand finals.

"But coaching was demanding, even in those days. By then I had developed a philosophy—whenever football interferes with business, get out of business. So I sold the pub and came back to Melbourne.

"St. Kilda asked me to coach. It was no big deal. The Saints were perennial losers. I spent the summer recruiting.

"It was easy in those days. There was no country zoning. All you needed was a pocketful of money, a car and smooth talk.

"I recruited so successfully that in the last practice game of 1956 the recruits beat the senior players of the previous year by eight goals.

"We dropped 26 of the 1955 players off the senior list and all hell broke loose. But it was the beginning of a new St. Kilda and we continued to recruit.

"In my first year we recruited Brian Walsh, a top back pocket player; 'Bud' Annand, a handy ruckman, Paul Dodd a star rover and Bill Young who won the V.F.L. goal-kicking in his first year.

"Next season we got Lance Oswald a top centreman, Jim Guyatt, a tough defender; Bill Stephenson who would have won a Brownlow Medal if he had not done a knee; Allan Morrow the best ruckman of his size I have seen and tough Eric Guy.

"Next year our best recruits were Verdun Howell, who could play almost anywhere but specialised at full-back, and centre half-back Ian Synman.

"It's not hard to build up a club. Get people to get money to get top players to get a top coach to get the best out of the players. Then you have yourselves a premiership. This is what North Melbourne did years later.

"St. Kilda had a tradition but it was a horrible one. They were losers. You would have almost thought they were playing football for laughs there were so many playboys and buffoons around the club."

It was at St. Kilda that Killigrew's colourful pre-match addresses drew big audiences.

He chose unusual themes, some not connected with football, but he sent players out determined to win.

One day I was at St. Kilda, "Killa" asked his players to win for a former Saint whose bones were "rotting alongside the Kokoda Trail".

Some players were crying as they ran down the race with "Killa" running after them and slapping each player on the back as he took the field with the cry, "Win for Harold, win for Harold".

Killigrew makes no excuses for his colourful pre-match speeches. "Julius Caesar used to address his troops before battle. Its been going on ever since," he says.

"I tried to inspire them—motivation is the new word. A lot of players can do well for a limited period but they can't keep it up all day. The muscles, sinews, tendons start crying 'enough'. Its then a coach's job to drown out those distress cries from aching muscles."

After three exhausting years at St. Kilda, Killigrew's health, which never was good, became worse. He was re-appointed for a fourth season but dramatically took off for Adelaide where he thought a warmer climate would help.

Norwood knew a good coach when it saw one coming and grabbed "Killa" as soon as he arrived. In four years he coached it to two grand finals and a third.

"The first year we lost our first seven games. So I grabbed some money and came back to Melbourne and recruited. The Victorians with their tougher approach to football lifted us. But I was charged with favoring Victorians. I replied that I had signed the only players in Australia who could get us quickly out of the poo."

Then came North Melbourne. North were grovelling on the

234

bottom and Jack Adams, the first of North's great administrators went to Adelaide and persuaded Killigrew to return to Victoria.

"I loved North Melbourne, I still do," reports Killigrew. "I got North to a middle of the list side but then we marked time. North were too loyal, too friendly. Nobody would rock the boat.

"So I began jumping up and down and a few top administrators started to emerge. Ron Joseph, the best cloak and dagger man in the business became secretary; then came Mick Aylett the best player I have coached and easily the best administrator I have seen.

"Then North got the top fund raiser in the business in Barry Cheatley. As a door knocker he is superb. He could squeeze 200 bucks from a cold door knob.

"Now, at St. Kilda, I have met up again with top administrators Graham Huggins and Ian Drake and an up-and-comer in new president Lindsay Fox. Already I call him Mr. Magic. He has performed miracles in the short time he has been there."

Killigrew has a lot of thoughts about football; its administration, its future, its image.

"I've heard people say football is becoming more violent: that's nonsense," says "Killa", settling comfortably for a warm appraisal of the game he loves.

"Society is a lot more violent than football. You can get whacked on the head going around the corner at night to buy a Herald.

"Too much red blood is being taken out of football. If footballers are not allowed to bump that does not make society a better place to live in.

"Ron Barassi is a great coach but I disagree with his policy of non-retaliation.

"If someone biffs you it is only natural to hit back. If you don't, they biff you again. Any school kid will tell you that.

"By not allowing his players to come back at ruffians on other sides Barassi is setting up his players to be shot at. Anyone can be a hero if he knows he is not going to cop one back— and there are more and more heroes playing against North Melbourne.

A LOUDICROUS INTERLUDE

LOU RICHARDS SWEEPS COLLINS ST WITH A FEATHER DUSTER.

Sun, August 11, 1959

When you stick your neck out, you've got to be prepared to take the consequences—well I did and I have!

I said that I'd sweep Collins St. with a feather duster if Footscray beat Melbourne—OUCH!

Will Footscray Football Club please send a nurse to massage my sore and sorry knees and a seamstress to repair the two pairs of pants I wore out yesterday doing my street-cleaning?

That Jack Collins, Footscray's fighting secretary, certainly drives a hard bargain. Collins and those Bulldog players Arthur Edwards, Jim Gallagher and Bernie Lee made me eat my words or that's what it felt like after I'd swallowed half the dust in Collins St. and that dashed duster!

I thought I'd get away with it by sweeping just a small section at the top of Collins St. but those Bulldogs made me kneel my sweeping way down to Swanston St.

And if you don't think it's busy at the corner of Swanston and Collins Sts. at 11 o'clock any morning, ask *Sun* photographer George Bugden and me.

I reckon we both deserve medals from Footscray F.C. for risking our lives in the middle of cars, buses, trams, pedestrians and policemen. I lost George at one stage and found him perched on the front of a tram heading for St. Kilda Beach.

I see that the Bulldogs, or Feather-Duster club, are meeting my old mates, South Melbourne, for whom I once wore a strait-jacket, next Saturday.

OK, I'll stick my neck out again!

If this match is a tie, and there won't be much between the two teams, I'll go for a swim in Albert Park Lake with the two skippers my old mates "Smokey" Clegg and Ted Whitten!

13
The Sixties: "you can buy anything in your club colours"

This was the decade which marked the height of football madness in Melbourne—an addiction which spawned the Anti-Football League of Keith Dunstan (and some remarkable writing by him for the Bulletin*), the novel of Barry Oakley (*A Salute To The Great McCarthy*), the play of Alan Hopgood (*And The Big Men Fly*). It also saw the beginnings of the modern, businesslike football club in the resurgence of Richmond and Carlton replacing the traditional suburb based loyalists.*

MELBOURNE'S FOOTY FEVER

By 'Batman', *Bulletin*, June 8, 1963.

It is only two or three weeks since we were introduced to the latest Melburnian football novelty—nappies for baby in club colours. Now, nappies are designed for one particular function, and the thoughtful may feel that club nappies are hardly a compliment to the club concerned.

But this is Melbourne in the winter, and nobody ever thinks that deeply. Nappies are just the latest idea. You can buy anything in your club colours—rugs, earrings, socks, towels, baskets, coffee tables, money-boxes, ties. Even when the gentlemen are drying the dishes at night they can mop up in the colours of the club dearest to their hearts.

Oh, yes, you can buy jackets for your poodle, all embroidered with the club colours. If your poodle is particularly devoted to any individual player, then he can have that player's number sewn on top. Or, if he is a fickle poodle, the jacket can be reversible; if, say, Melbourne is being thrashed by Essendon at three-quarter time, then it is a simple matter to turn the jacket over and, lo, up come the Essendon colours.

The great Essendon full forward John Coleman enthralled football followers in the fifties.

Football is blazing to such a degree in Melbourne this season that everybody is cashing in. It will help any business. For example, honey people sell their honey in glasses embossed with football emblems. There is barely a firm in town that does not bring out a fixture list. I have, maybe, 20 of them on my desk.

Even staid, august firms like Amalgamated Wireless have a "footy" list. The Bank of New South Wales hands out money-boxes in the shape of footballs. The ES & A Bank provides an elegant booklet giving a complete list of records, premierships and, most important, the rules. Coca Cola has produced a colour film to help with training at the clubs. Shell has a very nice autograph book, with special places where you can collect the names of all your favorite players.

Nor is it just a seasonal affair. The Melbourne *Herald* has Alf Brown. He writes football ALL THE YEAR ROUND. He does nothing else, and regularly he shifts the cricket off ·the back page. Football training with some clubs starts well before Christmas, and the players are put through commando courses across the sand dunes. Then, to make up for the long, arid, cricketing months, the TV stations put on special football summer programmes. One is called "Football Replay", which week by week regurgitates the old footy finals.

Naturally, the TV tempo is stepped up during the season. I think we have more time allotted to football than gun-play. The climax comes on Sunday mornings, when the vast post-mortems take place, when all the players are called in for questioning by the experts. I have a favorite bit on one programme. This is the run-down of all the injuries from the Saturday. The announcer dresses up in a white jacket, just like Ben Casey, and he wears a stethoscope about his neck. It gives the whole affair authenticity.

It is difficult not to get carried along by this enthusiasm. You can't ignore it in conversation. And it doesn't affect only one class of the community. Sir Harry Winneke, the Solicitor-General, is one of the top men in Hawthorn. You come across a man like Oliver Shaul, ex-managing director of Federal Hotels, in the dressing-room at North Melbourne. One of our economists gets behind the goals at Collingwood every Saturday, and he says you wouldn't believe the important people you see there. This man won't go into the stand. That wouldn't be exciting enough.

Politicians and all those in public view know that it is wise to associate themselves with one of the clubs. Sir Robert Menzies makes frequent mention of his devotion to Carlton. Mr. Bolte is for Fitzroy, Arthur Calwell is a North Melbourne man; Mr. Porter, the Police Commissioner, is for Essendon; Sir Maurice Nathan, the Lord Mayor, likes Carlton; and Sir Dallas Brooks, our recently retired Governor, was number one ticket-holder at Richmond. Sir Rohan Delacombe, the new Governor, hadn't been in town one day before he, too, declared his allegiance for Richmond. You have to do these things.

There are other towns in the world that take their football seriously. There's Auckland, Buenos Aires, Madrid, Rome, Glasgow, Moscow; but their enthusiasm is of a different kind. Our heroes are local heroes. We are completely introverted. All that interests us is the local competition. We don't want international football; heavens above, we can't even stand interstate football. Interstate football is a tiresome arrangement which interrupts the weekly competition. There was a newspaper here that ran a poll to decide what we should do about interstate matches. The result was clear-cut—42.3 per cent of readers suggested that we should scrap them altogether.

Why is Melbourne like this? To be honest, nobody has ever given an adequate explanation. The cynical fellow will tell you it's the cheap drug. What else is there to do in Melbourne? The enthusiast will tell you that the answer is obvious—here we have the most exciting, most spectacular game ever devised for mankind. Now, before you Rugby League and Union men stop reading at once, I confess, reluctantly, that there must be other reasons.

The great depression of the eighteen-nineties put a sudden stop to the expansion of Melbourne. There was the further depression in the thirties and, more than anything else, this had to be the cheap entertainment. Because of these difficult times there was a big population in the inner suburbs. Old clubs like Collingwood, Richmond, Carlton, Fitzroy and South Melbourne could draw their recruits and their supporters from within their own boundaries.

The people from Carlton would loathe the people from Fitzroy. The people from Collingwood would loathe the people from Richmond. The match between Collingwood and Richmond was a classic battle between players and spectators, worth going miles to see. North Melbourne did not come in to the League until 1925, but the Shinboners used to hate everybody. Many an old player will tell you that after the match at North Melbourne they were lucky to escape with their lives.

By 1946 it was no longer possible to place supporters into neat suburban compartments, but tremendous publicity gave it a new push. It is intriguing to compare the space given to football before and after the war. Before the war football got only nominal space, and never did it make the front page. Now it fills the newspapers front and back, and there is all the added impetus of radio and television. It makes the posters three or four times a week. Why, recently we had a poster which dealt with the fact that a Geelong full forward had a sore neck.

Five times in the last seven years the attendances at Grand Finals have been over 100,000. Take last year. You couldn't buy a ticket of any kind at the ground. All of them were sold beforehand. Even so, the queuers began to arrive on the Thursday at 4 a.m., 58 hours before the game was due to start. They went through hell. It rained most of that time. Bodgies pelted them with eggs. Yet they queued for one reason—so that they could get a good position behind the goal. We proudly put this forward as a world record for football queueing.

And it is still building. The average attendance at all weekly matches last year was 151,000. For the six matches on the first two rounds of this year they were 174,640 for the opening round and 214,484 for the split round on the Saturday and Anzac Day. These figures broke all records.

Now just compare these figures with Sydney Rugby League, played on Saturdays and Sundays. For the five matches on April 13 and 14 they were 50,915; for April 20 and 21, 53,090; the next week-end was almost washed out and for May 11 and 12 it was 59,216.

True, there are rival codes in Sydney, but then there are rival codes in Melbourne. The truth of the matter is that three times as many people in Melbourne spend their afternoons looking at the game.

Now to get back to reasons. Tradition has a lot to do with it. Look at the names of Sydney Rugby League clubs. Fair enough. St. George is a good one, and famous. But what can you do with Western Suburbs, Eastern Suburbs, North Sydney.

Take Collingwood. Visitors will hardly credit it, but the tradition there is almost a mystic thing. When you enter the Collingwood clubrooms it has something of the atmosphere of a church. Famous British regiments took centuries to build tradition, but with battles every Saturday, tradition here built with incredible speed. The walls are adorned with countless photographs and great names; names that really are revered like fallen revolutionary heroes. Lou Richards, a former Collingwood captain, has written that always it is impressed on players that the greatest sin of all is to lose.

One can gain a faint idea of this tradition by attending the pre-season Collingwood Football Club dinner. Usually it works this way. The club members turn up in force; black tie, wine, turkey, brandy correctly served in balloons. Then at the right moment there is a fanfare of trumpets and from the end of the hall enters a Boy Scout bearing high an embroidered cushion. On this cushion is the most cherished article in all Collingwood—the No. 1 black and white Collingwood guernsey. As the Boy Scout comes forward out steps the Collingwood captain to accept his guernsey from the club president himself.

And so it goes on—every man on the senior training list gets his guernsey in the same way. This helps him to appreciate that he is receiving one of the highest of all honors in Melbourne town. A graduation at West Point would be no less moving.

It is not often that the passions which rule this club come right out into the open, but an astonishing example was the campaign for the presidency last February. There is no point here in explaining all the complicated political manoeuvres which brought about this battle. They are known perfectly in Melbourne.

On the one side was John Galbally, 52, a top barrister in criminal actions, the Leader of the Opposition in the Legislative Council, a former State Minister, and, more important than anything, a former Collingwood player. On the other side was Tom Sherrin, 46, a football manufacturer, and, what's more, his business right there in Collingwood.

Backing Jack Galbally were John Wren, son of the famous John Wren, and Jock McHale, the greatest of all Collingwood coaches, and the present coach, Phonse Kyne. It was almost like a battle between the Tories and the workers. Behind Tom Sherrin were the players and most of the rank and file.

Elections in State politics can be awfully dull, but this was done in the grand style; the electors were really wooed. The Galbally team, for example, did a complete telephone canvass.

What else happened? Every club member received at least three letters in the mail. The candidates personally put their cases on the two commercial TV channels. There were men to hand out pamphlets at the railway stations all along the Collingwood line. Then on polling date the players paraded with placards asking the members to vote for Tom Sherrin. What's more, just like a Federal election, there were How to Vote cards.

It is history now that Tom Sherrin had an easy win. It all cost a great deal in time, effort and money. But this is the point to understand. Neither Tom Sherrin nor Jack Galbally had anything whatever to gain financially or in privilege by winning the election. There was just the prestige to be had in being PRESIDENT OF COLLINGWOOD.

If you want to understand the passions of Melbourne football it is interesting also to look at Alan Killigrew, the coach of North Melbourne. He's a spell-binder, a man who gains results by the almost unbelievable strength of his sincerity. He played for St. Kilda, then for a long time he was in hospital with a spinal disease. Many believe that it was only the power of his faith in the Roman Catholic Church that brought him back to health. He coached St. Kilda, then went to Norwood in Adelaide, and this year he returned to coach North Melbourne.

The results have been astonishing. Last year North Melbourne won only four matches and finished second last on the League ladder. This year North Melbourne won its first three matches by defeating Collingwood, Footscray and Richmond in that order. Unfortunately, it lost the next three, but it still fights on, mesmerised.

Killigrew depends on the psychological approach. In the North Melbourne room there are pictures only of *winning* sides, no failures. North Melbourne has never won a V.F.L. premiership so he has a slogan: *The Team that Wins North Melbourne's First Premiership Gains Football Immortality.*

But the thing to do is to see him in action giving his pre-play speech to the side. At this he is superb. He is Billy Graham, Percy Cerutty, Laurence Olivier all rolled into one. He knows how to build to a climax, how to time an impact and how to drop to an emotional hush.

When he is talking he can't stand still. He marches up and down the dressing-room. He wears no coat. His tie hangs down loose. He becomes red in the face. Here are some extracts from a recent speech as reported in the *Sun News Pictorial*:

"This is it. THIS IS IT. You're in the BIG time after today. Now I want you out on that ground in a body all tight together. I want you to look like a top V.F.L. side—the cream of Australian football. Let the whole WORLD know—it's US—against THEM.

"You're going to fight now for North Melbourne and believe me there's no better cause. North Melbourne always has been noted for GUTS. Don't you forget that ever. There's never been a North Melbourne team that didn't have GUTS. North Melbourne teams may have been beaten, yes they have been annihilated, but they have never been FRIGHTENED. Never.

"And if someone does something good, takes a good mark, give him a rap. Tell him. You're a team, remember. You got to LOVE each other. Yes. LOVE EACH OTHER.

"The silk is here to see you today. Great names. The world is your oyster—if you win. But this is a ruthless business, the jungle. DOG eat DOG. If you go down you're finished. NOBODY'S INTERESTED IN YOU. Already they're saying North Melbourne for the four. You can do it IF YOU BELIEVE IT. Well, I believe you can . . . It's the truth.

"All right, I can't tell you how to win. I can't put blood in your heart, I can't push the blood through to work your muscles. HEART IS SOMETHING YOU GOTTA HAVE ON YOUR OWN. Now North has won only five times here in 38 years. Well, what are you going to do?

(Very soft now.) "Are you going to be one of those teams who COULDN'T or one of those that CAN?" (Applause and shouts of enthusiasm as teams runs out.)

The Rewards

As you can see, a great deal is demanded. What then are the rewards? All V.F.L. players had a £2 rise this year, which

244

means that now they get £10 a match. However, on top of this are provident fund payments. Collingwood Club is the most generous in this. Each player gets £10 for a win, £5 for a loss. There is also £4 from the V.F.L. provident fund. When Collingwood wins every player earns £24.

Jack Dyer ("Captain Blood"), the renowned former captain of Richmond, is a little scornful of the rich rewards to be had now. In the old days it was the honor and glory. He could remember the time when the greatest of honor of all was just to rub shoulders in the bath with the champion. He'd play for the smell of the eucalyptus.

Now, of course, there are Ron Barassi fan clubs, Murray Weideman fan clubs, Ted Whitten fan clubs. The adoration is so great that the rewards to be had are rich. After every match various sponsors hand out rewards. There are electric razors, suits, shirts, ties, transistor radios. Some of the top players haven't bought a stitch in years. There's the sponsorship of all sorts of products—everything from motor cars to hair oil. The faces of footballers beam at you through the ads. It almost seems that every time one turns on the television there is a footballer enthusing, saying that he couldn't kick a goal but for milk.

There are personal appearances at lectures, at stores. There are the countless TV and radio panel shows. There are 10 shows on Thursday nights and 11 shows on Friday nights. An appearance here is usually worth better than £5. Then there are awards offered by newspapers, TV and radio stations. There are three cars going this year, plus an overseas trip for two and numerous awards of £200 and £100.

How much the top men earn is anybody's guess. These are points that are not advertised. However, Jim Cardwell, secretary of Melbourne, said in 1961 that Ron Barassi, the Melbourne captain, made £2000 a year out of football alone. It would be safe to say that he probably did better than that.

The real problem for most clubs is the finding of new recruits. Once they came by natural process from schools, technical schools and little leagues in the area. Now, with the great expansion of Melbourne, particularly for clubs like Fitzroy, North Melbourne, South Melbourne and Melbourne, these sources have dried up. So club representatives have to roam the State, in fact the entire country, looking for talent.

They have to be mighty circumspect about it. The Coulter law forbids clubs to make any cash payments. Other methods have to be found. Most of the clubs have groups of businessmen to handle this sort of thing. At Melbourne it is the "coterie"; at Collingwood, until they were recently disbanded, it was the Floreats—from the Collingwood motto, Floreat Pica (May the Magpie Flourish). Distinguished Floreats were John Wren and his brother Joseph.

The story goes that St. Kilda had to pay £1500 to get the three stars, Bill Stephenson, Alan Morrow and Bill Young, from the country. This was denied by the St. Kilda committee. Carlton this month wanted the rover, Trevor Best, from North Hobart Football Club. The Carlton president, Lew Holmes, said North Hobart demanded a big transfer fee. Best's father in Hobart said the sum demanded was £200.

There was the case this year of Terry Waters, the Dandenong ruckman. Waters wanted to transfer to Collingwood, but Dandenong, a rapidly rising Association team, wanted to keep him.

Collingwood finally won Waters by taking out two Supreme Court writs. The writs were issued by Frank Galbally, Jack's brother. The counsel engaged was John Winneke, the former Hawthorn ruckman. Things are done in the grand style in Melbourne football. Anyway, before the matter came to court, with the superb opportunity of seeing the young Mr. Winneke in action as a barrister, Dandenong relented and Waters got his transfer.

To acquire the stars from interstate is the biggest problem of all. The two biggest transfers in recent times have been Darrel Baldock, captain of Tasmania and now captain of St. Kilda, and Polly Farmer, who moved from Perth to Geelong. The story goes that Baldock and Farmer both cost about £3000. These figures were denied, and both players had to be made very comfortable. Yet, no matter what they cost, both were magnificent footballers and they drew the crowds.

Another incentive for the players is the trips. It is tradition for a V.F.L. team, plus officials, to go on a marvellous end-of-season junket. Surfers Paradise always has been the favorite, but just lately they have been getting grander and grander. Last year Fitzroy and Geelong went off to New Zealand. Collingwood went on a dreamy sea-cruise to Noumea. This year Melbourne and Carlton are going to Hawaii, and Geelong Football Club has just announced that a party of 50 players and officials will go to the U.S. as an end-of-season jaunt to play exhibition matches in San Francisco. This will be the first exhibition of Australian football on the mainland.

Cynics might say that the Victorian Football League is rolling in wealth. That's not true. Victorian football draws the biggest crowds, but it hasn't anything like the money of the Rugby League clubs. There are no one-armed bandits to drag in the money. So they resort to other methods, such as raffles and dances.

The old story is that Victorian football is still under the thumb of the cricket associations. Whether this is true or not, that extraordinary fanatic, the Melbourne football fan, watches the game under frightful conditions. The entertainment is fairly cheap, 6s. 6d. for the grandstand, 4s. 6d. for the outer. But there are only two grounds with real comforts—the Melbourne Cricket Ground and the St. Kilda Cricket Ground. At the others, often, the lavatories are horrible. To get a seat you would need to go three hours beforehand. At many of the grounds the outer is only partially terraced. You stand there hemmed in on a slippery slope in a welter of litter and beer cans.

Of course, the clubs feel that if they had full control of their grounds they would be able to provide better facilities. That's a matter for great argument. Collingwood has full control of its ground, but the improvements have been for the social club members rather than for the spectators.

Apart from the problems of accommodation, the game is in a very healthy state. The crowds and enthusiasm grow year by year. Mostly we are very well behaved. We don't have the riots like they have at Rome and in some of the South American countries. True, we put in wire races to protect the players from the kindly affections of the spectators.

It is also true that on May 4 a woman, wielding a cane decorated with Collingwood ribbons, whacked the president of Hawthorn, Dr A. S. Ferguson, on the head. Field umpire Schwab also was hit in the face with an apple. Hawthorn player Brendan Edwards, too, had to suffer a can on the back of the head and a slap in the face by a girl.

But these are minor aberrations.

THE PERFIDY OF RON BARASSI

By 'Batman', *Bulletin*, January 9, 1965.

I almost didn't write this week. I was too upset and miserable.
I have been through an almost unbearable shock. How can I
tell you? Ron Barassi has applied for the job and been accepted
as playing coach of Carlton. Sydney fellows wouldn't understand
the perfidy of this. There are two things that good fathers do
for their sons in Melbourne, neither thing more important than
the other, but both must be done on the date of birth and not a
day later. That is, put him down for a good school and put his
name on the waiting list for the Melbourne Cricket Club. The
M.C.C., dating from 1838, is the oldest club of any kind in Victoria. We invented the game of Australian Rules football back
in 1858 and Carlton was an upstart club that wasn't heard of
until 1864. This is why we look in horror at the departure of
Barassi.

Barassi, until last week, was the greatest demon of them all.
He was Mr. Football in Melbourne. When the electoral office
puts out sample forms they never use a name like John Doe or
John Smith. They put Ron Barassi. If you ask a Melbourne
newspaper man for the greatest news story of 1964 automatically
he will say: "Ron Barassi's move to Carlton."

You should have seen some of the letters that have been in
the papers. Here's a couple from the *Sun*. "A staunch Demons
supporter, I cried when I learned of Ron Barassi's appointment
to Carlton. If Barassi feels that he is too good for Melbourne,
then why go to a lower club? The victories won't be as frequent
nor will the praise and sympathy from his supporters, Carlton
and Melbourne alike.—Demons Supporter (Melbourne)."

"What does Ron Barassi think he is doing? How about the
thousands of Demon fanatics who have defended him when
attacked, backed him up when he is outspoken and supported
him when down?—Red and Blue (Burwood)."

But that's not all. Here in Melbourne we love our budgies
and it has always been our custom to make our little ones loyal
footy supporters. So there have been all sorts of letters from
budgie lovers. One lady at Lilydale reported how patiently she
taught her budgie to sing "Come on Ron". There was another
lady in the city who went even further. She taught her budgie

to say: "Come on the Demons", "Kick a goal Barassi", and "Good kick Barassi". What are these people to do now? As I understand it budgies can be taught only at a very early age, and it is too late for them to turn now. I hate to say it, but I think these budgies will have to be strangled.

And there's this problem. Every little kid in Melbourne as soon as he can walk is given a football sweater by his loving parents. Three out of four of all sweaters would be exactly correct Melbourne football sweaters. And of the umpteen thousand little Melbourne football sweaters, nine out of 10 would have the number 31 on the back. This is the number always worn by Ron Barassi in battle. It was also worn by his late father, Ron Barassi Snr, a former Melbourne rover.

Sweaters are one thing, but it goes further. They also make these football jackets for dogs in club colours. There was a shop here called Poodles Paradise and very nearly all the jackets they sold for divine poodles were Melbourne jackets with 31 on the back. Can you imagine all the unstitching that will have to be done?

Even now I find it all hard to believe. There have been many coaching offers before. Some time back there was an offer from Woodville in South Australia, but Ron made it clear that he wouldn't go under £5000 a year. Ron makes £1000 to £1500 a year from his TV and radio appearances alone. Then, last December 10, Carlton made Barassi this offer of playing coach for three years at £3000 a year; not bad for a part-time seasonal job. We were happy to note next day that he knocked the job back. After all, why should he want it? He is assistant coach at Melbourne, he is heir apparent to Norm Smith, who has been the brilliant coach for 14 years. He has only to bide his time to collect the most noble job in football.

Then, incredibly, right on the eve of Christmas, he changed his mind. Despite the fact that he had some powerful rivals like Murray Weideman, the former captain of Collingwood, Carlton appointed Barassi as their new coach, fast as you can bat your eyelid. Why did he do it. I have thought and thought about this one. Was it mere hunger for money? Barassi is 28, still at the height of his powers and still the inspiration and power of the Demons.

I remember all too well the 1963 disaster, the trial of Ron Barassi when he met the tribunal at Harrison House on a charge of striking John Peck of Hawthorn. You might say it was the biggest court case of 1963. Over 250 people waited outside on the result and every newspaper assigned three men to the job, to say nothing of radio and TV. Well, Ron was suspended for four matches, which put him out for the finals and unquestionably cost Melbourne the premiership. This mustn't happen again.

There's the theory that all this is part of a demonic plot. Ron is going to Carlton just as a coach. If he is a success, in three years' time he will be just beautifully ripened to take over as coach from Norm Smith on his retirement.

But already there have been threats from the Melbourne committee that never will they clear Barassi to Carlton. They couldn't afford to have such a player against them. It is all too much for me. I don't understand anything any more. How can I sustain a worthy loathing for the opposition if my idols start romping around from team to team?

A SALUTE TO THE GREAT McCARTHY

From the novel by Barry Oakley.

Before our first match against Wentworth we were presented with our jumpers, in turn, and all the school clapped. I'm going up the wooden steps to the low platform in the school yard, eyes down in an ecstasy of modesty before Valerie and all the girls, when behind Mr. Sims the headmaster I am appalled to note my father approaching, parking by the fence and spoiling it all by yelling good on yer boy in a foghorn of I-told-you-so triumph. I saw him for the first time with the eyes of others, a big man, florid, bellied, the successful businessman who just didn't look right in a suit. It was his first big moment in ten years, since the time he'd been elected mayor, in the days when he was younger and slimmer and he cared.

The big buses were rolling in from Wentworth by the time he could get across to shake my hand, invading us with their foreign green and gold colours as my father says to me: 'Just a start boy, just a start. At your age, I played for the town, remember that.' When he thumped me on the shoulder with his ham of a hand, I felt it was his back, not mine.

Horseplay in the dressing shed, cuffs over the head, football boots tossed high, the team song. In our new blue jumpers with intricate W. H. S. monograms, we thought we had changed into men—until a whistle blast cuts us to size. Stop that, says Mac-Guinness, pompous as a country mayor. What is this, a social match? We finish enrobing in silence, the new wool prickles the bare skin, boot-stops clatter the floorboards. We gather round him, this mad Moses. It is his moment, not ours or our fathers! We're his to mould, and he knows the exact shape.

'This is no Wednesday afternoon frolic, this is war. A struggle, a preparation. For life! You don't believe it yet, you're young—but you'll see.' Pacing up and down in a check suit, out of place in this creaking shed on the world's edge, yet loving every minute.

'In the next few minutes you get your first taste—of life! Team against team, man to man, will against will! Yours against the other fellow's, and winner take all! The prize? (He's red, his face is swollen, we haven't seen this man before, I want to look away.) Not premiership points, pennants, cups—confidence! Self-respect! Pride in yourself, your team! Determination! (He shouts it, bangs it against the tin roof, he's throwing a challenge to the whole world, this is *his* match and we are his counters.) Nothing, but nothing, can stop you if only you set your mind! Focus your mind, your will on the job to be done. Focus your mind and say it with me—win! win! win!'

Giddy with words, you tumble onto that flat dreary oval. It's your first real match, you're ten feet tall, the people round the boundary fence are tiny, there's nothing in that landscape save the goalposts, the cars parked round the incline, the old red rotunda where the timekeeper sits. A kind of theatre world. No props and just the wind blowing. A school match, take it easy—but my guts pay no heed to reason. The green-and-golds run out, a pride of young men, the enemy. I'm full forward, an exposed position right there in the goals, the kids' yells ripping through: 'McCarthy you slob! Tanglefoot!' I'm close to them and can see their faces but there's light years between the watcher and the watched. Valerie? Maybe in that group of senior girls. And there my father in his big top-of-the line Comet Special.

They fade. Big Norman fills my sights, round and solid and with a pig's white flesh, his face rashed in fiery pimples, not broad in the shoulders but solid through them, slightly humped.

One of the Wentworth hoods, that tatty frontier town, the poor relation over the river. Watch this guy, a great chopper from behind, slow on his feet but a ton-up man in his Dad's old Customline. Seventeen other fellows out here with you, where's the worry? Right here in the shrivelled gut. I feel frail and papery and short of breath, on the edge of the family's traditional asthma, my wind coming in tiny whistles. The number on my back, 16. That's me, that's all you are now, a numeral.

The umpire, who came with them from Wentworth, holds the ball high, blows the whistle; a yell from the pickets and off she goes—the ball tumbling my way. Come one, come on! The instinct takes an age to get to my brain and I hear the thump as Big Norman takes it on his chest. Wake up McCarthy! You mug! I hear the jeers as he moves back slow and confident to kick. I am an inch high, waiting, as whomp! he boots it hard, starts a chain reaction, mark, kick, all gold and green, exploding into a goal. Toot of horn, stamp of feet as the goal umpire, a clockwork man in white, waves his two white flags.

The ball goes back to the centre, the machine starts again, and I wish I were someplace else. Anything but this public humiliation. But look: there's Jenkin the bank manager driving past, old Mrs. Ring walking slow with her stuffed string bag. Life proceeds as usual, it's only a game. But what, are we downhill? Tumble, bounce, the ball's coming our way again—along the ground, awkward, erratic as a tossed grenade, over there in open country. Charge! Run! Thump thump and I beat him to it, bend to pick the thing up, fumble, I hear Norman's rhino gallop—what hits me, a tank? Flat out, the world spinning, the grass rising from me at forty five degrees. Mac Guinness running out, all righteous and protective. 'You dirty young so-and-so,' he screams, brandishing the fist at Norman, who stays impassive, only the jaw moving as he chews his gum.

'That's enough of that,' says the umpire, 'get off the field.'

'What are you, blind in one eye? That was a definite charge.'

'Get off the field or I'm reporting you for intimidation.'

'I'm attending my player,' says MacGuinness, dragging me to my feet, the saliva showing as he hisses: 'Come on damn you! Get up! Show him! Beat him! Kill the bastard!'

Norman watching close by, big and stolid, chewing, chewing. Shake the head to get the stars out. And feel the venom enter the blood, the lust to crush this guy. Atkins, the pigeon-toed farmer's boy, kicks the ball from the centre, and I wait. The right height, this one is mine. Norman moving out, doing his rhino trot. Lumber on ahead, you creep, and give me a run at you. He does. I run. The ball. His back. I take off, put a knee into his neck, sail up, hands outstretched; mine! Big Norman inert on the ground, and the kids are shouting. The great McCarthy! The monster levers himself up, slowly, muttering. And the Great McCarthy kicks it straight over his head: a goal.

Your perspective changes. It's not the match, the flags, the team. It's you and the other guy. Man to man. He waits his time, he's the patient type. We're losing, we drop back slowly over two quarters, but I have eyes only for Norman, he has eyes only for me. There's not long to go, we're four goals down, MacGuinness is pacing the boundary, he shouts, waves his arms, but the wind takes it from his mouth, he's powerless. We're going to lose, the tension's gone, it's just plod plod and the bump of bodies, a knot of us wheeling in the goal's mouth. I race into the turmoil foolish and wild, grab the hefty enemy body, Norman lifts his elbow; pow! McCarthy's down again, the planets wheeling red and blue and white in his head.

In the dressing shed. Kids are changing, teachers fussing, my head aches with a steady klaxon blare. My father appearing from nowhere, scent of beer on his breath as he leans over. 'You all right boy?' I nod, wanting him to go out. He understands and does. We've nearly finished dressing, the shame of defeat has almost left us, we're thinking of other things, I have Valerie in my mind, was she satisfied or did I shame her?— when stop, look, at the door: MacGuinness, his face the bone colour of the raincoat he's just put on, a going-away garment. He's quiet. He seems close to howling, he is Hitler after a battle, come back to give his generals his rage.

'Great fellers,' he says. 'Great. You horseplay all you like. Don't let it worry you. All you did after all was let yourselves down. And your school. And me. I work,' he says, getting louder. 'I give up my time, hour after hour, night after night. Try to mould you into men. And you fold! You let me down! Thanks. Thanks very much. I'll give you just one more chance. Hear me? One more. Play like you did today and you're not finished— I am. Get yourself another coach. A kid's coach. But not me!'

Wow. We're embarrassed rather than afraid. He goes out and runs into Hollingsworth, the umpire, on his way in for the after-game chit-chat and the quaffing of drinks. MacGuinness the mad brushes straight past him, so Hollingsworth turns and goes too. Five minutes later the enemy buses, offended, are roaring off for their home airfield. 'Hey,' says Turner, the kid next to me, 'how's it with all that crap about sport and friendship?'

'The man is mad.'

'He's what?' says Sayers the stupid, craning a long neck round to participate, 'who's mad?'

I repeat it for him slowly. 'MacGuinness is mad. He's not a coach, he's a madman.' All through us, high with sweat, rebellion rumbled.

I stand on the Warwick Football Ground, the month is March, a new year, MacGuinness has gone behind layer after layer of days. School is only two streets and five months back, but at nineteen this in an age. I am in training to play for the town, I must go on, in the only skill I seem to have: my life by February having come to a dead stop. The bright ones in my Matriculation year have gone on to university, careers, the city. Valerie has deserted me for Melbourne, where right now she walks the Monash University campus, a fresher, doing Arts. Two letters exchanged and then no answer—like MacGuinness, she's abandoned the town, where McCarthy wastes away the summer days by the river aboard Lenore the waitress, or underneath a car.

But here it is March and a new momentum starting, McCarthy the country nobody standing there holding a football, surrounded by men of muscle, in greens golds blues reds, all the colours of the minor leagues from miles around, listening to Tiger Thomas, the old pro from the city, past his prime but once a star. Thin legs, small hips but broad in the shoulders, slightly stooped over, tossing a ball from hand to hand.

'Boys. Last year, they tell me, you didn't do no good. Finished near the arse of the ladder. Last year, they tell me, you was inclined to let the other mobs call the tune, make a chopping-block of youse. Boys, no more. We're going to change all that. Down at Richmond where I come from, we play it only one way. Hard. Not like it was a social match. We're going to train harder than the other mobs. Play harder. We're going to climb up there to the top!'

He uplifts an arm and points skyward, the tattooed dragon ripples alive along his bicep. We follow it up to the always-blue

Murray Valley sky, and we cheer, and the quiet committeemen nod approvingly, and we start to train. Smell of sweat, animality; shouts, grunts of effort, thud of leather on leather and bone on bone as we work out, c'mon now get into it, running, kicking, jumping high to mark. You move arrow-fast, you twist and turn, you sink the boot hard into the leather, you poise four feet clear of the ground, arms up to take the ball, an old training ball, soft and deeply polished, a pleasure to the touch. You come off breathless and scarlet through the shadow of the gaping grandstand, silent now but soon to shout; into a closed world, linament, fat-armed trainers in singlets who caress and bully your body slap/slap with expert hands, modelling you into footballer's shape.

You lie there flat and look up at the honors boards and the sepia team photos of the past. And there he is, good morning, the great man, *the* great McCarthy, first ruck for Warwick 1937–38–39, the premiership days, folded arms, hair parted down the centre.

'In those days every man a champeen,' says Charlie, working my body, a trainer for thirty years, knowing every muscle. 'He would've made the city sides, they was after him in droves, then came the war. A very powerful footballer, with hands like pincers and a leap like a steel spring. Good to see another McCarthy peeling off for the town.'

That was it, it suddenly came to me, lying there in oil with a towel over the private parts. You didn't just play for Warwick, you stripped, bared the flesh and were nailed to a board. You had Warwick written up and down you in blue and white stripes, once a week, to suffer and die and rise again; you represented your tribe.

All through March, that lingering summer month, we train, with the narrowed eyes and puffed pipes of the selectors pointed straight at us. As the first match approaches the three of them seem to hunch closer together by the fence and merge into one: Matt the farmer, Norm the stock and station agent, and in the middle Leslie Grenfell, Valerie's dad, porkpie hat and Returned Soldiers badge, with a McCarthy in his gunsights at last. He gritted his teeth at my fancy pick-ups at speed, pretended to be distracted when I leapt high for marks, and punished me for my flashiness by making me first reserve.

We played Wentworth first up, the poor relation across the

river. The town that hated our wide streets and the irrigation greenness of our parks, our big schools, all glass, and our single supermarket. It was bred into them when they were kids and when we visited them for football it piped out with a high whistle; light a match and we'd all go up, boom.

The noise starts as our trojan-horse buses unload us at their hard-dirt oval (collapsed fence, lurching goalposts). Our dressing room a tin shack out in the open, and the cold inland wind is part of their hate, whistling in through every hole, trying to lift the roof. The battle begins while I sit and shiver on the reserves bench, the wind up the khyber, right in front of their ancient grandstand, the spare man, not in the crowd, not on the field, neither fish nor flesh, sitting next to the club officials in no-man's land, our backs to the enemy.

Fist, elbow and foot: their technique is simple. Pick out the talented Warwick guys, gun 'em down. By three-quarter time, sitting round in a circle sucking oranges, three of our players are out on their feet, look at Soapy Williams if you please, all you can see being the whites of his eyes. Things are bad, our supporters are silent, a tight group under the outer gum trees, near their cars and ready for rapid flight.

Thomas the Tiger talks quiet, spitting out pips for words: 'Listen you goddamn bastards, you have just 25 minutes left to show me you're not cream puffs. Never in all my life, Jesus, have I seen such a performance. Namby-pamby! You're going to get five goals, you're going to beat these hicks, and you got the wind behind you to help you do it. Passengers! Too many passengers! What is this, a picnic flight? You see their bruiser over there? Leave him to me. First, I iron him out, that's the signal. Then we run all over them. Now get out there and knock 'em down.'

They run back to their positions, I trot back to the reserves bench, turning my back on the insults from over the fence (What? You can't even get a game? Christ, he must have one leg). The ball is bounced, a punch-out, a quick kick, Soapy Williams sets himself, Baldy Adams their bruiser takes aim, runs and trundles right through him. Adams keeps on going, a loco-motive, while Williams pauses, buckles, drops. The crowd go mad, they love it, players gather, jostle, punch, while four of our trainers dash out, unfurl a stretcher, carry him off. Grenfell, two up from me on the bench and not a word between us till this moment, turns to me crimson: 'Get out there boy. Get out there fast!'

Who, me? I stand, peel off the mild-mannered Clark Kent dressing-gown to reveal my true colours: shorts a spotless white, blue jumper with W.F.C. on the breast, intricately worked. I'm on! The new man, McCarthy the immaculate, he gambols, a gazelle freed. My father's over there, in that cheering crowd, and fat Mrs. Wilson the football fanatic and Leon Moore the chainsmoking hairdresser and my enormous uncle and they'll talk about it all week.

To full forward! The goals! Tiger Thomas is yelling, but here's the ball, here, race over to it, scoop up, run, bounce, two approaching heavies, elbows up; twist, baulk, keep on running—open go! The goals, ahead, steady now, take aim and fire through the middle. McCarthy! Our mob go mad, there's a group of them in the derelict rotunda, it thunders with their stamping feet. Warwick revives! McCarthy's name flutters in the air, a flag, a sign towed by a plane.

The ball's bounced again in the middle. Watch out for Baldy Adams! I note the monster is close, aroused by the scent of blood. But I am on fire too, this game is mine, I am fresh and they're tired, moving spring-heeled amongst them, heavy of leg. Our wingman has it now, Eddie, the fleet part-aboriginal with the delicate bones; he's racing round the boundary, he kicks hard and high, I see Adams start his hippo wallow, we are on collision courses. The ball; him, both closer; start your spring—now! At the last moment I jump, Baldy's bulk hurls itself below me; I sit up there on his whale back and take the ball.

Gymnast! Acrobat! Loud noises from fence and rotunda, the crowd come to life, as the monster uprears from the turf, flat nose, tiny smile, a frog, a page from a textbook on evolution, his beady eye saying you are my dinner. But the divinity is in McCarthy, a wind; he has to stand and watch as I boot the ball fifty yards, a goal.

But we too have our hired gunman from the city, and as the ball's bounced again I see Tiger amble over slowly. A flurry, someone kicks the ball high. It hangs up there, a wheeling hawk, leaving me exposed below it. Chicken out, look behind even, and you'll be shamed forever. Stand there, waiting for death. Hear the thump of big boots. Tiger, it is time, a tank attack.

257

Baldy is charging me, Tiger is charging him. There's a noise, half thud, half explosion, while the ball drops plop in my lap. Uproar! I turn to see the two men on the ground, fallen trees. The trainers run out. Tiger hobbles off on one leg, Baldy gets up then folds over slow and majestic, dramatic as a TV death.

The crowd! Oh my! The wind is fresher, the beer cans tumble on, brawls whirlpool up and down the hill, the four local cops walk the fence tight-lipped, and from behind the goals a trumpet sounds. Headlamps Harrison, the lanky retarded bugler, calling his compatriots to arm—the boy-man I used kick a football with, the gangling peeper on girls; blast after blast as he races up and down the hill, his mad Marseillaise.

The last few minutes I give over to Scribe, hard of hearing, short of sight, his 4000 cliches at the ready for the Warwick Gazette: 'In those last hectic moments, Wentworth's cooler heads prevailed, and their greater steadiness in the crisis carried the day. The loss of T. Thomas, a tower of strength all day, proved a fatal blow to the Warriors, despite the impressive debut of McCarthy, who notched three goals. But he proved unable to pull the fat out of the fire, and the home side ran out winners by nine points.'

The big time at last for McCarthy? Not so. The next Thursday, when the selectors retire behind pipesmoke to pick the side, I can imagine it all. 'Time we considered young Jack McCarthy.' That would be Matt the farmer talking, tamping down the tobacco with stubby fingers, looking across at Norm the agent, crimson after half a hundred lagers. Aye, says Norm, with you there Matt; time we did. They wait. Grenfell not speaking, looking straight ahead, appearing to meditate. 'Nope. Not ready. Too green. Flash in the pan. Better a solid man like Wally Turner who'll give us four quarters of straight football!' Matt and Norm muttering, and McCarthy into the freezer for another week.

The next match is on our own ground, our own crowd behind me as I sweat it out on the reserves' bench. I get a game for twenty minutes, kick goals. We win, everyone is happy, except for my dad. He comes into the clubrooms afterwards, the first time for years, all booze and fight. I'm in the bath, wanting very much to submerge. He looks down at his amphibian son who is naked and ashamed.

'Great,' he says. 'Great. This time, you go in the side. Hear me? This time you go in. Discrimination,' he says loudly. 'Too much discrimination.'

BLACK NIGHT IN COLLINGWOOD

By John Morrison

Mrs. Brady turned from the stove and hurriedly placed a roasting-dish on the table. "Phew, that's hot!"

A rich odour of roast lamb filled the little kitchen. Mrs. Woods, in on a neighbourly visit from next door, sniffed appreciatively. "It smells good."

"It ought to. I paid plenty for it. Fifteen and six. You could buy a whole sheep for that once, wool and all."

Mrs. Woods, with an expression of disapproval, watched Mrs. Brady baste the sizzling joint. "I don't know how you can be bothered to cook a hot dinner Saturday night."

"You'd be bothered all right if you was in this house. You wouldn't get them two blokes of mine to sit down to this at twelve o'clock Saturday. Not young Jimmy, anyhow—not in the football season."

"I heard he was playing for Mordialloc again this year. I thought he was going to turn it up."

"That'll be the day! He'll turn it up when he gets his damn neck broke, not before."

"I suppose Pop's following Collingwood—they're playing Footscray, aren't they?"

"Fair dinkum, I wouldn't know if they was playing Dudley Flats. I've had football. I'm always glad when it's over. I get a bit of peace then."

Mrs. Brady returned the joint to the oven, glanced at the clock, and began moving the pots around on the stove.

Mrs. Woods, for the third time in half an hour, got up to go. "My God, just look at the time! That lot of mine'll be in any minute."

Mrs. Brady, just as reluctant to end the session as was her friend, promptly came back to the table and enquired, more affably, "Going out?"

"I wish I was. We've got Harry's folks coming. His old man's all right, but you know how I get on with his old woman. What're you doing?"

"Depends on Collingwood. Joe's been talking all the week of going to the flicks, but it'll be another story if that damn football team loses. He gets a bit full when they win . . ."

"They were leading thirty-two . . . . half-time."

"Thank God for that!" Mrs. Brady after another glance at the clock, sat down. Mrs. Wood also sat down but on the extreme edge of the chair, as if ready for . . .

"That Marlon Brando's on. I've never seen him yet . . ."

They got talking of pictures. It was very peaceful. Through the quiet give and take of the two gossips the clock ticked steadily on, the pots bubbled and hissed on the stove, and a muffled voice rose and fell on a radio in another room.

An inner door opened and a young girl came in. She was wearing a highly-coloured floral dressing-gown and pink mules, and had her hair set in butterfly-pins.

"Hello, Mrs. Woods."

"Hello, Dulcie. I was wondering who was in there."

Mrs. Brady was observing her daughter critically. "How're you feeling now?"

"All right. I told you I was all right. Done my frock?"

"I said I'd do it as soon as I got the table cleared, if you'll stop worrying. He isn't coming till after seven, is he?"

"Keep your wool on. I only asked." Dulcie rubbed her mother's cheek with the back of her hand and seated herself on the edge of the table.

Mrs. Woods was smiling at her in the interested, slightly-envious way of a matron watching a girl prinking herself up for an outing. "Still going with Bill, love?"

Dulcie smiled back, and winked. "He'll do me!"

"Good on you! What's up with the football this afternoon?"

"Oh, Mum says . . ."

"She come in with a sore head and a bit of a sniff last night," put in Mrs. Brady. "I told her if she wanted to go out tonight she could just content herself in the house for the rest of the day. It's no day to be standing looking at a football match."

Dulcie looked round at the yellow evening sunlight streaming in at the window, and winked again at Mrs. Woods. "They're winning anyway. They had a nine points lead at three-quarter time. Bobby Rose got a beaut goal in the second quarter."

"It'll be about over now." Mrs. Woods's eyes sought the clock again, and she fairly jumped off her chair. "Jeese. I'll get turfed out! Have a good time, Dulcie. See you tomorrow, Ruth. You can tell me about Marlon Brando . . ."

"If Collingwood wins! Ta-ta, Peg."

Dulcie, after a bit of chatter with her mother about what she was going to wear, went back to her room—and radio. Mrs. Brady began to clear a litter of dishes and cooking utensils from the table.

Five minutes passed. Then the radio suddenly stopped and the door was flung open. Dulcie didn't come in. She just stood there, looking in at her mother with an expression of horrified astonishment, wide-eyed and open-mouthed.

"Mum!"

Mrs. Brady faced her in guarded silence from the other side of the table. She knew.

"They got beat?"

With a grim face, she picked up the electric iron and tested it for heat by shooting a bit of spittle at it.

"That Trusler got a goal—oh, Mum, Dad'll have a fit!"

He came in at a quarter-past six. He was a big, slow-moving man, and entered with the weary "Thank God I'm home!" air of a workman at the end of a particularly exhausting day.

Mrs. Brady, seasoned veteran of a football home, brewed a pot of tea as soon as she heard him coming along the side of the house, and managed to be at the stove with her back to the door as it opened. By the time she turned round it was understood that he had already looked towards her, and both were saved the initial embarrassment of meeting each other's eyes. For the next few minutes she could study him to her heart's content; he wouldn't look at her.

"By jeese, it's cold outside!" he said as he pulled off his overcoat and hung it behind the door.

Her lips tightened as she noted that his voice was deliberately lowered to hide the rasp in it.

"Get a cup of tea into you then. I've just made it fresh. And your slippers are there on the side."

"That'll do me, mate. Me feet's like blocks of ice."

He had his head down now, and she watched him closely as he settled into an armchair near the stove and began unlacing

261

his boots. She had changed into her going-out frock, not to save time later, but just to remind him.

"So we lost," she said sympathetically as she poured a cup of tea and placed it at the end of the table where he could reach it.

"Lost?" Struggling with his laces, he repeated the world thoughtfully, as if it were the clue to a problem. "Yes, we lost. We lost all right. Three-quarter time we had it in the bag, and we finished up losing. I'm satisfied now we got the stiffest side in the League."

"Dulcie says Bill Twomey got hurt."

"Two goals in two kicks, in about five minutes. Then goes off hurt. Wouldn't it! And they don't need to talk to me no more about Jack Collins. Seven behinds and one goal—God spare me days . . ." in his excitement he raised his voice and it immediately cracked. He coughed in an effort to cover up, and picked up his cup of tea. "Anyhow, what's the use of worrying you about it—you wouldn't understand. We lost and that's all there is to it. Jim in yet?"

"Not yet. What d'you want to do—wait for him?"

"We might as well, there's no hurry. I'm not particularly hungry, anyway."

"There's a good hot dinner. You haven't been going and getting yourself upset again, have you?"

His head came up suddenly, and for the first time they looked straight at each other. "Now what d'you supposed I'd be getting myself upset over?"

"You sound like you've been bawling your head off. You can hardly speak."

"Well, that's all right, ain't it? I've been to a football match. What d'you want me to do—stand like a stunned duck all the afternoon?"

"All right," she said pacifically, "there's no need to get shirty about it. What about a gargle with an aspirin? I'll mix you some."

"Look, Mum, me throat's all right. I had a bit of a tickle in it this morning when I got up. I might have a cold coming on."

"If you thought you had a cold coming on you shouldn't have been to a football match," she said incautiously, and turned quickly to the cupboard so that she wouldn't meet the exasperated stare the retort was sure to provoke.

262

A minute or two passed while he rolled a cigarette with great concentration.

Then, in an effort to dispel an atmosphere which had already become difficult, she said. "Mrs. Woods has just gone out. She was here all the afternoon."

"Did she say anything about Geelong?"

"All she said was that Harry's still working on the truck. He thinks he might have it on the road next weekend."

He nodded, and silence fell again.

He was sitting crouched forward with his eyes fixed gloomily on the base of the stove. She could tell by the speed with which he was burning up his cigarette that he was thinking furiously, living over again the last fateful moves of the game, yearning backwards to that blessed moment around three-quarter time when it had been in the bag. Observing him at leisure from the far side of the table where she stood whipping an egg, she saw him involuntarily move his head forward, brows knitted, eyes fairly popping as if he were following a snake vanishing into the ash-pan. Then, as if the snake had suddenly turned and lunged at him, he drew back, with eyes tightly shut and face twisted with horror—Trusler's goal.

Absurd though it was, she couldn't but feel sorry for him.

"I wish you'd let me mix you some aspirin, Joe. It would help to steady your nerves, even if you haven't got a cold."

"Look, Ruth," he exclaimed irritably, "I wish you'd leave a bloke alone. I'm not worrying nobody, am I?"

"You're worrying *me*. You shouldn't be getting yourself stewed up like that at your age."

"Who's getting stewed up? Stone the crows, I'm just sitting here having a nice quiet smoke. I've told you before I don't like taking them aspirins unless I've got to. They play my guts up."

"They never did you any harm that I know of," she said stubbornly. "You're in no fit state to be going out like that, anyhow." She was going to say something more, but pulled herself up as she realized she had already conceded precious ground. And the fact that he let the remark pass in silence showed that he was wide awake to it.

She took Dulcie's frock through to the girl's room, and came back and began laying the table for the evening meal.

Ten minutes later the son came in. They could hear him

whistling all the way up the side of the house from the front gate.

"Sounds like Mordialloc won, anyway," she remarked cheerfully, glad of a chance to break the long silence.

He just grunted, but raised his head with a glimmer of interest as the door opened.

Jim came in with the headlong exuberance of youth, heeling the door behind him and flinging his leather bag into a corner so that both bumps sounded as one.

"Hi, there! Why don't you come and barrack for a winning side, Dad!"

His father gave him a sad smile. His mother, standing where only Jim could see her, was making signs to him to be careful what he said.

He was smartly dressed, more as if he were on the point of going out than just coming in, and after taking off his hat and raincoat strode across the room and stood looking down at the pans on the stove.

"How's dinner, Mum? I've got to be out again in half an hour. Ted's picking me up in the City."

"Aren't you having a shower?"

"I had all that at the ground. Dulcie in?"

"She's in her room. Give her a call and I'll dish up right away. It's all ready."

Mrs. Brady brought out the plates from the oven, and after going to the passage door and yelling: "Come on, Dulcie, it's on the table!" Jim returned to the side of his father's chair.

"The old Magpies had a bad day, Dad."

Joe nodded wearily. "We should've won. Seen the scores?"

"Yes. Led every quarter up to the last, eh? What happened to Bill Twomey?"

"Pulled a muscle in his leg. He got two goals almost before the whistle stopped blowing."

"What sort of a day did Jack Collins have?"

Joe pulled himself together. "One goal and seven behinds! Work that out for a so-called star forward! Footscray would have been better off . . ."

"He's still a star forward. You've got to give it in that the best of them have their off-days."

"They all have their off-days when they're up against Jack Hamilton!"

264

"I wouldn't say that." Jim flinched as his mother gave him a warning dig in the back, but finished what he had to say: "Collins didn't do too bad against Hamilton last time they met. He got eight."

Joe picked up his tobacco with the air of a man settling down to a formidable but not unwelcome argument. "How many times have you seen Collins play, mister?"

"I haven't seen a game this season, you know that . . ."

"All right—I have. Now then . . ."

"Collins gets the goals!"

"Pigs!"

"Joe!" Mrs. Brady, waiting for the last few seconds for an opportunity to break it up, seized on this just as Dulcie came into the room. "Can't you two talk football without doing your blocks?"

Jim gave her a hurt stare, caught the appealing wink, and shrugged his shoulders.

"Anyway, come and get your dinners. I want to get washed up." She shot a sharp glance at Joe. "We're all going out tonight."

"How did you go, Jim?" asked Dulcie as they pulled their chairs up to the table.

"We stoushed 'em, kid, we stoushed 'em. Mick Ryan was asking after you."

Dulcie wrinkled her nose to indicate how much Mick Ryan meant to her, and shifted her attention to her father. She liked the way he was looking at her frock.

"All right?" she asked, spreading the skirt and standing where he could see it.

"You're not bad for a wharfie's daughter, mate," he grunted. She sat down. "Cheer up, we're still in the four."

"What's special about that for Collingwood?"

"We've got an easy programme left, you know," put in Jim.

"We should be lying right up with Melbourne. A team that gets beat by the class of football that was played this afternoon . . ."

"Suppose you talk about something else till dinner's over?" suggested Mrs. Brady.

Joe was watching her carve the joint. "Not too much for me, Mum."

She stopped. "What d'you call too much? There's only one

slice there, I've given you the outside cut. You like it crisp, don't you?"

"Yes. Yes, I like it crisp. But I told you I'm not hungry. And only one spud."

"You was hungry enough last Saturday when you beat Melbourne." Then, before he could reply: "What about peas?"

"I don't think I'll have any at all. Just a bit of meat and a spud."

"That damn football'll be the death of you yet," she said as she took the plate to the stove.

Behind her back there was a swift exchange of glances. Jim gave his father a conspiratorial wink and made signs to Dulcie to keep talking. Dulcie showed the tip of her tongue to her father.

"Never mind him, Mum!" she called out. "He'll be all right once he gets out," and followed up by pulling a face at him that said quite plainly: "There, that'll cook your goose!"

"I'm not out yet!" he muttered defiantly.

They began to eat, but it was a far from happy meal. Jim and Dulcie ate heartily but hurriedly, with eyes every now and then seeking the clock. Joe "picked", head moodily bowed over his plate, selecting every portion with meticulous care, and looking at it for a moment before carrying it to his mouth, as if all the time he wanted to stop but didn't dare to.

Mrs. Brady sat bolt upright, watching his every movement out of the corners of her eyes, and disposing of her own food with a noisy and ostentatious relish. She'd given up hope, but if there were to be no pictures she would, at least, let him see how she felt about it. Football wasn't going to put her off *her* food.

Jim and Dulcie carried on what little conversation there was, but nothing flowed easily. It was the talk of people playing for time, the forced inconsequential talk of neutrals in the presence of an imminent quarrel. They tried in vain to make it four-cornered, but only Mrs. Brady came in. This made matters worse, because she did so with an exaggerated enthusiasm that obviously had no other purpose than to expose the silence of Joe.

When meat was finished, and two bowls, one of stewed fruit and one of custard, were placed on the table, everybody was conscious that another stage had been reached in a situation that

266

was rapidly approaching flash-point. Three pairs of eyes were on Joe as Mrs. Brady picked up the serving-spoon.

"What about some apricots?"

"No, thanks, I'm set. A cup of tea's all I want now."

"Spare me days, Dad," exclaimed Jim, "how would you be if you was barracking for St. Kilda! You'd be down to fly-weight!"

Joe glared, but before he could say anything, Mrs. Brady rallied.

"That's enough from you, Jim. You get on with your own tucker. And for Pete's sake stop staring at the clock, Dulcie! He can come in and wait for you, can't he, if you're not ready?"

"I was just looking," said Dulcie meekly.

"And see you keep inside, wherever you're going. Don't go running in and out of the night air."

"It'll be all right, Mum."

"You wouldn't be wearing that frock if I'd had my way. You'd have had something warmer on of a night like this."

"I reckon there's a storm blowing up," said Jim to his sister.

Mrs. Brady intercepted the half-concealed smiles, and frowned. "You was talking of being in a hurry when you come in."

She brewed a pot of tea and sat down.

"Excuse me," Joe murmured, "me feet's freezing." He retreated from the table to his seat at the stove, and the meal creaked along to a finish.

Everybody gave some indication of relief when a car tooted out on the street.

"There's Bill!" Dulcie got up, cup in hand, and stood hastily sipping the last of her tea.

"Ask him if he's going towards the City," said Jim.

A little later, after a whirl of last-minute titivating-up, and a few perfunctory kisses and not so perfunctory admonitions, the youngsters were gone and Mr. and Mrs. Brady were alone with their sorrows.

Mrs. Brady, with set lips, began to clear the table. She worked quickly, and with a certain intent deliberation as if all this were just a boring prelude to something much more important to be done next. Every now and then she looked at Joe, sitting with elbows on knees and face hidden in his hands.

267

With the departure of the children there was nothing now for either of them to shelter behind, and their quarrel, though not yet spoken, was right out in the open. Every touch of dish and pan sounded unnecessarily loud. Perhaps it was.

At the end of a difficult five minutes Joe raised his head and gave his wife a long offended stare. She was standing at the sink, in profile to him, and pretended not to be aware of it. But when he relaxed into his former position she seemed to think that an opportunity had been missed.

"You don't have to go out, you know, if you don't want to."

He ignored the remark, and after a little thoughtful contemplation of his bowed shoulders her expression slowly changed. She dried her hands and took down a small bottle from the mantelpiece. Dropping three tablets into a tumbler she watched them dissolve in a little water, filled up the glass with milk, stirred the mixture, and took it to him.

"Here," she said firmly, "get that into you."

He looked up at the glass suspiciously. The pressure of his hands had driven the blood from his face, making him pale and haggard.

"Go on," she said, "drink it up. Why didn't you say you had a headache when you come in, and be done with it?"

Still looking only at the glass, he took it from her and swallowed the medicine. "Thanks."

"And if you take my advice you'll get yourself straight into bed."

He didn't answer that, and nothing more passed between them while she finished washing up and put everything away.

He heard her go into the bathroom, and followed the trickle of water, the dropping of the soap into the rack, and the familiar rattle of the roller as she hung up the towel. Then her footsteps going up the passage to the bedroom, the moving about of things on the dressing-table, and the opening and closing of the wardrobe door.

When, all ready to go out, she returned to the kitchen, he hadn't moved.

"What's it like now? Has it eased off at all?"

"I'll be all right, Mum. You go out and enjoy yourself."

"I might as well. There's no sense in two of us sitting here moping."

"Yes, go on. I'll hit the cot."

268

"But, I'm telling you this, mister"—he kept very still as her finger prodded the nearest shoulder—"I'm not cooking no more hot dinners of a Saturday night. I've had it. Every damn Saturday night's the same now. You either come in full of beer and wind if they win, or full of pains and aches if they lose. If they lose next week you can just bring yourself in a packet of fish and chips, because . . ."

"Did you say you was going to the flicks?" he demanded sharply.

It was what she wanted. "Too right I am!"

"Then for God's sake, woman, go! Stop talking about it."

"I'm going all right . . ."

He could hear her muttering all the way down the passage, and gathered himself for the bang of the front door.

It shook the house.

She would have been gratified, though, if she had seen the despairing look he cast around the deserted kitchen before going back to his moody contemplation of the floor.

AND THE BIG MEN FLY

From the play by Alan Hopgood.

Scene III

(Lights up, and sound effects raised, as we return to COMMEN-TATOR, HARRY HEAD, and WOBBLY at the mike)

COMMENTATOR: And another one to Turner. Making his sixth goal. The Galahs seven goals one . . . forty-three points. And the Crows still to score. Turner's not even raising a sweat out there.

(Boos from the crowd)

What's going on?

WOBBLY: I see J. J. Forbes has finally decided to come back and face the music. He's sitting on the bench again. Someone threw a bottle . . . and there it goes . . . orange peels, beer cans . . . the crowd are taking out their spleen on Forbes, the quitter . . . the police are coming from everywhere to break it up.

COMMENTATOR: Forbes has sent a runner out to speak to Jones.

WOBBLY: Well, it had to come, Harry. Achilles Jones has just got to be taken off. A kid of four couldn't do worse than Jones has done today. Wait a minute . . . the runner's gone and Jones is still standing there.

COMMENTATOR: For Heaven's sake, look at that.

WOBBLY: Whatever that runner said to Jones has made him hopping mad. He's throwing a flamin' fit. You'd swear he had flea powder all over him. He's stamping the ground, snorting, waving his arms like he wants to kill somebody. The other players are killing themselves laughing. What is this, Harry? A football match or a sideshow?

COMMENTATOR: I just don't know any longer, Wob. But it stopped the crowd boo-ing. They can't boo because they're doubled up with laughter. Well, I never.

WOBBLY: There hasn't been a sound like this heard on the East Melbourne ground since back in '36, when Ocker Davis lost his strides, and played the rest of the match with one hand holding his jumper down over his hips.

COMMENTATOR: Umpire Begg's stopped the game. He's walking up to Achilles Jones.

WOBBLY: S'elp me, look at that. Jones is taking off his boots. He's taking 'em off! Begg's indicating that he's wasting time, but Jones is giving him his boots to hold. First one, then the other . . . and now he's taking off his socks. Begg's holding 'em up as much as to say, what do I do with these? But the runners coming back to collect them. Oh . . . I can't take much more of this.

COMMENTATOR: The runner's taken them off. Umpire Begg's standing there, scratching his head . . . and Jones is jumping up and down on the spot, ready to get on with it.

WOBBLY: And you people listening in, believe it or not, the Manangatang mystery man is standing there, in his two bare feet, waving his arms at the umpire to bounce the ball, and dancing round like a Maori doing a war-dance.

COMMENTATOR: Well, the best thing for Begg is to work it all out afterwards. He might as well bounce the ball and stop the farce as quickly as possible. Oh dear . . . I've described some strange incidents in my time . . . there's the bounce.

270

(*Stands in amazement*) Did you see that? Jones leapt about fourteen feet in the air and punched the ball before it even started to drop. What a beauty! It's gone forty yards. At least forty yards! What a hit-out! And Jones is off after it! Have you ever seen anyone move so fast. The crowd's stunned. Hypnotised. They can't believe it, and I don't know that *I* can. There's a pack of players smothering that ball, up on the half-forward zone . . . and Jones is up with them . . . the ball flies out of the pack. Jones has picked it up . . . Zanecchi for the Galahs has thrown everything he's got at Jones, but he's just bounced off him, and he's rolling on the ground . . . and Jones is still going. Stiffen the crows, he's kicked it . . . ten . . . twenty . . . thirty yards . . . *it's a goal*! The most amazing goal I've ever seen. That kick went sixty yards and it was still going . . . straight through the middle . . . and it came from the big bare toe of Achilles Jones!

The Crows have gone wild. I've gone wild. I'm either out of my mind or what we've just seen is the most amazing piece of play ever seen on a football field. Achilles Jones has goaled with one punch, and one kick, and all by himself . . . *in bare feet*. What do you say to that Wobbly? What do you say?

WOBBLY: (*downcast*) Yeah.

COMMENTATOR: The crowd's on its feet cheering. The other players are running in to pat Achilles on the back, but he hasn't even stopped for breath. He just turned and started running back to the centre, ready for more. Folks, don't ask me to guess at the speed with which he covered that ground. All I know is what I told you . . . by the time that pack had sorted out the ball, Jones was up with them . . . and you know the rest. Incidentally, Zanecchi is still in the hands of the trainers. The way he bounced off Jones, you'd have thought he had a collision with an express train. And look at J. J. Forbes down there. He's dancing up and down. *He's* gone mad, too. Jumping and yelling, and kissing everyone in sight.

WOBBLY: It's obviously not Friday.

COMMENTATOR: Say a few words, Wobbly, I'm exhausted.

WOBBLY: Er . . . yeah . . . well . . .

COMMENTATOR: One goal, six points to the Crows. They're thirty-seven points behind the Galahs, but it's only the first quarter. And by the look of the other Crows players, they're suddenly alive. They suddenly look like they *want* to play football.

And there's the bounce. And the big men fly! Jones again! And another forty yard hit-out . . . there it goes sailing straight up the ground. And Jones is off after it again. But Harrison has got it for the Galahs . . . Jones is dropping back . . . Harrison's kick is high . . . Jones changes direction and he's going after it! Jones marks it! Jones against six Galahs. Have you ever seen a pack flattened like that, Wobbly? Four Galahs are still on the ground, looking as if they've been hit by a swinging lump of concrete. And Jones, stands there, ready to take his kick . . . the bare-foot bomber . . . there it goes . . . oh, no, Wobbly I'm not seeing it . . . it's not happening. Jones has kicked another goal! A goal from practically the centre of the ground. Say something, Wobbly! I'm exhausted.

WOBBLY: I'd rather not. I've got a funny feeling it's all a nightmare.

COMMENTATOR: So, this is Achilles Jones. And by the look of him now, J. J. Forbes was *not* exaggerating. Not one bit. In fact, he was only giving us half the story, 'cause in three minutes Achilles Jones has staged the most remarkable exhibition of football ever seen anywhere. I know I'm safe in saying that because the distance that ball travelled is not only a record, it's a physical impossibility. But, we'll work out the story later. For the moment, this Jones has grabbed every single heart on this ground. Crows and Galahs alike, they're screaming with delight and amazement. You reckon he might be Superman, Wobbly?

WOBBLY: Well, this I *can* say. It's two goals. And I gotta admit, two of the weirdest goals I ever seen in my life. But it's only twelve points. The Crows are still thirty-one points behind. And that's a handy lead, in anybody's language. No matter if Jones can do all that again, he's only one man . . . It's a miracle. I'll give ya that. But it's not a miracle that can keep going for three quarters. That's what I've got to

say, Harry. Nobody could keep that up. And that includes
Achilles Jones. Nobody could keep that up.

(Stab music)

LIFE CYCLE

By Bruce Dawe

For Big Jim Phelan

When children are born in Victoria
they are wrapped in the club-colours, laid in beribboned cots,
having already begun a lifetime's barracking.

Carn, they cry, Carn . . . feebly at first
while parents playfully tussle with them
for possession of a rusk: Ah, he's a little Tiger! (And they
   are . . .)

Hoisted shoulder-high at their first League game
they are like innocent monsters who have been years
   swimming
towards the daylight's roaring empyrean

Until, now, hearts shrapnelled with rapture,
they break surface and are forever lost,
their minds rippling out like streamers

In the pure flood of sound, they are scarfed with light, a
   voice
like the voice of God booms from the stands
Ooohh you bludger and the covenant is sealed.

Hot pies and potato-crisps they will eat,
they will forswear the Demons, cling to the Saints
and behold their team going up the ladder into Heavan,

And the tides of life will be the tides of the home-team's
   fortunes

—the reckless proposal after the one-point win,
the wedding and honeymoon after the grand-final...

They will not grow old as those from more northern States
   grow old,
for them it will always be three-quarter-time
with the scores level and the wind advantage in the final term,

That passion persisting, like a race-memory, through the
   welter of seasons,
enabling old-timers by boundary-fences to dream of resurgent
   lions
and centaur-figures from the past to replenish continually the
   present,

So that mythology may be perpetually renewed
and Chicken Smallhorn return like the maize-god
in a thousand shapes, the dancers changing

But the dance forever the same—the elderly still
loyally crying Carn...Carn...(if feebly) unto the very end,
having seen in the six-foot recruit from Eaglehawk their hope
   of salvation.

14
Today: "A game of Russian roulette. The winner-take-all ethic rules supreme "

The modernised clubs North Melbourne, Carlton and Richmond, with the curiously old fashioned Hawthorn win everything from 1968 until 1982 modern business, modern football. Collingwood are the bridesmaids for most of the decade, giving rise to the extraordinary disease: the Collywobbles, and a deep interest in what went wrong. Sportswriting acquires a new, and possibly temporary, respectability.

WASSAMATTER WISEGUY

Robert Coleman, *Herald*, March 27, 1972.

You can't help wondering where they hibernate in summmer, Or, for that matter, for six days a week in winter.

But come Saturdays, from April to September, they emerge from unseen burrows in masses, like soldier crabs when the tide goes out.

The ubiquitous footy fan is a goldmine to students of human nature. In 100 minutes of play he can demonstrate almost every mood, emotion and characteristic known to mankind.

He can display ecstasy, frenzy, anger, sarcasm, anguish, stoicism, humor, loathing, contempt, astonishment, disbelief, happiness or grief—but never boredom or disloyalty.

A threatening cloud in the sky might keep him from weeding the garden, but a flood would not keep him from the football. Nor would fire or famine.

He is the most dedicated person on earth. He can stand all afternoon in the rain, drenched to the skin, and watch his team get beaten by 20 goals—and still find excuses for them.

Footy fans come in all ages, shapes, sizes and conditions of

North Melbourne full forward Phil Baker takes a magnificent mark in the 1978 Grand Final. But Hawthorn won the flag.

men—and women. Weekday inhibitions slip away to reveal all that is good and evil in the darkest recesses of their souls.

And there is no sound so terrifying as the raucous bellow of a football barracker in full cry.

If you look around you at the opening game on Saturday, the people you'll see will include:

THE WISEGUY. He has a wisecrack, filed and card-indexed in his head, for every occasion. He loves an audience and doesn't mind repeating the same jibe until everybody is sick of it. He thrives on encouragement.

THE SHIFTER. Can't stay in one place for five minutes; always looking for a better view.

THE BACKWARD-UPHILL-CLIMBER. Starts at the fence and backs his way up to the top of the hill, treading on every pair of feet on the way.

THE LEANER. Always leans on the bloke next to him.

THE WASSAMATTA MAN. Usually picks on a star player from the opposing team. Every time he fails to get the ball, the WM yells, "Wassamatta, Hudson? Won't he give you a kick?" Or, "Wassamatta, Nicholls? Can't you catch him?"

THE EAR PIERCER. Male or female. Bellows or shrieks in your ear from first siren to last. Follows you if you shift. You go home deaf on one side.

THE PUNCHER. Can't resist belting you one every time his team scores a goal.

THE DRINKERS. Usually come in schools of four to six, loaded with enough grog for five times their number. They start off in hearty good spirits. As the day wears on, and the pile of empties around them grows, their interest in the game diminishes; they became quarrelsome; their empties roll down the embankment under other people's feet; one or more get lost in the crowd trying to find their way back from the lavatory.

THE LATCHER-ON. You go to the footy with three mates and finish up with four. You don't know who he is or where he came from, but before you know it he's sharing your refreshments.

THE RULE BOOK MAN. Knows every law of the game covering every contingency. He would know exactly what the umpire should do if the scores were level and a player was having a shot after the final siren when a goalpost was shattered by lightning.

THE SPRAYER. Wants to share his beer with everybody.

With a favorable wind he can spray people 30 yards away.

THE SAUCE DAUBER. Tries to carry more hot dogs than he has hands for and gets sauce on everybody within reach.

THE DIPLOMAT. Agrees with everything everybody around him says, especially big blokes.

THE PLAYER'S MATE. Talks loudly about one of the players so everybody in earshot gets the message they're bosom buddies, and that the player wouldn't do a thing without first asking his advice.

THE CLUBMAN. Stands near the fence and calls out jocular remarks to the trainers and coach as they walk around the boundary impressing everybody that he has an "in" with the club.

THE GOAL UMPIRE'S ENEMY. From acute angle, with his view obstructed by an umbrella, swears "That wasn't a goal!" In the summer this bloke sits in the Outer at the M.C.G., in the vicinity of square leg, and disputes lbw decisions.

EAGLE EYES. Observes from 200 yards away on a dull day, things the umpire cannot see from a distance of five feet.

THE STATISTICIAN. Knows now many games every player has played, how many kicks he has had, how many goals and behinds he has kicked and how many grubbers. He can tell you that this is the fourth time Peter Hudson has pulled his right sock up before kicking for goal in a game against Essendon at Windy Hill—which you'll agree is a very handy thing to know.

THE ALOOF PROFESSIONAL MAN. A leading surgeon or lawyer. Imperturbable. Studies game analytically. Faintly murmurs approval or otherwise. Thoroughly enjoys himself but you'd never know it.

THE RATBAG. Loudmouthed aggressive, uncouth, usually two-thirds stoned and a thorough nuisance to everybody.

THE PUGILIST. Wants to pick a fight with anybody who'll be in it. If there are no takers he has one with his mate.

RELUCTANT WITNESS. Fellow drawn into somebody else's argument, ("YOU saw that, didn't you, mate?").

THE OLD PLAYER. "Listen, sport: I know what I'm talking about. I've played this game meself—against better players than this mob of goats, too."

THE WELL-EQUIPPED MAN. Comes prepared for all emergencies. Carries a folding stool, umbrella, overcoat, sandwiches, vacuum flask of hot soup, binoculars, Football Record and five pencils.

THE CRASHING BORE. It's no good shifting. He'll follow you.

THE MAN WITH FLU. He was too sick to work yesterday. Today he's spreading his germs generously. Tonight he'll sit up and watch all the replays. Sunday he'll watch World of Sport and more replays before he goes to an Association game. Monday he'll still be too sick to go to work.

THE LITTLE OLD LADY. Sweet, prim and demure; somebody's grandmother. Suddenly goes purple in the face and shrieks, "Flatten the rotten bloody mongrel!" Then goes on with her knitting.

YOUNGISH AND MIDDLE-AGED LADIES. Can be the most obnoxious, one-eyed, vociferous supporters of all. Frequently don't understand the rules and take every decision against their team as a personal insult.

SQUEALY CHICKIES. Go to watch their heart-throb player in action. What the other 35 players do is quite incidental. Anyone who bumps their man is a brute, and umpires who do not give him free kicks are cheats. They'll follow their man all the way to Harrison House if necessary.

THE LONER. Comes early stands high on the hill in the Outer; speaks to no one: doesn't barrack; intermittently reaches into his gladstone bag for another bottle; after game he is last seen heading through the park, going who knows where, with a slight list to starb'd.

THE CLERIC. Priests and clergymen are among the keenest of supporters. Some are extremely vocal and, when the going is really tough, one suspects they pray a little.

THE PUNTER. Turns his transistor on full blast for races in Melbourne, Sydney, Adelaide and Hanging Rock. Gathers a crowd around him to discuss horses while keeping one eye on the football.

THE LONELIEST MAN IN THE WORLD. Chap in the grandstand reserve at Collingwood who barracks for the visiting team.

WINTER HEROES

By Garrie Hutchinson/John Spooner, *Age*,
March 28, 1981

● *MUMS. She knows more about the private lives of her boys than the coach. She has sufficient food, blankets, changes of clothes, thermoses, umbrellas, rosettes, badges and souvenir programmes to survive a major catastrophe—such as losing. She has a voice louder than Dame Nellie's and puts the fear of damnation into the hearts of any umpire silly enough to come close. Rubbish any of her boys and you'll be lucky to escape retribution.*

● *THE PSYCHOPATH. Take a look at his eyes. Watch them become a shade lighter as he runs down the race, gleaming like a junkie after a fix. He's got an Everlast belt under his jumper for services rendered, and about to be rendered. He puts the opposition in fear of their lives, he has a long memory, a short fuse and would make the deaf hear footsteps.*

● *THE CATERER. The Lord Mayor's Dinner's got nothing on the feast available at any football ground, any Saturday. Pies so hot even Ronald Biggs wouldn't touch them; selected lagers and ales cold as a baby's bath; hot dogs drooping over both ends of a roll like an armful of dachshund; hamburgers so overwhelmed with fillings that Big Mac ought to take the hint and go home; chips fried fit for any pretender to the throne of France; donuts with jam better than mother makes .. there's no need to bring takeaways, everything has already been brought.*

• *THE VETERAN. You'll see him leaning on a goal post. Offering gratuitous advice to hungry young forwards. Chatting amiably with his old mate, the goal umpire. His knees resemble the skeleton of a fish; he has a catheter in his arm ready for the pain killing injection his arthritis craves. He's been around forever. He puts in a serviceable game every second week. Four kicks, two goals two, three hitouts earns his astronomical pay, and a shot at being next year's coach.*

SPOONER.

• *THUGS. Watch out for anyone lying unconscious near the toilets—he's sure to have some mates just looking for the reason why. And beware gap toothed long hairs sporting an ear-ring. They are so quick to take offence that you won't even know you gave them aggravation. And if you've wondered why there's less violence at the football than at the cricket it's because of the smoke. If a joint should flow your way, don't say you don't—just pass it along. Because someone will be watching. He'll look like a drinker with lace-up cuban heels, foam can-holder, trannie and button-up jeans, but he'll really be waiting for an insult to his generosity.*

● *THE INTELLECTUAL. Half time is your best bet to spot one of these, all corduroy and elbow patches, pipe and polysyllabic abuse. He'll be explaining the more esoteric points of the game to his son, or mistress. He'll buy a pie to keep in touch with his origins, but he'll bring his own wine. He'll read the* Guardian Weekly *during dull patches, but only after the social notes in the* Footy Record. *He stands in the outer in constant fear of someone behind him, someone who has listened to his aesthetic and political commentary without saying a word, someone he knows simply wants to kill him.*

● *THE SHOWPONY. Look for the open spaces. There he'll be spinning out of packs, taking towering marks over midgets, baulking at shadows, running on his toes, blind turning into brick walls. He's a receiver, as natural targets often are. You'll often see him in the hands of trainers, where the magic sponge starts him up again, the heroic little bloke.*

THE RON BARASSI MEMORIAL
LECTURE 1978

Text of Lecture Twelve, *Overland*, 1979.

*Ian Turner first delivered his Barassi Memorial Lecture at Monash
University in 1965. It was normally repeated annually thereafter, with
increasing fame, until 1978, when the final lecture was given at the
Prahran College of Advanced Education. Overland is indebted to Ken
Gott, who painstakingly made this transcription from the final tape,
checking references against Ian's notes and against the authorities quoted.*

Those who watched several years ago a TV show called "The
Big Game" in which costumed footballers—costumed in uniform, that is, and not in drag—were asked to answer quiz
questions for the honor of their clubs (and some slight material
rewards such as a see-through Whitmont shirt and a slightly-used
Holden by courtesy of Kevin Dennis's Autorama) would have
observed the following exchange:

"What team does Graham Kennedy barrack for?" "St.
Kilda." "Correct."

(Whereupon a scantily clad go-go girl danced onto the screen,
waving a pair of flags and leaving it open to some doubt as to
whether she was the prize for this segment of the show.)

"John Peck has four children. Are they all daughters or all sons?" "Daughters." "Correct."

"What famous scientist produced the theory of relativity?" "Don't know."

Those who observed this might well wonder whether there is sufficient intellectual content in the great Australian game to justify its inclusion in serious academic discourse.

However there is already a fair body of academic studies worthy of note. For example, Professor Dunn's pioneering work, *The Incidence of Brain Hernia Among Reserve Eighteens*; Professor Waller's definitive text, *The Brownlow Medal and the Rule of Law*; Professor Bradley's penetrating analysis, *Barassi and Hamlet—a Comparative Study in the Tragic Hero*; Professor Davis's distinguished monograph, *Informal Voting for the Collingwood Committee*; Professor Andrew's piledriving paper on *Minor Surgery of the Back Pocket*; and my own modest contribution, *The Tigers, the Blues and the Class Struggle*.

It is evident that academic exploration of this highly significant social phenomenon already provides a substantial proportion of the intellectual output of this university. And that is as it should be, because we are the inheritors of a long and distinguished tradition of intellectual inquiry, beginning with Joseph Strutt, the first historian of British sport, who published his *Sports and Pastimes of the People of England* in 1801. In it he said: "In order to form a just estimation of the character of any particular people, it is absolutely necessary to investigate the sports and pastimes most generally prevalent among them. When we follow them into their retirements, where no disguise is necessary, we are most likely to see them in their true state and may best judge of their natural disposition."

Here Strutt is urging the claim of recreation and leisure activities as keys to the national character. The claim is given respectability by some historians, not only those who might be thought to have a vested interest—as does Dr. Percy Young, the distinguished author of a history of British football, who says that when one is writing a history of football "one is in effect constructing a history of the nation"—but also from general historians, especially the Americans. Let me quote two examples.

In 1944 Dr. Dixon Wecter, an American, found that cricket was a game of "leisured boredom and sudden crises met with cool mastery to the ripple of applause", characteristic of the British national character. Whereas, "football with its rugged individualism, and baseball with its equality of opportunity" were seen as "valid American symbols". And in 1951, two other Americans, David Reisman and Reuel Denny, contrasted the democratic ideology prevailing in the United States with the class-ridden atmosphere of the United Kingdom. In Britain, they wrote, working-class audiences watched "gentlemen in action" and were looking particularly for good form and a respect for the law. For them, "legality was more important than power". By contrast, American audiences were on a level with the players and were power-oriented, while the American competitive spirit was reflected as much in the desire to win as in high production goals in industry.

But at an even more profound level, football illuminates not only character but life itself. Thus the Chinese poet Li Yu who wrote between A.D. 50 and 130 said: "A round ball and a square goal suggests the shape of the Ying and the Yang. The ball is like the full moon and the two teams stand opposed. Captains are appointed and take their place. In the game, make no allowance for relationship, and let there be no partiality. Determination and coolness are essential and there must not be the slightest irritation for failure. Such is the game. Let its principles apply to life."

Australian historians haven't gone so far, but other commentators have edged into the field. Thus, Donald Horne, writing in 1967:

It is only in sport (and as soldiers) that most Australians confidently see themselves as being of 'world class'. *Only* in sport? What else is there that matters as much as sport? The qualification would seem meaningless to many Australians. What else is there that matters as much as sport? It is only in sport that many Australians express those approaches to life that are non-Australian if expressed in any other connection. Here it is good to be unashamedly expert, ambitious and competitive, to proclaim faith, dedication and difference. It was almost as if the nation had been built on sport; had acquired international significance from sport; sport seemed to be what Australia was 'about'. Playing games or watching them was to play one's role as an Australian.

The comment is not altogether unjust.

The movement from sport to national character rests on a Rousseau "man was born free but everywhere is in chains" kind of assumption. Social life forces men to play roles which do not represent their true selves. Only in relaxation, freed from the demands of society, are their true selves revealed. But it's difficult to assert that football, in particular, is the key to Australian character—if there is any such thing. Firstly, because it replaced cricket only about thirty years ago as the most popular spectator sport; and secondly, because all spectator sports are now giving way to participant sports such as golf, yachting, surfing and skiing; and finally, because Australia is divided by a deep cultural rift between the north and the south known as the Barassi line. It runs between Canberra. Broken Hill, Birdsville and Manangrita and it divides Australia between Rugby and Rules.

I'd prefer to argue more empirically. Melbourne has a population of around about 2.5 million people. The major competition is that of the Victorian Football League. In the 1975 season, 12 clubs played 22 rounds of home-and-home and five finals matches to a total attendance of around three million. In my estimate, that means in terms of man-hours per week, somewhere between two and six million.

For those of you who are interested in the discipline of sociometrics, I should perhaps explain my method of calculation. I have taken myself at an average of eight hours per week. I have multiplied myself by about one-fifth of the population, equalling half a million people, and arrived at the figure of four million man-hours, and then I've allowed plus or minus two million man-hours just in case I've got the coefficients wrong. This could be made more precise by a survey, but unfortunately the V.F.L. won't play ball. It is, however, supported by some independent investigations.

For example, the late George Johnston captured the atmosphere thus:

In Melbourne, football is a fever disease like recurrent malaria, and apparently incurable. 'Aussie Rules' in the austere southern capital probably has a bigger and undeniably a more frenetic following than all the other codes in Australia put together. For six or seven months of the year, a mad contagion runs through press, television, radio, and everyday life. An acidulous Sydney man, himself a Rugby Union addict, put it to me that "Melbourne has no summer, only a period of hibernation between football seasons".

I had forgotten until I went back to a grand final on the Melbourne Cricket Ground what it was really like—that unbelievable roar of over 100,000 screaming zealots, baying for blood and bruises, the toss and tumult of partisan colors, the streamers, the hats, the emblems, the banners, frenzy, hysteria. No other sporting event in Australia draws a crowd as big or committed as this. For a time men become gods and heroes.

In Melbourne, the mythical conflict between winter and summer is institutionalized in the struggle between cricket and football clubs for the Saturdays of the spring and autumn—and winter is winning.

Indeed, Melbourne football has taken on something of the character of a primitive religion. Thus, on one occasion the distinguished Methodist divine, Rev. Alan Walker, addressed a Mission to the Nation at the V.F.L. grand final on the Melbourne Cricket Ground, "Ladies and gentlemen, gathered on this great occasion, whichever team we may support, whether it be the Saints or the Demons, we can surely all agree that we are joined together in this, that we are brothers and sisters in Christ." Whereupon there came a mighty voice from the southern stand: "What about the bloody umpire?"

And indeed football is already invading the territory of the sacred texts. Thus, Father Gerard Dowling, the historian of the North Melbourne Football Club, advised North supporters that they should place his book on their bedside tables alongside the family Bible—and further, they should consult it more often.

In historical terms the problem which interests me is the transition from football as a popular pastime, a folk game, to football as a recreation for gentlemen, and then to football as the most popular spectator sport, a major sector of mass entertainment. The questions which arise include these: What has caused this change in the character of the game? How has this change affected the game itself? Its organization, its rules, its style of play? How has it affected the players and spectators?

What is the function of football in modern society?

In 1969 I visited a small town called Ashbourne in Derbyshire in the United Kingdom. Izaac Walton had fished near Ashbourne and George Eliot had lived there whilst writing her last novels. (I didn't know that at the time—I'd gone there to watch a football match.)

An interesting game, an all-in-game. The town of Ashbourne was divided between the uppards and the downards, depending on which side of the river the people lived, and they all played. The game began at 2 p.m. on Shrove Tuesday and ran through until 10 p.m. on that night, with intervals for tea and other refreshments. It resumed at 2 p.m. on Ash Wednesday and ran through to 10 p.m. that night. The aim of the game was to score a goal by striking the ball against one or other of two mill wheels which were each at one-and-a-half mile's distance from the centre of the town. The method was to convey the ball to one of the mill wheels by any method bar motorization, which was regarded as being unsporting.

At one point of the evening the ball disappeared for an hour-and-a-half. It later emerged that a devoted supporter of the uppards had taken the ball to the local public dike, placed it in a cistern, and sat on it, re-emerging in time to score a goal at 9.55 p.m. At 10 p.m. on Ash Wednesday the game ended, after the players had ploughed for two days through snow and ice, with a characteristic British football score—drawn game, one-all.

Folklorists have often thought of games, not as conscious inventions, but as survivals from primitive conditions under which they originated in magical rites. And so it was at Ashbourne, and so it was with the kind of game that first came to Australia.

The early immigrants to this country brought with them the traditional English outdoor recreations of their time. They played these on Christmas and New Year holidays. Thus the first Melbourne sporting paper, *Bell's Life*, reported that at Christmas 1857 Bendigo miners engaged themselves in running, jumping, climbing greasy poles and "grinning through horse-collars in the manner of their ancestors". At the Duke of York in Prahran at Christmas 1858, the patrons were "climbing the greasy pole, the pig with the greasy tail, playing football and all the usual Christmas sports".

292

Unfortunately no details of these games survive and in any case they are not particularly relevant, except to confute those romantics who still persist in believing that Australian football grew out of the bucolic amusements of Irish-born miners on the goldfields of Bendigo and Ballarat.

In between these two Christmases, one Thomas Wentworth Wills, a leading member of the Melbourne Cricket Club, wrote to *Bell's Life* deploring the absence of a suitable winter recreation and suggesting the formation of a football club. Wills was a man of impeccable Australian nationalist connections. His grandfather, Edward, had been transported for life for highway robbery, after which he did well in sealing and shipping; his grandmother married (for the second time) George Howe, a convict and the first printer of the *Sydney Gazette*. His uncle Tom, for whom he was named, married a daughter of Thomas Reiby, a convict, landowner and a director of the Bank of New South Wales. One aunt married a Dr. Redfern, who had been transported for sympathising with the naval mutineers at the Spithead and the Nore, while another aunt married the aide-de-camp to Governor Lachlan Macquarie. Tom was also named for William Charles Wentworth, the great Australian patriot whose father Darcy had narrowly escaped transportation for highway robbery, being allowed instead to leave his country for his country's good. Tom's father, Horatio, was a successful pastoralist who overlanded the family and his stock to Australia Felix, now western Victoria, in 1836. Horatio was killed in the most famous of all Aboriginal massacres, that at Cullinaringo in 1861, when pioneering a new property in central Queensland. Tom was with him, but happily escaped. Indeed, Tom's ancestry was impeccable.

But unfortunately for radical Australian nationalists such as myself, the sins of the grandfather were not, in this case, visited upon the grandson. Horatio, having been freed of the convict stain, determined to make his son a gentleman and sent him "home" for education to Rugby. So what Tom Wills knew of football came from what he had learned of the game as it developed under Dr. Arnold in the decades following "The exploit of William Webb Ellis, who, with a fine disregard for the rules of football as played in his time, first took the ball in his arms and ran with it, thus originating the distinctive features of the Rugby Game. A.D. 1828.'' But Wills didn't propose the introduction of the Rugby game. This was thought to be, in the words of his cousin and brother-in-law, Henry Colden Antill Harrison, unsuitable for grown men making a livelihood; something with which one might concur, having read the description of the game in *Tom Brown's Schooldays*: ''It's no joke, I can tell you. Why, there's been two collar-bones broken this half, and a dozen fellows lamed. And last year a fellow had his leg broken.''

Australian football began with the Melbourne Football Club in 1858. Over the next few years new clubs formed and, as with soccer, the needs of interclub matches demanded a code of rules. The Melbourne code was adopted. By 1860 the fundamentals of Australian rules had been accepted—the mark, limited running with the ball, no throwing, the beginnings of the holding and dropping the ball law, no tripping, holding or hacking. Then it was closest to the Harrow game. Now the only similar game is Gaelic football, but the rules as evolved were a distinctive Australian creation.

It proved attractive to spectators right from the beginning. By the mid-1860s crowds of 1,500 were attending, by the mid-seventies 10,000, and by the mid-eighties 20,000. From the outset, many among them were women. The first admission charges were imposed in the mid-seventies—sixpence a head.

Admission charges were to be devoted to the improvement of facilities, but the entrance fees soon created temptations of professionalism among top players and officials alike. This was at the same time as the question of professionalism in soccer came up in the United Kingdom. It also arose in Rugby Union, where it caused a split and the formation of Rugby League. That was scarcely coincidental.

It arose out of the growing leisure and the desire of the urban masses for popular entertainment, the growth of the potential audience, the desire of working class men to have an entré into sport in something like equal terms with gentlemen. By the 1880's the game had developed in Australia, as in the U.K., along two lines—the professional game, which men played at least partly for reward, and the amateur game, which men played, as gentlemen had always played, for recreation.

It was the professional game which drew the crowds. Until the 1930's, cricket remained preeminent. Those were the heady years of the dramatic conflict between Bradman and McCabe of Australia and Mr. Jardine and Larwood of England—the bodyline series during which notes were exchanged between the Australian and U.K. Governments, and when Australia nearly left the Empire.

The turn came during the war years. Cricket never recovered from the break, except perhaps for the West Indian tours, and football is now many lengths ahead. The Grand Final crowd of 120,000 which will fill the M.C.G. later this year continues to establish new records for any sporting event in Australia.

So the mass demand for entertainment was there in the late nineteenth century, there was money to pay for it, and none to gainsay it. The Anglican Church was non-established, and in any case it inclined towards muscular Christianity; the non-conformists formed the social base for a peculiar Australian variety of moralism known as wowserism which objected to sex, drink, gambling, smoking and most other pleasures. But they were caught between the Anglicans and the Catholics, the latter being an Irish-based church which inveighed against unlicensed sex, but approved of drink and sport—provided they didn't interfere with Sunday mass. So given the climate—which, no matter what present-day Melburnians might think about it, seemed to new arrivals from semiarctic England suitable for outdoor sport all the year round—open air recreations were inevitable developments. Cricket, racing, hunting, athletics, cycling and aquatics were, along with football, soon on the scene. Among them, football finally came to reign supreme.

I want to move from that brief historical survey to some comments on the game today.

Firstly, to players. It is generally believed that professionalism is a turning point in the attitude of players to their games. Thus, it is assumed that amateurs would play by the code enunciated in what an historian of American gridiron described as "the imperishable words" of Grantland Rice:

> For when the One Great Scorer comes to mark against your name,
> He writes not that you won or lost, but how you played the game.

Whereas it is generally thought that professional players tend to react rather like Fitzroy's Ian McCulloch, who was reported last year as saying: "Most players are in it for the money. I know I am—I'm not in Victoria because I like the bloody place."

That's clearly much too simple. We must ask what is the nature of the pleasure that footballers of any sort get from their game; and is it really true that the cash nexus has obliterated pleasure for professionals? David Reisman shares this last doubt of mine. Of gridiron he says: "Yet it would be too simple to say that football has ceased to be a game for its players and has become an industry." Consider, also, this statement of that distinguished psychologist, Ron Barassi, a leading and most articulate Australian footballer: "I think retirement from football is just like death. You can't avoid it, no matter what you do. And just the same, it's hard to face when it comes. Luckily I've got the coaching which I enjoy very much. It's very fulfilling. I'm still in football. The game itself is not really enjoyable. I don't see how a sporting contest with a lot hanging on it can be enjoyable during the actual contest. The enjoyment comes afterwards. You're proud, you can remember all the good things you did. I reckon the Australian footballer is the greatest all-round athlete in the world. There's no question, our game's a great game."

Several things seem to follow from this. Firstly, pleasure probably needs to be defined in terms of power, domination, the mastery of one's physical talents in the situation within the game, and domination over the spectators. In both of these you have, of course, a strong element of sexuality, homo- as well as hetero-.

Part of it is the desire to win. I don't think it is ever true that players are indifferent to the outcome of the game, but if that *is* so, then sportsmanship is a code of behavior designed to regulate competition, rather than an ethic of indifference to the result. Barassi's point about the game not being pleasurable while the fight is on is well taken. But it applies equally to such amateur events as the old Davis Cup and the Olympic Games. A professional may well get the same sort of pleasure out of the game as an amateur: not the pleasure of a man at play, but the pleasure of a craftsman who takes pride in his skill and achievements.

One side benefit for the players is social mobility. Not only for the sons of New Australian players whose names are written in gold in the annals of Australian football, if not always pronounced terribly accurately by football commentators, but also for those whom the white supremacists of our society like to call "our Aborigines". Thus when Doug Nichols remonstrated with "Captain Blood" Jack Dyer for saying "Get out of the bloody way, yer black bastard", Dyer explained that he was not responsible for anything he said during the game and certainly didn't mean it. "Nichols was quite welcome to play."

At a Richmond-Carlton game I observed the following exchange:

Richmond supporter shouts to Aboriginal Sid Jackson of Carlton, "Leave him alone, you black bludger."

Carlton supporter to the Richmond man: "You can't say that to Sid Jackson! Come on Sunshine."

Mobility also has a spill off into politics. Traditionally ex-footballers became policemen. Today they tend to become publicists, publicans or politicians. Thus, three weeks ago I was scrutineering for my local, friendly councillor in Richmond and the opponent's scrutineer was sitting beside me. Kevin Sheedy came in, and I opened the electoral roll and ruled off his name. My opponent's scrutineer said, "Who's that?" and I said, "Kevin Sheedy." And he said, "Who's Kevin Sheedy?" At that moment, I knew we had taken Richmond.

Beyond this there is a consequence of professionalism in the growing involvement of the game and the players with the mass communications media. The players become pop stars. John Gould designs gear and Don Scott used to model it. Royce Hart and Neil Balme look more and more like [the international soccer players] Charlie George and Georgie Best, who in turn look more and more like the Beatles and the Stones.

The players themselves become charismatic heroes. A couple of years ago, outside a church in Hawthorn, the vicar had posted a notice saying: "What would you do if God came to Hawthorn today?" A graffitist had written underneath it: "Move Peter Hudson to centre half-forward."

The colleague who reported that to me said: "When I tell the story outside Hawthorn, they say, 'Who's Peter Hudson?', but when I tell the story in Hawthorn they say, 'Who's God?'"

Now this is half-time and at that point I usually have the RAAF Band playing selections from "Mary Poppins", but unfortunately today they had a prior engagement to play "Mack the Knife" and "Money Won't Buy You Love" at the annual general meeting of the Victorian Association of Surgeons.

Now let's look at the ideology of the game—apart from the attitudes of the players and the fans.

There are all the usual rationalisations—*Mens Sana in Corpore Sano*—which happens to be the motto of the Carlton Football Club. Muscular Christianity? But that's no longer terribly fashionable. The playing fields of Eton? Affable Alf Deakin said that when Australians were called upon to defend their country on the field of battle, the battles would already have been won on the Australian Rules playing fields. Thirty years later 'Honest' Joe Lyons said that the battle of Gallipoli had indeed been won on those same playing fields. (Note that Australians habitually count Gallipoli as a victory.)

As with American football and baseball, of which Cozens and Stumpf wrote in 1952 "The bleachers are equally cordial to coalminers, politicians and bank presidents", and with soccer, about whose basically democratic character Dr. Young has written, the adherents of Australian football proclaim it to be a democratic game. The V.F.L.'s motto is "*Populo Ludis Populi*"— "the game of the people for the people".

I don't believe this. The game's no more democratic than the society in which it is played. It's true that it's largely open to the talents, but it's not true that Snowy on the trams is as good as the chairman of BHP. The latter has a considerably better chance of making the club committee than Snowy, and can usually buy himself a better seat to watch the finals.

What the statement probably means is that these mass spectator sports have a broad cross-class appeal—and that certainly is true. As a New Zealand friend once commented to me: Australia is the only country he had visited anywhere in the world where the conversation in the gent's pissoir at the university staff club was the same as that at the local pub—football and racing.

Class differences, however, still find their expression in the vent between the outer and the stand at the M.C.G., and in the extra edge to matches from such factors as the differences between high-toned Melbourne and democratic Collingwood—as they were described as long ago as the 1870s.

The barrackers. Almost the only thing known about Australian football fans is how many of them pay to go in. And since they do pay to go and it's not yet compulsory, it's reasonable to assume they go because they get pleasure out of it. What the source of that pleasure is, nobody knows. When Ron Barassi was asked what pleasure spectators got out of football, he answered: "You'd have to be a psychiatrist to answer that." The usual psychological explanation has a historical basis in the view once widely held by anthropologists that games are a kind of imitative warfare. Thus, Dr. Gilbert Slater, in an article called "Concerning Golf (and Other) Balls" in the Sociological Review, 1911, thought of those participating in ball games as responding to "the very stimulus which maddened uncounted generations of your ancestors through ages of palaeolithic savagery in tribal warfare". The spectators, of course, shared in this by identifying with the players.

The argument is familiar. It was clearly stated by the psychoanalyst A. S. Brill in the North American Review in 1929. All men, he said, have "an aggressive component" in their psyche. This is one of the primary weapons in the fight for survival. However, this aggressiveness is potentially socially destructive. Therefore it needs to be socially manageable and to have socially approved outlets. One such outlet is spectator sport.

Roll says sports are a greatly necessary social catharsis, indispensable to civilised man, a salutary purgation of the combative instinct which, if dammed up within him, would break out in disastrous ways. To this I might add a couple of observations, one of them psychological: perhaps it is not merely a matter of securing a release for an existing tension, but also of a human need to *create* tension in order to obtain the pleasure of release, on the analogy of copulation. The other is sociological, suggested by Elias and Dunning in a paper at the British Sociological Association Conference in 1967—in a culture which disapproves of the public expression of emotion, and which offers progressively fewer occasions for excitement, the need for this release is increasingly concentrated in leisure activities. Indeed, that view has been confirmed by my own field work in this area. Catharsis is achieved, not only by players but by spectators.

Thus, at a moment during the final quarter of a St. Kilda and Richmond match at Moorabbin, when the Tigers, having been down five goals, were now drawing ahead, a St. Kilda supporter—thirtyish, short-back-and-sides, running to fat, white shirt, and clasping a can of Carlton Draught—addressed himself

299

to the umpire: "You rotten, bloody, commo, poofter, mongrel, bastard." He had thus given vent to all the Australian political, social, racial, sexual and made chauvinist prejudices. Moreover, he had projected them onto a representative of bourgeois, imperialist, fascist repression, and one hopes he had received a satisfactory purgation and didn't beat his wife that night.

Now for the meaning of the game. It has been a long-time lament of Australian socialists that if only the Australian workers transferred the thought they invest in picking winners and the passion they devote to football into politics, we would have had the revolution long ago.

The catharsis view of psychology perhaps lends weight to this belief, and there is some reason to think that Cozens and Stumpf are right when they say that "sport is an integrating factor in American democracy", that is, it cuts across class barriers and thus tends to dampen class hostility. Some support for this view comes from the Victorian football official, L. H. McBrien, who, in the American Rotarian of 1940, wrote: "As an emotional safety valve, football has tonic properties. Young people must have some outlet for their nervous energy. In other parts of the world, the outlet is politics. In Australia it is football."

I think we can probably dismiss such attributed meanings as "*Mens Sana . . .*", "training for leadership", learning how to play according to the rules (that is, the game of life in the guise of football), and the voice of the schoolboy rallying the ranks, as moralistic rationalisations. However, I would not like to omit from this discussion Dr. Gilbert Slater's claim that "other things being equal, the boy brought up on Rugby will make a better man and a better citizen" than the boy brought up on soccer.

Consider the manner in which individual combatants meet one another in the two games. In soccer, the defense meets the attacker by the shoulder charge. In Rugby, the defender clasps his arms lovingly around the attacker. If he knows how to collar properly, he puts his whole energy into that embrace and sinks gently to the ground with his opponents. The difference in psychic reaction is considerable. I am convinced the schoolboy feels just one degree more friendly to a schoolfellow when he has collared him, just one degree less friendly when he has charged him.

In modern anthropological terms, this is a structural functional explanation of the game. It needs to be rounded off by the dimension added by the Badminton Book of Football (1888), speaking of a game between bachelors and married men. The object of the married men was to 'hang the ball', that is to put it three times into a small hole in the moor. The aim of the bachelors was to drown it, that is, to dip it three times in a deep place in the river. The party which could first affect either of those objects won the game and the ball. If neither won, the ball was cut in equal parts at sunset. If my symbolism is correct, that's a very threatening concept.

Adrian Stokes, in an article called "Psychoanalytical Reflections on the Development of Ball Games" (1956), observed that for a fieldsman to catch a batsman out in cricket is an act of symbolic castration. I am attracted by these and other psychological explanations. Some have seen the ball itself as a symbol of perfection. Thus, Cicero in his "On the Nature of the Gods" says: "What can be more beautiful than the figure that encircles and encloses in itself all other figures and that can possess no roughness or point of collision on its surface, no indentation or concavity, no protuberance or depression?" Again, the Dutch philosopher F. J. J. Buytendijk, in a book called *Football: a Philosophical Study* published in 1954, says of the ball that it is the most simple and perfect of all forms, the qualities of which one can enter into by touching and fondling. The sphere also has an archetypal, magical significance; as sun and moon it is both ritual symbol and object of worship. (There is perhaps some support for this in the action of the Brazilian football fan who, in despair that his team was doing so badly, took out his revolver and shot the ball.)

When one considers that the ball in a football game spends much more of its time being kicked, punched, thrown and headed than being fondled, it seems that the explanation cannot stand. Perhaps R. W. Pickford comes closer to the truth in an article in the British Journal of Psychology in 1940 in which he discusses the difference between Rugby and soccer. He says that in Rugby the ball is lovingly caught and caressed, that the image is maternal. Whereas, in soccer the ball is kicked away, treated as a dangerous or unclean object, a symbol of paternal potency. My objection to this as a follower of Australian football might perhaps be dismissed as emotional. In Australian football, the ball is both caught and fondled, as well as being kicked and punched. Therefore Pickford's theory leaves me quite uncertain about my own sexual identity.

Personally it is the Freudian interpretation of the great Australian game that most strongly attracts me. We are dealing here with one of the four greatest minds of our era, and it is inconceivable that such an intelligence should not have been brought to bear on such a significant contemporary social phenomenon as the great Australian game. And indeed such was the case.

One of the elementary propositions of Freudian psychology is that nothing happens by chance. Thus, in the *Psychopathology of Everyday Life*, which has specific application to language and its use, Freud discusses the names that we give to everyday objects. Consider the vocabulary of Australian football—words, phrases and injunctions such as "Ruck", "Punt", "Forward Flank", "Ball Up" and "Put it Through the Big Sticks". These are indicative of, though not central to, the point I want to make.

The next significant revelation comes from Freud's theory of the personality which he developed in his *Introductory Lectures* to Psychoanalysis. Freud suggested a triple-tier personality, in appearance not unlike the outer stand at the M.C.G. There is a deeply submerged Id, situated at ground level, in which reside the instinctual drives towards aggression and sexuality. There is a Superego soaring high above, like a psychic scoreboard, on which we record the successes and failures of our repression or sex drives, depending on the criteria with which we start. Then there is the Ego, that part of the persona which we care to expose—or which we are allowed by the Superego to expose—to the public gaze. And if we think of the personality of Australian football, of course it fits the Freudian model.

Because, there, beyond the palings which represent the boundary between the conscious and the unconscious mind, stands the 100,000-headed Id, straining at the leash of its repressions, howling to its Ego for violent and erotic release. And there, strategically distributed over the green sward which represents the conscious mind, stand the five, chaste, white-clad figures of the Superego with their whistles and flags poised to warn at any moment, "Down, Id, Down." There, also within the realm of the conscious mind, stand the thirty-six multicoloured particles

302

of the Ego, representing all that the Superego wishes the Id to aspire to, revealing all the characteristics which the Australian football personality it represents is proud to profess—stoic endurance, heroic endeavor, a beauty akin to that of the Greek warriors, and in which the instinctual drives of aggression and sexuality are sublimated in the elaborate mime of the great Australian game.

But there are more insights to come. In his *Interpretation of Dreams*, Freud demonstrates that even the most innocent of objects conceal an elaborate erotic symbolism—and indeed, since everything appears visually as either a straight line or a curve it is difficult to see how it could be otherwise.

What then, is the symbolism of Australian football? I suggest that from the moment when the heroic figures of the rival teams burst through the thin membrane stretched by the Vestal Virgins across the entrance to the oval, to the accompaniment of the ritual waving of multicoloured beribboned phallic objects in an act of symbolic defloration, and the release of inflated spheres which bear mute witness to the potency of the celebrants, to that climactic moment when the acolytes carry the victorious high priest, still triumphantly erect, out of the oval and down the dark passage to the undressing rooms, that the game is one long playing out of the sex act. For those who have got the football message, its purpose and function are clear—Australian football is nothing more than an elaborate and arcane fertility rite.

A female-oriented liberationist interpretation might take a more complex form. Thus the ground, which is invaded by large numbers of men, is taken to be the symbolic body of the woman—which highlights an interesting difference between Australian and American characters. In American gridiron, men are required to capture one erogenous zone after another until they "score a try", while in Australian football the men, in an undisciplined and anti-authoritarian way, roam virtually at will across the field, acting out the Australian national fantasy of "Sydney or the bush".

But there are those who focus on the ball rather than on the ground and who see the ball as a symbolic womb. What, then, are the roles of those who contend for this symbolic womb?

They clutch the womb-symbol to them, they double up over it, they roll on it, they seek to transfer it to their fellow celebrants by striking it with legs or arms, which are themselves only thinly-disguised phallic objects. To the Freudian scholar there is only one mystery in the symbolism of Australian football—why is it that the victory goes to those who succeed most often in placing the womb-symbol between the central two of four upright poles? I was mystified by this myself and this is my principal original contribution to research in this area. My researches uncovered the fact that originally there were not four poles, but two. And once I had uncovered the truth of the early and essential reality of the great Australian game, it became clear that the poles were structural or dialectical polarities and that the real object of this weekly ritual, which has now been deeply repressed or perhaps overlaid by later cultural accretions, was not to place the womb-symbol between the two poles, but rather to impale it on one or other pole. Once we have grasped the true structural reality of the two poles—and not four—the hidden meaning of the ritual at last becomes evident.

The ball represents the wife and mother, Jocasta, and the real purpose of the celebrants is to determine the outcome of that oldest of all sexual battles—whether the ball should be impaled on the post representing Laius, the father, or on that of Oedipus, the son.

Finally a word on the totemic significance of Australian football. In his *Totem and Taboo*, Freud says: "Among the Australians, the system of totemism takes the place of all religious and social institutions"—an aphorism clearly derived from his observations of the great Australian game. Freud's analysis was also based on field work by some distinguished Australian anthropologists, including Lou Richards, who once said: "I was born in a Magpie family and reared in a Magpie nest."

Freud's message is all too clear: It is of fundamental importance—indeed, it is a totemic sin to do otherwise—for the Tiger man to mate *not* with a Tiger woman, but with a woman of some other totem. For otherwise, how can one's own totem increase? It is clear, however, that there are some special problems associated with Swans. Those who take the Swan totem unconsciously identify themselves with Zeus, who in the guise of this noble bird conducted an exhilarating affair with the delectable Leda. But I hope that those present who are of the

Swan totem will not forget the solemn warning of the porter of St. John's Oxford, that: "Them swans is reserved for the dons."

Finally, Freud draws attention to the prohibition against the adherents of a totem eating their ancestral father—except on those ritual occasions when the totemites, regaling themselves in symbolic representations of the fur or feathers of their totem, ceremonially consume a portion of the totemic creature, thereby taking unto themselves its potency and strength.

This is the final proof of the validity of the Freudian hypotheses in their application to the ritual life of Australian football adherents. For does not this sacred totemic practice survive in attenuated, but clearly apparent form, in that greatest of all Australian tribal chants: "CARN THE TIGERS! EAT 'EM ALIVE!"

BRUCE DOULL

By Garrie Hutchinson, *Age*, June 9, 1981.

Malcolm Blight's been given a coach's free kick, 35 metres out. Here's his chance to kick an easy one, a morale booster.

He lines up the perpendiculars, and goes through his checklist. He's holding the ball out in front, getting the correct angle for release close to the boot, measuring the breeze, making sure the place where he wants the ball to go is in a straight line between arms, boots and ball.

He looks up and down the line.

Suddenly he seems to notice a couple of things in the way. They are a pair of burning, determined, hypnotic eyes which fasten on Blight and the ball in his hands.

He kicks, and the ball, mesmerised, is pulled, like a yo-yo, into the arms of Bruce Doull. He's done it again. Mind over matter.

That's only one of his tricks. Doull has many ways of preventing the ball going straight, as many ways as a magician has of bending a spoon, or making a glass move across a table.

Like a magician, Doull's secret is getting the man with the ball to look where Doull wants him to look.

How does sleight of hand work? The magician makes you look at the wrong hand, the innocent hand, while the other one quickly produces a lighted cigarette. As long as Doull can fasten his lamps on his opponents eyes, he can make the ball go where he wants it to.

It might be as simple as selling him a dummy, or it might be preventing an important shot for goal.

The bloke's lining it up, and Doull's not even on the mark. All he does is run behind the mark just at the moment the kicker's eyes drop with the ball to look at it hit his boot—then he sees some flash of navy in the periphery of his vision, it distracts him ever so slightly, and the ball veers into limbo.

He did this twice on Saturday, showing that the adage, bad kicking is bad football, is sometimes a little off the mark. Sometimes bad kicking is because the kickers have been bewitched.

Magic isn't Bruce Doull's only skill, of course.

He's an elegantly fierce tackler, knowing how to apply the confidence snapping. "I've just got the ball in the open and now I'm sitting without it on the grass" tackle; and the "I'm going to run right through the pack but now I'm flat on my face and he's hand passed to someone running past" tackle, not to mention the "I haven't even got the ball and why is he doing this, whoops there it (and he) goes" tackle.

Doull also excels at getting what they now call "the hard ball". That is diving in where the boots are flying, chasing and harassing opposition players with the ball, knowing when to stand on your opponents toes and when to leave him for dead, at making position, spearing hand-passes, and especially, at the finger crunching punch out of the pack.

You can almost hear the sound from the boundary line. The Doull fist snaking its way through a forest of arms and groping hands cracking the ball out into the open, a few bodies thumping to the ground, and Doull landing on his toes, sprinting away after it.

You hardly ever see him fall or get bumped over—even get tackled. He has the skill to be out of the way, to administer feints and dodges; and his trademark, the knack of just standing still with the ball, letting everyone else go yards down the field, leaving him the time to use the ball to advantage.

And he never gets angry except when someone has a go at his emblem, the headband on the noble, balding scalp. Why is it there, when there is so little to keep out of his eyes?

I reckon he wears it to distract attention, part of the magician's uniform.

Maybe he wears it to attract the attention of umpires, though to remind them that the half-back line is still eligible for the Brownlow, that Bruce Doull is the successor to a great line of Carlton half-backs who did win it, and some great ones who didn't.

Certainly, if he had had blond hair he would do better.

He doesn't say much; he doesn't have to. He's the strong, silent type, he lets actions speak louder than words.

He's the unsinging hero.

ALEX JESAULENKO

By R.S. Whitington, *The Champions*.

It is a delight to write about some characters, some champions. Inspiration flows and ideas rush to the head like wine; one's mind and memory begin to race and revel. Such a character and such a champion is Alex Jesaulenko, captain of Melbourne's Carlton Football Club and captain of Victoria, where Australian Rules Football is a winter religion and perhaps the world's most gripping spectator sport.

Alex Jesaulenko was born in Salzburg, Austria, on August 2, 1945, the son of a Ukrainian father and Russian mother. They brought him to Australia in 1949 and settled in Canberra. Ten years later Alex had yet to grip a football. He found one, one day in an Australian field. His destiny was shaped. Another eight winters passed before Jesaulenko came to Melbourne and was invited to attend a Carlton Football Club social afternoon and to join there in a game of tennis. He had been playing football brilliantly with Canberra's Eastlake Football Club. But Canberra football, compared with Melbourne football, is as Australia's Mt. Kosciusko is to India's Everest.

Melbourne's 'Mr. Football'—its former State captain, Melbourne Football Club captain, Carlton Football Club captain, Carlton and North Melbourne premiership winning coach—the Italian-descended Ron Barassi, happened to see Jesaulenko, then eighteen, indulging in the game of tennis, during that social afternoon.

Alex Jesaulenko marks spectacularly in Carlton's winning Grand Final game against Collingwood in 1970.

Barassi saw the anticipation, the amazing speed, the eye for the ball, the lightning reflexes. And they were enough. A few weeks later, Alex was applying all these attributes to his kicking and marking and movement in Carlton's pre-season practice matches.

Surprisingly unsuccessful at centre, the pivot position of Australian football, Jesaulenko was moved to a half-forward flank and, as Barassi has written, 'The rest is history'.

He later was moved to centre-forward, to ruck-rover, back to centre—moved to every position where Carlton believed it needed him most. And the rest is also history. Confining 'Mr. Magic' to one position, one part of a football field, would be like caging a swallow. In movement, he reminded me of breaking surf—the first impelled and impulsive burst, the swoop, the flow and that final surge—that 'kick-on' which left his lessers in his wake.

Now, sixteen thousand kilometres away, in the country from which Ron Barassi and Serge Silvagni's ancestors came, I can remember and can see Alex Jesaulenko, as I remember and see no other footballer. 'Jezza' floated rather than ran.

I remember one day at the St. Kilda Football Club's Moorabbin Ground. 'Jezza' was a' roaming, as ever, on the left of Carlton's half-back line when the ball came to him—or, rather, he came to the ball. Most of the other thirty-five players were on the far side of the field. Alex had the way to goal to himself, except for three St. Kilda men. The stage was set for three miracles?

'Jezza' had sized the situation, the opportunity, before he gathered the ball. The first of his adversaries came at him on the wing of the centre line. He swept around him like a baseball pitcher's curve. Near half forward left, his favourite position, the second Horatius stood barring the way. 'Jezza' ran straight at him, handballed the ball over his head, swung around him, recovered the ball and ran on faster than before.

In front of him now, between him and the goal, was his old enemy, the giant and awkward 'Cowboy' Neale, custodian of the St. Kilda goal. This time 'Jezza' short-kicked the ball over his opponent, left him standing hands on hips like some bulldog guarding a gate, ran on, recovered the ball at a forty-five degree angle from the posts. Giving himself time to gain perfect balance at top speed, Jesaulenko torpedo-punted the ball low, no more than two feet from the turf, dead centre of those posts.

They're pretty patriotic down Moorabbin way. But patriotism, insularity, partisanship were forgotten, lost in a spontaneous, unstinting avalanche of applause.

I remember another occasion at the great Melbourne Cricket Ground. It came during the second quarter of the Carlton-Collingwood Grand Final of September 1970. All over the field, Carlton's champions were being outclassed. Collingwood were on their way to a 44 point lead at half time.

Suddenly against the gloom in midfield, a figure soared high above the head and shoulders of Collingwood's 6 ft. 4 ins. ruck-man Graeme Jenkin. His left foot was by Jenkin's waist, his upraised right foot level with Jenkin's head, his erect body high above. Next to his own head, he was grasping the ball as if it were his pillow. There was *one* Carlton champion who could compete.

Carlton coach, Ron Barassi, had something to base his inspiring speech upon when he addressed his team in the dressing room and said:

'Well that game's over. Now we begin another with a new team. Forget that first half. Go handball happy. The first player who hangs his head in shame will be taken from the field. We can peg them back four goals a quarter. Go out there and don't disgrace Carlton. Even if we lose, be proud of yourselves.'

But Carlton did not lose. They were five points ahead with minutes to play before the final bell. The ball came to Jesaulenko, unexpectedly, in centre field. He swooped on it and began one of those unpredictable, unanswerable, weaving dashes which no other modern footballer has emulated. Approaching a barricade of adversaries near goal, he veered left and, though he is by nature right-footed, snapped left-footed around the out- and upstretched arms and hands of the pack. The ball bounced on and on, through the heart of the goal. Now there was no fear of defeat. Carlton were V.F.L. Champions again—champions for the eleventh time.

Brilliance of the standard Jesaulenko brought to football, however, can bring retribution in its train. Elasticity and uncertainty of law, lax interpretation and imposition of law, leaves the champion, especially the audacious champion who thinks not of self-protection, open to persistent mauling. And 'Jezza' has suffered far more than his share from the footballing 'thugs' who, finding themselves powerless to match his genius, have resorted to brutal reprise.

'Jezza's' broad back and mercurial legs have become targets for the maimer. I also well remember an incident at the Melbourne Cricket Ground which occurred during a Preliminary Final some years ago.

'Jezza', stationed at centre-forward, was leading and marking magnificently, kicking goal after goal. Each time he marked the ball, a huge goal keeper butted him in the middle of his back, crashing him to the turf. After the fifth or sixth such assault, for that is what they were, the giant stepped forward to help Alex from the ground. When his offer was disdainfully refused, the giant extended his hand.

'Jezza' turned his back on his persecutor, limped and staggered back and booted yet another goal.

It is a tragedy for football, as a sporting spectacle, that umpires either cannot, or will not, extend greater protection to the champion. I still believe, hope against hope, that the millions who throng to Victorian football fields each winter would prefer to watch footballing artistry to the, at times, criminal methods employed to answer and destroy it.

Which brings me to another pertinent question. Though admitted universally to be the most brilliant and fair footballer of the past near decade, Alex Jesaulenko has yet, as I write, to win the Brownlow Medal for the 'fairest and most brilliant footballer' of any season.

There must be something wrong with the laws of football, the application of them by umpires, or with the system of selection of this highest of all footballing honors, surely, for this to be so?

I am sure I am but one of millions who like to hope that Alex Jesaulenko will win that honor before he retires. And one of millions who hopes he will be fit enough to enjoy a game of tennis when he forsakes his stage.

JACK DYER 1981

By Geoff Slattery, *Age*, June 18, 1981.

TEN years ago, when he was a football columnist with Truth, *Jack Dyer was called to give evidence in the Victorian Supreme Court. In the case, a libel suit against the paper's boxing writer "The Count", the prosecution was having difficulty finding out the defendant's identity.*

Dyer took the stand. His police days helped him race through the oath; then he was asked the identity of "The Count".

"I don't know, sir," he replied.

The court was flabbergasted.

"You mean you've worked there for so many years, and you don't know who a fellow writer is?" asked the prosecution counsel.

"Yes sir," said Dyer.

"Well," continued the barrister, "who are some of those you work with?"

"Aaah," said Dyer, "there's Mopsy, and Poge, and Bluey, and Big Steak and..."

The judge cut him short. "Mr. Dyer," he intervened, "you are turning this hearing into a Roman Holiday."

The phone rang for ages before the familiar voice answered: "Dyer speaking". We exchanged a few wisecracks before we got down to what Dyer likes to call "business". It was time for the Jack Dyer story to be reconsidered. After all, it was 16 years since his life story *Captain Blood* had been published. And the Legend is bigger than it's ever been before. Dyer was momentarily taken aback. "After all these years," he said, "someone wants to talk about me." Then he laughed. Dyer can't be serious for long these days.

We began at South Vermont, where Dyer has been living for the past two years. Wide, quiet streets, rolling hills empty of life, big cars in big garages, brown bricks sitting in clay, and a day's march to the nearest pub. Dyer lives out here with his daughter Jill, son-in-law Warren and their three children. It couldn't be farther from Dyer's Richmond.

Two pairs of low-cut boots stand drying on the front porch, immediate evidence of the tradition continuing. A dedication dominates the fly-wire screen: "Bless this house, Oh Lord we pray, make it safe by night and day."

Again, a long wait before the door opens. Dyer never worries about haste or time. "Hello-how-are-you-are-you-well?" he says. It's a typical Dyer greeting, covering the lot in one mouthful. Ten years earlier, when I met him for the first time, he used exactly the same words. And nothing else about Dyer had changed. The wide nose, big ears, grey sideburns supporting the brushed-back steel-grey hair, the kind eyes, the fast-moving mouth, the slow laugh and the delight in stories from the past.

Dyer was cleaning the potatoes, getting things ready for tea. It was strange to watch the vegetables treated so tenderly in the big, rough hands. But that's Dyer—the Captain Blood part of him started and finished on the football field.

The invitation to start from the beginning was all he needed. "Right," he said, "right from the start—Yarra Junction State School." Then came the Dyer definition of education in the twenties. Like most things Dyer says, nobody could put it better. "Mum wanted us to go on, so she sent me to Richmond. Put me into St. Ignatius's, to see if I could play football and cricket. Brother Peter was the sportsmaster. He took me straight down to Surrey Park, and arranged a scratch match. He was very happy with the performance. We went on to win the premiership. He said he had only wanted a ruckman. After six months at St. Igs, he was transferred to De La Salle, so he took me with him. He said 'we might as well go on with the business'." That last line sounded more like Dyer's than Brother Peter's.

Memories of school days for Dyer don't go much further than footy and fighting. Big wins and big losses, interspersed with tales of hiding college cap and blazer as he came home to Richmond, for fear of "mobs waiting for you on the corner". They were the Depression days and, whether he liked it or not, Dyer had to leave school after his Intermediate year to provide for the family. You get the impression it didn't worry him too much. "I wasn't a bad scholar, but I lost interest," he said.

It's probably fortunate that Dyer went into the workforce at 14. Had he taken the option of a scholarship to Xavier, and perhaps further, his great broadcasting lines would never have caused so much mirth for so many. It doesn't worry Dyer in the least that his quaint use of the English language—his so-called Dyerisms—create so much humor. Last year we took great delight in publishing quite a few lines from the man's broadcasts. Did he feel we were ridiculing him? Not at all. In a pub in North Melbourne last week he said: "We were starting to slip away a bit. They put us back on the map."

Dyer's amazing ability to slip the tongue has lasted as long as the man himself. He started on radio in 1952, three years after his retirement from the game, after much persuasion from Phil Gibbs, now sports director of Channel 10. "He wasn't keen to do it," said Gibbs. "He reckoned he couldn't speak on radio. So we finally convinced him to have a practice first. We went to a game at North Melbourne. Jack was terrible. Even then he had a language of his own. I'll never forget him saying: 'Pass the benicolars, Phil.' But we went back and listened to the tape, and despite it all, you could tell even then he had that quality about him."

Part of the deal with Gibbs was that he would teach Dyer the art of radio if Dyer would teach him the finer points of football. "The lesson started at a social match at Keilor," said Gibbs. "All the old stars were playing. Jack told me to play in the ruck with him. We were waiting for the first bounce and Jack said to me to take the knockout. Up I went, and I felt this whack across the ear. It nearly knocked me out. Dyer had hit me a beauty. I couldn't believe it. I said to him: 'What was that for?' He replied: 'Now you know what it feels like.' It was part of his teaching."

Dyer doesn't teach football with such fury these days, but according to Gibbs his radio style hasn't changed in those 30 years. "He is certainly more confident, but nothing else about him is different". "More confident" is verging on gross under-statement. Gibbs used to run a Saturday night football show called 'Pelaco Inquest' in those days; naturally he wanted Dyer on the panel. Again Dyer resisted, saying he couldn't possibly speak on a game for five minutes straight. The answer was simple. Immediately after the match 3KZ would send a typist to Dyer who would recount the story of his game. She would type it out "in English" and, at 8 o'clock that night, Dyer would read it out on air. Twenty-five years later he was using the same methods to record his morning footy talks for 3KZ's breakfast show. (Despite the need for "on air" scripts, Dyer is rated one of Melbourne's best after-dinner speakers.)

Of all his media activities—radio, TV, newspapers—Dyer prefers radio. "It's just like playing the game," he says, "you're always with it, and you can abuse the umpire." People listen to Dyer not for what he says about the football but how he says it; some find him infuriating, most don't. Dyer's knowledge of football also causes debate. It's safe to say he knows more about players than he does the modern game. "Nothing new has happened in football," he says, "they are just a bit more polished. In the old days they all bounced the ball, and kicked it, and handpassed it. They thought just as quickly."

What doesn't provoke debate is discussion of Dyer's football prowess. He is universally agreed to be a champion, in the real sense of the word. In the foreword to *Captain Blood*, the late Hec De Lacy, of the *Sporting Globe*, wrote of Dyer: "Jack Dyer, Richmond's giant, was the greatest big man in Australian football. He stands supreme, he's the greatest of the great." Not surprisingly, Dyer rarely polled in the Brownlow Medal, although it is not generally recognised that he finished fourth (with 17 votes) to Marcus Whelan (23), in 1939. (Dyer was also a very good cricketer. Before football took over early in the thirties, he had scored a double century in the mid-week league. His most prized trophy is a cup which names him "best all round athlete" of St. Ignatius.)

Dyer will be 68 in November. He is fit and strong, and looks years younger. There is no hint of the illness which, in the late fifties, had him close to death. He was more than 108 kilograms (17 stone) then—now he is under 83 kilograms (13 stone). He is in the 50th year of the sport he loves. "The most satisfying thing in my life is to be able to have kept in football," he admits, "and the ultimate was life membership of the V.F.L.". Dyer puts that above his 311 games with the Tigers, above the fact he led and coached the Tigers to premierships.

There is more to Dyer's life than football, but it needs considerable prodding to get it out of him. Ask Dyer about football and he'll talk for ever. Ask him about his family, his friends, his other life, he just smiles, mumbles a few lines, and then looks blankly at you, waiting for the next question. His wife of more than 30 years, Sybil, died 10 years ago. His friends say her death left him flat. Says Dyer slowly: "Everything was all nice until she died. Suddenly it was . . ." His family kept him going. "I'm pretty lucky," he said, "I've never had to live by myself."

But it's plain that Dyer could not be happier with life. He is forever smiling, joking, always relaxed. He will talk to anyone about anything, and is forever confronted in pubs by people

talking about football. He is never more content than when he is
holding forth at the bar with friends or, more likely, drifting
acquaintances. Friends Dyer knows by name, others by nicknames. Those who know him are always amused by his inability
to remember names. The story of Dyer in court is no different
when Dyer is at work, at the pub, or in the street.

Every week Dyer makes the trip to Richmond for lunch at
Craig McKellar's pub in Swan Street. It's there he picks up all
the gossip, maintains the links. If it were up to him, he'd rather
live in Richmond. "But the kids love it out there," he says.
When he retires from the media round ("I'd like to stay in it
forever, but the mind won't let you. The mind takes over.")
he'd be happy to "get right out of town. A bit of shooting, a bit
of fishing . . . beautiful . . ."

Dyer's closest friends remain the men of his playing days,
men like Ted Rippon and Laurie Nash and Lou Richards,
although Dyer says: "Don't say that. He's my bread and
butter", and Richards says: "You're writing about Jack. That'll
take about three paragraphs."

Dyer and Richards are the two who have kept TV's longest
running programme 'World Of Sport' from tedium. Ron Casey,
the show's compere and HSV-7's general manager, describes
Dyer as "the gentle humorist". But there is nothing gentle
about a battle of wits between Richards and Dyer after a Colling-
wood-Richmond contest.

The popularity of the duo can be measured in the number of
advertisements they do together, and the number they knock
back. Richards says Dyer is "the funniest bloke in the world to
do advertisements with. He's forever changing the script in
midstream. We were doing an ad for a chain saw, and I'm
saying something like 'you use it with your partner', and Jack's
supposed to reply with: 'Is it any good for camping?' And lo
and behold, he adds after camping 'and fishing'. I nearly fell
through the floor. I had to ad lib to Jack's fishing line. I ended
up saying 'yes it's great if you catch a whale, it really makes the
filleting easy'. The funny thing is, whenever he throws in these
lines, the ad is always much better".

Casey is another at 'World Of Sport' with undisguised
affection for Dyer. "Every year," says Casey, "at the end of
the football season, Jack says he's got to have holidays. He says

he's suffering 'industrial fatigue'." Casey never says no, and so Dyer goes for his annual holidays, fishing at Bemm River, through Albury, up to Queensland.

One year, Casey recalls, he wanted Dyer to do some promotion for Channel Seven. "He wasn't on the phone, so I sent an urgent telegram to ask him to come to the studio. We received no reply, so I sent another. Still no answer, so in the end I went over to his house in Richmond. I knocked on the door, hardly knowing what to expect, and Jack answered. Behind him, on the mantle, I could see the telegrams—unopened.

"I said to him: 'Jack, I sent you those urgent telegrams, why didn't you open them?' Straight away he replied: 'Oooh, I never open urgent telegrams, you never know what might be in them'."

Most Dyer's stories have been heard or read before. One he told me on Tuesday seemed a new one. "We were playing out at Carlton," he said, "and I had to catch the train to the ground. You had to in those days. I only had a deener, and I caught the train out there. Then I looked out the window, and I couldn't see any houses. I thought 'This is not Carlton'. Eventually the train stopped at Reservoir. I didn't know what to do. Eventually a bloke put me on the right one, and I arrived just in time."

On to the field he went, getting into the game. "I was so riled up, I had a lovely time. Blokes were going down everywhere (despite the nonsense, Dyer appears to have a genuine delight in recounting stories of on-field violence). Anyway, we won easily, and I've left the ground feeling marvellous. On the train again, and you wouldn't believe it—the carriage was full of Carlton supporters. They never stopped abusing me—kids, old ladies, the works. One bloke said to me: 'You must have eaten your babies, Dyer.' I said to him: "Me. I'm gentle. I go to church on Sundays.' The train stopped. I was out like a shot, and into the next carriage. It was full of Richmond supporters. The rest of the trip home was lovely."

No story on Dyer would be complete without a few of his lines: The following come from the 1978 Grand Final between Hawthorn and North Melbourne:

"On the kickout, it's out towards the wing position, the pack fly again, over the top of the pack and a good mark has been taken here. It looks like . . . it is . . . Cowton with the ball. He immediately handballs

*it in the air, away they go as Henshaw comes down the ground. He's
going for the short pass. It's not a good one at all. It's punched away
by Martella (sic). Another punch up in the air. In goes Demper...
dipier... ier... domenico... in after it again."*

AND...

*"Up they go in the air, it goes over the top of the pack and the mark
has been taken. Here's a handball going across, gets it across to Moore,
Moore has one bounce, two bounces, comes right up the field. He's looking
for a kick here to Ablett, Ablett makes position beautifully too, and he's
got the ball Ablett, right on the wing position again, here's the kick by
Ablett, sending it right up. He's getting pushed out of the road, Moncrieff
again. It goes down to the ground. In they go in after it. A chance for a
handpass, gets it across to Russo, Russo lines 'em up, kicks into the man
coming towards him. Knights comes in, he's showing plenty of pace, too
Knights, at this stage. He picks it up, he's tried to play on, he got pulled
by the leg, the umpire gives a handpass to Hendrie..."*

Can't you just hear him saying that? Richards has heard
Dyer for 30 years, but he never tires of the man. "You couldn't
buy what he's got," he says, "you couldn't make it up."

Despite his years, Dyer remains a busy man. During the
week, the *Herald* tried to trace him to get him photographed
with the new Premier, Lindsay Thompson, an avid Richmond
fan. Dyer wouldn't be in it: "Don't they know I'm a Labor
man?" he wailed. On Tuesday, he was up at dawn, filming a
commercial for Tattslotto with Richards. ("That's the first time
I've seen a million dollars," he said. "We tried to pinch some,
but they had two armed guards"), then out to St. Albans to
present some guernseys to a primary school on behalf of 3KZ.
Then to North Melbourne to do his column for *Truth*. ("It's
getting harder. Once upon a time there was only one writer you
had to beat. Now there are thousands.")

Then to Richmond for some photographs. We met at
McKellar's pub. The old blokes around the bar cheered when
Dyer arrived, 40 minutes late. Dyer was prepared for anything.
We went from one bar to another, then for a walk down Swan
Street. Dyer was self-conscious as he posed outside Dimmy's.

Several people went past. He knew none of them.
Occasionally one would greet him.

"How-are-you-are-you-well?" asked Dyer.

MARK JACKSON

By Mike Coward, *Age*, April 22, 1981.

Mark Alexander Jackson pounded the sweat-splattered blood-red leather bag with the same fury as Rocky pummelled a side of beef.

Jackson, the man and the footballer, is different, intimidating, perhaps awesome. He is as formidable as was Stonewall Jackson yet speaks with a voice pitched as high as Michael Jackson.

Comic, stirrer, acrobat, eavesdropper, strongman and regular goalkicker, he looks tough and talks tough. He is tough.

An off-beat character, he evokes a frenzied, nearly hysterical reaction from the horde of devotees he has unwittingly gathered. He really would be more comfortable on the set of the Dirty Dozen than going out of his way not to make small talk to Melbourne's Havana and cherry brandy brigade.

"I'm me, I'm how I turned out. I can't help it if I'm not the run of the mill," snorted Jackson as he continued to belt all hell out of the punch bag in the little gymnasium off the kitchen of the family home at Nunawading.

"I'm not a he-man. I don't go round punching guys in the mouth, but I think I can handle myself all right.

"I'm just a battler with a bit of nous. Personally I don't think I've projected an image. I'm just what I feel at the time, that's all.

"I don't care what other people think. They can think, that's their own business. That's why God gave them a brain. They can think what they want. But I'm me.

"Whether I'm going on the ground or walking around the street, I'm me. If I do something bad, I do something bad. If I do something good, I do something good. It's as simple as that."

Jackson, who doesn't drink alcohol or smoke, has no illusions about his football ability. He is successful because of his strength. He knows it and continues to work to get stronger.

He is as mean in looks as he is in his approach to the ball. Standing at 192 cm (6 ft. 3½ ins.) and weighing 93.5 kg (14 st. 10 lb.) he leads with an angular jaw which houses very few of his

319

Jacko.

own teeth. A crewcut accentuates the shape of his ears. His features suggest he is much older than 22.

Jackson had his top teeth kicked out while playing for the under-15s at Mitcham.

He doesn't care how he looks with his teeth out. "I feel more comfortable without them anyway," he says. "I might go and live up in the hills and have them out all the time," he adds with a toothy grin.

Jackson, a roof tiler by trade who has established his own roof recolouring business, is a member of a closeknit family.

His father George, secretary of the Slaters, Tilers and Roofing Industry Union of Victoria, and his vivacious mother Frances— "my old lady is the only woman I've ever known that can tell me honestly what went wrong or right at footy"—have obviously had a strong influence on the development of their six children.

Traditionally Sunday night is reserved for a family dinner, and Ann, 23, Cathy, 21, Josie, 20, Stephen, 18, and Monica, 16, enjoy their time together, often talking about the fortunes of brother Mark and Melbourne.

"I have a lot of respect for my family, and I like being home," Jackson says. "It's a big family and with four girls you've got to look after them you know."

Jackson thinks highly of his father—whom he considers as shrewd as "Crackers" Keenan—and would like to emulate his union interests.

"If the job came up as a union rep, I'd take it. I'm learning. I go to union meetings with the old man and sit down the back and have a listen and make sure he doesn't get cleaned up."

But his father is not the only man Jackson has on something of a pedestal. He has great and obvious affection for Mal Brown— who coached him in his one season with South Fremantle—and Brent Crosswell, his all-time hero. He believes them to be changeless people, and that impresses him greatly.

They also have helped him greatly with his development as a footballer.

"Football means a lot to me," he says. "But it's not everything. I'm not one to put all my eggs in one basket.

"I play my guts out for the side who's paying me the year I'm playing. You can't get any fairer than that.

"I'm professional in my approach to football. When I'm on

the ground and at training, I know what I've got to do to be a good footballer.

"Kevin Sheedy taught me to do extra work. I know I got to do extra because of the fact I got a few things missing, like my pace and I got to make it up with strength.

"Browny taught me you don't go out punching blokes like I did in the under-19s, which was stupid. You can do it, but you can do it fair, too.

"I like playing the game hard. I think I'm just one of those blokes who likes to have a go.

"I've always played at full-forward and when I was coming through the juniors there were a lot of tarts as full-forwards. As a kid I thought to myself that if there was ever a tough full-forward, you might be able to get a few.

"Once you start playing a backman like a backman, some blokes can take it, but there's a lot that can't. That's the way I play."

Jackson, proud and modest, doesn't see himself as a star player and is genuinely surprised that he has such an avid following.

"The fans are paying their money to get through the gate, and I think they're getting their money's worth. I try to give them their money's worth. But I play for the club first. I'm not an entertainer, although I can see some of my ways turning into something regarded as that."

Jackson enjoys playing his football at Melbourne, and for Ron Barassi, whom he describes as a "solid coach".

But he has clashed with Barassi although perhaps, not as often as has Crosswell. Invariably the disputes have involved Barassi as a figure of authority.

Jackson quickly reaches breaking point in any discussion on figures of authority whether they be policemen, umpires, football coaches or whatever. His coarse language becomes more coarse, his fists flail and the punch bag threatens to break clear of its ceiling moorings as he prepares to explode on the subject of authority.

"It's got to be there, but it depends what authority," he says. "Barass is authority and you've got to respect him. There's things when he hits home hard and you don't like, of course you're going to have a go back.

"That's your right to, I think. I don't like authority being exerted on you. I don't like that at all."

Jackson was as determined not to talk about umpires as he was to keep private the identity of his girlfriend. ("There's too much pressure, I keep my girl away from footy as much as I can.")

But he drops his guard—but not his left—when he talks about football the way it is played today.

"I'd like to see football played as a man's game. At the moment, you might as well be playing netball.

"Some of the restrictions are terrible. It's meant to be a man's game, not a tart's game. If I knew football was going to be played like it is today. I would probably have played rugby."

With that off his expansive chest, he unleashed a straight right that would have demolished much more than a stick of fairy floss. He enjoys boxing, having learned the skills in a Perth gymnasium.

Jackson, who until this year had not been reported in a League match—he kicked 76 goals in an outstanding first season last year—first clashed with football authority at Nunawading South Primary School, where, because of a lack of strength, he often struggled to get a game.

"I wagged school for 10 minutes to get some lollies and got caught and suspended for a week. That was a nice start, I was in grade four. I cried for a week."

Jackson graduated to Melbourne via the Mitcham Technical High School, Mitcham, Heatherdale, Richmond—to which he won a scholarship—and South Fremantle football clubs and prefers to spend most of his time with his old mates.

"I spend a bit of time with my team-mates but really I don't like socialising with any footballers. If you get too friendly with footballers how are you supposed to go out and knock their heads off? After all, it's a man's game, not a tart's game.

"I don't believe in all this mixing with players. I don't agree with it, I'm sorry, but that's the way I think.

"I've got my own mates, and I know they would look after me if anything went wrong."

His wish to keep to himself does not offend his Melbourne team-mates—to whom he refers as "brother"—who speak well of him. His praises are sung enthusiastically by Crosswell and captain Robert Flower in particular, who speak about his great pride, modesty, loyalty, humor, concern for his team-mates, strength and courage and football shrewdness.

And what ambition has this remarkable, exuberant and theatrical fellow who has the respect of Barassi, a man who always has admired the genuine characters cum comics cum eccentrics of football?

"Other than to play with my brother Stephen (now doing his football apprenticeship in the colts at South Fremantle) I want to be Prime Minister and have Tiger (Crosswell) and Crackers (Keenan) in my Cabinet."

Barassi will be glad to have him off the back bench and in action against Carlton this week. When Jackson was last in the team, Melbourne won.

MALCOLM BLIGHT

By Garrie Hutchinson, *Age*, April 9, 1980.

Who will ever forget that sunlit afternoon at Princes Park when Carlton were goals in front, and Malcolm Blight still won the game for North, while most supporters were reaching for the final celebrating can?

The mark on the siren, the question to Keith Greig, and the answer: kick it. And the kick, a 70-metre torpedo that sank Carlton when they had one foot on the wharf, and one arm around a friend.

Or that muddy game against Hawthorn in 1977 Blight was pushed in the back as he kicked the behind that drew the game. Should he leave it a draw or go for the win? He, of course, went for the win, kicked it out of bounds, and North lost.

Malcolm Blight is a footballing genius, a man whose anticipation, skill, reflexes, vision, concentration and lateral thinking make him one of the players we travel a long way to see.

Even to the Arden Street Oval, perhaps, the most uncomfortable ground in the League when the wind blows.

Where there's a sign outside that says: "No representations are made that there is space available in the ground suitable for viewing the match."

It also says that they can refuse to let you in, and that if you do go in it's at your own risk, and that if you don't like it you can't get your money back.

Inside it's more or less impossible to get a drink, a pie, or to perform nature's necessary functions because of the dreaful amenities.

But, as always, we will put up with anything to see a good game, or even a bad game. And maybe Malcolm Blight will give us another moment, another example of the impossible come true.

Because beyond commitment to a team (to a point of view) football is about being amazed. It's like the circus used to be.

The magic chain of handpasses, the giant mark, courage. Maybe we'll see some today.

After a minute the ball is kicked down towards the North Melbourne goal. Blight has a look, leans forward, then takes a step or two back. He sticks his foot in the back of his opponent Craig Stewart, levers himself creakily into the air, and watches the ball bounce off other hands in front of his own, some time after he has returned to earth.

Blight shakes his head, purses his lips, and trots back towards the goal square.

A few minutes later, the ball flies out of the centre towards Blight and Stewart. Stewart goes after the ball with a pack of players. Blight feints forward, drops back and waits. The ball does not come to him.

Collingwood goals, and Blight runs to the opposite flank to where the play appears to be heading after the bounce. The ball explodes out of a scrimmage, hits Blight on the chest and bounces off.

Now he marks on his chest standing in the forward pocket, Stewart instinctively having followed the ball. Blight allows himself a smile, and seeing a colleague in the goal square gently hoofs it towards him. The colleague can't get near it. The ball swings and bounces through for a goal. Clarrie Grimmett would have been proud of the ball.

Blight looks, smiles, does a little swooping movement with his hand. Maybe the tide's turned. He shrugs his shoulders.

Seconds later, the ball bounces off Blight's chest again. He goes after it, gets it, a handball out, he shouts, makes position, gets it back, a hard handball, muffs it.

He trots back towards the centre, eyes on the ground.

He's not playing well. He goes to where the ball should be and it isn't there. He pushes and prods the ball to where someone else ought to be, and they're not there either.

His opponent watches the play, and you can see his legs lead him to where he judges the ball will go.

Blight, on the other hand, lurks behind and moves to where the ball ought to go. Somehow his physics let him down. Maybe there's a problem with the person kicking it at him.

Blight's problem is North's problem. They seem to have only spasmodic interest in the game, whereas fierce Collingwood players concentrate and say nasty things through clenched teeth. They just keep batting the ball forward more often than North can. It's a grim struggle.

It's obvious that Blight or Dempsey or Dench or Greig or someone is going to have to win it by themselves. Maybe they could win it together.

Two minutes into the second quarter Blight gets the ball, blind turns, side steps, handballs out, runs on, and on, waiting to get the ball back. It doesn't come. He kicks a divot.

He runs past the pack a couple of times, takes a mark, has a blind kick and then after 23 minutes of frustrating football, he gets a free kick at centre half-forward. This is nice, a big kick, and maybe...

Then, strangely, Ron Wearmouth climbs on to the shoulders of Bill Picken standing on the mark, and is penalised for the antic. Blight accepts the gift and dobs it through. Such a peculiar incident should have been a turning point. It wasn't.

The third quarter opens with Blight and Picken both desiring to stand on the same square foot of ground. A time-honored V.F.L.-style wrestling match ensues while the game begins again.

Picken stamps his foot, lets go a straight right that whistles past Blight's chin. Thus surprised, Blight slams Picken to the ground. The ball passes nearby, an umpire lets the boys know. They get up, look around, and now that the particular square foot of soil has become irrelevant, jog after the ball.

Blight running the wrong way grabs the ball as it slides off the top of the pack, whacks it with his left foot and drills it through for a goal.

But it was a flash in the pan.

For a quarter Blight handballs to where he thinks someone

might be, stages for free kicks, taps the ball forward and finally has a blind shot over his shoulder for an out of bounds on the full. His heart doesn't seem in it, and it's a great surprise to everyone that Collingwood leads by only five points at three quarter time.

In the last quarter Blight has four kicks and a handball, and each one of them might have resulted in a goal. But the fates were unsympathetic. A handball went begging, the boot didn't connect sweetly with the ball, the ball bounced unkindly.

And North Melbourne lost by five points.

Not Blight's fault, but still...

For the game, Malcolm Blight had 14 kicks, seven marks and seven handballs. He kicked three goals.

He didn't win the game. Someone should have.

PETER HUDSON

By Athol Meyer, *Australian*, September 22, 1979.

"If you go into football to achieve things on a personal basis you are doomed to failure."

These are the words of a man whose personal achievements in Australian football are unsurpassed—Peter Hudson, now at the end of a 17-year career, and with nearly 2000 goals to his credit.

At 33, Hudson is giving the game away. He plays his final club match on Saturday—his last goal being to help his club, Glenorchy, win the Tasmanian Football League premiership in the grand final against Clarence.

It was of little importance to him that on the eve of this match his personal goal tally for the season was 196 and he was on the verge of becoming the first senior footballer to kick 200 or more goals in a season.

Perhaps having achieved so much, it is easy for Peter Hudson to play down the importance of his individual performances over the years. But, there is little reason to doubt his sincerity when he says that being part of a winning team, and particularly a premiership team, is the greatest thing in football.

"Football is a team game and you rely so much on your team mates particularly a full-forward like myself. There's no place for the greedy individual in a team sport," he says.

With this philosophy towards the game it is not surprising that Hudson rates Hawthorn's Victorian League premiership win in 1971 as the greatest football highlight of his career.

"To me that premiership was everything—even to be part of a team that plays in a V.F.L. grand final is something never to be forgotten. Look at Bobby Skilton—he once said he would swap his three Brownlow Medals for a place in a premiership team."

There are parallels for Hudson in the seasons of 1971 and 1979. He went into the 1971 grand final needing only four goals for 151 for the season—a total that would have smashed the great Bob Pratt's 150-goal V.F.L. record of 1934. Instead he kicked only three to equal Pratt's record.

But then, and still now, Hawthorn's victory overshadowed any personal disappointment.

"Really, it wouldn't have been a true record anyway because Bob Pratt kicked his goals in fewer matches. But I equalled it, and my name is bracketed with Pratt's—and they don't come much better than that."

The record should have been Hudson's and probably would have been, but for a stunning blow in the first quarter that left him dazed and with double vision for the whole match.

"You know, one regret I do have is that I remember so little about what was such a great day for Hawthorn."

Hudson joined Hawthorn early in 1967. He was 21 but had already had four seasons of senior football behind him with New Norfolk in the T.F.L. He went to Hawthorn having worked hard at developing the basic football skills passed on to him by his father, Bob Hudson.

They played together in district football in 1962 when Peter, in his second last year at high school, was full-forward for Upper Derwent and his father captain-coach.

In 1963 Peter, at 17 and still at high school, was in the New Norfolk senior side. He made his senior football debut on the same day as another high school boy, ruckman Peter Jones still with Carlton.

Peter topped the T.F.L. goal-kicking list in each of his four seasons with the club and in 1966 was awarded his first All-Australian blazer after kicking 20 goals in the national football carnival in Hobart. This total included six against Victoria so it is no wonder five other V.F.L. clubs beside Hawthorn were also after the sharp-shooting young Tasmanian.

Hudson's move to Melbourne was an on-again, off-again event, particularly when Hawthorn and New Norfolk seemed unable to agree on transfer terms. Eventually the deal, reputed to cost Hawthorn $8000, went through and Hudson, having established residential qualifications, played his first V.F.L. match against Carlton.

The Blues rugged full-back Wes Lofts gave Hudson a vigorous introduction to V.F.L. football but he still managed four goals.

"I don't think I ever considered failing in Melbourne. I was confident and having this confidence helped me make it from the start."

Hudson was a young member of a young side, which included such future V.F.L. stars as rover Peter Crimmins, half-forward Bob Keddie, centre half-back Peter Knights and rover Leigh Matthews, which was to form the nucleus of the team that coach John Kennedy would mould into premiership winners in five years.

"We were all young, all very enthusiastic and I think we knew that eventually we would get there."

Hudson was a key man in the Kennedy strategy, because as he gained in confidence and experience it became clear that in one-for-one contest his positional play, body control and uncanny anticipation gave Hawthorn a distinct advantage.

The Hawthorn players were under instructions to move to centre-field taking their opponents with them and leaving Hudson and the full-back alone in front of goals.

The congestion around the centre bounces became so great that eventually the V.F.L. introduced the centre square rule, but only after Kennedy's strategy had paid off handsomely.

There also was a growing understanding between the Hawthorn players, particularly Hudson, Keddie and Crimmins.

"We played together so often in the same position, we knew exactly what each other would do. This has made me a great advocate of leaving players, if they are doing okay, in the one position. I'm against a lot of the shifting around of players that goes on today. I don't see how anyone can specialise and develop specialist talents when he's being moved around every week."

Hudson was given every encouragement by Kennedy and Hawthorn to develop his particular talent—kicking goals. He succeeded in a way which is unlikely to be equalled in the V.F.L.

In each of the four seasons from 1968 to 1971 Hudson kicked

more than 100 goals and repeated the effort when he returned to
Hawthorn for one season in 1977. He is the only to player in the
V.F.L.'s long history to have kicked more than 500 goals in five
seasons—but that fifth century should have come up in 1972.

"I really felt that was going to be the year. During the summer I trained harder than I ever had. By the start of the season
I was fitter than at any time in my career."

The first match of the season was against Melbourne at
Glenferrie Oval and by late in the second quarter Hudson had
kicked eight goals.

Then he flew for a mark, landed heavily and did not get up.

He had torn the cruciate ligament in his right knee and the
injury, with later cartilage trouble, was to keep Hudson out of
football for the best part of three and a half seasons.

However, there was one notable comeback attempt. Late in
the 1973 season, nearly 17 months after the knee injury, the call
went out from Hawthorn for Hudson to come back in a bid to
get the Hawks into the final five.

Kennedy flew to Hobart, jogged around the oval with a
rather portly Hudson, and put him on a tough two-week training
program to get him somewhere near playing fitness.

On August 25, 1973, after missing 41 matches with Hawthorn,
Hudson flew from Hobart on the morning plane. When he
arrived at Melbourne Airport, he was flown by helicopter to
V.F.L. Park and a crowd of 48,000 saw the No. 26 jumper in
action against Collingwood again.

Those who saw an overweight, unfit Hudson mesmerise the
Collingwood defence and kick eight goals will never forget
it—but his magnificent effort was in vain. Hawthorn was beaten
and missed out on the finals.

Hudson started the 1974 season with Hawthorn but played
only two games before cartilage trouble forced him out for the
season.

Those missed three and a half seasons were one of Hudson's
big disappointments.

"That perhaps is my biggest regret because I feel that I missed
playing at a time when I could reasonably have been expected to
be at my top."

But there were compensations. An offer to manage a large
modern hotel on the northern outskirts of Hobart giving him the

opportunity to be his own boss, the second of his ambitions after playing in the V.F.L.

"By 1975, though, I was back to football. I felt I was spending too much time at the hotel. I needed some other interest."

He became non-playing coach of Glenorchy and by mid-season was back on the field, a little slower, considerably more bulky, but still possessing all the old skills. Glenorchy won the premiership that year but was beaten in the grand final the following season by Sandy Bay.

But for Hudson 1976 was another personal triumph. He proved he could stand up to a full season of hard football, and still kick more than 100 goals. Little wonder Hawthorn was back on his trail, and in 1977 Hudson became the fly-in full-forward, making 29 return plane trips between Hobart and Melbourne in 27 weeks.

Again he personally triumphed—kicking 135 goals for the season and topping the V.F.L. goal-kicking list. However one such season was enough.

"It was not fair on the family. I was spending just too much time away from the hotel and putting too many demands on them."

So came the final break with Hawthorn, but, it was not the end of football for Hudson, far from it. Last year he surpassed even his own great statistical heights, and though Glenorchy was again beaten by Sandy Bay in the grand final, Hudson finished with an all-Australian season record of 191 goals including, just to show he could still do it, seven against Victoria in an interstate match.

Hudson was tempted back again this season mainly by the prospect of that premiership—and what a season it has been. In representative matches, he has kicked 23 goals and for Glenorchy 173 including bags of 12, 12, 15 and 18 in the four roster matches against the Hobart club.

But this time it really is the finish. As Hudson said half-jokingly, half-seriously a few nights ago: "You can't come back after they've made a one-hour film to mark the end of your career."

Not for Peter Hudson the tag of a has-been. He quits while right at the top—to be remembered by his Tasmanian fans, as he is remembered in Melbourne, as a football great, right to the end.

MAGPIE MAGIC

By John Powers, *Age*, June 7, 1980.

Collingwood—pre-season favourite at 3–1 odds to win the 1980 flag—plummeted down the League ladder with early losses and a draw. They had lost not only premiership favoritism, but pride. Defeat hurled them back to their traditional role of playing "battlers" football—cast once again as "the underdogs".

Outside the arena fans block all movement of traffic. They arrive in hordes, flaunting their allegiances and taunting each other with dire predictions of unbearable humiliation ahead. They exude a carnival spirit of expectation in which the possibility of their own team's defeat will not be entertained.

Supporters chant in unison as they buy buttons and ribbons and scarves and miniature team flags and 'Football Records'. They continue goading and chanting as they queue impatiently at the turnstiles. Inside they queue again for one of the 13,000 pies that will be eaten or an armful of the 24,000 cans of drinks required to slake their shout-torn throats. Then they elbow their way to their favorite viewing spots. From there they will urge, abuse, cheer, groan, hoot and laugh.

They have come, through rain or sunshine, to take part in that most desirable emotional experience—winning.

Journeying straight from this carnival spirit into the grim purposefulness of the Collingwood rooms proves too rapid a transition—like coming from a Walt Disney comedy back to the real-life world of triple fatalities on the roads and dire rumblings in the Middle East. It's too sudden, too sharply contrasted.

The mood of the changing rooms prohibits laughter, even smiles.

Informed opinion tips Collingwood to lose again. Down here there is no false optimism. Just defiance—the "rage" Hafey wants to stoke.

Club administrators huddle in small groups, watching the players change wordlessly from street clothes into their playing gear. Twenty of them. The 20 Hafey and his co-selectors believe deserve places in the team ignited to place Collingwood back into premiership contention.

As the players lace their boots and tug black and white guernseys over their heads Tom Hafey prowls among them, preparing them for the blitzkrieg.

Looking more visibly anxious than any of his men, Hafey appears desperate to give advice of monumental importance. He looks haunted by the fear that something might be overlooked.

He's spoken to each player by telephone the previous night— reminding them in turn of the task ahead. But now it's time for final words. He sits briefly beside each of them, whispering for either a moment or a minute—checking that they are emotionally and mentally primed. A few words, a nod, a reassuring pat.

Sometimes he almost springs forward in his urgency to impart a thought. Some players answer, some just grunt. Then Hafey begins prowling again. His head and shoulders twitch ceaselessly.

The result of the 100 minutes of imminent combat will be determined by innumerable and totally unpredictable factors, but the responsibility for sending these 20 men on to the arena with unshakable determination to emerge victorious rests squarely on one man—Tom Hafey.

The bracing smell of liniment thickens in the air as trainers apply it unstintingly on to the shoulders and bare arms of their players. The team manager constantly checks his watch to ensure that each stage of the final preparation begins precisely on schedule. He remains within a few paces of Tom Hafey, whispering the countdown each time Hafey flashes past him.

Players begin handballing and kicking as the dull boom of the outside crowd indicates that the Reserves match has entered its dying minutes. An atmosphere of charged adrenalin builds perceptibly in the changing room. Menace as tangible as a bunched fist can be felt now.

"Come on, Ronnie . . . Come on, Peter . . . Big one today . . . Give the bastards nothing . . . Build it up, build it up . . . Come on, Butch."

The brevity of everything spoken reflects the tension.

The siren wails.

Ray Mooney, the physical conditioning expert, shepherds the players into one large circle. The noise of footballs being kicked, punched or hurled against brick walls accelerates into a bedlam of noise as the players' deliberately restrained vocal encouragement swells to constant shouting. Individual words don't matter any more—collectively they announce the gladiatorial readiness to crush any opposing force.

333

Dozens of little boys who've scaled the outside walls to watch the last-minute preparations of their heroes through the wire-meshed windows of the changing room look suddenly awed by the passion erupting beneath them.

And as the players lower themselves to the floor to begin the obligatory stretching exercises Tom Hafey moves agitatedly around the circle his players have formed.

"Give it everything you've got today, fellers," he yells. "Fight them . . . FIGHT them all the way . . . Throw EVERY-THING at them . . . RIP into them . . . HARD into their bodies! . . . And RUN all day . . . lead for the ball . . . and help each other . . . WORK for each other . . . It's desperation stuff today, boys—DESPERATION STUFF!"

Between Hafey's shouts—thunderous in the confined space of the changing-room—Ray Mooney barks his commands for each new stretching exercise. Then he orders them to their feet to begin knee-to-chest jumping. Then a burst of sprinting-on-the-spot. At the end of each set of jumps, and each sprint, the baying of voices increases in volume as they individually and collectively pledge themselves to give it to the opposition the way the great Collingwood teams of the past have always dealt it out—hard, mean, tough, remorseless.

Then it's time for Hafey's speech.

The players sit, squeezed tightly together on wooden benches. Their faces, arms, shoulders and legs gleam with sweat and liniment.

Hafey centres himself in front of them. He looks uncommonly small in this room packed with twenty match-hardened foot-ballers. But he beams with the pride of being their coach. Proud of them. Proud for them.

"This's it, boys," he begins. The first words are subdued. But then he shouts: "THIS'S IT! I don't know if you've had enough of the sledging and rubbishing we've been getting . . . but I HAVE!"

He gets an affirmative roar of support.

"When we lose, the Press says we're nothing to beat, and when we win they say the opposition 'played poorly'. Well, I've had enough of it—enough losing and enough sledging. Today's the day we prove we're a bloody good side . . . a winning side . . . a PREMIERSHIP side!"

He let them roar endorsement. Then—in a quieter but quickened and more urgent tone—he reminded them:

"The thing we were noted for last year was the PRESSURE we placed on the opposition—the chasing, the bumping, and the aggressive tackling. They were the things that made us a good team, because a lot of people believed we lacked the ability of some of the other top sides—the number of star players in those other teams. We got where we did by combined team aggression. And THAT'S what we've got to produce again this year—RELENTLESS AGGRESSION!"

He allowed another roar of approval, but quickly cut across the roar.

"Personnel doesn't mean a bloody thing in the opposition, or in any team if it comes to that," he assured them, accelerating the speed of his words. "If you've got a team of goers, that's enough. Where you got last year was a result of just go, go, go . . . and not giving up . . . NEVER giving up! And that's the way it's got to be again.

"That's our game—hard, tough, and never giving in. We're the toughest side in the competition—you proved that last year. There's no worries about that. And most of the other teams don't like it to be as tough as we play the game. They don't like it when we flex our muscles at them. But THAT'S OUR GAME, THAT'S our racket—FIRST to the ball, and HARD into the ball. Everybody putting in. Goers, goers, GOERS! Then, no matter who's the opposition we've got, it's THAT that'll make us CHAMPIONS this year!"

The team manager called. "Time, Tom."

Hafey didn't turn away from his players but his face registered a flicker of dismay that time was running against him.

Then, spilling words into each other in his desperation to plant his final imperative message into their heads, he galloped into his finale as a great swell of roaring from outside told him that the opposition had entered the arena.

"I want our style stuck to as much as possible—that's play-on desperately at every opportunity, using long kicks straight down the field, straight down the centre. From the half-back line to the half-forward line, then straight into the goal square, or maybe even through the goal posts. But no lairising. No short passes.

"Fearlessly into the ball, fellers. Fight for the ball all the time. Fight all the way. Fiercely contest everything. It's 1980, boys—THE YEAR OF THE MAGPIE! So fight, fight, fight. Be up there all the time. Straight for their bodies. Nothing sissy about it. Don't go for their heads, just body to body. Tough football, Collingwood football. INTO them! All for the team. Attack, attack, attack. NEVER STOP attacking!"

"Time, Tom!" the team manager yelled, urgently now, pointing to his watch. And the players sprang to their feet, shouting defiantly in chorus.

But Hafey shouted louder than even their collective voices as they moved towards the race. He yelled:

"FIGHT them!... fight all the way!... PLOUGH into them!... RIP into them! GRIND them into the earth!... Fight!... NEVER STOP FIGHTING!

He kept shouting as they formed their line—the proud line of "battlers" and "underdogs"—and ran on to the oval to contest another of their seemingly endless battles for survival.

THE CLUB

From the play by David Williamson, 1978.

The scene: The boardroom of a famous football club. The players: Ted, club president; Laurie, the coach; Jock, former coach, committeeman and club stirrer; Gerry, new whizz-kid administrator.

TED: I *would* like to put harmonious somewhere in that press statement, Laurie.

LAURIE: You're a trier, aren't you?

TED: It would make me feel a lot better.

LAURIE: Say we've had a long talk and have resolved our differences. That's as far as I'll go.

(JOCK *comes in the left door.*)

JOCK: I got on to Geoff and he's on his way in.

TED: You're a hard man, Laurie. I'll write it out and give it to Gerry.

LAURIE: I want to check it before it's released.

TED: Don't worry. I won't slip anything in.

(TED *leaves through the right door.*)

JOCK: Geoff's on his way in.

LAURIE: Ted tells me that you were the one who held out for him.

JOCK: Yeah, I did. He is good, Laurie. He's got so much talent he's a bloody freak. He just needs to be motivated properly.

LAURIE: What's this I hear about Parker resigning?

JOCK: Parker resigning? Is he?

LAURIE: Come on, Jock. I'm not an idiot. Gerry said there's some sort of storm blowing up that's going to force him to resign.

JOCK: Yeah, I did hear a whisper to that effect.

LAURIE: Come on, Jock. You don't *hear* whispers, you start 'em. What's going on?

JOCK: He's got himself into some sort of trouble but I don't know the details. Thank Christ is all I can say. I mean let's face it. The man's a buffoon. He's got to go.

LAURIE: And when he goes you'll be standing for President?

JOCK: If it's the wish of the Committee. I'll tell you something, Laurie. With Parker out of the way things'll start ticking over smoothly again and we'll come out of this trough. You wait and see. Gerry's got some great ideas for next year.

LAURIE: Oh he has?

JOCK: Yeah. A great administrator, that lad. Getting him's one of the smartest things the Club ever did.

LAURIE: You were the one man on the Committee who voted not to appoint him.

JOCK: A man can be wrong.

LAURIE: Not many can manage it as often as you.

JOCK: I'm glad I laid you out behind the lockers.

LAURIE: What are some of these great ideas of Gerry's?

JOCK: We're going to buy up big.

LAURIE: Buy more players?

JOCK: No, sheep. We're going to graze 'em on the oval and save on lawn mowing costs. Of course we're going to buy more players. We're going to go on the biggest buying spree in the history of the game, and what's more it's good economics.

LAURIE: Why?

JOCK: If we win a premiership it'll arrest the membership decline and members mean money. As a businessman myself I can see the logic of it.

LAURIE: As a businessman yourself. God help us. I was one

of the mugs who invested in your import business. A hundred dozen pop-up Taiwanese toasters that burnt the bread then fired it like mortar shells. No wonder the Chinese don't invade them. There's probably a hundred thousand of those toasters permanently trained on the mainland. Then we had the forty gross of Russian alarm clocks that ticked so loudly that the alarm wasn't needed because there was no bloody way you could get to sleep, and the eighty dozen pairs of toy handcuffs from the Philippines that had to be withdrawn from sale after three days because forty-seven kids had to be hacksawed out of them.

JOCK: I'm glad I laid you out behind the lockers.

LAURIE: Well you haven't exactly distinguished yourself in your business career.

JOCK: You won't make fun of me when you hear some of the names we're negotiating with.

LAURIE: (*sharply*) Negotiating? Who's negotiating? Listen Jock, I'm supposed to be consulted—(*when there's*)

JOCK: Not negotiating. I didn't mean negotiating. All we've done is started to think of some names.

LAURIE: Who has?

JOCK: Gerry and I.

LAURIE: What names?

JOCK: Try these for size. Cam Donaldson, Mickey Dimisch and Andy Payne. How'd you like that lot on your goal-to-goal line?

LAURIE: I'd love 'em on my goal-to-goal line but I'd like to be consulted.

JOCK: You are being consulted. Right now. Cam Donaldson, Mickey Dimisch and Andy Payne. Good enough?

LAURIE: Are they available?

JOCK: No, but they will be. Gerry's amazing, but for Christ's sake keep those names under your hat. There's half a dozen clubs after all of 'em. Next year's going to be a good one, Laurie. With you at the helm and players like that in the team there'll be no stopping us.

(GERRY *enters through the right door holding a notebook in his hand.*)

GERRY: Is this all you're prepared to say to the press, Laurie?

(LAURIE *reads the statement.*)

338

LAURIE: Yes.

GERRY: You're not very generous. Ted's pretty upset.

LAURIE: Tough. What's this I hear about Donaldson, Dimisch and Payne?

JOCK: Sorry, Gerry. It just slipped out.

GERRY: (*coldly*) The rate at which things slip out around here makes me wonder if members of this Club aren't fitted with a special circuit that goes straight from ear to tongue and completely bypasses the brain.

LAURIE: What's the meaning of starting to plan next year's team without even consulting me?

GERRY: I was going to talk to you about it today, only you went and got yourself into this mess with Ted.

LAURIE: Where are you getting all the money for this spending spree?

GERRY: We'll get it.

LAURIE: How?

GERRY: Leave that to me.

LAURIE: Be buggered I'll leave it to you. Listen. I've been around here for twenty-seven years and I'm coach of this bloody Club, not the office boy. How are you getting the money?

GERRY: Keep it quiet then. It's all touch and go at the moment. We had two of the biggest property developers in the country in the members bar last Saturday—

LAURIE: Arthur Mowbray and Dick Tanner?

GERRY: Yeah, and despite what Ted thinks they didn't get there by accident. I fossicked around and found out that they're both old supporters so I've been courting them, and doing it pretty well even if I do say so myself. Most guys of that age and in their position are looking for an interesting sideline, pastime, hobby—and these two are no exception, except that they won't have anything to do with us while Ted is President. They haven't said anything directly but it was quite obvious what they were feeling and I can't say I blame them. He was fawning on them like a drunken toad on Saturday.

LAURIE: What sort of role in the Club are you planning for them?

GERRY: If we get rid of Ted we can put Mowbray in as Vice-President and make Tanner an honorary life member.

LAURIE: Where's his twenty-five years active service?

GERRY: We'll get around that. Shit, Laurie, let's not be bush lawyers when there's this sort of money involved.

LAURIE: What sort of money?

GERRY: Two hundred thousand each for starters. If we can't buy ourselves a premiership with that nobody can.

JOCK: We'll collect a bit of cash from our sales as well.

LAURIE: What sales?

GERRY: (*glaring at* JOCK) I was going to discuss the possibility of offloading one or two of our older players who are still looking good but who are just about over the hill.

LAURIE: Such as?

GERRY: I don't know. I'm just an administrator, you're the expert. Given that we get Donaldson, Dimisch and Payne, who could we do without?

LAURIE: Tony Harper, I suppose.

GERRY: Hardly worth the effort. His market price is somewhere under five thousand.

LAURIE: Market price?

GERRY: I've been making a few enquiries.

LAURIE: They're men, not pigs.

GERRY: All right. If you want to mince words we'll call it something else, but the fact remains that there is a market mechanism operating, there is a price on every player and the price on Tony Harper is so low it's not worth negotiating his sale. The only player we've got that has big money on his head is Danny.

LAURIE: We're not selling Danny.

GERRY: Why not? With the players we're getting do we really need him?

LAURIE: (*angry*) Yes of—

GERRY: It's a question. I wouldn't know whether we need him or not. I'm just the administrator and you're the expert. There's no need to get angry. I'm merely posing a question.

LAURIE: We need him.

GERRY: Fine. A few of the wise heads around here seem to think he's looked better than he really is for years because he hasn't exactly been playing in a team full of champions. They're worried that if he plays too many more games like last Saturday a lot of people will start to realise it and his market price, or whatever you like to call it, will plummet.

340

LAURIE: Which of the "wise heads" around here believe that little theory?

JOCK: I do. I say sell him while he's still worth something. Let's face it, Laurie, when we were winning our medals it was in a team full of champions. Danny's little more than a talented hack.

LAURIE: Come off it, Jock. He's bloody near as good as either of us were in our day. I know what's worrying you. If he stays around for another couple of years he'll beat your two hundred and eighty-two games.

JOCK: Yeah, well you couldn't beat it and he's not going to either. Bloody leaves his wife and kids for an Avis girl. When my record goes it'll be to someone with a bit of moral fibre.

LAURIE: Moral fibre? I don't seem to recall that you were famous for your celibacy in the old days Jock. In fact if my memory serves me—

GERRY: That's enough. Laurie, what if I told you I could swap Danny for Tony Marchesi?

(LAURIE *looks at* GERRY.)

That's made you stop and think, hasn't it?

LAURIE: Can you?

GERRY: No, but it made you stop and think, which goes to show that the central assumption of the science of economics— that we'd all sell our grandmothers if the price is right—isn't all that far wide of the mark.

LAURIE: (*defensive, irritated*) The only reason I'd want Danny to go is if Danny wanted to go. I don't care if you could swap him for Jesus Christ.

JOCK: With the team we'll have next year, Jesus Christ will be pushing to make the reserves.

(*There is a knock at the left door.*)

That's probably Geoff. How do you want to handle this, Laurie? I'll have a chat to him first if you like.

LAURIE: I'll talk to him, if you don't mind.

JOCK: Suit yourself. I just thought that a fresh viewpoint....

BRAVE NEW FOOTBALL

By Barry Dickins, *Age*, April 9, 1981.

I haven't seen a game of footy since 1900, when Fitzroy tied with Lort Smith dog pound, so I guess I'm a trifle out of touch.

But many was the time we watched the old Lions lose to whoever from the bridge over the North Fitzroy briquette yard at the old ground and barracked ourselves hoarse, or perhaps donkey would be a better word because we followed Fitzroy through 10,000 losses straight.

Not that they were a bad team. They were just poor, that's all. They just couldn't seem to be able to afford to win. Anyway, Carn the mighty Roys!

A grease and oil change, a million bucks and better pies, and who knows? They might beat the Combined Briquette Workers, best of three. Those were the days when Kevin Murray (Old Gummy Shark) was the indomitable captain, or was it Butch Gale? As I said, it's been a long while. Anyway.

I still love the game, and last Saturday saw a miracle. It was like meeting Christ in Frankston. The Mighty Lions won. Had done Melbourne. At V.F.L. Park at Waverley. I was so happy I ate my pies right through the bag. Six tins and a win! Too much! Yahoo! But yahoo to whom?

This is where George Orwell steps in. V.F.L. Park is like playing footy on the moon. I was frightened. You needed a computer print-out sheet to order a hot dog! A buck for a pie, too frightened to do you any good. I watched the game seated. Perhaps that was the trouble. But Fitzroy won, and I felt beaut.

But won where? That's the question. It was like trying to relax on Saturn. Brave New Footy. Nuclear scoreboard, intellectual pie boys, existentialist frankfurt men, Jungian umpires, Freudian boundary umpires. One felt too withdrawn to boo. One whispered, as one has always whispered to oneself "Come on Fitzroy". It's like a rosary. A prayer. (Soft) "Fitzroy a dark horse for the flag".

The ground was too big. I missed the old footy intimacy. I hereby reproduce the old dialogue, circa 1960, at the old Brunswick Street ground, in the outer, shoulder to shoulder, inner and outer, members stand and pickpocket stand. Captain Blood (Jack Dyer) is on every tranny. Every supporter has a two-buck transistor to their cauliflower earhole. There are roars like volcanoes when Fitzroy score a goal. You hear the radios everywhere all round the ground.

"And Butch Gale's got the ball, he can't do a thing wrong or right with it terday and full credit must go to him. Butch Gale's sandwiched by Ray Gabelich, the only footballer for Collingwood who can sandwich a player from both sides on his own, and the old Butch is after the footy, it's nearly time-on, and Murray Weideman boots the ball out of his grasp and the ball's slithering across the grass like a bag of wet briquettes here terday.

"It's thrown in, up they go, Butch gets the tap down and it's booted into the air, and ooooghhh, arghhh . . . an incident, someone's dead out there, this sort of thing gives the game a bad name, don't you agree, Bill Twoomey?"

"Arghhh, yes, too right Butch, I mean Smoke Rings Hickey, I mean Captain Blood, um Jack, the Saint John Ambulance is administering oxygen, and hello, what's up now, Kevin Murray's pulled down a screamer right on the siren. Fitzroy and Collingwood level here terday. Could hear a pin drop. Not a can hits the gravel as The Gummy Shark comes in, steadies, steadies and boots a major article and the goal umpire makes no bones about bringing up the twin calicos. Wait on, it was only his footy boot and wet old sock. The footy's still on the ground, and the old Muzzah's booted his left sock and boot through the goalsquare. Bad luck Lions!!!"

Yeah, and the smell of buns, franks, snags of all sorts, women that screamed like ferrets on heat. One bloke I saw at the Waverley game last Saturday was the frankfurt man, and he got excited and ran on and marked the ball as if it were some gigantic bun. In the old days that sort of behavior was encouraged. He would've had his kick.

I can imagine the old Captain Blood saying "And the frankfurt man coming in now, steadies, steadies, lines it up and boots the bun right through the high diddle diddle and full credit must go to him and each and every frankfurt concerned".

Yeah, wish they were at their old home ground. Buses and trains and Orwell make it hard to support the old lions!

BIG MEN FLY, AND THE ROT STARTS

By Les Carlyon, *Age*, April 6, 1974.

What would you say to a newspaper photograph of a grown man in bed with a football?

A grown man wearing number 28 guernsey, crooking the ball in his left hand so that it nuzzles into the floral sheets.

And a caption to explain that young Fred Smith, the boy they recruited up at Goornong, has been having cartilage trouble . . . so he thought he'd have an early night.

Nothing about the ball or the guernsey, the omissions suggesting that EVERYONE sleeps with a footy—and in a number 28 guernsey.

What would you say? A trifle contrived perhaps?

Well, what would you say to a photograph of young Billy Brown, the raw-boned sensation down at Victoria Park, milking Dad's Friesians on an icy Colac morning in his number 33 guernsey—sleeveless, mind you, and the blow wave still in place?

Or a photograph of two opposing captains, both travelling salesmen, who just happened to park next to each other in the city on Friday and stopped for a yarn about the "big game" just as a photographer walked by.

No, they aren't wearing guernseys, although now that you mention it there is a number 18 guernsey lying obtrusively across the back seat of one of the cars.

What do you say? A lot of contrived nonsense?

Well don't. The footy season starts today, and this is what you are going to see and read in the papers for what will seem an eternity.

Sometime in the next few months you will doubtless see a headline which screams: *"SMITH TOLD TO CUT THEM OFF"*.

Do not—repeat do not—be alarmed: they will be talking about his sideboards.

You will read about coaches "reading the riot act" (it happens every Thursday night actually); about cartilages and hamstrings; about athletes whose names, it seems, can only be mentioned if preceded by a string of adjectives.

Words like "high-marking", "hard-bumping" and "nimble footed".

[I understand that "never-giving-anything-in-the-crunches" was once submitted, but the sporting editor was stricken with apoplexy and this pearl was never published.]

And it will all be so po-faced.

Scoff as much as you like; football is a serious business.

Football—that great ritual of the Victorian winter—in some senses lives off the charity of the media.

Yet it is perhaps also true that nowhere is football taken more seriously than in the newspapers and on TV.

Which brings us to TV. There are a few things you should prepare for there, too.

The video cavalcade; the inquests, the club corners, the post-mortems that would make any coroner pall.

And the cliches, those Melbourne winter cliches that reverberate around your diningroom . . . "the big men fly" . . . "it's stacks on the mill" . . . "the umpire says: 'I'll have it' . . ." . . . "he's taken two bites of the cherry" . . . "the ball is out of bounce" (sic) . . . "a penetrating drop kick."

And there are the commentators. They were nobodies in summer; now they are gods.

Just as newspapers suspend standards, so do TV stations. Many of the commentators—selected not because of their fluency so much as the fact that they once pulled on a jockstrap for Collingwood or wore dirty bandages for Richmond—have fearful trouble with their tenses. Who cares. They're footy commentators, aren't they?

Raw-boned and jocular fellows they are too, oozing a sort of pie-night-bonhomie, sharing private jokes and experiences.

They are so clever at creating this pie-night atmosphere that sometimes you almost think you can hear the clink of cans off the set.

Like football writers, they too have a bent for theatrical gravity.

Only they can ask straight-faced: "What really happened out there today Fred?".

Of course, what really happened out there was that Fred and his mates were inept and flat-footed and, besides, half a dozen of them had consumed several dozen the night before.

But Fred isn't captain for nothing: he knows what to say. And so he begins: "Well, Jack, we just couldn't play 100 minutes of football . . .".

Yes, footy—more precisely football as it appears in the media—is truly a ritual.

It is also the essence—for some, the life-force—of a Melbourne winter. It is as totally predictable as leaden skies and drizzling rain.

So prepare yourself. Even as I write, pictorial editors are briefing their top men.

"Now listen, I want you to go out and get a picture of young Cowboy Jones, the kid who kicked all the goals on Saturday. He's done a bit of scuba diving, so we want to get him under water, but don't keep him down there too long because he reckons it mucks up his blow wave. Incidentally, you can pick up a number 14 guernsey for him on the way . . ."

Actually, I quite like football: it's the media that upsets me.

UP IN THE MEMBERS

By Garrie Hutchinson, *Age*, April 7, 1982.

Robbie Flower is loping after the ball. It's caught in a clump of players who cannot decide how to pick it up, and so stand around talking and pushing each other.

Robbie parts the melee like Moses did the Red Sea, and discovers the ball rolling gently along the turf minding its own business.

Flower bends to gather it in. Just then the slow motion excitement around him suddenly becomes noisy, and falls over, and frightens the ball so much that it slips from Flower's sticky fingers.

Not giving a hoot for the pack around him, Flower pats the ball softly, pushing it along, bending it to his will. Maybe he fills it with static electricity so that it is attracted to his hand, because wherever Flower goes, so does the ball.

Through a maze of legs and arms, boots and bad breath, the ball follows Flower, or rather goes in front of him.

He has it on a string, like a dog on a lead, like a yo yo, like a juggler with hoops.

He can change direction, stop, go backwards, and the ball will follow. It's amazing, and it's happening right in front of the green plastic seats of the Members Stand.

After such an exhibition of football wizardry, clean and graceful, the members stand as one, can applaud as if they've just heard La Stupenda shatter the crystal chandeliers of the Princess.

"This is the kind of football they like to see," I think, "not the antics of Jacko."

Just then Tiger Crosswell takes a mark, wheels around and kicks the ball to where David Cordner should be, and very nearly is.

You can almost see the mists of memory clear, and the vision of teams full of Cordners winning flag after flag, as the blond grabs the ball, has a ping at the goals, and misses.

He gets a round of applause, but the members don't stand up. This Cordner has a way to go before the deeds of his forefathers are replaced by his own in the subconscious of the Long Room.

The Members. Anyone can be a member if they are patient enough, or had a dad with foresight 20 years ago.

Which means that anyone can climb the historic stairs to the Long Room and reserve a station on the leather armchairs with a copy of 'Wagner's Ring' and sample the Roast of the Day, $6.50.

Anyone can stand at the bench behind the leather armchairs, look through the glass at most of the field, drink copious numbers of pots, and admire the form of the Greek god, Con Gorozidis, who happens to play for St. Kilda.

Being a member doesn't necessarily mean you barrack for Melbourne.

You have to wear a tie (or a visible cravat), and so young members tend to adopt the Old Sports Coat syndrome. These checked and houndstoothed numbers are often coupled with white pants and riding boots, a casual uniform unseen since the fifties outside the public schools and the Law School of the University of Melbourne.

Older members tend to go for the more subdued greys and browns and matching tops and bottoms, although the silver buttoned reefer jacket and the three-piece Dior suit are not unknown.

For all that, it is a very pleasant, unhurried way to watch the football. You could learn to like the uniform, the environment (steeped, as they say, in history) and the feeling of privilege.

It's just like a Men's Club where, if during the game, your

language becomes a little strong, even indiscreet, then you're a least among friends. They understand.

So the members roar and shout, out in the open, inventing prolix sexual insults about umpires and opponents, by turns loud, raucous, profane and for some inexplicable reason, antisemitic.

And carried away by it all, they enthusiastically cheer the Redlegs on for the first win at home in a couple of years.

They cheer on the win, and in doing so have to cheer on the two most un-Flower-like players in the V.F.L., Jacko and Tiger.

Jacko gets reported early on, for something too far away to see, and makes the ground shake as he paces furiously up and down. Something is burning deep inside his heart, and when he gets the opportunity, at the quarter-time gathering, he's off calling the offending umpire names, it seems. He's restrained in this make-believe game by his co-conspirator, Tiger.

A member voices his approval: "You go and stand on his toes, Jacko." Others are not so enthusiastic. "Put Cordner at full-forward," says one, "Put Jackson in the zoo."

Jacko and Tiger beat their chests like Tarzans.

Luckily, Jacko comes good with a bag of goals, doing what a full-forward of his copious bulk does best—taking marks with one or both paws, standing his ground when all around him flyweights struggle to gain a foot or hand hold.

Some members find Jacko distasteful because he isn't a graceful swallow-like high mark, and he isn't a brainy forward like Hudson. He just stands and takes half a dozen marks for four or five goals nearly every week.

All the other business, like handstands and chest beating, is so much show business, a foot-balling skill much underrated but highly desirable.

Where would we be without "colourful" players?

Jacko was one of the great actors of all time as a mentor in the form (or bulk) of Crosswell. The old Tiger. Towards the end he was so puffed out it looked as if he was pleading with St. Kilda to keep the ball up the other end, to give him a breather.

But can the old fellah play! Can he take a mark! Can he get off a handball over the shoulder to an extremely surprised team mate jogging past! Can he organise a forward line!

Can he commit a handpass in the direction of Jacko, call out to the lumbering giant to catch it, then receive the ball back from the Sherman tank, and kick a goal himself!

348

The old one-two, a close facsimile of team work, of organisation, of football.

The members stood as one, clapping and cheering as if it were September. They might like Robbie Flower, and have hopes for David Cordner, but they surely know winning football when they see it.

Even from Jacko and the Tiger.

THEY DON'T NEED TO SPEAK

By Garrie Hutchinson, *Age*, July 6, 1982.

There's a lot to watch on the football field besides goals and behinds, marks and kicks. There's acting, for example.

Not just the time-honored dive into the mud when a player feels a touch on the back; or the agonised lack of motion (one eye cocked for the umpire) after feeling the whistle of a left hook; or even the seemingly incapacitating limp developed between the message from the runner and the journey to the bench.

Footballers are, as everyone knows, professional entertainers, and have the full lexicon of acting devices at their disposal. As actors, though, their biggest problem is in communicating with their audience the full range of emotions and facts that they want to.

Like mimes and silent movie actors, footballers do not have the undoubted advantage of speech. They must perform in dumbshow.

But they have developed a whole range of acting devices, gestures, displays—which communicate to their audience how they feel at the more important moments of the game.

We might divide these into Displays of Triumph, Displays of Despair, Displays of Control and Displays of Concentration.

A lot of them are fairly ostentatious messages to the coach, who can presumably see straight through them.

DISPLAYS OF TRIUMPH

These are employed at moments of extreme joy, such as scoring of goals, or the taking of important grabs.

The Bum Slap: After scoring a much needed goal, the scorer

349

runs back to his position as his team mates smack him on the bottom. He does not blink an eye. A variation is where a rover, say, has to run a gauntlet of slaps, a corridor of team mates, all the way back to the centre. These slaps are meant to propel the scorer, using a high back lift and a satisfying 'smack!'

Thanks Mate: A goal scorer, the recipient of a piece of hard work by a team mate, will point out his pal, look him in the eye, clap his hands and thank him for the assist.

The High Handclap: Developed by the legendary Percy Jones, this involves watching the ball sail over his head, through the goals while he raises his hands above his head, claps very fast, sometimes jumping in the air as well.

The Hug: A goal scorer can be greeted with degrees of affection, depending on his status in the team. If a goal is particularly important and is scored by a team favorite, he might be hugged. It is sometimes followed by a headclasp, hands holding the scorers head, employing eye to eye contact.

The Group Hug: Other players might join in, in whole-team contact—a group expression of love and joy.

The Horizontal Hug: If the scorer has fallen over in the act, happy comrades might dive on him for a full length expression of satisfaction.

Gimme some skin: A scorer holds out one or two hands after the event, depending on its importance, to have the palms slapped. Imported direct from the USA. A good goal scores five, a great goal 10 fingers.

Look At Me: A player takes what he regards as a screamer, or is paid a mark after being denied several by the umpire. He gets up from the turf and holds the ball aloft on one hand. A variation is to spin it on one finger. Sometimes regarded as a device only used by show-ponies.

Easy: After scoring an easy or not particularly vital goal, the scorer might point to the sky with one finger, one fist, or simply shake the fist more or less to himself. No one else notices.

Air Punch: If a goal scorer thinks his work is very meritorious, he might run and punch the air, at the same time as doing a bicycle kick while jumping in the air.

Two Fisted Air Punch: Similarly, a scorer might shoot through the goals after kicking one, and wheel around, all the time shaking both fists in the air.

Two Fisted Sidestep: A variation is to shake both fists in the air, but to jump from side to side. All these air punches require particular determination from team mates if they are to catch up and give the scorer a good slap.

Hair Ruffle: Not very important goals might be greeted, especially if scored by a team junior, with a fatherly ruffle of the locks.

Hand Shake: And, even in recent years, old comrades might still acknowledge good play with a man to man shake of the paws.

DISPLAYS OF DESPAIR

These are messages designed to indicate degrees of disappointment, missed opportunities, incorrect decisions.

Head Shake: After missing a particularly hard shot for goal, an old hand will shake his head. "I should have got that one".

Hands on Head: A more gloomy display is watching the ball sail where it was not intended, with hands clasped behind the head. Used for missing easy shots.

Hands on Face: For missing a shot for goal from the square, for example, a player will cover his face, unable to witness his shame.

Forehead Slap: A variation on the head shake—should have got that one.

He Fell Over: A free kick is given against a player. He might hold his arms out horizontally, shaking his head, looking at the umpire. "He fell over ump. Should be my free".

Heads Down: After having been out run, or after a game has been lost, players walk about staring at the ground, a gesture of defeat.

DISPLAYS OF CONTROL

These are gestures used by players to protect, control, or try to gain possession of a piece of turf, the initiative, the umpire's eye.

Chesting: This is the pigeon-like aggression display where players puff out their chests, and hit each other with them, arms being held backwards. Violence is seen to be intended without being done.

Not Me Ump: A player lies seemingly unconscious on the ground, and his opponent stands above him like a triumphant gladiator. No one else is within cooee. The victor saunters off shaking his head. It wasn't me ump, he fainted.

Stand There, Kid: old hands will direct the umpire's attention to where the mark should be.

Wrong, Ump: Players will gesture to the umpire, indicating with swishes of the arms what the decision should have been.

Right, Ump: Sometimes when a free kick is earned after a period of not getting any, the umpire will receive a round of applause. About time.

DISPLAYS OF CONCENTRATION

These are gestures used to indicate that a player is taking a strong interest in the game, or in a particular passage of play. Often they are for the benefit of the coach. Look at me, I'm really trying.

Pawing the Ground: A ruckman, especially at centre bounces will bend forward, paw the ground with his stops, let his arms hang loose, growl and stare mightily at the ball, waiting for the signal to pounce.

Arms Akimbo: When play is at the other end of the ground a lot, the players, especially old rivals at the other end, stands arms crossed, leaning on one leg, staring up the field. They might chat a bit while concentrating, or else share a jug when offered by any trainer.

Hands On Hips: A gesture of tiredness or recovery. A player has done his bit, and now watches the results upfield, resting his hands on his hips.

I'm Really Trying To Handball. A player when tackled strongly, having failed to get rid of the pill makes a strenuously obvious attempt to handball it while on the ground. He never succeeds in disturbing the ball.

They might not be able to talk, but there's a lot said in the art of body language.

IN RED AND BLACK

By Garrie Hutchinson, *Age*, July 28, 1981.

Essendon has always managed to create a great army of young supporters when it looks like being successful. I know, I was one.

The reason is more obvious now that it was in my day. Essendon is probably the sexiest team playing today. The players are young, big, winning and they play with a kind of edgy aggression that seems to be just waiting for some slight, or look, to tip it over the edge.

Essendon has featured in some of the great brawls of the past, but this year it looks more dangerous than ever, like a dormant volcano.

I've been trying to remember what it was like in the Red and Black Armies of the 60s when John Coleman was king coach, and the idols were an odd, not at all sexy assortment of great players.

John Birt, Hugh Mitchell, Ken Fraser, Geoff Leek and Jack Clarke, Alex Epis, who must surely have taught Kevin Sheedy a trick or two, Ted Fordham, Charlie Payne, Barry Davis and Bluey Shelton.

I can remember two stages of supporting Essendon, before the Carlton schism. One as a titchy kid, one as a just-turned teenager. Things were different in those days in Essendon, as they were everywhere else.

Little kids could go to the footy, and were encouraged to go, by their parents. Dad might take you to the foreign fields of Arden Street or Victoria Park or Brunswick Street where you'd get an early view of terrace houses, pubs and other ways of life, but you went to Essendon on your own if you wanted to.

Rough as the games inside and outside the ground might be, there was no thought that anything would happen to you. You weren't going to get kidnapped or molested. I can remember being passed hand to hand over the heads of the crowd to the front row so "the kid can have a look at a great football team."

You just ducked and wove past the riots outside the ground, outside the pub, on the roundabout, under the railway bridge.

But when you're a little kid, footy's pretty dull. It was great to get right down on the fence, close to the players as they thundered by, seeing how big they were, smelling the sweat and linament, hearing the crunch of hip and shoulder, seeing how far a 60 yard torp really was with your own eyes.

After that it was generally time to search for a real pollywaffle and a bottle of drink (was it Boon Spa?) and then have a great time endlessly scurrying through the legs of grownups on forgotten errands.

I remember nearly getting bowled over by a muddy Jack Clarke one day, and saving a neighbor from getting a Sherrin in the face with a timely fist—the only time I have ever touched the match ball.

Then there was the uniquely Melbourne sound of a thousand footies being kicked dangerously by a thousand little kids, tongues out in concentration, dobbing dropkicks through the big ones from 15 yards out on the sacred turf, on the angle. And imagining the real thing, commentating on yourself. 'He grabs the pill off the pack. Bounce, bounce, dummies round a lumbering backman, steadies, and hits Coleman on the chest with a daisy cutter . . .'

I can remember thinking that lunch time kick to kick at Doutta Galla State would have been much more enjoyable if we'd had turf as smooth and soft as this, with its unique pattern of stop marks.

Saturdays was a day of freedom on a little kid, meeting pals, catching the bus, emerging through the underpass from the bus stop in Rose Street to a world of red and black crowds, hurrying excitedly through Essendon junction.

But as we grew older, Saturday afternoon freedom wasn't just to eat a pie and run non-stop for a few hours, it was the freedom to talk to girls, behind the goals.

That was something, especially in a year when the Bombers had won a flag, and you'd just turned into a teenager.

This was round the time of the great feuds between Jazzers and Rockers. Jazzers used to get around in desert boots, black socks, black skivvies, blue V-neck jumpers and duffel coats with badges on them. And shades. And washed hair.

That made us easily distinguishable meat for the duck tailed, greasy, white socked, red shirted, leather coated, pointy toed Rockers lying in wait.

Walking down the street outside the ground was really running the gauntlet. There you'd be in your decorated coat, a few badges, and a flogger on a stick, and there they'd be. The Footscray boys or the Collingwood boys, arriving just in time to chase and whack a few suburban semi-long hairs. We represented everything these visitors hated, through choice of suburb, music, team, clothes, attitudes.

But the after-game horrors were worth it for the few hours of bliss behind the goals.

354

Not the cheer squad girls—whose eyes were strictly on the game—but the others, from local schools you'd never heard of, and nearby suburbs you'd never been to.

You'd spend games manoeuvring around, hoping to catch an eye, jog an arm as a prelude to a chat, see what dances they went to, see whether they'd like to come and listen to your 78s of Bunk Johnson and Kid Ory.

It was all quite innocent, in the days before the Beatles transcended the categories.

Doubtless the same kind of thing is still going on behind the goals, though it's hard to believe it is still as innocent as it was. The music has changed, and so has the team.

But I get the distinct impression that this team of aggressive, skilful, arrogant slightly crazy young players might be the sort of team that will make a mark on the 80s. And we'll have to put up with similar behavior from the Red and Black Army, growing larger by the week. Modern times.

THE JOHNSON STREET BUS

By Garrie Hutchinson, *Age*, August 26, 1981.

Down at the grassy end of Victoria Park on Saturday it was a combination of carnival and World War One.

There were conga lines of singing little Magpies, trailing plastic bags of cans; a man with a black and white scarf wrapped over his head as if he feared toothache; a group of Greek children dancing after every goal; a man in a gaberdine overcoat drinking from a bottle extracted from a lovingly preserved ANA flight bag; gap toothed lads in Collingwood guernseys shouting themselves hoarse in the convivial atmosphere of a big win.

And who could blame them? It was freezing. The rain kept coming in over the R. T. Rush stand, thankfully obscuring the high rise Housing Commission flats from time to time, turning the grassy banks to mud slides so that the pressure from a fast opening can might send an enthusiast sliding down to the more stable terracing.

It was a football Woodstock.

The colder and wetter it got, the happier everyone seemed to be. Their team slips further ahead, turning what was anticipated as a tough game into a cakewalk. The players turned it on in a celebration of most un-Collingwood like football.

Several times attacking handball sent the ball up the ground at great velocity. Rene Kink played like a ferocious young bull. Peter Daicos took a couple of Greg Chappell-like marks. And that larrikin Craig Davis actually tipped the hat of the goal umpire in an affectionate way to make sure he paid a full pointer. Everyone smiled.

Carnival in the trenches, and a last game to be played at home before the sun comes out and the great springtime passion is played out.

For now the Collingwood legions can see no obstacle to their happiness. They brook no pessimism from fellow Pie fans, and any scepticism from non believers is contemptuously disregarded.

The bedraggled Hawks should have known they were in trouble once the cheer squads erected their banner, which promptly ripped.

It said: 'Collingwood—You're lower than the basic wage.' It was curiously insulting, coming from the leafy eastern suburbs.

It hardly seems right to blame Collingwood, either team or suburb for the spartan basic wage, if there is such a thing anymore.

It seems the Hawthorn Cheer Squad had a more squalid purpose in mind. They seem to have meant that Collingwood were lower than the idea of a minimum wage, less than subsistence, a bunch of poor working class kids about to be squashed by the mighty Glenferrie steamroller.

It was not to be. The worm turned.

A couple of Hawthorn supporters close by would hardly have noticed.

At first they seemed just to be ordinary Hawks. They pulled a whole roast chicken from their bag, ripped bits off it and stuffed them into fresh rolls. I should have observed the lack of plaid blanket and thermos, for they soon passed a refreshment between themselves that had them smiling more and more broadly as the Hawks went further and further behind.

I imagine that is why such condiments will only catch on among supporters who don't enjoy the difference between winning and losing. It's all the same to the dope smoker; it's all beautiful.

Nearly everyone walked from the ground happy. It was as

cold as an M.C.G. pie, but the prospect of the warm Johnson St. bus promised relief.

It had a comedian for a conductor. It's often occurred to me that once we've gotten all the trams and buses painted, it will be time to train the connies as performers, so that for the price of a ticket into town you get a show as well. You sometimes do even now.

"That'll be 40 cents to Lygon St." says the conductor in a voice from the north of England.

A very large bloke in a Collingwood beanie says "Yoonited or Ssitty, mate?".

"I thought you wanted to go to Lygon Street?"

"Nah, seriously, whodja barrack for, you know, Manchesteer Yoonited or Ssitty?"

"I'm from South Africa," says the conductor.

"Haw. Haw. No you're not. You're a pom. Gotta be a pom. You can tell from your voice, you know".

"What's a pom?" asks a little girl in an Essendon jumper.

The bloke looks at her with a pained expression on his face.

"What would you know. Wearin' those colours."

"Liverpool," says the conductor.

"Liverpool. We'd better get off then."

A bloke gets on "I'm a bit drunk," he says, "I'm a little bit drunk." He looks around the bus. "But brother am I happy. Carna Pies, Eh! Eh?" "Carna Pies," says someone up the back.

"This bus go to the city?" he asks the conductor.

"This bus only goes to the city," he says.

"Yeah, but does this bus go to the city?"

"Certainly sir. This bus definitely only goes to the city."

"But does this bus go to the city."

"Yes this bus only goes to the city."

"Well how much to the city?"

"How about 50 cents?"

"Ahh. I've only got 60 cents here to get to the city."

"Look you give me that 60 cents and I'll give you 10 cents back."

"But does that 60 cents get me a seat?"

"It's only going to cost you 50 cents."

"I'll pay the extra for a seat."

"Here's your change."

"I'm a bit drunk. I think I'll sit down right here."

"Here's your seat sir."

"Geez, that's cheap. You get to the city with a seat for 50 cents."

"Fares please."

Someone starts singing 'Good old Collingwood forever', someone else is giving a deep statistical analysis of everyone else's chances, before concluding there is no way Collingwood can lose this year, someone says 'I'm not a fan of nobody' and is stared at as the worst kind of renegade.

It's the Johnson Street Bus; as entertaining as Barry Dickins, as certain as Joe Brown, as committed as Vincent Van Gogh, as enthusiastic as Errol Flynn.

There's no way they reckon they'll lose, this week.

IT'S JUST A GAME FOR SHEILAHS

Ron Saw, *Bulletin*, May 3, 1975.

Bumper Mulligan, the Savage of the Second Row, put down his Sunday paper and gazed gloomily at his ghost-writer. "They're at it again down in Melbourne," he said. "The season's hardly started down there and they're serving up stories about what a rough, brutal game Aussie Rules is. Same old words they're always dishing up: mayhem, rampant, acrimonious, ber . . . berserk. Jeez, they don't even know how you spell beresk."

"So we'll write a piece," said the ghost, "about how it's really just a game for girls."

The Bumper knotted his brow, laboring with the thought. It was, he suspected, a bit of a girl's game, but they reckoned it was pretty good all the same. He'd seen a bit of it played and he wouldn't mind a lash now and then, mattera fack. Anything for a quiet life—anything, after the way those Rabbitohs had given him the stick yesterday. By now he must have more scar tissue than Henry Cooper. Why not a bit of the ole aerial ping-pong?

It would be preposterous to pretend (wrote the Bumper's ghost-writer) that Aussie rules was a rough game, compared with Rugby League. But it would be just as preposterous to pretend that it was anything but a magnificent ball-game: fast, scientific, accurate and spectacular.

The great thing about it, from the player's point of view, is that the rules don't allow a lot of body contact to slow down the play. Probably the most terrible contact in the world of sport is that of a Rugby League player, say a nicely-warmed-up centre, taking a pass on the burst and crashing into the defence—which is coming at him, head-on, at approximately the same speed. It is, for either participant, rather like being driven into a brick wall at 40 mph while you sit on the front bumper.

You're stopped, as Ken Howard used to say of horses, like a shot out of a gun. The game is stopped. True, it's stopped for only a few seconds; and the true excitement, the beauty of Rugby League comes out in those moments of speed when the aforementioned centre, or anyone with the ball, beats the defence and goes like billy-oh for the line. And the only way to stop him is to grab him and try to kill him as fairly as possible.

If you grab someone in Aussie Rules, if you play the man instead of the ball, you run the risk of committing some sort of offence and giving away a free kick. And that makes it a game that's, well . . . not actually gentle but not ludicrously brutal, either.

It's not right to get a bloke round the neck, or over the shoulder, or around the arms. You break the rules, and slow up the game and give away a free kick, if you trip someone or push him in the back. The only way you can make life really unpleasant for another player is by bumping him sideways, and that's the kind of football I, for one, fancy.

Mind you, nobody's going to trip you or push you in the back in Rugby League, either—mainly because one good, flying trip could keep you going for yards; and a decent shove in the back could damn near send you over for a try.

The trouble with League is, they stop you in other frightful ways. They'll do it with direct, frontal assault, with teeth bared. They'll make a point of taking you head-high, getting you round the neck, over the shoulder and round the arms—mainly because that way you can't get rid of the ball and also because that way they're doing nothing against the rules.

Because every yard is vital, they'll make a point not only of stopping you but of driving you backwards. So they'll grab you front-on, get you round the neck and the arms, pick you up and slam you down like a sandbag. Two or even three of them at a time will perform this frightful violence. It's called dumping.

With just a little extra energy and skill they can manage to turn you up and over and drive you head-first into the ground. This is called spearing the bastard. How in the name of God would you like to play a game like that?

There are, of course, rules against some forms of violence. Some referees impose penalties for round-arm tackles or head-high tackles or stiff-arm tackles—three different ways of trying to tear your opponent's head off—but the rules seem pretty vague.

And when it comes to actual punching, the most terrible work is done in struggles called scrums.

Well, what I want to say is that I'm acting purely in self-defence in the scrums. When I, in the second row, swing a punch at the face of the first-rower on the other side, I'm swinging one only because I know damn well he's manoeuvring his shoulder and arm in order to be able to swing one at me.

Punching and cuffing is, of course, denied—as it's denied in Aussie Rules. But almost every one of us who's played League for more than three years has a nose like an ironing board and ears like cauliflowers, and we're not getting those noses and ears at poetry-readings.

What I like about Aussie Rules is that someone can take a swing at me, or just look as if he's about to take a swing at me, and I can fall down with a loud cry and stay there, apparently senseless. (In soccer writhing and jerking on the ground is fashionable.) If the umpire falls for it I can cop a free kick. If he doesn't I can just spring up and get on with things and nobody but my supporters will care one way or the other.

But in Rugby League you need to be unconscious—they can always tell—and some referees actually need to hear bone crack before they'll slow the game by awarding a penalty. It makes things very hard and bitter.

Finally I draw attention to the matter of ear-biting in the scrums. I can't think why it should be so popular. It can't be easy—even with the most myopic referee in the raggedest of scrums—and it hardly ever stops an opponent for long. I've bitten a few good ears in my time, and the longest I've ever kept anyone off the field, while they've patched him up, or tacked the thing on again, has been four and a half minutes.

Again, there are claims that it's all talk; that it doesn't happen any more and wouldn't hurt much if it did; that is would be a waste of time gnawing at a cauliflower ear anyway. You can offer all those theories until someone bites off your ear for you.

And then (said Bumper Mulligan's ghost-writer) you Melbourne girls'll really know what it is to go beresk.

GOAL UMPIRES

By John Lahey, *Age*, September 4, 1982.

Did you hear about the man who wanted to be a goal umpire, but failed the eyesight test? "Crikey," they said, "when can you start?"

No no, says Jim Mahoney, the V.F.L.'s coach of goal umpires, it isn't like that. Every year before the football season starts, all the goal umpires troop off to Coles and Garrard's, the opticians, to have their eyes tested, under orders from the V.F.L.

"It lasts a long time," says Mr. Mahoney. "We have to look at lines moving up and down and identify what's happening. We look at all sorts of colours and have to pick them exactly. You can't have a colour-blind umpire. It is a very severe examination. We come out first-class or our careers are finished. I have known only one man to fail the test."

This one failure saddens him. The man it concerns was a friend on top of the world because he had just been promoted from the reserves to the seniors, and the way Mr. Mahoney tells it you nearly cry. You think of a violinist struggling along for years to become leader of the orchestra and then when everything is within his grasp, and the world is at his feet, he breaks his fingers.

"It was the end of his football career," Mr. Mahoney says. "He was not allowed back in the reserves..."

I thought he was going to ask me to whistle the 'Last Post'. The setting was appropriate. A huge red sun was sinking behind the M.C.G., the holy of holies, on a warm, still evening in the holy month of September, as we waited for all the goal umpires to arrive for their weekly training session. I wouldn't have minded whistling the 'Last Post' if Mr. Mahoney had really urged me to.

This is a surprising thing about goal umpires. They are deadly serious. Oh, they laugh and all that, but their job is no joke, it is a passion. They discuss technique with the dedication of a micro-surgeon. And yet they are the most lovable—some people would say comical—of all the men in football. In their absurd hats and white coats, they do incredible and unexpected things with their necks, legs and arms as they bound about the four posts which are their little shrines. I once showed an Australian football film to some Nigerian students, and the only time they became animated was when the goal umpire came on. They clapped. They didn't think much of the players.

In 23 years as a goal umpire, Mr. Mahoney dodged missiles which included Jaffas, banana peel, pieces of pie and occasionally a can, and he has suffered what appears to be the goal umpire's ultimate indignity: tomato sauce in his flag holders.

Picture the scene. Refreshed from his half-time rest, and eager to see the rest of the action, the goal umpire returns to his posts, plunges the flags into the flag holders and . . . dear, oh dear.

It is worse in Sydney, he says. There is only a small area behind the Sydney goal. In one game, supporters were hanging their floggers over the umpire's face as a rival player came in to kick. They also took to pulling his hat over his eyes.

Sadly for Mr. Mahoney, those days are gone. Last November soon after officiating at the Grand Final, he turned 50, the mandatory age for goal umpires to hang up their holsters, and he then took on the coaching job.

Yes, holsters. They are only imaginary, but you will know what I mean if you watch a goal umpire using his two hands to signal a goal, before he grabs the flags and waves them. He stands perfectly still, hands at his sides, like Wyatt Earp facing a showdown. The crowd goes quiet. What is the man going to do? Will he raise two hands or one? Flash! The hands grab imaginary guns from imaginary holsters and suddenly his forefingers are pointing out from his chest. He has the drop on everyone.

Studying Mr. Mahoney's technique at the M.C.G., I made a marvellous discovery: two actions are involved, not one. The forefingers, after flashing from the holsters, actually reach shoulder height, then they come down, quiver once and stop. What this means is that the goal umpire is marrying the art of gunslinging to the art of conducting an orchestra. Mr. Mahoney agrees that this is a good description.

The goal umpires actually receive instructions about this, which explains why you can put a group together and they will act in unison. Their instructions are to do nothing showy, just be neat and smart. They must bring their rigid forefingers to shoulder height, arms bent and at body width.

Two observers are at every match to watch how umpires perform, and if a report comes back to Mr. Mahoney criticising some aspect of technique—and appearance or anticipation—the unfortunate fellow is told to smarten up his forefinger.

Their training is very regimented. Do you know that Bill Mather, who handles their physical development, makes them run as much as seven miles some nights? Then he brings them back and gives them a few sprints. They have nicknamed him the Sadist.

They had a little break from this the other night, though. They did aerobic dancing. Roy Ferguson, 42, who will be one of the two goal umpires at the M.C.G. today, was rapt. It lasted 45 minutes, he says, and they all had to keep changing pace as the music changed tempo.

Oddly enough, they do not run at the M.C.G. They are not allowed to. They run outside, around the parks and streets and across the bridges.

This means, says Mr. Mahoney, that "we do four-fifths of our training in the dark".

Make what you will of that statement. He said it, I didn't. One of their number, Ted Johnson, tripped in a hole while running in the dark recently and needed nine stitches near his eye. The rest of them discuss this as a grave event. Anything to do with the eyes is grave.

Off the training field, they all have a set of exercises to do at home, mainly to relax their necks and shoulders and stretch their hamstrings. It is just as well, for their neck movements are often very sudden.

Roy Ferguson, who has played League (Fitzroy), Association (Northcote) and Saturday morning football, says he is training harder now than ever. "More intense. Solid all the time." Physically it is tiring, but mentally it is worse, he says. "I can't go out on a Saturday night. I'm done for. When you are on the ground, you can't relax for a minute even if the ball is at the other end."

One of his compensations, however, is the barrackers. "They are beautiful, just beautiful, I love them."

He tells the story of a tense moment when a player was going for a difficult goal. In the hush, a voice bellowed: "Give us a goal and you can have my wife for the night." The player missed. A different voice called out: "He must have seen your wife."

THE COACH

By John Powers, from *The Coach*, 1978.

On Saturday 24 September Collingwood and North Melbourne played one of the most dramatic football matches of all time.

North Melbourne began the first quarter with a crushing speed and strength that made them look like the all-the-way winners they had been against Richmond and Hawthorn in the preceding weeks. Leading Collingwood by 4.4 (28) to 1.5 (11) at quarter-time they looked headed for certain victory. But in the second quarter they kicked a lamentable 6 points straight to Collingwood's 3.3 to leave the ground only 2 points ahead.

In the dressing-room Barassi roared and screamed at the ineptness of his men. 'You're all crawling back into your shells the moment you make a mistake!' he bellowed at them. 'That's not the way men with any guts play this game . . . I'm talking about *mental* guts . . . that's what I'm looking for! . . . When you make a mistake you fight back *harder* next time, you don't put your heads down!'

In his fury Barassi grabbed one player and slammed him bodily against the mental lockers, roaring about the player giving away unnecessary free kicks. 'That is lack of mental discipline!' he roared into the player's startled face, 'and I *will not put up with it!*'

Still fuming, Barassi ordered his men into the coach's room and told them bluntly: 'Nobody's running! . . . and I won't hear of it that you're tired . . . I will *not hear of it!* . . . I want *running* and *attack!* . . . You've got just one half of football left to *run your hearts out!*'

In the third quarter North did run but, in the total unpredictability that is one of the glories of the game, they kicked nothing but points—5 in the quarter!—whilst Collingwood, with its army of supporters deliriously in full cry behind them, surged forward to lead by 8 points, then 14, and finally, at the end of the quarter, by 27 points. The 1977 Grand Final appeared to be over.

But in the remarkable last quarter Barassi's coaching genius revealed itself fully. He had always urged his players to take risks—now he took mammoth ones himself. Stripping his back line by throwing Darryl Sutton to full-forward and David Dench to centre-half forward, and relying on a last desperate appeal to his players to take *any* risks . . . anything! . . . he left them to try to salvage the Premiership.

Sutton goaled almost immediately. Then Baker. Briedis had a great chance but kicked only a point. Then Dench stormed through an opening with the ball under his arm and slammed through North's third goal in seven minutes. In that crucial seven minutes North Melbourne had reduced Collingwood's lead from 27 points to 8 points.

Briedis and Dench each kicked a point, and then Baker kicked a goal at the 14-minute mark that levelled the scores.

With the 108,000 people in the stadium suddenly erupting with excitement, and the millions watching on television forgetting about everything else in life, the struggle narrowed to the question of which team could summon the mental and physical energy to mount the final drives to victory and glory.

Collingwood kicked a point, and North replied with a point. At the 22-minute mark John Byrne kicked North to the lead by a point. Then, at the start of time-on, Phil Baker marked and scored what everyone believed must be the winning goal.

Now, as Collingwood mounted desperate counter-attacks, the question re-defined itself—could North Melbourne's defence withstand these desperate Collingwood attacks for the remaining minutes of time-on? For the supporters of both teams the time clock had now become the focal point of interest.

And somehow, from somewhere within previously untapped reserves of energy, Collingwood launched the final attacks, broke through North Melbourne's resistance and got the ball to Peter Moore who scored a point. Now, with only one straight kick the difference, every yard the ball moved towards either goal became critically important. Exhausted players flung themselves onto the feet of opponents trying to kick the ball forward. It became a battle of street-fighting desperation, totally reliant on guts and the heart to compete. Yet finally North's defence cracked. Collingwood's Bill Picken kicked high into the goal square and somehow—miraculously it seemed to everyone watching—Collingwood's 'Twiggy' Dunne got his hands to the ball in the centre of the contesting pack and held the decisive mark.

From point-blank range Dunne goaled and, for the third time in 15 minutes, the scores were level. And stayed level until the siren. For only the second time in V.F.L. history—the first being between Melbourne and Essendon in 1948—a Grand Final ended in a draw.

With the scoreboard above them reading North Melbourne 9.22 (76) to Collingwood's 10.16 (76), many of the players of both teams lay prostrate on the M.C.G. turf for a few moments before rising and slumping dejectedly into their dressing-rooms. Nobody—neither players, spectators nor officials—wanted a no-decision result. On Grand Final days everyone is geared for either total joy or total disappointment. No emotional provision is made to cope with the weird never-never land of draws.

So it would be a replay the following Saturday.

A desolate mood pervaded the dressing-room. Players took cans of beer from the officials and slumped onto the benches in front of their lockers. As they gulped mouthfuls of beer they stared disconsolately at the floor, at the movement around them. Hardly anyone spoke, because nobody knew precisely what to say. Somebody floated the possibility of: 'We'll kill them next week!' but it sounded hollow. Nobody was ready to think about next week just yet.

They waited for Barassi.

When he finally called them into the coach's room his voice sounded drained as he congratulated them on the magnificence of their fight back in the last quarter. 'It should have won you the match', he told them. 'It did in fact win us the match . . . then *we lost it!* But it was still a magnificent quarter . . . bloody magnificent. And I'm very grateful that we're still here with another chance next week. And *that's* when we'll win it. Okay?'

They all filed quietly out of the coach's room. A jumbo-sized plastic rubbish bin filled with iced champagne for the celebration toast remained unopened. It, like everything else, had to wait one more week.

Reigniting his players with an appetite for more football, and a potentially more gruelling match than the first drawn encounter with Collingwood, became Barassi's immediate objective. Even for a Ron Barassi that task was formidable. Through the last grinding weeks of the season 24 September had loomed as an oasis, a respite. Win or lose, playing in a Grand Final offered recompense for those weeks of pushing to the outer limits of exhaustion, running with bruises, running on torn and strained muscles and ligaments, making the final effort to gain extra inches of speed and extra minutes of endurance. But always, for them all, 24 September would have ended it. The agony would have stopped. Then the good times started—no more curfews on socialising, no more having to organise lives around Tuesday, Wednesday and Thursday training, and matches on Saturday. For a few months their lives could become normal.

So a mood of incredulity and mild resentfulness permeated the dressing-room when the players togged for training on Tuesday night. Nobody felt they should be there. Even the administrative staff, geared to relax after the strain of the additional work through the Finals weeks, looked vaguely shell-shocked as they geared themselves to handle thousands of demands for tickets, and made hasty decisions about the social functions and the hundred-and-one other problems created by this unprepared-for week.

A perceptible hollowness sounded in the players' voices as they warmed up to begin another three nights of intensive training. They tried to rev each other with cries of, 'We'll do the job properly next Saturday!' and 'Let's show them what we can really do this time!' But the mood remained sluggish and anti-climactic. And on the oval, at the start of the first training session, handpasses lacked precision, the kicking looked lethargic and even the marking lacked the authority of the previous few weeks.

To snap this insidious mood Barassi first harangued them after each sloppy mistake. This sharpened the mood a little but not enough. So, for the first time since the start of the Finals series, Barassi imposed penalty push-ups. The sight of players like Brent Crosswell and John Cassin—who only three days previously had thrilled millions of viewers on live television— prostrate on the ground to atone for slackness, shocked everyone into total application. Within minutes the entire squad transformed itself from plodding competence to zestful brilliance. Yet Barassi kept yelling: 'Faster! . . . More talking! . . . You should be hitting him on the tits with those passes!'

Later, after a dinner in the social club, Barassi and the players returned to the coach's room for a video replay of the Grand

Final, throughout which Barassi drew the attention of individual players to glaring errors they made: 'Watch this atrocious kick coming up . . . You should've held that mark, Johnnie . . . How did Wearmouth get clear there? Who was supposed to be minding him? . . . Look at that—nobody running past to help him or take a handball . . . Too slow. Too *slow!* . . . No talking caused that mix-up. There's no other reason it could happen . . . *That's* what comes from playing behind your man. You've *got to be in front!*'

But he didn't berate constantly, as he had through screenings of earlier matches, instead he let the players realise their own mistakes as they watched. But he made one point that had a perceptible impact: 'Let's remember that every time we do something that costs us a goal, or miss a chance to score a goal, it cost us the match. This is a classic way of emphasising how bloody important *everything* is at this level of football. What you do, or fail to do, at any point of the game can cost us the match . . . or win us the match. If you make a mistake in the forward pocket, and they put together a string of passes that results in a goal, it should register on you that it was your mistake, a hundred and sixty yards away, that cost us that goal. If you have this attitude, and are *positive* about it, you'll make fewer mistakes . . . and we'll win the tight games.'

He also quoted from the sheets of figures his statisticians had prepared about the drawn game. 'Collingwood has changed its style of play. Instead of going around the flanks they rely on the big mark, the handball to someone running up the ground, and then the long kick to position. They're much more direct than us. Collingwood's possessions per player averaged 10½ kicks and 3 handballs, while we averaged 13 kicks and 4 handballs. This indicates that we need 15 more possessions than Collingwood *per quarter* to stay on level terms with them in scoring.' Flipping through the sheets he found another interesting fact: 'By the 20-minute mark of the third quarter Collingwood have normally sewn up the game. They have *never*, throughout the season, been able to come from *behind* at that point and win! That's something for us to bear in mind. So if we can go into that last quarter on Saturday with a lead, things are going to look pretty rosy for us.'

Barassi replayed all of the match except for the last minutes of time-on, when Collingwood's two scoring shots equalised the score. He switched off the set while North was still in ascendancy.

'Well', he said to them as they shuffled anxiously on their benches—it was 10.30 and they obviously wanted to be home in bed—'watching that game through again, and seeing all the mistakes we made—mistakes that should not happen in a professional league football team, coached by Ron Barassi... a North Melbourne football team... footballers in a Grand Final —must make you confident that, if we play anything like we're capable of playing, we can *eat* this mob on Saturday!'

After a chorus of support Barassi nodded. 'All right', he said. 'We don't need to do any more talking about it. We've seen where we fell down. Let's just sharpen ourselves up in the two nights we've got left, then get out there on Saturday and do the job properly this time.'

Before training on Thursday, following a sustained hard-running night on Wednesday, Barassi announced that the team to face Collingwood in the replay remained unchanged from the previous week. Probably nobody expected changes but Barassi's announcement nevertheless brought a tangible sense of relief into the coach's room. Twenty chests seemed simultaneously to release held breath. For many of the players such as Gumbleton, Henshaw, Cowton, Sutton, Nettlefold and Baker, who had been in and out of the team throughout the season, there could have been no certainty until that moment that they would contest the replay of the Grand Final.

'That decision to make no changes', Barassi told them challengingly, 'shows an enormous act of faith on the selectors' part, because at least three of you don't deserve a game after last week's performance. But we're backing you. We believe you've all got too much professional pride to let us down again. And if you three lift your games, and the rest of you drive something extra out of yourselves, we're going to *win* this Premiership!'

Barassi's energy in the shout of '*win*', followed by the team's energetic shout endorsing his confidence and the way they now punched each other's shoulders and thighs, showed that no vestige of their earlier despondent mood remained. They wanted to play football again now. And they wanted to win the Premiership. 'Come on!... We're going to do it!... Just one more!' they shouted to each other eagerly.

'We're looking good', Barassi told them, speaking excitedly now, 'but in this final training session I want to see the total

369

eradication of errors, so that our game on Saturday will be as near perfect as any team's ever played. We'll need to be that good, because they're going to improve too. They'll play better than they did last week. So if *ever* there's a day for every one of you to produce your super-best it'll be Saturday. *Nothing* less will be good enough to win us that Flag!'

He let them urge each other on again for a few seconds, then said: 'We've got a big crowd of spectators out there tonight, so when you run out and do your laps, and then throughout the session, I want you to show them just how a real team of professionals looks and performs. I want these people to see that we are the *number one* club in this competition!'

An estimated 4000 people applauded the team as it trotted onto the ground for the last training night of 1977. Looking into the crowd from the side lines Jack Brearley, the property steward, shook his head in amazement. 'Before Barassi came', he said, 'we didn't have crowds much bigger than this when we played a *match!*'

Each time the team passed the grandstand during their three warm-up laps the crowd boosted the players with sustained clapping and shouted encouragement. 'It was a helluva sensation', one of the players commented later, 'to feel that weight of support out there. It made you realise the debt you owe people as loyal as that. It really stoked us up.'

It stoked Barassi up as well. He'd intended a light work-out on Thursday, but the crowd's enthusiasm buoyed him up. With every passage of skill drawing applause, and every mistake a groan, he goaded his players into a 30-minute burst of end-to-end handballing and passing and he seemed reluctant even then to stop. He appeared to be waiting, and hoping, for several minutes of sustained brilliance that would convince everyone—on the field and off—that he had indeed blended from the twenty idiosyncratic temperaments and talents an intricate and interdependent masterpiece of a team. So it was not until nearly 6 o'clock that he called the squad to the centre of the Arden Street oval for the last time of the year and assured them that they were perfectly tuned to beat *any* team.

Physically, Barassi could do no more for them. Only the work on their minds remained.

As the players trotted off the ground impatient youngsters waving authograph books besieged them. Dozens of children

370

surrounded each of the players, yelping for attention, while in the background camera bulbs flashed and the cheer squad members clapped and shouted in unison. Barassi couldn't have hoped for a better wind-up to the punishing and often agonisingly frustrating eight months that led to this final confrontation, now less than 48 hours away.

Again, as on the previous Saturday morning, the players and coach met at the Old Melbourne Inn for the pre-game breakfast. Nothing differed except the mood—perceptibly less nervous, tangibly more meanly determined than before the first Grand Final. Immediately the doors of the room shut you felt the harsh and unified gladiatorial spirit of the team. Today there seemed to be positive menace in the atmosphere. Uncharacteristically, several of the players requested—and requested firmly—that smoking be banned in the room. That request epitomised the mood of the day—no compromise.

After breakfast and the playing of a short film on American football, Barassi rose to speak. Sensing the mood of his players, he opted for a low-keyed address at this early meeting. Speaking with uncommon gentleness he reminded them that: 'Last week you had the Premiership in your mitts, and you let it slide out. *That's* the reason you must win today. There're a million other reasons, but that alone should be enough—because you're the guys who let it slip. So you should feel anger inside yourselves about that. It'll be no use looking back after a loss today and saying about that first match: "God, why didn't we do it then!", because that'll be too late. It's always too late afterwards.'

Turning to the blackboard behind him on which the names of the Collingwood players had been chalked in the positions they were expected to play, Barassi began analysing the strengths and weaknesses of each man and contrasting them to the strengths of the North Melbourne player opposing him. And the further he went through the list of names the more his face looked puzzled, until finally he stopped speaking and stared at the board in incredulous silence.

'The more I look at that side', he said with a sudden note of genuine admiration in his voice, 'the more I'm convinced that Tommy [Hafey] has done a marvellous job . . . a *marvellous* job! Because who've they got who are top-class footballers . . . real superstars? Just one forward and one ruckman, that's all. They can all play well, but they've got just two superstars. And seeing that I can understand Hawthorn looking at Collingwood and saying: "We should *eat* this mob!" But they bloody didn't. And the reason they didn't is that Collingwood *jump*—they kick the ball long and they go down the centre as much as they can with their long kicks, pumping them up to Moore, and keeping the pressure on the opposition defence.'

'But *today*', he said, raising his voice for the first time of the morning, 'the pressure is to come from *us*. Today we build our game around attack. Go for broke! By putting pressure on through our running and tackling, we'll carve this mob up! So I want blokes *chased* and *hammered into the ground!* They've got several sore guys—so have we got sore guys—and if we're not doing it they'll be doing it to us. They'll be demanding that every tackle is a hard-hitting tackle . . . so it's going to get back to who does it first and who does it best.'

All the while he spoke of pressure and tackling Barassi's eyes and teeth flashed and the note of battle sounded in his voice. But then he returned to the low-key again, obviously sensing from his players that he was boosting their adrenalin too high with the game still nearly two hours away. So he brought the emotional level down a fraction by stressing the need of complete team involvement—encouraging each other in every way they could through the game, and reprimanding each other if necessary to ensure that maximum concentration levels were maintained for the full hundred minutes. 'We've got to all help each other out on the field, because today's D-Day—Desperation day'.

He paused then before concluding: 'I've told you that I believe this will be the greatest Premiership to win—certainly the greatest mental test footballers have had to face since the war. So if you win you should gain enormously out of it . . . as people. It's something you'll carry with you for the rest of your lives. It's a test of you as a person. And you should recognise the historic importance of this match, and realise all the acclaim you'll be given by people who love sports—they'll acclaim you for having won after playing through five Finals in a row. That should give you a well-earned sense of pride. And in the process of earning that pride you'll prove the lie of those people who say we're front runners. We are *not* front runners! We are at our best when the going gets tough . . . and it won't ever get tougher than it'll be today.'

He paused then, staring down at them with almost gentle affection. He was cementing the emotional bond between them, using his eyes and the sudden gentleness of expression to increase the highly-charged mood of commitment to each other—twenty players and a coach striving for a victory worthy of permanent pride. Then, after a full half-minute of silence, he nodded his head slowly, as if wordlessly telling them that it was agreed, and that they all knew what this afternoon was irrevocably about.

'In between now and when you line up to go down that race', he told them very calmly, 'I want you to think of desperation, of running, of attack, of hitting with the body. And think of winning. That's all I want from you.' His eyes flashed quickly over their faces. 'Are you ready to give it?'

The twenty of them yelled affirmatively.

'Okay', Ron Barassi said. 'Let's go.'

You sense Grand Final fever miles from the M.C.G. Drivers honk their car horns to anyone sporting the colours of the club they support. Men clamber onto trams lugging plastic Eskies jammed with chilled cans of beer to slake the quenchless thirsts that develop through an afternoon of non-stop shouting. A mood of rare conviviality pervades. Strangers speak to each other without any of the customary reserve. And little boys have their heads patted fondly by people they have never seen before, and probably will never see again.

A high percentage of the fans streaming through the parkland surrounding the M.C.G. on Grand Final day support neither of the two contesting teams. Through the twenty-two Saturdays of the home-and-away season most of them follow other clubs, but on the great 'One Day of the Year' they come gleefully to the Mecca of Australian Rules Football to witness the culminating moment of the winter struggle for football supremacy. The Grand Final is everyone's game, and everyone's day.

The fans come not only to watch, but to participate. A league Grand Final may not always produce the greatest football of the year, but the sense of event remains unrivalled. This is the day when the heroes of the season win the main event. And lovers of the sport come to watch history being made.

In North Melbourne's dressing-room the players radiated the same mood of intense purposefulness that characterised them before the vital Richmond Semi-Final. Today, you felt, these players would die on their bayonets before they conceded defeat.

The dressing-room pulsed with their nervous energy. Well-wishers received curt handshakes, brisk nods, and were then immediately ignored. Even the highest officials in the club stood back, awed by the mood of barely suppressed hostility. The players behaved, collectively, like men obsessed with some smouldering grievance. They generated an air of potentially explosive emotionality.

Barassi himself seemed engulfed in the mounting tension. He couldn't remain still for longer than a few seconds at a time. His face looked uncharacteristically middle-aged—tight with strain. Nobody except the players could command his attention. He listened distractedly to the many people whispering information and news to him and, often, he walked away from them whilst they were still in mid-sentence. He continuously rolled his shoulders and wriggled his arms in his efforts to reduce his own tension, exactly as he must have done twenty years before when, as Vice-captain of Melbourne, he prepared himself to play in his third Grand Final.

Throughout the players' warm-up Barassi watched tensely from inside the metal barrier separating the players from the trainers and officials. Normally he paced amongst them, urging them to get the mood right, but today that wasn't necessary— the mood in the room was electric as the players yelled to each other: 'Everybody together today! . . . Like brothers out there! . . . Give them nothing! . . . Come on! . . . Let's be aggressive to-day! . . . Come on! . . . Make them chase *us* all day! . . . Let's back everybody up! . . . Big team effort!' Watching and listening to them from the side lines, Barassi's breathing was rapid and shallow, like a man in a high temperature.

As soon as the players had finished their warm-up Barassi ordered them to study the list of game requirements he'd chalked on the blackboard in the coach's room. He left them alone for nearly a minute to read and absorb the mental and physical requirements that he believed would win them the league Premiership in the battle ahead. And while they read the lists he paced agitatedly outside the room, now thrashing his arms up and down in an effort to shake the excessive tension out of himself. Then, abruptly, he rushed back into the coach's room, closed the door and ordered the players to stop reading and concentrate on what he said.

'More than any other game of football', he began emphatically, 'a Grand Final is a game of fundamentals—of ability, of the mind, and of fitness. We've got the ability, and we've got the fitness, so the only question is whether we are tough enough in the *mind!* And, by Christ, our record proves—*surely!*—that we bloody well *are!* . . . Tougher than *they* are!' And, as he roared 'they', a thrust of his arm indicated the Collingwood dressing-room on his left. '*They* haven't gone through what we have.' Now his arm pointed directly towards the arena. 'Out there is the perfect setting for you to prove just what sort of a club this is . . . because more than anything else this is now a battle of clubs. The older blokes know what I'm talking about—Stan Alves, Frank Gumbleton, Ross Henshaw, Gary Cowton, Arnold Briedis, Phil Baker, Ken Montgomery, and Barry Cable. They know what it's bloody like to be in the shit. And I really believe, and we've said this for a few years now—that our first aim is to become a consistently *successful club* . . . *not* a Johnny-come-lately; a oncer, and then to slip back into being a middle-of-the-list team, a bottom-of-the-ladder club. We have not slipped back. We are now what we set out to become. But I believe today—I *really* believe this—that this game could put the seal on the greatness and solidity of the North Melbourne rise. If *ever* there was a day to prove yourselves, *this is it!* That's why I want the David Denches and the Ken Montgomeries to be so *proud* after today, when they see their club finally and irrevocably arrive as a league *power!*'

The players roared their support, waved their clenched fists determinedly in the air, then hunched forward with clenched jaws as Barassi prepared to speak again. And now his voice rose to a continuous shout. 'As a league *power!*' he repeated, thrusting his own clenched fist out towards them. 'Which, of course, is the keynote of today, isn't it—*power* . . . in the physical sense! And I want it displayed in all its full flowering in the opening *ten* minutes! . . . in the opening *twenty* minutes! . . . and throughout the first quarter! I want the *running* and the *hitting* and the *tackling* to be like we did it against *Richmond*—who we've conquered in the past four years—and against *Hawthorn*—who we've knocked off in three out of the last four years Finals! Now it's Collingwood . . . it's their turn to feel the North Melbourne *power* . . . the North Melbourne bloody *heat!*'

The players were now making continuous sounds underneath Barassi's bellowed words. Sometimes the players' support swelled loudly, as when Barassi crashed his emphasis on 'power!' and on 'heat!', bending his body towards them and thrashing his right fist through the air wildly. Sometimes their support came in abandoned shouts. At other times they growled a muted support that sounded like timber straining under the pressure of high wind.

'I want the North Melbourne heat *turned on!*' Barassi screamed into their faces. 'I want them *fried* by the heat! . . . I want *fried Magpie!* . . . fried Magpie's what I want for my supper . . . and it'll go beautifully with *champagne!*'

He let them roar steadily now. Their energy had to be allowed release. He had built their tension close to the unbearable, so now he let them shout, waited while the excess level of excitement bellowed out of them like steam from an overheated boiler. His eyes danced with their own frenzy, but they still checked each contorted face in front of him. And, while he watched them shout, he panted like a runner who had just completed a fast sprint.

At some point in those seconds while he waited for their shouts to subside Barassi must have decided that they could tolerate only one last goad, one final pump of his energy. He could now have asked them to punch down brick walls with their bare fists and they would have tried it unquestioningly. They were ready. They were primed. They could take just one more spur.

'If you're not inspired by the occasion', he yelled at them, 'nothing in this world will *ever* lift you! . . . And I believe you're going to be *fantastic* today!' The players sprang to their feet, roaring noises rather than words, and Barassi pointed to David Dench, then the door, and thundered above their combined noise: 'Follow David out *there* . . . and take that bloody mob apart!'

Some of the players actually wrestled each other to get out the door more quickly. At a run they formed into a line behind David Dench and, as soon as the line was formed, and with the encouraging shouting of the trainers and officials adding to the noise of the players' own ceaseless shouting, Barassi ordered them onto the ground.

As the door swung open a sledgehammer of sound walloped into the room, unbelievably loud—solid like the steady crash of some monstrously amplified wave breaking continuously around

376

you. But David Dench, five-times veteran of this numbing shock of noise, started his irreversible run with his team behind him. As soon as the crowd sighted them, and as they burst through the paper banner held aloft by the North Melbourne cheer squad, the noise of the crowd intensified with the cheering and booing and just plain excited shouting of the 98,000 spectators.

Thousands of blue-and-white and black-and-white helium-filled balloons soared into the air as both teams ran their customary sprints across the oval, and the cheer squads of both sides thrashed their paper floggers through the air incessantly as the running stopped and the teams lined up for the playing of 'Advance Australia Fair' and 'God save the Queen'. And then, to an accompanying thunderclap of roared voices, the field umpire bounced the ball to start the replay of the 1977 Grand Final.

From the opening bounce the match—watched by an estimated four million viewers in addition to the 98,366 official spectators at the ground—established its claim as a sports classic. Playing in bright sunshine, under a cloudless summer-blue sky, and with no wind giving a scoring advantage to either end of the ground, both teams attacked relentlessly to gain the vital early break.

The conditions of sporting greatness are forged by various elements, various pressures—the quality of the opposing forces, the intensity of the desire to win, the historical significance of victory, the sense of 'occasion' and the emotional commitment of the competitors. When all these factors—and perhaps dozens of less definable ones—peak at the one time, greatness becomes possible. Such moments sometimes occur at the Olympic games, at World Cup Finals and at Wimbledon. But they can occur at such unlikely places as a boxing ring in Kinshasa, Zaire, at 4 a.m. when Muhammad Ali faces the awesomely destructive might of George Foreman's punching and, against all odds, regains the Heavy-weight Championship of the World. And now, such a moment occurred when the golden teams of Ron Barassi and Tom Hafey clashed for the second time in eight days at the Melbourne Cricket Ground on 1 October 1977.

Something magnificent, yet not quite communicable, about the spirit of man reveals itself when levels of competition reach the superlative. Nobody can adequately define it. It is a 'felt' thing. But when contests rise to a pitch where the ordinarily

377

accepted 'best' is not enough, and when the desire for victory becomes indomitable on both sides, and the technical skills of the combatants are adequate to produce something from within themselves that even they didn't know they possessed, new levels of excellence become possible. Men suddenly do run faster, and jump higher, push themselves through the second and third levels of effort, absorb pain that at lesser moments would be unendurable, and somewhere, somehow, find previously untapped resources of courage and endurance.

Everyone—participators and spectators—recognises the uniqueness. Together they combine to create an atmosphere of heightened excitement, of mounting euphoria, which makes the great event collaborative. The crowd emotion infects the players, helping to lift their performances to the unrepeatable. And somehow, in a succession of moments that reaffirm man's ability to perform the seemingly impossible under intolerable pressures, an element of grandeur sparkles momentarily into life. An imperishable event is created—greatness.

Every quality that Ron Barassi advocated in sport, every ideal that convinced him that competitive sport is a noble activity of man rather than just two hours of frivolous impermanence, gained credence as the battle between North Melbourne and Collingwood seesawed through the October afternoon.

North gained the vital 'jump'—a goal and a behind, to lead by 7 points to nil—but by the halfway mark of the first quarter Collingwood, matching everything North threw at them in speed, skill and brute strength, levelled the scores to 2.1 (13) each. Only slowly, but inexorably, could North Melbourne draw ahead to lead by 5.5 (35) to Collingwood's 3.4 (22) at the end of the first quarter.

Gaining momentum and confidence, North surged forward to open what appeared to be a winning lead of 36 points midway through the second quarter. But, playing ferociously, Collingwood reduced the lead to 17 points and then, almost on the siren, to a mere 11 points. At half-time the scoreboard read North Melbourne 9.12 (66) to Collingwood's 8.7 (55).

While the spectators stretched the stiffness out of their bodies, and opened fresh cans of beer, and ate meat pies, and speculated about the infinite possibilities of the fifty playing minutes ahead, Barassi worked daemonically to rouse his men to achieve the greatness he believed they possessed.

Initially he carped about the players who had received too few handballs because they had refused to run enough. Then he announced that Collingwood had twice fought itself back into contention by outplaying North in the time-on periods. 'In the time-on of the first quarter they gained thirteen possessions to our *four!* And in the second time-on period they got *twenty-three* to our *eleven!*'

But he quickly pushed aside the statisticians' sheets and concentrated his message on the vital quarter ahead. 'We *have* to put the kibosh on them this quarter!' he told his players urgently. 'This quarter is their big hope . . . so I want everyone to marshal every fibre of force and energy within you, and *pump it out* . . . for bloody North Melbourne and yourselves! I want that crowd out there to come alive—clapping and cheering—because the way you're playing deserves it.'

His team roared encouragement to each other—no longer the feverish encouragement that preceded the match but the defiant encouragement of men now locked in a battle demanding 'every fibre of force and energy'

'Some of you', Barassi continued urgently, 'are down because you're sore, and you've got headaches, and you've got all sorts of bloody things wrong . . . I *know*—I've *been there!* . . . and it's *worth* it! This's the *ultimate* in football. You will never get better football in any code in the world . . . or a bigger occasion. You can take bloody Wembley, and you can take your Superbowl', he told them defiantly. With a sweep of his right arm he pointed to the playing arena behind them, then shouted: '*Here* you've got 100 000 people urging and putting out energy to you! Suck everything of it that you can *in* . . . and then *pump it out!* You can achieve *miracles* in this world! . . . particularly in football . . . because you can knock a bloke aside, you can catch him, you can grab fiercely and win the ball back for your team . . . if you bloody *want* to! . . . if you want to *enough!* But now this has gone past the stage of wanting—it's something we *have to do!* . . . because we won't be able to *live with ourselves if we don't!*'

The players roared and smashed their fists on their thighs in an explosion of enthusiasm. Whatever griefs they had brought into the dressing-room with them had now completely vanished as Barassi, by his ranting and fierce physicality of movement, pumped his energy and dynamism into them. And now, as the volume and intensity of that roar sustained itself, he spoke more quietly, but with immense urgency.

'Last week we threw it away, and in that last five minutes

today [Collingwood snapped three goals in the final three minutes of the second quarter] if we have to look back and think: "If..."' The 'if' caused Barassi's face to look momentarily agonised. Still thinking about the 'if', he clamped his eyes shut and moaned 'Oh, what a *word!*' And now, in front of him, the players shouted that they refused to accept the possibility of having to say 'if'. Barassi nodded and, with both fists bunched again, he said: 'We mustn't have to look back and say: "Jesus, we had them on toast... and *again* we didn't polish them off!"' So, instead of making the colliwobbles strike in the last quarter, make it *this* quarter!' The players roared again. 'You've done it twice already... against Hawthorn and Richmond', Barassi continued, even more urgently now as Max Ritchie called 'Time, coach!' 'You ran over both those teams in the third quarter... and now you've got to do it *again!*' he demanded. 'Run... run... *run*... forwards leading... everybody lifting... everybody giving it *everything you've got* in this last half of football for the year... and for the ultimate *prize* in football!'

North, reinvigorated by its coach, goaled in the first minute and continued to sweep the ball around the field and goalwards, but always against ferocious Collingwood resistance. With the crowd in full voice behind them, both teams lifted the contest to the level of the superlative. And, little by little, score by score, North crept ahead. By the end of the quarter North had opened a 30-point lead. They had scored 15.19 (109) to Collingwood's 12.7 (79).

Now the question was put squarely to Collingwood—could they fight back as North had the previous week?

Their answer came emphatically—in less than ten minutes of play they reduced the North Melbourne lead to a mere 12 points. Two kicks! Once again, as it had the previous week, the M.C.G. became the scene of high drama as the vital, desperate second half of the last quarter began. Anything could still happen. Once again play reached the gut-level of competitiveness.

A goal gave North Melbourne an 18-point lead with eighteen minutes played—still not a winning margin. And even with a 21-point lead at the start of time-on they still did not look safe. Collingwood continued to attack, still threatened. They goaled, but North immediately retaliated with a goal to keep its 21-point lead. And only when the clock showed that eight minutes of time-on had been played, and another North Melbourne goal by

Arnold Briedis made the difference 27 points, did the possibility of a last minute boil-over become totally impossible.

North Melbourne were the Premiers of 1977.

The contrast between victory and defeat revealed itself graphically within seconds of the siren ending the Grand Final. While the North Melbourne players cartwheeled around the fringes of the oval, sprang into the air gleefully, wrapped their arms around each other and hugged in pairs, then knotted into a euphoric pack, the Collingwood players tramped wearily up the race leading to their dressing-rooms.

Exaltation created new waves of North Melbourne energy while despair etched the Collingwood faces with agonised tiredness. Arnold Briedis, Wayne Schimmelbusch and John Byrne all suddenly looked capable of playing another feverish hundred minutes of football, but many of the Collingwood players seemed barely able to muster the energy to stumble from the ground. And as Ron Barassi was hoisted onto the shoulders of his ecstatic players and chaired to the front of the grandstand to receive the applause and rapturous cheers of the spectators, Tom Hafey strode briskly up the Collingwood race, flanked by trainers, and refused to glance either right or left in response to the consoling shouts from Collingwood stalwarts near the fence.

Many people later criticised the Collingwood team for not remaining on the oval while their conquerors received their trophy and ran the traditional lap of honor. But anyone studying those twenty anguished faces, and seeing the grimness of Hafey's expression as he rushed to console them, could not be harsh. For eight months each of the forty players on the arena had toiled, sacrificed pleasure and dreamt of this one supreme moment—winning the 1977 Premiership. And, as Royce Hart knew from experience, 'For the twenty men on the losing side in Saturday's Grand Final, the sickening taste of defeat can never quite be erased.'

League football must be played with passion—a passion to win. And the reactions of champions to loss must also be passionate. No team could have fought harder, or with greater tenacity, than Collingwood. A better team beat them on the day and, vanquished, Collingwood chose to retreat into privacy rather than act as if they were not mortally disappointed.

Now, in front of the M.C.G. members' stand, the ritual of the presentations began. Most of the 98,000 spectators stayed to watch and pay homage to North Melbourne as, one by one, the players mounted the dais to receive their trophies from the Governor. The crowd roared as each player's name was announced, but a special cheer sounded for the veteran ex-Melbourne captain, Stan Alves, as he leapt exuberantly into the air with his arms up-raised in uncontrollable delight at finally, after twelve years of league football, playing in a Premiership team. As Alves was to say later: 'All my life, all my football life, *this* is the day I've waited for.' But the big moment, now as always, came as the captain of the team, David Dench, accepted and held aloft for the world to see, the 1977 Premiership cup. He firstly displayed it forward, then turned it right and left. Vast roars swelled from the crowd. This was the great communal moment of Australian Rules football when everyone—supporter and rival—acknowledged the Champions of the season.

The sustained roar continued as Dench bounded down the steps of the dais and, with his team, began the lap of honor. As each player in turn ran a few yards with the cup upraised in his hands, and the crowd at each section they passed increased the volume of its cheering, dozens of unathletic photographers sprinted in almost comic pursuit to try to record the moment of triumph. Many of the players admitted later that *this* was the moment, above all others, when they felt themselves to be the princes of the earth, when moments of greater exaltation seemed unimaginable.

And that, for the public, ended season 1977. But for the victorious players, clattering up the concrete race together, nights and days of heady celebrations lay ahead. Immediately they entered the dressing-room they faced the glare of television lights and the new wave of more intensely personal, more concentrated, cheering and handshaking and backslapping from their officials, their teammates who missed selection in the final twenty, their relatives and friends and the hundreds of ecstatic fans already jamming the room to welcome them.

Here every face beamed, and the masses of blue and white streamers and balloons draped around the walls and lockers looked suddenly festive. The champagne bottles were already open and waiting, and as the players took them and gulped from them eagerly the room became chaotic with noise as hundreds of voices bellowed the club song. If you didn't know the words of the song it didn't matter, you just shouted, made as much noise as possible, joined in, shared the moment of exaltation.

As soon as the singing ended everyone tried to push forward to congratulate the players personally, but the door stewards and trainers held them back, telling them they would have to wait a few more minutes. And, for the last time of season 1977, officials summoned the players to the coach's room. There they took their usual places on the benches while the president, Lloyd Holyoak, congratulated them on their victory which, he said, 'Would have to go down as the greatest and best Grand Final ever seen.' And then, turning to Barassi but still addressing the players, he said: 'I read in the papers just recently: "You either love him or hate him", but there's no doubt about one thing—he only roasts you and gives you the blast for one reason, and that's to get the best out of you. You all know he's the greatest coach of all time—*Ron Barassi!*'

All twenty players, most of them holding up champagne bottles or beer cans in salutation, cheered wildly and then broke into a spontaneous 'For he's a jolly good fellow'. And, as they sang, tears rolled down Ron Barassi's face. He smiled at his players while they sang, but his hands kept jerking up almost ashamedly to brush away the steady roll of tears from his nose and cheeks. And after the players finished thundering out three boisterous 'Hip-hip-hoorays' for him, Barassi moved forward to speak. But for the first time of the year he appeared to be faltering, uncertain of what to say. And when he spoke his voice sounded thick with the effort of trying to control his emotions.

'I just want to say', he told them very quietly, 'that you've been absolutely fantastic today.' He paused then for several seconds, again looking uncertain and troubled about which words he should choose, and how he should phrase them. But finally he made the effort: 'I know I'm probably hard on you . . . '

'But look where it's *got us!*' John Cassin shouted gleefully, brandishing his bottle of champagne.

'It's the only way!' Stan Alves endorsed quickly.

Barassi's head nodded 'thank you' to both of them, but when he spoke again the emotion he felt had completely robbed him of his usual articulateness. 'As you think back on this day', he began tentatively, 'which has been one of the great spectacles in Australian sport . . . I hope you'll agree that all that hard work . . . and all that shit put on you by the coach . . . was worth it . . . And I want you to know . . . very sincerely . . . that I love you all.'